<INTRODUCTION to anatomy of reversENGLISH>

This book is a never-before-seen attempt at visualizing the process of English interpretation. Although most of our daily conversation and mechanically recited words and phrases by poor actors and the second-rate narrators simply develop as pure sounds in our ears, consciously understood English is visually seen through our mind's eye. Even those who are linguistically blind could still get used more or less to the very simplest of daily give-and-take conversation in English; but truly meaningful English could only be taken in by those who can see through its semantic structure with anatomically scrutinizing eyes. Those who can see can really command English; those who can just hear can't actually go anywhere. This book may take you somewhere you have never dreamt of going before. After you've seen it you will never be the same again. Although it is primarily written as a visual aid to **"reversEnglish (でんぐリングリッシュ)"**, a guidebook for Japanese students on how to master English written in English, it may also serve as an eye-opener for those who can only hear and say what they hear said but can't really command English the way those who can see deal with it. You'd be well-advised to check and see for yourself, with your own eyes, not through idle hearsay.

<でんぐリングリッシュ解剖編　ごあいさつ>

本書は、英文解釈のプロセスを（未だかつて誰も見たことのないような形で）可視化しようとするユニークな試みである。日常会話の大部分も、大根役者や二流朗読者の棒読みする単語や言い回しのほとんども、耳に流れるただの音として展開するばかりだが、意識して理解する英語というものは、我々の心の目を通して視覚的に認識されるものである。言語学的に盲目の人々でも、ポンポン飛び交う日常的英会話（の最も単純なもの）ならば（ある程度は）慣れることもできるだろうが、真に意味ある英語を理解できるのは、その意味構造を解剖学的視点で吟味し見通す目を持った人々だけである。意味を見抜く眼力を持つ人々のみが、真の英語使いたり得るのだ。漫然と聞く耳しか持たぬのではまるでラチが開かない、というのが実際のところなのである。本書を通して諸君はいまだかつて夢想だにしなかった境地に到達できるかもしれない。本書を見る前と後とでは、諸君は別人になっているにちがいない。本書は本来**『reversEnglish（でんぐリングリッシュ）』**（日本人学生のために英語で書かれた英語修得の方法論の指南書）の「視覚的補助教材」として書かれたものではあるが、英語を耳で聞いては又聞きの口ずさみに終始するばかりで、「吟味する目」を持つ人々並みには英語を真に使いこなせずにいる人々にとってもまた、本書は「開眼の書」たり得る可能性を秘めている。諸君も、安易な又聞きに頼らずに自分の目を通して実際本書の中身を見て独自に確認してみるのが賢明というものだろう。

<INTRODUCTION to anatomy of reversENGLISH>

(S) < This book > (V) is (C) 『 a { never-before-seen } (id)attempt at < ‡(V) visualizing‡ (O) « the process of < English interpretation > » > 』. Although (S) < (id)most of < (1)our daily conversation and (2)(*){ (mechanically) recited } (1)words and (2)phrases ((*)by (1)< { poor } actors > and (2)< { the second-rate } narrators >) > > (simply) (V) develop (as < pure sounds (in < our ears >) >), / (S) < { (consciously) understood } English > ＼ (aV) is (visually) (V) seen ／ (through < our mind's eye >). (Even) (S) < ^those^ { (S) < ^who^ > (V) are (C) 『 (linguistically) blind 』 } > (aV) could (still) ＼ (V) get (V) used 【 (id)more or less 】 to ／ < (id)the very simplest of < daily { give-and-take } conversation (in < English >) > >; but (S) < { (truly) meaningful } English > (aV) could (^only^) ＼ (aV) be (id)(V) taken in ／ (^by^ ^those^ { (S) < ^who^ > (aV) can (id)(V) see through < its semantic structure > (with < { (anatomically) scrutinizing } eyes >) }). (S) < ^Those^ { (S) < ^who^ > (aV) can (V) see } > (aV) can (really) (V) command (O) « English »; ^those^ { (S) < ^who^ > (aV) can (just) (V) hear } (id)(aV) can't (actually) (V) go (anywhere). (S) < This book > (aV) may (V) take (O) « you »(◎somewhere { *[(that)]* (S) < you > ↑ (aV) have never (id)(V) dreamt of ↑ < ‡(V) going‡ > (before) }). (After (S) < you > ↑ (aV) 've (V) seen ↑ (O) « it ») (S) < you > (aV) may never (V) be (C) 『 the same 』 (again). (Although (S) < it > ＼ (aV) is (primarily) (V) written ／ (as < (W)a { visual } aid to < "reversEnglish (でんぐリングリッシュ)", *[(S) < which > (V) is]* (C) 『 ◎a guidebook (1){ for < Japanese students > } (2){ on < how to (V) master (O) « English » > } (3){ *[(S) < which > ＼ (aV) is]]* (V) written ／ (in < English >) } 』 > >)), (S) < it > (aV) may (also) (V) serve (as < an eye-opener for < ^those^ { (*)(S) < ^who^ > (1)(*)(aV) can (only) (1)(V) hear and (2)(V) say (*)(O) « (O) « what » (S) < they > (V) hear (C) 『 ＼ (V) said ／ 』 » but (2)(aV) ca^n't^ ^really^ (V) command (O) « English » (◎the way { *[(in < which >)]* (S) < ^those^ { (S) < ^who^ > (aV) can (V) see } > (id)(V) deal with < it > }) } > >). (S) < You >(id)(aV) 'd (V) be (C) 『 well-advised 』 to (id)(V) check and*(= to)* (V) see (1)((id)for < yourself >), (2)with < your own eyes >, not (3)(through < idle hearsay >).

＜legends of anatomy（解剖学的解釈記号一覧）＞

＝4 main elements of a sentence（文の4大主要素）＝

(S)＜（S）subject＝主語 ＞

(V) （V）verb＝動詞

(O)≪（O）object＝動詞の目的語 ≫

(C)『（C）complement＝補語 』

＝subsidiary elements of a sentence（文の副次的要素）＝

(aV) （auxv）auxiliary verb＝助動詞

<(po)prepositional object＝前置詞の目的語 >

＝accessory elements of a sentence（文の装飾的要素）＝

(adverb＝副詞)

{ adjective＝形容詞 }

＝particular combination of words and phrases（語句の個別的連携）＝

(id)idiomatic expression＝熟語的表現

(w)specific word / phrase＝定型句

correlative — expression＝相関表現

＝semantic / grammatical units（意味別・文法別構成要素）＝

◎antecedent / what is modified by adjective＝先行詞／形容詞被修飾成文

{ relative (pronoun/adverb/adjective) clause }＝関係代名詞節／関係副詞節／関係形容詞節

comparison＝比較表現

components (*)of (1)common–(2)relation＝共通構文構成要素

[omittable elements]＝省略可能成文

[ellipsis。。。in italics]＝被省略成文補足（。。。斜字体にて表記）

〖 parenthesis 〗＝挿入成文

paraphrase*(= to put it another way。。。in italics)＝換言（。。。斜字体にて表記）*

＝modal units（様相別成文）＝

＼ passive voice ／ ＝受動態

↑ perfect tense ↑ ＝完了形

| progressive form | ＝進行形

†present participle†＝現在分詞

‡gerund‡＝動名詞

= INDEX =

— How this book is composed – p.2-p.5

1. School teaching curricula are made exclusively for teachers and schools, not for learners p.6-p.10
2. Japanese avoidance of personal pronouns p.11-p.19
3. Lack of future in Japanese tense p.21-p.26
4. The past and the future are equal with everyone, only the present divides us apart p.27-p.39
5. Lack of plurality in Japanese nouns p.40-p.47
6. English articles are too much for novice comprehension p.48-p.53
7. Let “be” alone, and the rest will “do” their job p.54-p.60
8. Always be aware of the duality of “-ing”(the present participle/gerund) p.61-p.67
9. It takes proficiency to discern the past participle from the past form p.68-p.71
10. SPAT-5: five sentence patterns are a magical set of molds to comprehend English in p.72-p.84
11. Backbone of English comprehension: 5 kinds of sentences, 6 sentential elements and 8 parts of speech p.85-p.98
12. Respective manners of study and memorization for eight parts of speech in English p.99-p.119
13. Be always aware what you are studying – terms (vocabulary), idioms (collocations), sentence patterns (SPAT-5), constructions, grammar, or anatomical interpretation of English sentences p.120-p.145
14. E-to-J translation vs. English interpretation, literal translation vs. paraphrasing: learn their difference through anatomical interpretation p.146-p.164
15. Input before output – EI”SHAKU”BUN rather than EI”SAKU”BUN; English recitation rather than J-to-E translation p.165-p.175
16. To consult a portable electric dictionary is too tentative to be meaningful: make wise use of a PC-based electric dictionary along with its consulting log p.176-p.187
17. On entering a junior high school, acquire touch-typing skill: learn to type English without seeing the keyboard p.188-p.203
18. English ought to be spoken, not written: minimum memos, maximum memory & no notebooks (4m2n) is the way for 'em to English mastery p.204-p.220

anatomy of
reversENGLISH

Beneath
Umbrella
of
Zubaraie LLC.

可視化解釈図つき **解剖編**

英語デキン日本人の感じ方

でんぐリングリッシュ

英語出来る人々の考え方

by 之人冗悟

Noto Jaugo

http://zubaraie.com

ReversENGLISH

◎the way { [*in* < *which* >] (S) < { English illiterate } Japanese > (V) feel }

VS. ◎the way { [*in* < *which* >] (S) < { English capable } people > (V) think }

by Jaugo Noto

Beneath < Umbrella of < ZUBARAIE LLC. > >

http://zubaraie.com

– How (S) < this book > ＼ (aV) is (V) composed ／ –

(S) < This > (V) is (C) 『 ◎a book (1){ (1)on 〖 (and (2)in) 〗 (*)< English > (2){ for < (1)starters and (2)restarters > 〖 (especially the latter*(= restarters))* 〗 } } (3){ to ˆ(V) enableˆ (O) « them » (C) 「 ˆtoˆ (*)(V) have (1)(O) « a clear-cut image of < (O) « what » (S) < they > | (aV) are (V) studying | > », (2)(O) « (id)a { reliable } set of ◎methodology { to (V) guide (O) « them » to < English mastery > } », and (3)(O) « ◎a mental attitude *[(S) < which > (V) is]* (C) 『 (id)common to < ◎all ˆthoseˆ { (S) < ˆwhoˆ > (id)(V) succeed in < linguistic studies > } > 』 » 』 }... / ((id)in { conscious } contrast to < ◎the (1){ time-honored } 〖 (and (2){ corpse-ridden }) 〗 (*)way *[in < which >]* (S) < the Japanese > (generally) (V) fail in < ‡(V) mastering‡ (O) « English » > >), / ((*)[with] < (1)(S) < the original English sentences > *[＼ (aV) being (V) placed ／]* ((id)on the left) and (2)(S) < Japanese translation > *[＼ (aV) being (V) placed ／]* ((id)on the right) >) 』. (Hence) *[(V) comes]* (S) < the title of < ◎"ReversENGLISH (でんぐリングリッシュ:DENGLENGLISH)" >, { (*)†(V) meaning†*(= (S) < which > (V) means)* (1)(O) « "ENGLISH { UPSIDE DOWN }" » or (2)(O) « "A (w)Copernican revolution in < your { English ‡studying‡ } attitude" > » } >.

(S) < This book > (V) is (C) 『 (id)full of < { (quite) bookish } (*)knowledge (1){ about < English > }, (id)or rather, (2){ about < ‡(V) studying‡ (O) « English » > > } 』. (S) < It > (V) is (C) 『 no ◎workbook { (id)full of < ◎practice { to (1)(V) introduce and (2)(V) inure (*)(O) « you » to < actual English usage > } > } 』, (nor) (V) is (S) < it > (S) < (id)a kind of < ◎"(w)placebo" { †(V) giving†*(= (S) < which > (V) gives)* (O) « you » (O) « a

(1){ sweet } 〚 (but (2){ vain }) 〛 (*)hope of < English mastery > » (through < (incredibly) (id){ small } numbers of < magical formulas > >) } > >.

(S) < This book (alone) > (aV) does not ^(V) enable^ (O) « you » (C) 〚 ^to^ (V) command (O) « English » 〛; (S) < it > ^(V) enables^ (O) « you » (C) 〚 ^to^ (correctly) (1)(V) study 〚 (and (consequently) (2)(V) master (eventually)) 〛 (*)(O) « English » 〛. (S) < It > (V) shows (O) « you » (O) « a summary of < (*)(O) « what » (S) < all Japanese (w)junior high school graduates > (1)(aV) should ↑ (aV) have (V) known ↑ 〚 ((id)at least, (2)(aV) should ↑ (aV) have ＼ (aV) been (V) taught ／ ↑) 〛 > » / but (S) < it > (aV) does not (V) expound (O) « such knowledge » ((id)in detail). (S) < It > (only) (V) shows (O) « you » (O) « (O) « what » to ^(V) make^ ^of^ < ◎^those^ separate (id)pieces of knowledge { *[(O) « ^which^ »]* (*)(S) < you > (1) ↑ (aV) have ＼ (aV) been ／ ↑ 〚 (or (2) ＼ (aV) are | (aV) being | ／) 〛 (*)(V) taught (at < school >) } > ». (S) < It > (V) shows (O) « you » (O) « "(w)a big picture" of < the world of < English > > », / (id)instead of < ‡(V) telling‡ (O) « you » (O) « ◎{ what } pigments { to (V) use (to (V) draw (O) « some particular corners of < the world > ») } » >.

(S) < This book > ＼ (id)(aV) is (V) composed of ／ < eighteen(18) sections >. (S) < The first one > (V) is (C) 〚 (purely) introductory 〛, (id)a sort of < (w)preface to < the book > >. (S) < The following ten(10) sections (2 – 11) > (aV) will (V) give (O) « you » (O) « a general view of < (1)(O) « what » and (2)how (*)(S) < you > (V) study ((id)at the onset of < your { English ‡studying‡ } career >) > ». (S) < A complete beginner in < English > > 〚 ((w)the 1st grader (in < (w)a junior high school) (in < Japan >) >) 〛 (aV) may (still) (V) find (O) « them » (C) 〚 intangible 〛, / while (S) < others > 〚 ((especially) restarters) 〛 (aV) will (V) find (O) « them » (C) 〚 (confidently) familiar 〛, ([(V) being] (C) 〚 assured 〛 *[that]* (S) < they > ↑ (aV) have not (V) missed ↑ (O) « much » (in < their past (id)attempts at < English mastery > >))... (*[even]* if (S) < they > ↑ (aV) have *[(V) missed (O) « much »]* ↑), (S) < they > ^have only to^ (1)(id)(V) read through < these 10 sections > and (2)^(V) try^ (O) « ‡(V) review^ing^‡ (O) « their old English textbooks » » ^to^ (V) get (C) 〚 (comfortably) reassured 〛.

(S) < The next four(4) sections (12 – 15) > (aV) will ^(V) lecture^ (O) « you » not so much (^on^ < (*){ particular } (1)facts and (2)knowledge (*)of < English > >) as (^on^ < ◎desirable attitudes { to ^(V) enable^ (O) « you » (C) 『 ^to^ (V) master (O) « this language » 』 } >). (Though *[(S) < they > (*)(V) are]* (1)(C) 『 (rather) abstract 』 and (2)(C) 『 (partly) difficult (for < beginners >) 』), (S) < all Japanese students of < English > > (id)(aV) would (V) be (C) 『 well-advised 』 to (V) read (O) « these instructions » (first). (S) < Most readers > (aV) may (V) find (O) « themselves » (C) 『 (shockingly) (id)averse to < (id)most of < (O) « what » (S) < the author > (V) says (in < these sections >) > > 』; (then(*= if so*)), (S) < that > (V) is (C) 『 *[◎the point]* { where(*= at < which >*) (S) < the ^difference^ > (V) lies (^between^ < you > ^and^ < ◎me, { (S) < who > ↑ (*)(aV) have (1)(V) written ↑ (O) « this book » (in < English language >) and ↑ (2)(V) offered ↑ (O) « Japanese translation » (for (S) < you > to (V) follow (O) « me ») }) > } 』.

(S) < The last three(3) sections (16 – 18) > (aV) will (id)(V) focus on < how to (id)(V) make (O) « the best [use] » of < (w)‡learning‡ materials – (1)dictionaries, (2)typewriters, and (3)textbooks > >. (Although (S) < some Japanese > (aV) may (V) find (O) « section 16 (on < (*)the (1)electric dictionary and (2)(w)personal computer >) and 17 (on < (*)the (1)(w)typewriter or (2)(w)word-processor >) » (C) 『 (id)irrelevant to < themselves > 』), (S) < this author > (V) (strongly) recommends (O) « you » (C) 『 (*)to (1)(V) read (O) « them » and (2)(V) reconsider (O) « your attitudes » (accordingly) 』. (S) < The last section (18) > (1)(aV) will ＼ (aV) be (V) found ／ (C) 『 *[to (V) be]* (C) 『 most shocking 』 』 (by < most (*){ Japanese } (1)students and (2)teachers >), and(*= and yet*) (2)(aV) will (V) be (C) 『 (id)of { the greatest } help 』 (to < ◎^those^ { (S) < ^who^ > (V) get (O) « the message » (right) } >).

((id)All in all), (S) < this book > (V) is more (C) 『 ◎guideposts { standing(*= (S) < which > (V) stand*) (at < the most critical points) > } 』 than (C) 『 a (*){ constant } (1)guide or (2)attendant ((*)in < your journey to < English mastery > >) 』. (Though (S) < it > (aV) will not (V) accompany (O) « you » ((id)all the way)), (S) < it > (V) shows

(O) « you » (1)(O) « ◎the right direction { [in < which >] (S) < you > (aV) should (V) go } » and (2)(O) « ◎the correct methodology { for (S) < you > to (V) follow ((id)at the (very) beginning of < your (id)attempt at < (1)‡(V) conquering‡ 〚 (or (2)(id)‡(V) revenging‡ on) 〛 (*)(O) « < English > » > >) } ». ^(V) Take^ (O) « a wrong step », ^and^ (S) < you > (id)(V) are (C) 〚 sure to (id)(V) go (astray) 〛. (If (S) < you > (id)want to (V) reach (O) « your desired goal »), (id)(V) read through < this book > and (V) take (O) « the right step » ((id)at the start of < your (*){ English } (1)studying 〚 (or (2)re-studying) 〛 (*)career >). (w)Bon voyage *(= (V) Have (O) « a nice trip »).*

October 18, 2012
Jaugo Noto(之人冗悟:のと・じゃうご)
Beneath < Umbrella of < ZUBARAIE LLC. > >
http://zubaraie.com

...addition... (There) (V) is (S) < ◎(id){ another } version of < this book > { (id)†(V) consisting† *(= (S) < which > (V) consists)* (entirely) of < ANATOMICAL INTERPRETATION for < (w)each and every sentence of < it > > > } >. (V) See (O) « it »*(= THIS BOOK: Anatomy of reversENGLISH)* (to (V) gaze into < the lucid mind's image of < { ENGLISH LITERATE } intellectuals > >).

1.(S) < School (w)‡teaching‡ curricula > ＼ (aV) are (V) made ／ ((exclusively) (1)for < (1)teachers and (2)schools >), not ((2)for < learners >)

(S) < ◎The first thing { for (S) < English learners (in < Japan >) > to (V) consider } > (V) is (C) 『 (id)◎the last thing { (O) « *[that]* » (S) < any ordinary teacher > (aV) would (ever) (V) teach (O) « you » } 』: NEVER ^(V) put^ (O) « easy ^trust in^ < your teachers' curricula > », / for (S) < they > ＼ (aV) are (V) made ／ (1)(id)for the convenience of < (1)teachers or (2)schools >, not (2)(id)for the benefit of < learners >.

(S) < A school's basic functions > (V) are (C) 『 twofold 』. ((w)First and foremost), (S) < it > (aV) should (V) be (C) 『 ◎a place { for (S) < learners > to (*)(V) acquire (O) « (1)knowledge and (2)skill » } 』. ((id)Secondary to < the (*){ first } { (1)‡learning‡ and (2)‡teaching‡ } (*)function >), (S) < a school > (V) is (C) 『 ◎a place { for (S) < teachers > to (V) give (O) « grades » (to < learners >) } 』. (S) < Good grades (at < schools >) > (V) give (O) « (w)social grace (to < learners >) ». (S) < Poor marks (in < exams >) > ^(V) encourage^ (O) « idle learners (^into^ ‡(V) studying‡ (harder)) ». (S) < Schools > (V) maintain (O) « such social interactivity » ((id)on the strength of < their function (as < grade providers >) >). (Therefore), (S) < schools > (aV) must (V) have (O) « criteria { for < ‡(V) deciding‡ (O) « (O) « { what } grades » to (V) provide (to < learners >) » > } ». (When (S) < schools > (V) prepare (O) « (w)‡teaching‡ materials »), (1)(S) < fragmentation >, (2)(S) < separation > and (3)(S) < ‡grouping‡ > (*)of < ◎things { to (V) teach } > ＼ (aV) are (V) made ／ . (S) < They > ＼ (aV) are (V) divided ／ (into < such small parts >) ((just) ^in order for^ (S) < teachers > ^to^ (V) (efficiently) judge (O) « the performance of < learners > »). (If (S) < 8 ((id)out of < 10 ◎things { to (V) master } >) > ＼ (aV) are (V) shown ／ 【 in < an exam > 】 to ↑ (aV) have ＼ (aV) been (successfully) (V) acquired ／ ↑ (by < a particular learner >)), (S) < ◎the grade { to ＼ (aV) be (V) provided ／ } > (aV) should (V) be (C) 『 EXCELLENT 』; (S) < two ((id)out of < ten >) > (aV) should ＼ (aV) be (shamefully) (id)(V) branded as ／ < FAILURE >.

(If (S) < mastery of < English > > (V) is (C) 『 the real goal 』), (however), (S) <

◎anything { less than < PERFECT > } – ◎10 things { ＼ (V) mastered ／ ((id)out of < ◎10 things { ＼ (V) taught ／ } >) } – > (aV) should not ＼ (aV) be (V) accepted ／ . ((id)In actuality), (S) < schools > (V) give (O) « ^such^ benevolent grades ^as^ < (1)(w)SATISFACTORY or (2)(w)AVERAGE or (3)(w)PASSING > (to < ◎learners { (S) < who > (V) (^only^) marked (O) « (1)^5^ or (2)^6^ (*)((id)out of < 10 >) » } >) ». (S) < FAILURE (of < learners >) > (V) brings (O) « shame » (to < schools >) (too), (id)so that (S) < schools > (id)have (*)to (1)^(V) brand^ (even) (O) « { (w)BELOW AVERAGE } learners » (^as^ < (w)CONDITIONALLY PASSED >) and (2)(aV) let (O) « such (w)low achievers » (id)(V) get (C) 〚 away 〛 with it; 【 or (aV) should (S) < we > (V) say 】 , (just) (3)(id)(V) get (C) 〚 rid of < such encumbrances > 〛.

(In < the world of < English grammar > >), (S) < some things > (aV) should, 【 logically 】 , ＼ (aV) be (*)(collectively) (1)(V) taught and (2)(V) comprehended ／ ((1)in < one (id)set of < knowledge > >, not (2)(id)in < { many } { separate } pieces >), ((C) 〚 (*)however (1)tough and (2)daunting 〛 (S) < they > (aV) may ((id)at first) (V) appear). (S) < They > ＼ (aV) can't, ((id)of course), (aV) be (V) mastered ／ ((id)at a time). But (S) < to (V) offer (O) « such { (essentially) collective } (id)set of < knowledge > » ((id)in { (too) many (seemingly) unrelated } fragments) > (aV) will (only) (V) make (O) « their mastery » (C) 〚 all ^the^ more difficult 〛 (^for^ < the number of (1)< separate lessons > and (2)< the lapse of < time (between < them >) > > >).

^(V) Take^, (^(id)for example^), (O) « the subject of < (w)tense > ». (In < English >), (S) < they > (V) have (O) « the (1)(w)past tense, (2)(w)present tense, (3)(w)future tense and (4)(w)perfect tense ». While (S) < (w)the perfect tense > ＼ (aV) is (further) (id)(V) divided into < (1)(w)the present perfect, (2)(w)the past perfect and (3)(w)the future perfect > ／ , / (S) < (w)the past perfect tense > ＼ (aV) is (intricately) (id)(V) associated with ／ < (w)subjunctive mood >. (S) < These temporal elements of < English > > (aV) may (V) seem (C) 〚 *[to (V) be]* (C) 〚 ^too^ ◎complicated { ^to^ (1)(V) teach and (2)(V) master ((id)at a time) } 〛 〛. But (S) < (1)perfect ^separation^ of < (w)the (1){ present } (*)(w)tense ^from^ < (2){ future } or (3){ past } > > and (2)‡^(V) spending‡ (O) « several months of < lessons > » ((solely) ^in^ < (w)the present tense >) ((id)at the { total } exclusion of < (w)(*)the (1){ past } or (2){ future } (*)tense >) > (id)(V) makes (O) « ^no^ sense » (^(id)at all^) ((id)from { logical } point of view). ((id)From { practical } point of view ((id)on the side (*)of < (1)teachers and (2)schools >)), (however), (S) < such nonsensical separations > (id)(V) make { perfect } (O) « sense »: (S) < they > (V) make (O) « ^it^ » (C) 『 easier 』 ^(*)to^ (1)(V) judge (O) « the performance of < learners > » and (2)(V) give (O) « them » (O) « grades » (accordingly). (^If^ (S) < (*)the (1)past, (2)present and (3)future > (id)were to ＼ (aV) be (id)(V) dealt with ／ ((id)at a time), (just like *[(S) < they > ＼ (aV) are (V) dealt with ／]* in < the world of < { (actually) spoken } English > >)), (there) (V) (aV) would (V) be (S) < chaos > (in < classrooms >) (for < ◎(*){ some }(1)weeks or (2)months >, (during < { which } time >) (S) < no exact grades > (aV) could ＼ (aV) be (V) awarded ／ (to < learners >) ((id)according to < their respective performance >)). (S) < ^It^ > (V) is, (therefore), (C) 『 logical 』 ^for^ (S) < teachers > ^to^ ^(V) separate^ (O) « (*)the (1){ past } and (2){ future } » ^from^ < (w)the (3){ present } (*)tense >, ((id)with ◎the result { that (S) < (*)the (1){ future } and (2){ past } (*)tenses > (in < Japanese ‡teaching‡ of < English > >) (V) have (O) « their presence » (with < considerable (w)time lag (after < (w)the present tense >) >) }).

(If ^(S) < it > (V) is^ (C) 『 mastery of < English > 』 ^(O) « that »^ (S) < (1)learners and (2)teachers > (V) have (as < their aim >)), (S) < (*)the (1)arrangement and (2)management (*)of < ◎things { (*)to (1)(V) teach and (2)(V) learn } – ＼ [(*)(aV) being] (actually) (1)(V) taught but (id)not exactly (2)(V) learnt ／ – (at < most Japanese schools >) > > (V) are (C) 『 ^too^ problematic (^to^ (V) be (C) 『 practical 』 』). (S) < They > ^(V) present^ (O) « learners » (^with^ < ◎(w)jigsaw puzzles { with < ^too^ many (w)missing pieces (^to^ (V) imagine (O) « < what > (S) < the whole picture > (id)(V) looks like ») > } >). *[(S) < ^It^ > (V) is]* (id)(C) 『 No wonder 』 *[^that^]* (S) < few Japanese > (aV) can (fully) (V) draw (O) « realistic pictures » (in < English words >).

(S) < (*)The (1){ actual } and (2){ practical } (*)(w)world-picture of < English > > (aV) ought to ＼ (V) be (V) treated ／ ((1)(id)as a whole), not ((2)as < ◎fragmented pieces { ＼ [(S) < which > (aV) are] (id)(V) put together > ／ (after < (1){ long } (2){ patient } (*)efforts of < (w)garbage collection > >) }). (S) < (*){ Perfect } (1)comprehension and (2)mastery (*)of < the whole picture > > (aV) will (V) take (O) « some time » (anyway), but (S) < that (w)time-table > (aV) should ＼ (aV) be (V) set ／ (1)(by < (*){ learners' } (1)ardency and (2)intellectual capacity >), not (2)(by < (S) < (1)teachers and (2)schools > ‡(V) cutting‡ (O) « a picture » (into < ◎pieces { ＼ [(S) < which > (aV) are] (conveniently) (V) arranged ／ for < (1)‡(V) judging‡, not (2)‡(V) improving‡, (*)(O) « learners' performance » > } >) >).

(Now), (S) < you > (aV) must ↑ (aV) have (V) understood ↑ : (S) < (S) < what > (V) is (C) 〖 important 〗 (in < English ‡learning‡ >) > (V) is not (1)(C) 〖 (id)preparation for < ◎lessons { to (V) come } > 〗, but (2)(C) 〖 reviews of < ◎lessons { [(S) < which > ↑ (aV) have]] (already) ＼ [(*)(aV) been] (1)(V) taught ／ ↑ but (id)not quite ＼ (2)(V) learnt ／ (yet) } > 〗. (S) < This book > (id)(V) deals with < collective knowledge of < English > > ((id)in a bulk). (S) < They > (aV) may (V) fly (C) 〖 past 〗 (before < you >) (like (S) < (w)runaway horses >) ((id)at first): (S) < you > (aV) may (V) feel ＼ (id)(V) run over ／ (by < them >) (once), but (S) < (id)‡(V) going‡ over < them > (twice) > (aV) will (id)(V) get (O) « you » (somewhere); ((id)†(V) running† (O) « them » over ((id)again and again)), (S) < you > (aV) will (id)(V) come to (V) know (O) « (1)where and (2)how (*)to (V) go ». (With < { each } { additional } review >), (S) < you > (aV) will (V) get (C) 〖 the nearer (to < the goal >) 〗. (S) < The test of < an English textbook > > (S) < is > (in the ‡(V) re-visiting‡): (S) < a good one > (V) gives (O) « you » (O) « ◎(w)the big picture { (O) « [which] » (S) < you > (id)(V) failed to (V) see (at < the first ‡reading‡ >) } »; (S) < a poor guide > (id)(1)(V) insists on < ‡(V) teaching‡ (O) « you » (O) « how to (V) move (O) « your feet » » > but (2)(V) gives (O) « you » (O) « no idea [about] (1)< where (S) < you > | (aV) are (V) going | > and (2)< how far (S) < you > ↑ (aV) have (V) come ↑ > or (3)< (S) < ◎how much > ＼ (aV) is (V) left ／ { to ＼ (aV) be (V) conquered ／ } > ». (S) < This book > ＼ (aV) is (V) written ／ ((id)in { conscious } opposition to < such poor guidebooks of < English > (as < { tedious } ◎(w)contrary teachers { to (V) avoid > }) >); (S) < ^whether^ (S) < it > (V) is (C) 『 a good guide 』 ^or not^ > ＼ (aV) is ^(V) left^ ／ (^for^ (S) < you > ^to^ (V) judge)... after < several reviews >, with < the visual assistance of < the { (incredibly) meticulous } anatomical interpretation guide of < this book > > > – Anatomy of reversENGLISH – 【 (id)that is 】 .

2.{ Japanese } avoidance of < (w)personal pronouns >

- (S) < Japanese language > (V) has (O) « no (w)personal pronouns » -

(As (C) 『 incredible 』 as (S) < it > (aV) may (V) be (to < native English speakers >)), (S) < Japanese language > (V) has (O) « no "人称代名詞(NINSHOU-DAIMEISHI: (w)personal pronouns)" »: (S) < Japanese people > (V) use (O) « ^so^ many (w)nouns » (as < substitute (w)personal pronouns >) ^that^ (S) < ^‡(V) regarding‡^ (O) « them » (all) (C) 『 ^as^ < (w)personal pronouns > 』 > (aV) would (id)(V) make (O) « ^no^ { linguistic } sense » (^(id)at all^). (There) (V) is (S) < no definite rule (for < ◎(w)nouns { to ＼ (aV) be (V) used ／ (as < (id)substitutes for < (w)personal pronouns > >) } >) >: (S) < (only) personal choice of < the speaker > > (aV) will (V) decide (O) « ◎{ what } substitute (w)personal pronoun { to (V) use (for < (*)(w)any given (1)person or (2)persons >) (in < Japanese language >) } ».

- *[(There) (V) is]* (S) < (*)No (1)mystique or (2)mistake (*)(with < (*)English (1){ personal }/(2){ impersonal } (*)(w)pronouns >) > -

(S) < (*)English (1){ personal } and (2){ impersonal } (*)(w)pronouns > (V) are (C) 『 (definitely) fixed 』. (S) < It > (aV) can ＼ (aV) be (further) (id)(V) divided into < four forms > ／ ((id)according to < its function (in < the sentence >) >), (w)namely, (1)" 主格:SHUKAKU: (w)the subjective case" (I, we, you, he, she, it, they), (2)"所有格:SHOYUUKAKU: (w)the possessive case" (my, our, your, his, her, its, their), (3)"目的格:MOKUTEKIKAKU: (w)the objective case" (me, us, you, him, her, it, them) and (4)"所有代名詞:SHOYUU-DAIMEISHI: (w)the possessive pronoun" (mine, ours, yours, his, hers, its, theirs).

(S) < All (*){ English } (1){ personal }/(2){ impersonal } (*)(w)pronouns > (aV) can ＼ (aV) be (*)(systematically) (1)(V) defined and (2)(V) memorized ／ ((id)in ◎the { following } manner), { (with < which >), (as < a reference >), (S) < this author > (aV) will (V) enumerate (O) « possible counterparts (in < Japanese pseudo (w)personal pronouns >) (in < (*)the (1){ subjective }/(2){ objective } (*)case >) » } 〖 (((aV) should (S) < you >(= *if (S) < you > (aV) should)* (id)(V) want to (V) use (O) « them » (in < (*)the (1)(w)possessive case /(2)(w)possessive pronoun >)), (simply) (V) add (O) « "の:NO" » ((id)at the end)) 】:

一人称(ICHI-NINSHOU: (w)the first person) = ◎the person { [(S) < who > | (aV) is] (V) speaking | ((1)(id)along with or (2)(id)on behalf of (*)< ◎the person(s) { (id)on the side of < the speaker > } >) }:

単数(TANSUU: (w)singular): I - my - me - mine

Japanese substitutes: 私(WATASHI),私(WATAKUSHI),あたし(ATASHI),僕(BOKU),俺(ORE),俺っち(ORECCHI),あっし(ASSHI),あちき(ACHIKI),手前(TEMAE),自分(JIBUN),当方(TOUHOU),小生(SHOUSEI),儂(WASHI),うち(UCHI),こっち(KOCCHI),こちとら(KOCHITORA),etc,etc.

複数(FUKUSUU: (w)plural): we - our - us - ours

Japanese substitutes: 私達/ら(WATASHI TACHI/RA),私達/ら/ども(WATAKUSHI TACHI/RA/DOMO),あたしたち/ら(ATASHI TACHI/RA),僕たち/ら(BOKU TACHI/RA),俺たち/ら(ORE TACHI/RA),あっしら(ASSHI RA),我々(WAREWARE),我等(WARERA),手前ども(TEMAE DOMO),自分たち/ら(JIBUN TACHI/RA),当方(TOUHOU),儂ら(WASHI RA),うちら(UCHI RA),こっち(KOCCHI),こちとら(KOCHITORA),etc,etc.

二人称(NI-NINSHOU: (w)the second person) = ◎(*)the (1)person or (2)persons { [< whom >] (S) < the speaker(s) > | (aV) is (directly) (id)(V) talking to | }

単数/複数(TANSUU/FUKUSUU: ˆwhetherˆ (w)singular ˆorˆ (w)plural): you - your - you - yours

Japanese substitutes: 単数(TANSUU: (w)singular): あなた(ANATA),あなたさま(ANATA SAMA),あんた(ANTA),君(KIMI),お前(OMAE),貴兄(KIKEI),兄(KEI),貴殿(KIDEN),おたく(OTAKU),汝(NANJI),そっち(SOCCHI),そちらさん(SOCHIRASAN),自分(JIBUN),われ(WARE),うぬ(UNU),おのれ(ONORE),おんどれ(ONDORE),おんどりゃー(ONDORYAA),きさま(KISAMA),こいつ(KOITSU),て

めぇ(TEMEE),おめぇ(OMEE),この野郎(KONOYAROU),こんにゃろう(KONNYAROU),なろう(NAROU),こんちくしょう(KONCHIKUSHOU),こなくそ(KONAKUSO),etc,etc.

複数(FUKUSUU: (w)plural): あなたがた/たち/ら(ANATA GATA/TACHI/RA),あんたがた/たち/ら(ANTA GATA/TACHI/RA),君たち/ら(KIMI TACHI/RA),お前たち/ら(OMAE TACHI/RA),貴兄ら(KIKEI RA),兄ら(KEI RA),おたくたち/ら(OTAKU TACHI/RA),汝等(NANJI RA),そっち(SOCCHI),そちらさん(SOCHIRASAN),自分ら(JIBUN RA),われ(WARE),うぬら(UNU RA),おのれら(ONORE RA),おんどれ(ONDORE),おんどりゃー(ONDORYAA),きさまら(KISAMA RA),こいつら(KOITSU RA),てめぇら(TEMEE RA),おめぇら(OMEE RA),この野郎ども(KONOYAROU DOMO),こんにゃろうども(KONNYAROU DOMO),こんちくしょうども(KONCHIKUSHOU DOMO),こなくそ(KONAKUSO),etc,etc.

三人称(SAN-NINSHOU: (w)the third person) = ◎the person(s) or thing(s) { < *[that]* > (*)(s) < the speaker(s) > (1) | (aV) is (indirectly) (id)(v) referring to | , not (2)(directly) (id)(v) talking to }

男性単数(DANSEI TANSUU: (w)masculine (w)singular): he - his - him - his

Japanese substitutes: 彼(KARE),あの男(ANO OTOKO),あの人(ANO HITO),あの方(ANO KATA),あのお方(ANO OKATA),氏(SHI),彼氏(KARESHI),あの者(ANO MONO),その者(SONO MONO),あの御仁(ANO GOJIN),あいつ(AITSU),あやつ(AYATSU),やつ(YATSU),きゃつ(KYATSU),そやつ(SOYATSU),やっこさん(YAKKO SAN),あんちくしょう(ANCHIKUSHOU),あんにゃろう(ANNYAROU),あちらさん(ACHIRA SAN),あの子(ANO KO),あの野郎(ANO YAROU),etc,etc.

女性単数(JOSEI TANSUU: (w)feminine (w)singular): she - her - her - hers

Japanese substitutes: 彼女(KANOJO),あの女(ANO ONNA),あの人(ANO HITO),あの方(ANO KATA),あのお方(ANO OKATA),あの者(ANO MONO),その者(SONO MONO),あの御仁(ANO GOJIN),あいつ(AITSU),あやつ(AYATSU),やつ(YATSU),きゃつ(KYATSU),そやつ(SOYATSU),やっこさん(YAKKO SAN),あんちくしょう

(ANCHIKUSHOU),あんにゃろう(ANNYAROU),あちら(ACHIRA),あちらさん (ACHIRA SAN),あの娘(ANO KO),あのアマ(ANO AMA),あのスケ(ANO SUKE),etc,etc.

非人称単数(HININSHOU TANSUU: (w)impersonal (w)singular): it - its - it - its

Japanese substitutes: あれ(ARE),それ(SORE),あいつ(AITSU),そいつ(SOITSU), その物(SONO MONO),その何か(SONO NANIKA),etc,etc.

男性・女性・中性または非人称複数(DANSEI・JOSEI・CHUUSEI or HININSHOU FUKUSUU: (w)plural ^whether^ (w)masculine, (w)feminine, (w)neuter ^or^ (w)impersonal): they - their - them - theirs

Japanese substitutes: 彼ら(KARE RA),それら(SORERA),そういう人たち(SOUIU HITO TACHI),そういう物たち(SOUIU MONO TACHI),あの人たち(ANO HITO TACHI),あの方たち(ANO KATA TACHI),あの男ども(ANO OTOKO DOMO),彼たち(KARE TACHI),あの女ども(ANO ONNNA DOMO),彼女ら/たち/ども(KANOJO TACHI/DOMO),あの連中(ANO RENCHUU),ああした連中(AASHITA RENCHUU),ああいう者ども(AAIU MONO DOMO),あいつら(AITSURA),あやつら (AYATSURA),やつら(YATSURA),きゃつら(KYATSURA),そいつら(SOITSURA), やっこさんたち(YAKKOSAN TACHI),あんちくしょうども(ANCHIKUSHOU DOMO), あちら(ACHIRA),あちらさん(ACHIRA SAN),あちらさんがた(ACHIRA SAN GATA), あんにゃろうども(ANNYAROU DOMO), etc,etc.

- ◎The essential reason { why (S) < the Japanese > (V) avoid (O) « ‡(V) calling‡ (O) « someone » (by < (*){ definite } (1)names or (2)(w)pronouns >) » } -

(To < ◎English speakers { [(S) < who > (V) are] (C)『 (id)at a loss 』*[about]* < how to (V) make (O) « conversation » (C)『 possible 』(with < so many possible substitutes >) (without < definite (w)personal pronouns >) > } >), (id)(V) suffice (O) « ^it^ » ^to^ (V) say (O) « [that](*)(S) < most Japanese sentences > (1)(V) are (C)『 complete ((*)without < (1)SHUGO((w)subjects: I, we, you, he, she, it, they) or

(2)MOKUTEKIGO((w)objects : me, us, you, him, her, it, them) >) 』 and (2)(id)^(V) consist^ (mainly) (*)of (1)< DOUSHI((w)verbs) > and (2)< its accompaniment > ». ((Quite) incredibly (for < English natives >)), (S) < "(S)I (V)love (O)you" > (V) is ((almost) always) (C) 『 "(V)好きです(SUKI DESU)" 』 ((id)instead of < ＼ (aV) being (V) expressed ／ (in < ^such^ (perfectly) formal Japanese ^as^ < "(S)私は(WATASHI WA) (O)あなたが(ANATA GA) (V)好きです(SUKI DESU)" > >) >).

While (S) < (1){ subjective } or (2){ objective } (*)ellipsis > (V) is (C) 『 (quite) ◎rare { to (V) find } 』 (in < English sentences >), ／ (S) < their formal existence > (V) is (C) 『 rarer (still) 』 (in < Japanese >). ((id)In essence), (S) < Japanese people > (positively) (id)(V) hate (*)to (1)(V) call or (2) ＼ (aV) be (V) called by ／ (*)(O) « < definite names > ». *[(aV) Do (S) < you > (V) think (O) « [[that]] (S) < it >] (V) Sounds (C) 『 crazy 』 »?* (w)Maybe*(= (S) < It > (aV) may (V) be (C) 『 so 』)*, (to < Indo-European speakers >); but (S) < the avoidance of < direct name-‡calling‡ > > (V) is (C) 『 ◎a { time-honored } custom of < Japanese language > { (S) < which > (id)(V) has (O) « its root » (in < ◎their spiritual belief { *[(S) < which > ＼ (aV) is]]* (V) called ／ (C) 『 "言霊(KOTODAMA: ◎spirit { *[(S) < which > (V) is]* (C) 『 (id)inherent 』 in < (w)each and every word > })" 』 } >) } 』.

(S) < The history of < Japanese (id)belief in < ◎KOTODAMA > > > (V) is (presumably) (C) 『 as old as (S) < the Japanese language (itself) > 』, (S) < which > (V) tells (O) « us » 【 ((even) today, (id)more or less) 】 (O) « that (S) < we > (aV) can (V) capture (O) « the spirit of < (w)any given entity > » (by (simply) ‡(V) uttering‡ (O) « ◎the word { †(V) signifying† *(= (S) < which > (V) signifies)* (O) « the entity » } ») ». (S) < A name of < (1)someone or (2)something > > ＼ (aV) was (V) believed ／ to (id)(V) have (O) « { some magical } power (over < ◎the (1)person or (2)thing { < *[that]* > (S) < the name > (id)(V) stood for } >) ». ((id)In fact), (in < ancient Japan > 【 ((id)up until < the early years of < (w)the Heian Era > >) 】) ◎the terms (1)"事(KOTO: thing)" and (2)"言(KOTO: word)" ＼ (aV) were ^so^ (closely) (V) associated (together

) ／ ^that^ (S) < they > ＼ (aV) were (V) felt ／ to (V) be (C) 『 (virtually) the same thing 』. (S) < That > (V) is (C) 『 *[the reason]* why (S) < ^it^ > ＼ (aV) was (V) thought ／ (C) 『 *[to (V) be]* (C) 『 blasphemous 』 』 ^to^ (V) call (O) « persons (in < high positions >) » (by < (directly) (id)‡(V) referring‡ to < their names > >) 』. ((Even) today), (S) < ‡(V) calling‡ (O) « someone » (by < their real name >) > (V) is (C) 『 ◎a privilege { *[(S) < which > ＼ (aV) is]]* (only) (V) allowed ／ (to < ◎someone (C) 『 { *[(S) < who > (V) is]* ((so) intimately) (C) 『 near 』 } 』 >) } 』. (When (S) < any other boys > (V) call (O) « a girl » (by < (1){ affectionate } but (2){ general } (*)nickname "花子ちゃん (HANAKO CHAN)" >)), (S) < (only) her (w)true love > (aV) can (intimately) (V) call (O) « her » (C) 『 ◎"花子(HANAKO)" 』, (S) < which >, 【 in < English > 】 , (aV) can ＼ (aV) be (bravely) (id)(V) translated into < "HANAKO, my dear" > ／ . (S) < Direct name-‡calling‡ (in < Japan >) >, (while *[(S) < it > (V) is]* (id)not strictly (C) 『 a taboo 』 (today)), (aV) could (still) (V) invoke (O) « ◎feelings { *[(S) < which > (V) are]* (C) 『 (id)beyond < the wildest imagination of < Western folks > > 』 } ».

(When (S) < name-‡calling‡ > ＼ (aV) was 【 thus 】 (consciously) (V) avoided ／), (S) < ^it^ > (V) was (C) 『 (only) natural 』 ^that^ (S) < (w)personal pronouns > (id)(V) had (O) « no chance of < development > » (in < the history of < Japanese language > >). (Moreover), (by < ‡(V) giving‡ (O) « someone » (O) « any definite pseudo (w)personal pronoun » >), (S) < Japanese people > (aV) will (V) make (O) « their mental stance » (C) 『 clear 』 (toward < that person >): (S) < ^whether^ (*)(S) < they > (1)(V) respect(eg.あなたさま:ANATA SAMA), (2*)(V) feel (1)(C) 『 (id)affectionate to 』 (eg.君:KIMI) or (2)(C) 『 (id)distant from 』(eg.おたく:OTAKU), ^or^ (even) (positively) (3)(V) hate(eg.てめぇ:TEMEE) (*)(O) « < that person > » >, ＼ (aV) is (V) made ／ (C) 『 clear 』 ((*)by < the (1)choice and (2)use (*)of < a particular denomination > >). ((id)Rather than < ‡(V) putting‡ (O) « themselves » (in < a (possibly) awkward position >) (by < improper name-‡calling‡ >) >), (S) < Japanese people > (instinctively) (V) avoid (O) « ‡(V) using‡ (O) « any (w)personal pronouns » », /

(id)with ◎the { logical } consequence { that (S) < Japanese sentences > ((so) frequently) (V) omit (O) « (1)(w)subjects or (2)(w)objects », (id)only to ＼ (aV) be (V) supplemented ／ (by < the reader's imagination > ((id)according to < the context >)) }.

(For < Japanese learners of < English > >), (therefore), (S) < ◎the first thing { to (V) remember } > (V) is (C) 『 never to (V) omit (O) « ◎(1)(w)subjects or (2)(w)objects » (in < English >) 』, { (S) < which >, 【 in < most cases > 】 , (V) take (O) « the form of < (w)personal pronouns > (I, we, you, he, she, it, they / me, us, you, him, her, it, them) » }. (w)(S) < The good news > (V) is (C) 『 *[that]* , (S) < they > (*)(V) are (1)(C) 『 (definitely) fixed 』 (in < English >) and (C) 『 (2)^so^ ◎easy { to (V) understand } 』 ^that^ (S) < Japanese people > (id)(aV) will (V) find (O) « { little } difficulty » [in] ‡(V) mastering‡ (O) « them », / and (once (S) < they > (id)(V) get (C) 『 acquainted with < their use > 』), (S) < they > (aV) can (V) feel (O) « the ^freedom^ of < English > ^from^ < ◎^those^ crazy variations of < (1)nuances and (2)restrictions > { ^(S) < which >^ (V) make (O) « Japanese conversation » (C) 『 (*)^too^ (1)cramped and (2)(dishonestly) unnatural (^to^ (V) reach (O) « people of < different social status > ») 』 } > » 』.

(w)(S) < The bad news > (V) is (C) 『 *[that]* , (S) < ◎people { *[(S) < who > ＼ (aV) are]]* (once) (id)(V) liberated from ／ < such crazy chains > } > (aV) will never (id)(V) want to (id)(V) get back to < their old { suffocating } ◎restraints of < the Japanese > >, { linguistic (id)or otherwise } 』. (S) < ◎^Those^ Japanese { ^(S) < who >^ ↑ (aV) have (id)(V) acquainted (O) « themselves » with ↑ < English freedom > } > (aV) could 【 (id)no longer 】 (id)(V) put up with < (suffocatingly) absurd customs (in < their native country >) >. (S) < A possible solution > (V) is (C) 『 [that] (S) < all Japanese >, 【 beyond < any social status > 】 , (aV) should (id)be able to (V) communicate (freely) (in < English >) 』, ^not^ ((id)in order to (V) desert (O) « Japanese ») ^but^ ((id)so that (S) < they > (aV) can (V) understand (O) « (id)< what > (S) < ^it^ > (V) is (C) 『 like 』 ^to^ (V) be (C) 『 Japanese 』 »), and(= *and then*) (S) < they > (aV) will (id)(V) try 【 consciously 】 to (V) make (O) « themselves » (C) 『 ◎better, (linguistically (id)or otherwise) 』. [(aV) Do (S) < you > (V) feel (O) « [that] (S) < it >] (V) Sounds (C) 『 impossible 』»? (w)Maybe(= (S) < It > (aV) may (V) be (C) 『so 』)... but (S) < it > (aV) may (id)(V) turn out to (V) be (C) 『 nothing 』 ([when (S) < it > ＼ (aV) is]] (id)(V) compared to ／ < ◎the ^difficulty^ { (O) « [which] » (S) < foreign people > ^(V) find^ (^in^ < ‡(V) deciding‡ (O) « ◎{ what } pseudo (w)personal pronoun { to (V) adopt (in < their Japanese conversation >)) } » > } >).

- ^(V) Get^ (C) 『 ＼ ^(V) acquainted^ ^with^ ／ < English > 』 (through < (w)pronoun pronouncement >) -

(If (S) < you > (V) are (C) 『 a complete beginner (in < the study of < English > >) 』), (S) < ^it^ > (V) is (C) 『 a (very) good practice 』 (*)^to^ (1)^(V) change^ (O) « ◎anything { (O) « [that] » (S) < you > (V) see } » ^into^ < a (w)pronoun(we, you, they, he, she, it... 【 (S) < "I" > (aV) will ^(V) play^ (O) « no ^role^ » (^in^ < this practice >) 】) > and (2)(instantly) (V) pronounce (O) « it ». (S) < It > (V) seems (C) 『 easy (enough) 』, but (S) < it > (V) takes (O) « some ＼ (id)‡(V) getting‡ (C) 『 used to 』 ／ » (before (S) < you > (V) are (perfectly) (C) 『 (id)familiar with < the notion of < English (w)pronouns > > 』). (id)(aV) Shall (S) < we > (V) take (O) « some examples »?

(S) < (id)One of < ◎the commonest ^mistakes^ { (O) « [that] » (S) < beginners > ^(V) make^ } > > (V) is (C) 『 "personal association of < (w)impersonal pronouns >" 』: to ^(V) confuse^ (O) « (w)an impersonal pronoun(it, they, its, their, them) » ^with^ < ◎the person { [< whom >] (S) < it > ＼ (id)(aV) is (V) associated with ／ } >. ((id)For example), ([in ◎a case] where (S) < "(S) < Your lips > (V) look (C) 『 ^so^ charming 』. [^that^] (S) < I > (id)(V) feel like ‡(V) kissing‡ (O) « <them> »." > (V) is (C) 『 the correct English 』), (S) < beginners > (V) (often) say (O) « "...(S) < I > (id)(V) feel like ‡(V) kissing‡ (O) « <you> »" » ((simply) because (S) < "your lips" > (id)(V) belong to < "you" >). (Likewise), (S) < "(S) < My nose > | (aV) is (V) running | . (S) < <It> > (simply) (aV) wouldn't (V) stop" > (aV) will ＼ (aV) be (id)(V) mistaken for ／ < "... (S) < <I> > (simply) (aV) wouldn't (V) stop" > (by < novice learners of < English > >). (S) <

(1)"Your lips" and (2)"My nose" > (*)(V) are (1)(C) 〚 objects of < perception > 〛, not (2)(C) 〚 (id)identical with < ◎the person { [< *whom* >] (S) < they > (id)(V) belong to } > 〛.

(S) < This objectification process > (V) is (C) 〚 (initially) difficult 〛 (for < ◎Japanese people >, (S) < who >(= *because (S) < they >*) (rarely) ^(V) make^ (O) « mental ^distinction^ (^between^ < themselves > ^and^ < (1)things or (2)folks ((*)around < them >) >) »). [*(aV) Do*] (S) < You > (V) doubt (O) « me »?... OK, (then), (O) « what » (aV) do (S) < you > (V) feel (about < ^this^ English >^:^ "(S) < Our company > (V) is (C) 〚 (id)in { great } danger 〛 (now). (S) < <It> > (id)has to (V) regenerate (O) « <itself> ».")... (aV) didn't (*)(S) < you > (1)(V) feel (O) « it » (C) 〚 strange 〛 and (2)(id)want to (V) say 【 instead 】 (O) « "...(S) < <We> > (id)have to (V) regenerate (O) « <ourselves> »" »? (S) < ^Identification^ of < oneself > ^with^ < (1)things or (2)folks ((*)around < them >) > > (V) is (C) 〚 ^so^ deep-rooted (in < Japanese consciousness >) 〛 ^that^ (S) < "(w)pronoun pronouncement" > (V) is (C) 〚 important 〛 (for < beginners >).

(S) < To (id)be able to (w)(V) paraphrase (O) « anything » (in < the correct form of < (1){ personal }/(2){ impersonal } (*)(w)pronoun(I, we, you, they, he, she, it) > >) > (V) is (C) 〚 (w)the cornerstone of < your (w)command of < English > > 〛. (aV) Do 【 consciously 】 (V) practice (O) « (w)pronoun pronouncement » (while (S) < you > (V) are (C) 〚 (still) (id)awkward with < English language > 〛). (S) < It > (aV) won't (V) take (O) « much effort », (S) < it > (aV) won't (V) take (O) « too much time », but (S) < it > (aV) will (certainly) (id)(V) take (O) « you » (somewhere), (when (S) < you > (V) are (C) 〚 (completely) sure [*that*] (S) < you > (aV) can (V) handle (O) « English (w)pronouns » ((1)instantly and (2)instinctively) 〛).

3.(id)Lack of < future > (in < Japanese (w)tense >)

(S) < "時制(JISEI: (w)tense)" > (V) is (C) 『 ◎another dimension { (in < which >) (S) < Japanese language > (V) is (C) 『 (impossibly) (id)different from < English > 』 } 』. (S) < English consciousness > ＼ (aV) is (clearly) ^(V) divided^ ／ 【 by < temporal distinctions > 】 ^into^ < three (w)tenses >, (w)namely, ◎(1)"現在(GENZAI: the present)", (2)"過去(KAKO: the past)" and (3)"未来(MIRAI: the future)", { (S) < each of < which > > *[being]* with < possible accompaniment of < "完了形(KANRYOU-KEI: (w)the perfect tense)" > >*(= and (S) < each of < them > > (aV) can ＼ (id)(aV) be (V) accompanied by ／ (w)the perfect tense)* }, ／ while (S) < contemporary Japanese language > (id)(V) is (essentially) (C) 『 lacking in < (*)the (1){ future } and (2){ perfect } (*)(w)tenses > 』.

- (S) < (*)The (1)present and (2)future > (V) have (O) « no boundary » (in < Japanese >) -

(id)(aV) Let (O) « us » (C) 『 (V) take (O) « ◎English examples » 』 (to (V) see (O) « the temporal difference (in < their language >) », { (below < which >) (aV) will (V) come (S) < their Japanese equivalents >) }:

過去形(KAKO-KEI: (w)the past tense)

(S) < I > (V) worked (yesterday).

私は昨日働いた(WATASHI WA KINOU HATARAITA)

現在形(GENZAI-KEI: (w)the present tense)

(S) < I > (V) work (every day).

私は毎日働く(WATASHI WA MAINICHI HATARAKU)

未来形(MIRAI-KEI: (w)the future tense)

(S) < I > (aV) will (V) work (tomorrow), (too).

私は明日も働く(WATASHI WA ASU MO HATARAKU)

(For < each of < the { above-mentioned } forms of < (*)the (1)past, (2)present and

(3)future > > >), (there) (aV) can (V) be (S) < "完了形(KANRYOU-KEI: (w)the perfect tense)" > ((id)in the form of < "have+過去分詞(KAKO-BUNSHI: (w)the past participle)" >) (with (S) < "have" > ＼ [†(aV) being†] (id)(V) changed into ／ < "had/have/has/will have" > ((id)in accordance (*)with (1)< the (w)tense > and (2)< the (w)subject >)):

過去完了形(KAKO-KANRYOU-KEI: the past perfect tense)

(S) < I > ↑ (aV) had (V) worked ↑ (eight hours) (by < then >).

その時点までに私は既に8時間働いていた(SONO JITEN MADENI WATASHI WA SUDENI HACHI JIKAN HATARAITE ITA)

現在完了形(GENZAI-KANRYOU-KEI: the present perfect tense)

(S) < I > ↑ (aV) have (V) worked ↑ (three hours).

私は既に3時間働いた(WATASHI WA SUDENI SAN JIKAN HATARAITA)

未来完了形(MIRAI-KANRYOU-KEI: the future perfect tense)

(S) < I > ↑ (aV) will (aV) have (V) worked ↑ (eight hours) (at < 5 P.M >).

午後5時の時点で私は8時間働いたことになる(GOGO GOJI NO JITEN DE WATASHI WA HACHI JIKAN HATARAITA KOTO NI NARU)

(Now), (S) < ◎(*)the (1){ first } and (2){ easiest } thing { for (S) < Japanese learners > to (V) consider } > (V) is (C) 『 the English ^distinction between^ < "現在形(GENZAI-KEI: (w)the present form)" > ^and^ < "未来形(MIRAI-KEI: (w)the future form)" > 』: (S) < simple addition of < the (w)auxiliary verb "will" > (before < (w)any given (w)verb >) (in < its "原形:GENKEI=(w)root form" >) > (aV) will (V) ^change^ (O) « (1)the { present } » ^into^ < (2)the { future } (*)(w)tense >. While (in < Japanese >), (there) (V) is (S) < not (even) a ^distinction between^ < the present > ^and^ < the future > >, ((S) < as > (aV) can ＼ (aV) be (V) seen ／ (in < the translations { above } >)). (S) < The future (in < Japanese language >) > ＼ (aV) is ^not^ (V) shown ／ ((1)by < the "語尾変化(GOBI-HENKA: (w)inflection)" of < (w)verbs > >) ^but^ ((2)by < the presence of < "時の副詞(TOKI-NO-FUKUSHI: temporal (w)adverbs)" > >). (If (S) < "明日

(ASU:tomorrow)" > ＼ (aV) is (V) found ／ (within < the sentence >)), (S) < the (W)tense > (aV) will ＼ (aV) be (automatically) ^(V) interpreted^ ／ ^as^ < (id)‡(V) belonging‡ to < "the future" > >, ／ (id)so that (S) < "私は明日働く(WATASHI WA ASU HATARAKU)" > (id)does not have to ＼ (aV) be (meticulously) (V) written ／ as < "私は明日働くだろう(WATASHI WA ASU HATARAKU DAROU)" >.

- { Volitional } "will" and { expecting } "will" -

(*[If (S) < it > ＼ (aV) is]]* (Precisely) (V) interpreted ／), (S) < the English (W)auxiliary verb "will" > (aV) can ＼ (aV) be (id)(V) translated into ／ < two (id)types of < Japanese expressions > >: (1)volitional "つもりだ(TSUMORI DA)" and (2)expecting(non-volitional) "だろう(DAROU)".

(When (S) < the "will" > ＼ (id)(aV) is (V) meant as ／ < volitional declaration >), (S) < its Japanese equivalent > (aV) should ^either^ (V) be (1)(C) 『 "つもりだ(TSUMORI DA)" 』 ^or^ (2)(C) 『 "" 』 – nothing { added }. ((id)In fact), (S) < "つもり(TSUMORI)" (in < Japanese >) > (id)(V) has (O) « a way of < (id)‡(V) sounding‡ (more) like < a pretext > than < a declaration of < firm will > > > », ／ (id)so that, (in < normal contexts >), (S) < (volitionally) imagined future (in < Japanese >) > ＼ (id)(aV) is (rarely) (V) accompanied by ／ < "つもりだ(TSUMORI DA)" >. (If (S) < you > (V) find (O) « a Japanese sentence "私は明日働くつもりだ(WATASHI WA ASU HATARAKU TSUMORI DA)" »), (S) < you > (aV) may 【 reasonably 】 (V) expect (O) « [that] (S) < ◎the person { *[(S) < who > | (aV) is]]* (V) speaking | (like < that >) } > | (aV) WILL NOT 【 (id)in fact 】 (aV) BE (V) WORKING | (tomorrow) ».

(When (*)(S) < English "will" > (1)(V) has (O) « ^no^ volition » (in < it >) ^but^ (2) ＼ (id)(aV) is (V) meant as ／ < an objective expectation of < future events > >), (S) < the Japanese equivalent > (V) is (C) 『 "だろう(DAROU)" 』, (as < (id)in the case of < "(S) < It > (aV) will (V) rain (tomorrow)" ＼ *[(aV) being]* ^(V) translated^ ／ ^into^ < "明日は雨が降るだろう(ASU WA AME GA FURU DAROU)" > > >).

((id)In summary), (S) < (w)the future tense (in < English language >) >, 〖while ＼ [(aV) being] (V) expressed ／ by < the addition of < the same (w)auxiliary verb "will" (before < (w)the root form of < a (w)verb > >) > > 〗, ＼ (aV) is ^(V) divided^ ／ ^(*)into^ (1)< "volitional future"="つもりだ(TSUMORI DA)" > and (2)< "(simply) expected(non-volitional) future"="だろう(DAROU)" >. (In < actual Japanese >), (S) < volitional future > (V) is (C) 『 no (id)different from < (w)the present tense > 』, ＼ *[(aV) being]* (usually) (V) used ／ (without < "つもりだ(TSUMORI DA)" >), / and (S) < non-volitional future > (aV) can (often) ＼ (aV) be (V) used ／ (without < "だろう(DAROU)" >) ((id)in case (there) (V) is (S) < ◎some temporal (w)adverb { to (V) show (O) « [that] (S) < the sentence > (V) develops ((id)in the future) » } >, †(V) making† *(= (S) < which > (V) makes)* (O) « it » (virtually) (C) 『 (id)identical with < (w)the present tense > 』, (too)).

- (S) < English (w)past tense > (V) has (O) « ^so^ many variations » ^that^ (S) < conscious ‡memorizing‡ process > ＼ (aV) is (V) required ／ -

(In < Japanese language >), (S) < (w)the past tense > (aV) can (quite simply) ＼ (aV) be (V) expressed ／ (by < ‡(V) modifying‡ (O) « the DOUSHI((w)verb) » (with < ^such^ inflections ^as^ < "た(TA)", "だ(DA)" or "した(SHITA)" > >) >):
eg."(S) < He > (V) says (so):彼はそう言う(KAREWA SOU IU) into < (S) < He > (V) said (so):彼はそう言った(KARE WA SOU ITTA)" >,
"(S) < She > (V) dies:彼女は死ぬ(KANOJO WA SHINU) into < (S) < She > (V) died: 彼女は死んだ(KANOJO WA SHINDA)" >
or "(S) < We > (V) evacuate:我々は避難する(WAREWARE WA HINAN SURU) into < (S) < We > (V) evacuated:我々は避難した(WAREWARE WA HINAN SHITA)" >.

But (in < English >), (while (S) < most (w)verbs > (aV) can (V) signify (O) « (w)the past tense » (by < the simple addition of < (1)"d" or (2)"ed" > > ((id)at the end of < its (w)root form (規則変化:KISOKU-HENKA: (w)regular conjugation) >))), (S) < some (w)verbs > (aV) must (V) take (O) « (completely) different forms (不規則変化:FUKISOKU-HENKA: (w)irregular conjugation) » (to ＼ (aV) be (*)(V) used ／ (1)in < (w)the past tense > 〖 ((w)namely, (w)the past form) 〗, (2)in < (w)the perfect tense > or (3)in < (w)the passive voice > 〖 ((w)viz (w)the past participle) 〗). (Although (S) < their variations > (aV) must (respectively) ＼ (aV) be (V) memorized ／), (S) < they > (aV) can (loosely) ＼ (aV) be (id)(V) grouped into ／ < the following four patterns >:

(1)A - B - B: (S) < (w)the past form and (w)the past participle > (V) take (O) « the same form »

eg. catch - caught - caught, hear - heard - heard, sit - sat - sat

(2)A - B - C: (S) < (w)the past form and (w)the past participle > (V) take (O) « different forms »

eg. break - broke - broken, fall - fell - fallen, lie - lay - lain

(3)A - B - A: (S) < (w)the present and (w)the past participle > (V) take (O) « the same form »

eg. become - became - become, come - came - come, run - ran - run

(4)A - A - A: (S) < (w)the present, (w)the past and (w)the past participle > (all) (V) take (O) « the same form »

eg. cut - cut - cut, let - let - let, read - read - read

(S) < The more detailed list of < these (w)irregular conjugations > > (aV) can ＼ (aV) be (V) found ／ (in < (*){ most } (1)(w)reference books or (2)dictionaries >). ((id)Now that (S) < you > ↑ (aV) have (V) known ↑ (O) « why (S) < ^it^ > (V) is (C) 〘 necessary 〙 ^to^ (id)(V) learn (O) « them » (by heart) »), (to (V) make (C) 〘 clear 〙 (O) « the temporal distinctions »), (V) (aV) do (V) memorize (O) « them » (all) (by < (rhythmically) ‡(V) singing‡ (O) « "ring - rang - rung, sing - sang - sung, sink - sank - sunk[en], etc, etc..." » >)

- (S) < Chinese language > (aV) does not (even) (V) have (O) « (w)the past form » -

(Although (S) < Japanese language > (V) is (C) 〘 (structurally) (id)different from <

Chinese language > 』), (S) < it > (V) borrows 【 from Chinese 】 (O) « its (w)ideographic ‡writing‡ system: 漢字(KANJI=(w)Chinese characters) ». But, (unlike < Chinese >), (S) < Japanese language > ＼ (id)(aV) is not (V) composed (solely) of ／ < KANJI >: (S) < it > (also) (V) has (O) « かな(仮名:KANA), ◎(w)phonographic ‡writing‡ system { *[(S) < which > ＼ (aV) was]]* (originally) (V) invented ／ (from < (w)Chinese characters >) (in < ancient Japan >) } ». ^(S) < It > (V) is^ (C) 『 this latter 』, KANA, ^(S) < which >^ (V) makes (O) « ^it^ » (C) 『 possible 』 ^for^ (S) < Japanese > ^to^ (V) act (like < English >) (in < its (w)inflection >) (to ^(V) differentiate^ (O) « (1)the { present } (*)tense » ^from^ < (2)the { past } >), (as *[(S) < it > ＼ (aV) is]]* (V) seen ／ (in < the examples *[of]* (1)"私は働く(WATASHI WA HATARAKU: (S) < I > (V) work)" and (2)"私は働いた(WATASHI WA HATARAITA: (S) < I > (V) worked)" >)). (In < this case >), (S) < the addition of < the KANA *[of]* "た(TA)" > > (V) functions (as < a symbol of < the past > >), (just like (in < English >) (S) < "ed" > (V) signifies (O) « (w)the past tense »).

But ((id)in the case of < ◎Chinese { (S) < which > (V) is (C) 『 (totally) (w)ideographic 』 (without < any (w)phonographic supplement (for < ‡(V) making‡ (O) « (w)inflection » >) >) } >), (S) < (w)verbs > (aV) can't (V) show (O) « any ^distinction between^ (1)< the present >, (2)< the past > ^and^ (3)< the future > ». ◎(S) < A Chinese > "我働" (V) (aV) can (V) mean ^either^ (1)(O) « "(S) < I > (V) work (the present)" », (2)(O) « "(S) < I > (V) worked (the past)" » ^or^ (3)(O) « "(S) < I > (aV) will (V) work (the future)" » (in < the same form >), { (S) < the ^distinction^ of < which > > (aV) must ＼ (aV) be ^(V) made^ ／ (from < contextual judgment >) }. (More (id)(specifically) *[†speaking†]*), (S) < the (w)Chinese character "了(LA)" > (V) works (to (V) signify ^either^ (O) « (1)"the past"(過去:KAKO: (S) < I > (V) worked) ^or^ (2)"the perfect"(完了:KANRYOU: (S) < I > ↑ (aV) have (V) worked ↑) (*)context »), but (S) < it > (*)(V) is (1)(C) 『 (merely) a temporal (w)adverb 』 — a Chinese (id)equivalent (*)to < (1)"(id)in the past" or (2)"already" (*)(in < English >) >, not (2)(C) 『 an (w)inflected form of < a (w)verb >

』. (S) < (w)Verbs > (themselves) (aV) can never (V) change (in < Chinese language >), ((id)due to < the (purely) (w)ideographic structure of < their ‡writing‡ system > >).

(In < Japanese >), (S) < the presence of < KANA > > (aV) can (V) modify (O) « "我働" » ((*)into (1)< "我ハ働ク(WARE WA HATARAKU:(S) < I > (V) work)" > or (2)< "我働カン(WARE HATARAKAN: (S) < I > (aV) will (V) work)" > or (3)< "我働ケリ(WARE HATARAKERI: (S) < I > (V) worked, or (S) < I > ↑ (aV) have (V) worked ↑)" >) ((S) < as > ＼ (aV) is (V) well-(id)known to ／ < ◎all Japanese folks { with < ◎ordinary (w)educational background { *[(S) < which > (V) is]* (C) 『 ^enough^ 』 (^to^ ↑ (aV) have ＼ (aV) been (painfully) (V) trained ／ ↑ in < "漢文(KANBUN, (locally) modified Chinese sentences)" > (at < school >) } >) } >).

(Anyway), (S) < temporal distinctions > (V) are (C) 『 *[◎the point]* { where (S) < the speakers of < (1){ Chinese } and (2){ Japanese } (*)languages > > (*)(V) need (1)(O) « special attention » and (2) ＼ (id)‡(V) getting‡ (C) 『 used to 』 ／ } 』; (S) < they > (aV) should ＼ (aV) be (V) examined ／ ((id)in { more } detail) (in < the next section >).

4.(1)(S) < The past > and (2)(S) < the future >

(*)(V) are (C) 『 (id)equal with < everyone > 』,

(S) < (only) the present > (V) divides (O) « us » (C) 『 apart 』

- The { (w)gender-free } characteristic of < English > -

(*[When (S) < it > ＼ (aV) is]]* (id)(V) Compared with ／ < ^such^ (1){ old } (2){ Indo-European } (*)languages ^as^ (1)< French >, (2)< Spanish > or (3)< Italian > >), (S) < English language > (V) is (C) 『 (relatively) new 』. ([While] (id)†(V) taking† over(= *(S) < it > (V) takes over)* (O) « (id)lots of < linguistic elements > » (from < those traditional languages >)), (S) < English > ↑ (aV) has (id)(V) given up ↑ (O) « (id)lots of < complexities of < other European languages > > », †(V) making†(= *(S) < which > (V) makes)* (O) « it(= *English*) » (C) 『 ◎(far) easier { to (V) master } (for < foreign speakers >) 』.

(id)(aV) Let(O) « 's » (C) 『 (id)(V) take (O) « French », (for example), (to (V) see (O) « (C) 『 how simpler 』 (S) < English grammar > (V) is ») *[than (S) < traditional Indo-European languages >]* 』. (*)(S) < All examples { below } > (1)(V) develop (in < (w)the present tense >) and (2) ＼ (aV) are (V) shown ／ (in < (1)French/(2)English (*)combination >).

(S) < ◎The first point { to (V) consider } > (V) is (C) 『 the absence of < (w)gender > (in < English language >) 』.

(S) < Il > (V) est (C) 『 un monsieur 』. / (S) < He > (V) is (C) 『 a gentleman 』.

(S) < Elle > (V) est (C) 『 une fille 』. / (S) < She > (V) is (C) 『 a girl 』.

(V) See (O) « the French ^difference between^ < "un" > ^and^ < "une" > ((id)according to < the (w)gender of < ◎the (w)noun { †(V) coming†(= *(S) < which > (V) comes)* (after < them >) } > >), ((id)as *[(S) < it > ＼ (aV) is]]* (V) opposed ／ to < the { fixed } "a" of < English (w)indefinite article > >) ».

(S) < Il > (V) est (C) 『 le monsieur 』. / (S) < He > (V) is (C) 『 the gentleman 』.

(S) < Elle > (V) est (C) 『 la fille 』. / (S) < She > (V) is (C) 『 the girl 』.

(S) < (w)Definite article > (V) is (C)『 (always) "the" same 』(in < English >), ／ while (S) < French language > ^(*)(V) coordinates^ (1)(O) « "le" » and (2)(O) « "la" » ^(*)with^ < the gender of < ◎the (w)noun { (O) « [*which*] » (S) < they > (V) modify } > >.

(S) < Il > (V) est (C)『 grand 』. / (S) < He > (V) is (C)『 tall 』.

(S) < Elle > (V) est (C)『 grande 』. / (S) < She > (V) is (C)『 tall 』.

(id)(V) Take (O) « notice » of (S) < < the English (w)adjective "tall" > > (*)‡(V) being‡ (1)(C)『 "grand" 』 or (2)(C)『 "grande" 』(in < French >) ((id)according to < the (w)gender of < the (w)subject > >). (S) < This (w)sexual difference ((id)at the end of < the same word >) > ＼ (aV) is (also) (V) seen ／ (in < one's name >): while (S) < "Jean" > (V) is (C)『 a man 』, (S) < "Jeanne" > (V) is (C)『 a woman 』.

(In < French language >), (S) < (w)each and every (w)noun > (V) has (O) « its "性(SEI: (w)gender)" » — (1)"男性(DANSEI: (w)masculine)" or (2)"女性(JOSEI: (w)feminine)". (S) < ^It^ > (V) seems (C)『 (quite) natural 』 ^that^ (S) < (1)"彼(KARE: il=he)" or (2)"彼女(KANOJO: elle=she)" > (V) has (O) « (w)gender », (w)masculine or (w)feminine, but (S) < (even) ^such^ { (apparently) (w)neuter } (w)nouns (*)^as^ (1)< "太陽(TAIYOU: the sun: (w)masculine : le soleil)" > and (2)< "月(TSUKI: the moon: (w)feminine : la lune)" > > (*)(V) have (O) « their own (w)genders ». (S) < The same (w)adjective "背が高い(SE GA TAKAI: tall)" > (id)(V) changes (O) « shapes » ((id)according to < the (w)gender of < ◎the (w)noun { (O) « [*which*] » (S) < it > (V) modifies } > > 【 ((1)"grand" (for (w)masculine) { [(S) < *which* > ＼ *(aV) is*]] (V) pronounced ／ as < "GU_RAN" > } / (2)"grande" (for < (w)feminine >) { [(S) < *which* > ＼ *(aV) is*]] (V) pronounced ／ as < "GU_RAN_D" > }) 】), ／ (S) < (even) (1)"不定冠詞(FUTEIKANSHI: (w)indefinite articles: un/une... French (id)equivalent of < "a/an" >)" and (2)"定冠詞(TEIKANSHI: (w)definite articles: le/la... "the" (in < English >))" > (*)(V) are (all) (C)『 (w)gender-sensitive 』.

(id)(S) < ^It^ > (V) follows (from < this >) ^that^ (S) < learners of < French language > > (id)has to (V) memorize (O) « (w)each and every (w)noun » ((id)along with < (1){ his

}/(2){ her } (*)gender > (respectively))...! (S) < English learners > (V) are (id)(C)〘 free from < such (w)mnemonic nightmare > 〙, / for (S) < grammatical (w)gender > (V) is (C)〘 extinct 〙(in < English >). Although (S) < English (w)indefinite article "an" > (V) is (id)(C)〘 similar to < French "un" > 〙 ⟦ ((S) < both > †(V) meaning† (O) « "one" »(= *for (S) < they > (both) (V) mean (O) « "one" »*)) ⟧ , / (when (S) < ^it^ > ＼ (aV) was (V) found ／ ^that^ (S) < "an" (before < "子音(SHIIN: (w)consonants)" >) > (V) sounded (C)〘 (rather) mouthful 〙(ng.(= =*NOT GOOD*) "~~an man~~")), (S) < English > (bluntly) (1)(id)(V) gave up (O) « the original form of < "an" > » and (2)(id)(V) cut (O) « it » (down) into < "a" (eg. "a man") >, / (id)with ◎the result { that (there) (V) is (S) < no ^such^ English ^as^ < "~~(There) (V) is (S) < an man >~~" } ⟦ (although (S) < ^it^ > (V) is (C)〘 possible 〙 ^to^ (V) say (O) « "(There) (V) is (S) < one man >" ») ⟧ > >.

(S) < ◎The only case { *[(that)]* (S) < English > (still) (V) uses (O) « the (w)indefinite article "an" » } > (V) is (C)〘 before < "母音(BOIN: (w)vowels, ^not^ (1)in < (w)spelling > ^but^ (2)in < (w)pronunciation >)" >, (id)such as < "(S) < I > (V) have (O) « an (id)appointment with < an FBI agent > »" > 〙. (id)(V) Beware of < (S) < "an FBI agent" > ‡not (V) being‡ (C)〘 "~~a FBI agent~~" 〙 >; (if (S) < it >(V) 's (C)〘 CIA 〙), (S) < "an (id)appointment with < a CIA agent >" > (aV) will (V) be (C)〘 (just) fine 〙. (Thus), (S) < ◎the different use ⟦ in < English > ⟧ of < (1)"a" > and < (2)"an" > > ＼ (aV) is (solely) (V) determined ／ (by < (w)pronunciation >), { (S) < which > (aV) can ＼ (aV) be (V) decided ／ ((id)without (any) difficulty), not (id)according to < ◎the (w)gender of ◎the (w)noun { †(V) coming†(= *(S) < which > (V) comes*) (after < "a/an" ⟦ (or (aV) should (S) < we > (V) say (O) « "un/une" ») ⟧ >) } >, { (S) < which > (aV) can never ＼ (aV) be (correctly) (id)(V) dealt with ／ (without < ‡(V) remembering‡ (O) « ^whether^ (S) < it >(V) 's (*)a (1)(C)〘 "he" 〙 ^or^ (2)(C)〘 "she" 〙 » > }) }. (How studiously) (S) < students of < French > > (aV) must (V) study!... (w)Tough luck for < them >, and (w)(V) thank (O) « our lucky stars ».

((id)As for < the English (w)definite article "the" >), (S) < it > (aV) can ＼ (aV) be (indiscriminately) (V) used ／ (before < any (w)noun >), ((quite) unlike < the French "le/la" >). (S) < ◎The only ˆdifferenceˆ { (O) « [that] » (S) < English "the" > (aV) can ˆ(V) makeˆ } > (V) is (C) 『 the three variations (in < its (w)pronunciation >) 』 ("ZI" only difference English "ZEE" can make is "ZA" three variations in its pronunciation). *[(aV) Can (S) < you >]* (*)(V) See (1)(O) « (C) 『 how simple 』 (S) < English > (V) is » 【 (or (2)(O) « (C) 『 how complicated 』 (S) < French > (V) is ») 】 ?

- (*)(S) < { English } "be" > (1)(V) is (C) 『 the most complicated of < its kin > 』, but (2)(V) is (C) 『 (far) simpler than (S) < its French counterpart > 』 -

(id)(aV) Let (O) « us » (C) 『 (id)(V) proceed to (V) check (O) « the possible variation of < (id)(O) « what » (S) < we > (V) call (C) 『 "(w)be verb" 』 (in < English >) > » ((id)in comparison with < French >) 』: (S) < you > (aV) will (V) (easily) see (O) « (C) 『 how complicated 』 (S) < French (w)verbs > (aV) can (V) be ((id)according to < the (1)(w)gender and (2)number (*)of < (w)subjects > >) ».

(w)The 1st person ((w)singular):

(S) < Je > (V) suis (C) 『 a la < TAMAGAWA JOUSUI > 』. / (S) < I > (V) am (C) 『 (id)at the edge of < Tamagawa waterworks > 』.

(w)The 1st person ((w)plural):

(S) < Nous > (V) sommes (C) 『 a la < TAMAGAWA JOUSUI > 』. / (S) < We > (V) are (C) 『 (id)at the edge of < Tamagawa waterworks > 』.

(w)The 2nd person ((w)singular):

(S) < Tu > (V) es (C) 『 a la < TAMAGAWA JOUSUI > 』. / (S) < You > (V) are (C) 『 (id)at the edge of < Tamagawa waterworks > 』.

(w)The 2nd person ((w)plural):

(S) < Vous > (V) êtes (C) 『 a la < TAMAGAWA JOUSUI > 』. / (S) < You > (V) are (C) 『 (id)at the edge of < Tamagawa waterworks > 』.

(w)The 3rd person ((w)singular (w)masculine or (w)impersonal):

(S) < Il > (V) est (C) 〚 a la < TAMAGAWA JOUSUI > 〛. / (S) < He > (V) is (C) 〚 (id)at the edge of < Tamagawa waterworks > 〛. / (S) < It > (V) is (C) 〚 (id)at the edge of < Tamagawa waterworks > 〛.

(w)The 3rd person ((w)singular (w)feminine):

(S) < Elle > (V) est (C) 〚 a la < TAMAGAWA JOUSUI > 〛. / (S) < She > (V) is (C) 〚 (id)at the edge of < Tamagawa waterworks > 〛.

(w)The 3rd person ((w)plural ^whether^ (w)masculine ^or^ (w)feminine):

(S) < Ils > (V) sont (C) 〚 a la < TAMAGAWA JOUSUI > 〛. / (S) < Elles > (V) sont (C) 〚 a la < TAMAGAWA JOUSUI > 〛. / (S) < They > (V) are (C) 〚 (id)at the edge of < Tamagawa waterworks > 〛.

(S) < The rule for < "(w)be verb" > (in < English >) > (V) is (C) 〚 (quite) simple 〛: (if (S) < the (w)subject > (V) is (C) 〚 (w)plural 〛(We, You, They)), (V) use (O) « "are" »((S) < We > (V) are, (S) < You > (V) are, (S) < They > (V) are); (if (S) < the (w)subject > (V) is (C) 〚 (w)singular 〛(He, She, It, I)), (V) use (O) « "is" »((S) < He > (V) is, (S) < She > (V) is, (S) < It > (V) is) / (id)with the { sole } exception of < ◎(S) < (w)the 1st person > ‡(V) accompanying‡ (O) « "am" »((S) < I > (V) am) >. While (in < French language >), (S) < the grandiose varieties of < (1)"suis, es, est"((w)singular) and (2)"sommes, êtes, sont"((w)plural) > > (aV) must ＼ (aV) be (V) handled ／ (meticulously) ((id)according to < the (1)(w)gender and (2)number (*)of < the (w)subject > >).

(S) < Such { forbidding } perplexities > (aV) will ＼ (aV) be (V) felt ／ (C) 〚 [to (V) be] (C) 〚 nothing 〛 〛, ((id)to be sure), (once (S) < one > ＼ (id)(V) gets (V) acquainted with ／ < their use > (by < practice after < practice > after < years of < practice > > >)). But (S) < the presence of < ◎(w)gender-specific expressions { *[(S) < which > ＼ (aV) are]]* (V) shown ／ (above) } > > (aV) will (V) be (C) 〚 more than ^enough^ 〛 (^to^ ^(V) convince^ (O) « you » ^of^ < ◎the relative ^ease^ { (^with^ < which >) (S) < you > (aV) could (V) master (O) « the (w)gender-free language of < English > », ((id)as opposed (*)to < ◎(1)French, (2)Spanish or (3)Italian { (S) < which > (V) are (all) (C) 『 (w)gender-sensitive 』 } >) } >).

- (S) < { English } "be" > (V) is (C) 『 simple (enough) 』: (S) < "do" > (V) is (C) 『 simpler (still) 』 -

While (S) < "(w)be verb" (in < English >) > (V) has (O) « three possible forms((1)am/(2)is/(3)are) ((id)according to < the (w)subject >) », / (S) < "(w)do verbs" > (V) have (O) « (only) two forms: (1)"do" or (2)"does" ». (S) < All (w)"do" verbs > (aV) should (basically) ＼ (aV) be (V) used ／ (in < its "(w)root form" >, ◎a form { *[(S) < which > ＼ (aV) is]]* (V) written ／ (on < the dictionary >) }), / (id)with the (only) exception of (S) < the (w)subject > (*)‡(V) being‡ (1)(C) 『 in < (w)the 3rd person > 』, (2)(C) 『 (w)singular 』 and (3)(C) 『 in < (w)the present tense > 』, (w)namely, (C) 『 "(1)He/(2)She/(3)It" 』: (1)(S) < these three (w)subjects >, 【 and (2)these 3 (only) 】, (*)(V) demand (O) « [that] (S) < the (w)"do" verb > *[(aV) should]* ＼ (aV) be (w)(V) inflected ／ ((id)in the form of < "does" >) »:
eg. "(S) < I/We/You/They > (V) think (so). (S) < He/She/It > (V) thinks (otherwise)".

- ((id)Apart from < (w)the present tense >), (S) < all English (w)verbs > (V) are (C) 『 (perfectly) equal 』 ((*)in < (1)the past and (2)the future >) -

(Here) (V) is (S) < another (id)piece of < (w)good news (about < English >) > >: (S) < ^such^ variations ^as^ < (1)"am/is/are"((w)be verb) or (2)"do/does"((w)do verb) > > (aV) do not (V) exist ((*)in < (1)the { past } and (2)the { future } (*)tenses of < English language > >): (S) < inequality > (V) (^only^) exists (^in^ < "the present" >)... (C) 『 how (idealistically) wonderful 』 (S) < it > (V) sounds! (There) (V) is (S) < perfect equality > ((1)in < the future > and (even) (2)in < the past > (*)(in < the world of < English > >))!... Ooops! (S) < I >(id) ↑ (aV) 've (V) made ↑ (O) « a mistake »: (S) <

"perfect" equality > (aV) does not (V) exist (in < ◎everything { (S) < that > (V) is (C) 『 "not in < (w)the present tense >" 』 } >), / for (S) < "(w)the present perfect tense" > (id)(V) consists of < ^such^ varied forms ^as^ < (1)"(S) < I/We/You/They > (id) ↑ (aV) <have> (V) made ↑ (O) « a mistake »" or (2)"(S) < He/She/It > (id) ↑ (aV) <has> (V) made ↑ (O) « a mistake »" > >. ((id)But then again), ((id)from { grammatical } point of view), (S) < "(w)the present perfect tense" > (id)(V) belongs ^not^ (1)to < the past > ^but^ (2)to < the present >, / (id)so that (S) < the { "(S) < inequality > (V) exists ((only) in < (w)the present tense >)" } theory > (still) (id)(V) holds (C) 『 true 』.

(In < (*)the (1){ future } or (2){ past } (*)tenses >), (S) < you > (id)don't have to (V) worry (about < how to (V) change (O) « the form of < English (w)verbs > » ((id)according to < (*)the (1)(w)gender and (2)number (*)of < (w)subjects > >) >)... *[(S) < It > (V) is]* (C) 『 (w)Good news 』, (V) isn't (S) < it >? (In < (w)the future tense >), (*)(S) < you > (1)(id)don't have to (V) make (O) « any change (in < the (w)verbs >) » and (2)^have only to^ (V) add (O) « "will" » ((immediately) before < them >) (^to^ (V) make (O) « "(S) < I/We/You/They/He/She/It > (aV) will (id)(V) make (O) « a mistake »" »)!... *[(S) < It > (V) is]* (C) 『 ^Too^ simple (^to^ (id)(V) make (O) « { any } mistakes ») 』, (aV) don't (S) < you > (V) think?

(w)(S) < The bad news > (V) is (C) 『 *[that]* , 【 although (S) < English (w)verbs > (id)don't have to (id)(V) change (O) « { their } shapes » ((id)according to < (*)the (1)(w)gender or (2)number (*)of < (w)subjects > > (in < (*)the (1){ past } and (2){ future } (*)tenses >)) 】 , (there) (V) are (S) < ◎three(3) cases { [where] (S) < (w)verbs > (id)have to (V) take (O) « two(2) forms » { *[(S) < which > (V) are]* (id)(C) 『 different from < (w)the root form > } } 』 > 』. (id)(S) < That > (V) is (C) 『 [to (V) say] (O) « ,

(1)(when *[(S) < they > ＼ (aV) are]]* (V) used ／ (in < the past >)), (S) < (w)verbs > (id)have to (V) take (O) « "過去形(KAKO-KEI=(w)the past form : ◎"made" { (id)as opposed to < "make" > })" »;

(2)(when *[(S) < they > ＼ (aV) are]]* (V) used ／ (in < "受動態(JUDOUTAI=(w)the passive voice)" >)), (S) < (w)verbs > (id)have to (V) take (O) « ◎"過去分詞形 (KAKOBUNSHI-KEI=(w)the past participle: "made" not "make")" { *[(S) < which > ＼ (aV) is]]* (id)(V) preceded by ／ < "is/am/are/was/were/will be > }:

eg. (S) < ^A mistake^ > (aV) will ＼ (aV) be ^(V) made^ ／ " »;

and (3)(when *[(S) < they > ＼ (aV) are]]* (V) used ／ (in < "完了形(KANRYOU-KEI=(w)the perfect tense >)")), (S) < (w)verbs > (id)have to (V) take (O) « ◎"過去分詞形(KAKOBUNSHI-KEI=(w)the past participle: ^not^ "make" ^but^ "made")" { *[(S) < which > ＼ (aV) is]]* (id)(V) preceded by ／ < "have/has/had/will have:

eg. (S) < He > ↑ (aV) had ^(V) made^ ↑ (O) « ^enough^ ^mistakes^ (^to^ ＼ (aV) be (V) fired ／) »" > } » 』 ».

(V) Take (O) « the example of < "(id)‡(V) making‡ (O) « a mistake »" > », (again), ((id)so that (there)(aV) 'll (V) be (S) < no mistake > (in < your perception of < English (w)inflection > (in < various (w)tenses >) >)).

未来((w)the future tense):

(S) < I/We/You/They/He/She/It > (aV) will (V) make (O) « a mistake ».

過去((w)the past tense):

(S) < I/We/You/They/He/She/It > (V) made (O) « a mistake ».

現在((w)the present tense):

三単現(SAN-TAN-GEN: (w)the 3rd person, (w)singular and the present):

(S) < He/She/It > (V) makes (O) « a mistake ».

三単現以外の現在(the present { (id)in general } = (id)other than < SAN-TAN-GEN >):

(S) < I/We/You/They > (V) make (O) « a mistake ».

(In < (*)the (1){ past } and (2){ future } (*)(w)tenses >), (S) < (*)the (1)(w)gender or (2)number (*)of < the (w)subject > > ^(V) has^ (O) « no ^influence^ » (^on^ < the form of < the (w)verb > >). (S) < ◎The only (w)tense { < *[that]* > (S) < you > (id)have to (id)(V) pay (O) « { special } attention » to } > (V) is (C) 『 "the present" 』, but (S) < the rule >

(V) is (C) 『 (rather) simple 』. (id)With the exception of < ◎"三単現(SAN-TAN-GEN: (w)the 3rd person, (w)singular and the present)" { †(V) requiring†(= (S) < *which* > (V) *requires*) (O) « the (w)inflection of < "s/es" > ((id)at the end of < (w)the "root form" of < the verb > >) » } >, / (S) < all English (w)verbs 【 (except <"(w)be verb: am/is/are">) 】 > (V) take (O) « the same form — ◎the one { †(V) appearing†(= (S) < *which* > (V) *appears*) (on < the dictionary >), { *[(S) < which > ＼ (aV) is]]* (V) called ／ (C) 『 (w)the "root form=原形:GENKEI" 』 } } ».

- (To (V) master (O) « the general rule »), (V) conquer (O) « the exceptions » -

(There) (V) is (S) < ◎an English proverb { (S) < which > (V) says (O) « "(w)(S) < The exception > (V) proves (O) « the [general] rule »" » } >: (S) < to (V) say (O) « "(S) < this > (V) is (O) « an exception »" » > (V) is (C) 『 to (V) say (O) « "((id)except (*)for (1)< this > 【 (or (2)< these >) 】), (S) < everything { else } > (V) follows (O) « (1){ the same } (2){ general } (*)rule »" » 』. (In < the case { above } >), (S) < ◎the general rule { that (S) < all "(w)do verbs" > (V) take (O) « (w)the "root form" » (in < (w)the present tense >) } > (id)(V) holds (C) 『 true 』 ((id)with the { sole } exception of < (S) < SAN-TAN-GEN((w)the third person, (w)singular and the present) > ‡(V) taking‡ (O) « "s/es" (w)inflection » >).

(In < such cases >), (S) < you > ^have only to^ (id)(V) pay (O) « { special } attention » to < the exception >, ^and^ (S) < the rest > (aV) can ＼ (aV) be (collectively) (id)(V) dealt with ／ (as < the general case >). ((id)For example), (S) < the statement "(To < ◎^those^ { ^(S) < who >^ ↑ (aV) have (id)(V) passed ↑ (O) « the test » } >), (S) < we >(aV) 'll (V) give (O) « a phone call » (by < Friday >)" > (V) contains (O) « ◎the general message { that "^◎those^ { ^(S) < who >^ ↑ (aV) have not (id)(V) passed ↑ (O) « the test » } (aV) will never (V) get (O) « a phone call » (from < us >) (by < Friday >)" } », { (S) < which > (also) (V) means (O) « "(if (S) < you > (aV) don't (V) receive (O) « a phone call » (from < us >) (by < Friday >)), (id)(V) be (C) 『 advised 』 [that] (S) < you > ↑ (aV) have (V) failed ↑ (O) « the test »" » }. (In < this case >), (S) < the exception > (V) is (C) 『 "‡(V) receiving‡ (O) « a phone call » (from < us >) (by < Friday >) ((id)in case of < ‡(V) passing‡ (O) « the test » >)" 』 and (S) < the general rule > (V) is (C) 『 [that] "(S) < we > (aV) will (V) make (O) « no phone call » (by < Friday >) (to < ◎ˆthoseˆ { (S) < ˆwhoˆ > (V) failed (O) « the test » } >)" 』. (S) < General rule 【 (‡(V) making‡ (O) « no phone call » (by < Friday >)) 】 > ＼ (aV) is (automatically) (V) proved ／ by < the existence of < the exception 【 (‡(V) making‡ (O) « a phone call » (by < Friday >)) 】 > >.

(S) < This { "(w)(S) < Exception > (V) proves (O) « the [general] rule »" } formula > (V) is (C) 『 ˆsoˆ (1)important and (2)handy 』 ˆthatˆ (*)(id)(aV) let (O) « us » (1)(C) 『 (V) coin (O) « an (*){ original } (1)verb/(2)(w)noun *[of]* "EXPROGER" » 【 (by < Jaugo Noto >, 2012) 】 』 and (2)(C) 『 (id)(V) put (O) « it » to < good use > 【 ((id)free of charge, (id)of course) 】 』. (In < the case { above } >), (S) < "SAN-TAN-GEN's s/es" > (V) EXPROGERS (O) « [that] "(S) < all { English } (w)do-verbs (in < (w)the present tense >) > *[(aV) should]* ＼ (aV) be (V) used ／ (in < (w)the root form >), (without < any (w)inflection >)" ».

[(V) Are (S) < you >] (C) 『 (Still) uncertain 』 *[about]* < how to (V) use (O) « "exproger" » >?... OK, (then), (id)how about < ˆthisˆ >ˆ:ˆ "(S) < He > (V) is (C) 『 ◎(quite) an exceptional Japanese { (S) < who > (V) has (O) « (w)command of < English > » } 』": (if (S) < ◎"he", { (S) < who > (aV) can (V) command (O) « English » } >, (V) is (C) 『 (quite) exceptional (as < a Japanese >) 』), (id)(S) < ˆitˆ > (V) follows ˆthatˆ (S) < Japanese people { (id)in general } > (V) have (O) « no (w)command of < English > ». (S) < "His exceptional (w)command of < English >" > ↑ (aV) has "(V) exprogered" ↑ (O) « ◎the general rule { that "(S) < the Japanese folks > (aV) cannot (V) command (O) « English »" } ».

(S) < ˆItˆ > (V) is (C) 『 (quite) important 』 ˆforˆ (S) < an English learner > ˆtoˆ (V) be (C) 『 a good EXPROGERER 』, / since (S) < (1)the abundance of < exceptions >, or (2)unique (id)deviation from < the general rule > >, (V) is (C) 『 (id)one of < the notable characteristics of < English language > > ((id)in comparison with < ^such^ (rigidly) formal languages ^as^ < (1)French or (2)Spanish > >) 』.

- (S) < No EXPROGER > ＼ *[(aV) is]* (V) needed ／ (for < { English } (w)future tense >) -

(Where(= *If*) (there) (V) is (S) < no exception >), ^(there) (V) is^ (S) < ^no^ *[means of]* ‡(V) prov^ing^‡ (O) « the general rule » (by < the exception >) >. (S) < (w)The future tense (in < English language >) > ＼ (aV) is (totally) (V) ruled ／ by < ◎the simple principle { that (S) < all (w)verbs > *[(aV) should]* ＼ (id)(aV) be (V) preceded 〖 (in < (w)the "root form" >) 〗 by ／ < the (w)auxiliary verb "will" > } >... (Well), (there) (aV) might (id)(V) appear to (V) be (S) < an exception >: ((*)in < (1){ British } or (2){ legal } (*)English >), (S) < "shall" (id)instead of < "will" > > (aV) will (often) ＼ (aV) be (V) used ／ . But (S) < most of < those "shall"s > > (aV) could 〖 safely 〗 ＼ (aV) be (id)(V) substituted with ／ < "will"s >. (S) < The use of < "shall" > (to (V) signify (O) « (w)the future tense ») > (id)(aV) is ^not^ to ＼ (aV) be (*)(V) seen ／ ((1)as < (id)an exception to < the general rule > >, ^but^ (2)as < a special feature (*)of (1){ British } or (2){ legal } (*)English, { *[(S) < which > (aV) ^is^]]* (only) ^to^ ＼ (aV) be (*)(V) learnt ／ (1)by < advanced speakers of < English > >, not (2)by < novice learners > } >).

- (1)(S) < (w)Past form > and (2)(S) < (w)the past participle > (*)(aV) must ＼ (aV) be (V) conquered ／ by < EXPROGER > -

(In < (w)the past tense >), (S) < all English (w)verbs > (V) take (O) « "過去形(KAKO-KEI=(w)the past form »:

eg. "(S) < I > (V) finished/did (O) « my homework »")";

(^in^ < ‡(V) express^ing^‡ (O) « the meaning of < "受身(UKEMI=(w)passive)" > » >),

(S) < all English (w)verbs > (V) take (O) « "過去分詞形(KAKO-BUNSHI-KEI=(w)the past participle »:

eg. "(S) < His homework > ＼ (aV) was (actually) (V) finished/done ／ by < his sister

>")";

and (when [(s) < they > | (aV) are]] (V) expressing | (O) « the meaning of < "完了(KANRYOU=perfect)" > »), (S) < all English (w)verbs > (also) (V) take (O) « "過去分詞形(KAKO-BUNSHI-KEI=(w)the past participle »:

eg. " ↑ (aV) Have (S) < you > (V) finished/done ↑ (O) « your homework » (yet)?")".

(S) < The shape (*)of < (1)(w)the past form and (2)(w)the past participle > > ＼ (*)(aV) are (1)not (V) influenced ／ by < (*)the (1)(w)gender or (2)number (*)of (w)subjects >, (2)(always) ＼ (V) used ／ (in < the same form >), (^whether^ (S) < the (w)subjects > (V) are (1)(C) 『 "I/We/You/They/He/She 』 ^or^ (2)(C) 『 It 』"). [(S) < It > (V) is] (C) 『 Simple 』, (right)?... (Well), [(S) < it > (aV) would (V) be] (C) 『 simple (enough) 』 (if (S) < all (*){ English } (1)(w)past forms and (2)(w)past participles > (aV) were (V) created (C) 『 equal 』 ((id)according to < the { single } { general } principle >)).

((id)In fact), (S) < the general rule of English ((*)(id)as regards < (1)(w)the past form and (2)(w)the past participle >), (w)namely, "◎d/ed { [(S) < which > ＼ (aV) is]] (id)(V) added to ／ < the end of < (w)the root form of < a (w)verb > > > }"(eg. "finish - finished - finished") > (aV) must ＼ (aV) be (V) EXPROGERED ／ by < ^so^ many (exceptionally) formed (1)(w)past forms and (2)(w)past participles 【 (like < "do - did - done" >) 】 > ^that^ (S) < the { long } { daunting } list of ◎< such (irregularly) shaped (1)(w)past forms and (2)(w)past participles > ([(S) < which > ＼ (aV) are]] (V) called ／ (C) 『 "不規則変化:FUKISOKU-HENKA=(w)irregular conjugation" 』) > (V) is (C) 『 (id)one of < ◎the first ordeals { < [that] > (S) < all English learners > (id)(V) stumble upon 【 (and (S) < (id)not a few [learners] > never (id)(V) stand up (again)) 】 } > 』.

But (S) < this (w)irregular conjugation > (V) is (C) 『 ◎the only realm of < English > { [(where(= that))] (S) < (w)each and every verb > (V) demands (O) « respective memorization of < its unique forms > 【 ((1)(w)past form /(2)(w)past participle) 】 » } 』: (S) < (id)other than < those exceptional English (w)verbs > > (aV) should (simply) ＼ (aV) be (V) added ／ (C) « "d/ed" » ((id)at the end) (to (V) form (O) « (w)regular conjugations of < (*)the (1)(w)past form and (2)(w)past participle > »). (S) < You > ^(V) have only to^ (id)learn (by heart) (O) « (w)the irregular conjugations » (^to^ (V) EXPROGER (O) « (w)the regular conjugations »); (although (S) < the number of < the former > > (V) is (C) ⟦ (quite) (id)a lot ⟧), (S) < the latter > (V) are (C) ⟦ (^too^ much more) numerous (^to^ (V) remember (respectively)) ⟧.

(When (S) < the variation > (V) looks (C) ⟦ complicated ⟧), (aV) let (O) « your attitude » (C) ⟦ (V) be (C) ⟦ simple ⟧ ⟧: (just) ^(V) EXPROGER^, ^and^ (S) < the general rule > (aV) will (id)(V) take (O) « care of < the rest > ». (If (S) < you > ↑ (aV) haven't (id)(V) learnt (by heart) ↑ (O) « a particular (w)verb » (as < (id)‡(V) belonging‡ to < (w)the irregular conjugation > >)), (S) < you > (aV) should (automatically) (V) consider (O) « it » (C) ⟦ to (id)(V) belong to < (w)the regular conjugation > ⟧: (S) < ◎all { (O) « *[that]* » (S) < you > (id)have to (V) do (to (V) make (O) « (*)the (1)(w)past form /(2)(w)past participle ») } > (V) is (C) ⟦ [to] (V) add (O) « (1)"d" or (2)"ed" » ((id)at the end of < its (w)root form >) ⟧.

(Conversely), (S) < you > (aV) must (id)(V) pay (O) « ^such^ { special } attention » to < "the exception" 〚 ((w)irregular conjugation) 〛 > ^as to^ (id)be able to (V) declare (O) « (w)any given case » (C) ⟦ to (V) be (C) ⟦ "the general" 〚 ((w)regular conjugation) 〛 ⟧ ⟧ (because (S) < you > ↑ (aV) have never (V) memorized ↑ (O) « it » (as < "an exception" >)).

5.(id)Lack of < plurality > (in < Japanese (w)nouns >)

- (S) < All Japanese (w)nouns > (V) are (C) 『 (w)singular 』 ((id)by nature) -

(S) < The notion (*)of < (1)"単数(TANSUU: (w)singular)" and (2)"複数(FUKUSUU: (w)plural)" > > (V) is (C) 『 (yet) another (w)twilight zone (for < Japanese learners of < English > >) 』. (In < Japanese language >), (S) < all (w)nouns > ＼ (aV) are (innately) (V) felt ／ to (V) be (C) 『 "the (w)singular" 』; (S) < ◎{ (consciously) (w)plural } form of < (w)any given (w)noun > 【 ((O) « which » (S) < (id)not a few foreign speakers of < Japanese > > (invariably) (V) make) 】 > (V) sounds (C) 『 (singularly) strange 』 (to < Japanese ears >). (S) < No Japanese > (ever) (V) says (O) « "私の<本たち>のコレクションを御覧ください:WATASHI NO <HON TACHI> NO KOREKUSHON WO GORAN KUDASAI: (aV) Let (O) « me » (C) 『 (V) show (O) « you » (O) « my collection of < books > » 』" ». (In < Japanese consciousness >), (S) < "本(a book)" > (id)(*)is (1)(always) to ＼ (aV) be (V) used ／ (in < the (w)singular >), (2)(never) to ＼ (aV) be (V) treated ／ (as < the (w)plural >).

- (S) < (w)nouns > ＼ (aV) are (V) born ／ (C) 『 "(w)plural" 』 (in < Japanese language >) -

((Even) (id)in ◎cases [where] (S) < a Japanese (w)noun > (id)seems to ＼ (aV) be (V) used ／ (in < (w)the plural form >), (like < (1)"友だち(TOMODACHI: friends)" or (2)"子ども(KODOMO: children)" >)), (id)(S) < ◎the fact > (V) is { [that] (S) < such (w)nouns > ＼ (aV) are not (V) recognized ／ (as < (w)the plural forms of < (1)"友(TOMO: a friend)" or (2)"子(KO: a child)" > >) }. (S) < You > (aV) can (easily) (V) verify (O) « this fact » (by < ^such^ expressions ^as^ < "彼は私の<友だち>です:KARE WA WATASHI NO <TOMODACHI> DESU: (S) < He > (V) is (C) 『 <a friend { of mine }> 』" or "彼女には<子供>が一人います:KANOJO NIWA <KODOMO> GA HITORI IMASU: (S) < She > (V) has (O) « <one child> »" > >). (S) < These Japanese sentences > (aV) would (V) be (C) 『 impossible 』 (if (S) < (1)"TOMODACHI" or (2)"KODOMO" > (V) were (C) 『 (w)the plural forms of < (1)"TOMO" or (2)"KO" > 』). (S)

< Such { (apparently) (w)plural } forms of < (w)nouns > > (V) are (C) 『 (actually) not "(w)plural" 』; (S) < they > (V) take (O) « those forms » (^not^ (1)(id)in order to (V) show (O) « plurality », ^but^ (2)because (S) < the Japanese folks > (V) feel (O) « *[that]* (S) < they > (aV) should ＼ (aV) be (V) used ／ ((*)in (1)< those forms > and (2)< nothing { else } >) »). (In < the natural consciousness of < Japanese people > >,) (S) < plurality > never (V) exists ((*)in < (1)"TOMODACHI" or (2)"KODOMO" >).

(To < English speakers >), (S) < Japanese { "(w)plural" } (w)nouns > (V) look (C) 『 (id)not unlike < ^such^ English words ^as^ < ◎(1)"corps" or (2)"months" { (in < which >) (S) < plurality > (V) is (C) 『 ◎obscure { (*)to (1)(V) see or (2)(V) hear } 』 } > > 』. But (S) < the reality (about < Japanese plurality >) > (V) is (C) 『 (far) stranger than (S) < (w)the wildest imagination of < English speakers > > 』: (S) < the number((1)(w)singular/(2)(w)plural) of < Japanese (w)nouns > > (V) are (C) 『 ^not^ (1)changeable ^but^ (2)fixed 』 — (S) < { (seemingly) (w)plural } (w)nouns > ＼ (*)(aV) are (simply) (1)(V) born ／ (that way), not (2) ＼ (V) made ／ (C) 『 so 』 (from < some (w)singular forms >). (S) < "木々(KIGI: trees)" > ＼ (*)(aV) are (1)(V) born ／ (C) 『 "KIGI" 』, (id)not exactly (2)(C) 『 (w)the plural form of < "木(KI: a tree)" > 』; (S) < ◎the fact { that (S) < (1)"森(MORI: a forest)" or (2)"林(HAYASHI: a wood)" > (aV) can never (V) take (O) « (w)the plural forms of < (1)"森森(MORIMORI)" or (2)"森たち(MORITACHI)" or (3)"林林(HAYASHIBAYASHI)" or (4)"林たち(HAYASHITACHI)" > » } > (id)(V) goes (to (V) show (O) « [that] (S) < Japanese plurality > (V) is (C) 『 an innate attribute of < a given (w)noun > 』 »: (S) < it > (just) (id)has (1)to ＼ (aV) be (V) memorized ／ , not (2)to ＼ (aV) be (id)(V) tinkered with ／).

- Suffixes (*)for (1)< plurality > or (2)< mentality >? -

((id)(Theoretically) speaking), (to (V) signify (O) « plurality »), (S) < Japanese language > (V) has (O) « ^such^ suffixes ^as^ < (1)"たち:TACHI: eg. 君たち(KIMITACHI: you)" or (2)"ら:RA: eg. 彼ら(KARERA: they)" or (3)"ども:DOMO: eg. 私ども(WATAKUSHIDOMO: we)" > ». But (S) < these expressions > ＼ (id)(aV) were (

originally) (*)^(V) meant^ (1)to ／ (V) show (O) « mental attitude of < the speaker > », not (2)^as^ < ‡differentiating‡ symbols of < plurality > >. (S) < (Exceptionally) cultured Japanese > (aV) should (V) know (O) « ◎the terminological fact { that (S) < "たち(達:TACHI)" (in < Japanese >) > ＼ (aV) is (exquisitely) (id)(V) associated with ／ < ◎"どち(DOCHI)" { †(V) meaning†(= (S) < *which* > (V) *means*) (O) « ◎"どうし(同士: friends, colleagues, comrades, one's company, kin)" { †(V) signifying†(= (S) < *which* > (V) *signifies*) (O) « affectionate respect (for < ◎(id)a group of < people > { [(S) < *which* > ＼ (aV) *is*]] (id)(V) referred to ／ (with < "たち:TACHI" >) } >) » } » } > } ». ([*When* (S) < *it* > ＼ (aV) *is*]] (id)(V) Compared with ／ < this >), (S) < the suffix "ら(等:RA)" > (V) is (C) 『 (rather) insulting 』 ((id)in nature), (id)dealing with(= (S) < *which* > (V) *deals with*) < (id)a bunch of < folks > (as < ◎nothing { to ＼ (aV) be (respectively) (V) treated ／ (with < respect >) } >) >.

(S) < No ordinary Japanese > ever (V) says (O) « "彼たち(KARETACHI)" » / because (S) < (w)the plural form of < "彼(KARE: he)" > > ↑ (aV) has (aV) been ↑ (traditionally) (C) 『 fixed 』 (in < Japanese >) (as < "彼ら(KARERA: they)" >). ◎^Those^ { (S) < ^who^ > (V) use (O) « "彼たち(KARETACHI)" » } | (aV) are (V) using | (O) « that expression » (^for^ < three possible ^reasons^ >):

(1)(since (S) < (w)the plural form of < "彼女(KANOJO: she)" > > (V) is (C) 『 (generally) "彼女たち(KANOJOTACHI: they)" 』), (S) < the (w)masculine (w)plural form > (aV) should (also) (V) be (C) 『 "彼たち(KARETACHI: they)" 』 ((id)from the standpoint of < (w)sexual equality >) — (w)VIVA (w)[WO]MEN'S LIB!;

(2)(when (S) < everyone { else } (in < Japan >) > (id)(V) sticks to < "彼ら(KARERA: they)" >), (S) < the novel expression [of] "彼たち(KARETACHI: they)" > (aV) should (V) sound ^so^ (C) 『 unique 』 ^as to^ (V) make (O) « the speaker » (C) 『 (id)(V) stand out (among < the crowd >) 』 — COOL!; and

(3)(*)(S) < they > (simply) (1)(aV) didn't (V) know (O) « the traditional Japanese expression "彼ら(KARERA: they)" » and (2)(V) thought (O) « ^it^ » (C) 『 (just) fine 』 ^to^ (V) add (O) « the suffix "たち(TACHI)" » ((id)at the end of < "彼(KARE: he)" >) (

to (V) form (O) « (w)the plural form of < "彼たち(KARETACHI: they)" > ») – BOO!

(If (S) < the last one > (id)happens to (V) be (C) 『 ◎the paramount reason { why (S) < ^such^ a queer expression ^as^ < "彼たち(KARETACHI)" > > (aV) should (V) prevail (in < the { present day } Japan >) } 』), (S) < the possible result of < such linguistic anomalies > > (aV) might (V) be (C) 『 [that], ((id)some day), (S) < all ◎Japanese (w)nouns 【 ((S) < which > (V) are (essentially) (C) 『 (w)singular 』) 】 > (*)(aV) could (1)(id)(V) change (O) « shapes » and (2)(V) mean (O) « (w)plural » (freely) (by < the simple addition of < "たち(TACHI)" > > (as < the Japanese (id)equivalent of < "s/es" in < English > > >)) 』... (S) < I > (aV) must (V) warn (O) « you », (however), (O) « [that] (S) < such > (V) is (C) 『 not (id)the case with < the contemporary Japanese > 』 »: (S) < ◎a (w)noun > ＼ (aV) is (innately) (V) felt ／ to (V) be (C) 『 the (w)singular 』, { (S) < the { (forcibly) pluralized } form of < which > > (V) sounds ^too^ (C) 『 singular 』 (^to^ (V) be (C) 『 a legitimate Japanese 』) }.

(S) < Most Japanese people > (V) are (C) 『 (totally) (id)ignorant (*)of (1)< these linguistic facts of < traditional Japanese language > > or (2)< their latent (id)influence upon < their own speech > > 』, but (S) < they > (aV) could (still) (*)(V) discern (1)(O) « the { (aggressively) wild } tone of < "野郎ども:YAROUDOMO: those bastards" > or (2)< { (hypocritically) condescending } tone of < "私どもに言わせていただければ:WATAKUSHIDOMO NI IWASETE ITADAKEREBA: (S) < we > (humbly) (V) say (O) « that... »" > > ».

- (There) (V) is (S) < no real notion of < (1)(w)singular /(2)(w)plural > > (in < Japanese consciousness >) -

((id)In summary), (*)(S) < the { (apparently) (w)plural } suffixes of < Japanese language >(たち:TACHI, ら:RA, ども:DOMO) > (1)(V) are (id)^not^ really (C) 『 plurality modifiers 』 ^but^ (2) ＼ (id)(aV) are (V) meant as ／ < symbols of < ◎mental attitudes, { ^†(V) ranging† from^ *(= (S) < which > (V) range from)* (1)< disdain > through (2)< humility > ^to^ (3)< respect > } > >. (id)(S) < ^It^ > (V) follows (from < this >) ^that^ (S) < the Japanese people > (V) have (O) « no actual ^distinction between^ < the (w)singular

> ^and^ < the (w)plural >) in < their concept of < (w)nouns > >) »: (S) < their world > ＼ (id)(aV) is (V) composed (solely) of ／ < (w)the singular form >. (^For^ (S) < them > ^to^ (id)(V) migrate into < the world of < English > >), (therefore), (S) < the concept of < plurality > > (id)has to ＼ (aV) be (V) established ／ ((wholly) anew).

(Conversely), (S) < learners of < Japanese language > (from < { Indo-European speaking } nations >) > (aV) should (id)(V) make (O) « ^it^ » (C) 『 a rule 』 ^to^ "(id)(V) switch (C) 『 off 』" (O) « their attitude (*)of (1)< (id)‡(V) counting‡ up (O) « (w)nouns » >, (2)< ‡(V) adding‡ (O) « "s/es"(TACHI, RA, DOMO) » ((id)at the end) > »: (S) < all Japanese (w)nouns > ＼ (id)(aV) are (V) meant to ／ ＼ (aV) be (V) used ／ (in < the (w)singular >), (although (sometimes) (id)†(V) seeming† to (V) be *(= (S) < they > (sometimes) (id)(V) seem to (V) be)* (C) 『 the (w)plural 』).

- (S) < English (w)nouns > (id)had best ＼ (aV) be (V) memorized ／ ^not^ (1)(in < the (w)singular >) ^but^ (2)(as < (id)a pair of < (1)determinative/(2)numerical (w)adjective (*)+ < (w)plural form > > >) -

(For < ◎Japanese people { (S) < who > (V) have (O) « no real concept of < plurality > » } >), (here) (V) is (S) < one great (id)tip (*)for (1)< ‡(V) overcoming‡ (O) « that lethal handicap » > and (2)< (id)‡(V) building‡ up (O) « their vocabulary » ((id)along with < some useful expressions >) > >: ^never^ (V) memorize (O) « "a (w)noun" » ((id)as is), ^but^ (always) (id)(V) learn (O) « it » (by heart) (*[＼ (aV) being]*] (id)(V) coupled with ／ < ^such^ (w)adjective modifiers ^as^ < "some/(id)lots of/(id)a pair of/etc, etc." > >) (eg. "some handkerchieves", "(id)lots of photos", "(id)a pair of trousers"), ((thereby) †^(V) imprinting^† (O) « (w)nouns » ^upon^ < the memory > ((1)in the (w){ plural }, NEVER (2)in the (w){ singular } (*)form)).

((id)Along with < the concept of < plurality > >), (S) < Japanese language > (V) is (C) 『 (absolutely) (id)devoid of < "冠詞(KANSHI: (w)articles)" > 』; (more specifically), (1)"不定冠詞(FUTEIKANSHI:(w)the indefinite article: "a" and "an")" and (2)"定冠詞(TEIKANSHI:(w)the definite article: "the")". (S) < That > (V) is (C) 『 *[the reason]* why (S) < ordinary Japanese people > (id)(V) are (C) 〚 prone to (V) use (O) « (w)nouns » (in < (dually) wrong ways > 〛) 〛:

(1)(in < (w)the singular form > 〚 (the { "raw" } form { *[(S) < which >* ＼ *(aV) is]]* (V) written ／ (on < the dictionary >) }) 〛) and

(2)(without < (*)any (1)indefinite/(2)definite (*)article >):

ng. "~~(S) < I > (V) 'm not (C) 〚 (id)good at <computer> 〛~~".

(For < ◎Japanese people { *[(S) < who > (V) are]* (C) 〚 (id)unfamiliar with < English > 〛 } >), (S) < (1)‡(V) remembering‡ or (2)‡(V) pronouncing‡ or (3)‡(V) spelling‡ (*)(O) « an English word » > (V) is (C) 〚 "an accomplishment" ((id)in itself) 〛; (S) < their mental (w)attention span > (V) is ˆsoˆ (C) 〚 limited 〛 ˆthatˆ (S) < they > ＼ (1)(aV) are (already) (C) 〚 (V) satisfied 〛 ／ (when (S) < they > (aV) can (correctly) (1)(V) remember/(2)(V) pronounce/(3)(V) spell (*)(O) « "computer" »), and (2)never (V) realize (O) « [that] (S) < they > ↑ (aV) have (id)(V) failed to (V) add ↑ (O) « (1)"a" or (2)"the" » (before < "computer" >) ». (S) < This (id)type of < incorrect English > — ◎a (w)singular (w)noun { ＼ *[†(aV) being†]* (V) used ／ (without < ‡(V) accompanying‡ (O) « any article » >) } — > (V) is (C) 〚 (id)typical of < ◎Japanese folks > 〛, { (S) < { whose } language >*(= because (S) < their language >)* (*)(V) has (1)(O) « (absolutely) no (1)indefinite/(2)definite (*)articles » or (2)(O) « actual concept of < plurality > » }.

(S) < The best (id)cure for < this linguistic propensity > >, (again), (V) is: (C) 〚 "(always) (1)(V) remember/(2)(V) use (*)(O) « (w)nouns » (in < (w)the plural form >), ／ unless (S) < ˆitˆ > (V) is (C) 〚 (absolutely) necessary 〛 ˆtoˆ (1)(V) remember/(2)(V) use (*)(O) « them » (in < (w)the singular form >)" 〛. (S) < This { (simply) practical } remedy > (V) is (C) 〚 most effective 〛 (when *[(S) < it >* ＼ *(aV) is]]* (V) applied ／ (in < the earliest stage of < ‡(V) learning‡ (O) « English » > >)). (When (S) < a (w)noun > ＼ (aV) is (id)(V) stored up ／ (in < your memory >) (in < (w)the singular form >) — (without < ‡(V) accompanying‡ (O) « "s/es" » > ((id)at the end)) —) (S) < it > (aV) MUST (V) be (C) 〚 ◎a (w)noun { (S) < which > (aV) CANNOT (V) take (O) « (w)the plural form (eg. "deer" or "John" or "mail" or "democracy" or ◎any such (w)nouns { without < (*)the (1)form or (2)concept (*)of < the (w)plural > > }) » } 』. (If (S) < your memory > ^(V) presents^ (O) « you » ^with^ < a (w)noun (in < (w)the singular form >) >), (id)^(V) it^ (aV) must (automatically) (V) follow ^that^ (S) < the (w)noun >(id)is to ＼ (aV) be (V) used ／ (in < (w)the singular form (only) >); (S) < anything { else } > (aV) should (id)(V) come up to < your memory > ((in < (w)the plural form >) (with < "some" (id)types of < determinatives > (before < them >) >))... (S) < this (id)type of < attitude > > (*)(V) is (1)(C) 『 (quite) useful 』, 【 (2)(C) 『 (indeed) indispensable 』 】 , (^for^ (S) < Japanese learners of < English > > ^to^ (V) overcome (O) « their innate (id)lack (*)of (1)< articles > and (2)< plurality concept > »).

- (S) < The (w)plural > ＼ (aV) is (generally) (id)(V) preferred to ／ < the (w)singular > (in < English >) -

(S) < The (w)plural forms of < some English (w)nouns > >, 【 just like < the "不規則変化(FUKISOKU-HENKA: (w)irregular conjugation)" of < the (w)verb > > 】 , (V) take (O) « (totally) ^different^ shapes ^than^ (S) < their (w)singular forms > (eg. "a child/children", "a mouse/mice", "an ox/oxen") ». (In < such cases >), (1)(S) < the (w)singular > and (2)(S) < the (w)plural > ＼ (aV) must (both) (*)(aV) be ／ (1)(id)(V) paid (O) « { equal } attention » to and (2)(id)(V) stored up (in < your memory >) ((id)side by side), 【 (id)of course 】 . But (always) (V) remember: (O) « (S) < practical usefulness of < the (1)(w){ plural } > > (V) (far) exceeds (O) « (2)the (w){ singular } (*)form of < most (w)nouns > » ».

(In < actual English >), (S) < people > (rarely) (V) use (O) « ^such^ expressions ^as^ < (1)"(S) < I > (V) am (C) 『 (id)good at <the computer> 』" or (2)"(S) < I > (V) am (C) 『 (id)good at <a computer>" 』 > »; (S) < they > ((almost) always) (V) say (O) « "(S) < I > (V) am (C) 『 (id)good at <computers> 』" ». (S) < The (w)plural > (V) is (C) 『 (*)the (1){ most ordinary } and (2){ most useful } (*)form of < a (w)noun > 』. (S) < Learners of < English > > (aV) ought to (V) acquire (O) « the habit of < (*)^‡(V) preferring‡^ (O) « the

(1)(w){ plural } » ^to^ < the (2)(w){ singular } (*)form > > » (in < the early stage of < their studies > >). (S) < This > (V) is (C) 〚 (also) (id)true with < ◎French natives > 〛, (S) < who(= because (S) < they >) > (V) are (C) 〚 (id)in the habit of < (always) ‡(V) using‡ (O) « ◎a (w)noun { [(S) < which > ＼ (aV) is]] (id)(V) coupled with ／ < ^such^ articles ^as^ < "un/une/le/la/les/du/de la/des" > > } » > 〛; (S) < English speakers > (aV) don't (V) use (O) « "a/an/the" » (^so^ (frequently) ^as^ (S) < French people > (V) imagine). (S) < The overuse of < "the" > > (V) is (C) 〚 (id)one of < the most conspicuous characteristics of < ◎foreign speakers of < English > { [†(V) coming†] from < (1){ traditional } (2){ "article-tight" } (3){ Indo-European language speaking } nations > } > > 〛.

(For < anyone { (id)other than < native English speakers > } >), (S) < ^it^ > (V) is (C) 〚 the best practice 〛 ^to^ (1)(V) remember and (2)(V) use (*)(O) « English (w)nouns » (in < the (w)plural >), ／ except when (S) < (w)the singular form > (V) is (C) 〚 (absolutely) necessary 〛.

6.(S) < English articles > (V) are (C)『 (id)too much for < novice comprehension > 』

- (1)Indefinite/(2)Definite (*)article: its possible danger < for < beginners of < English > > > -

(S) < (id)One of < ◎the reasons { why (S) < the Japanese people > (id)are (generally) unable (*)to (1)(V) comprehend and (2)(V) command (*)(O) « English » } > > (V) is (C)『 their (1)^fuzzy notion^ 【 ((id)not so { clever } (2)‡understanding‡) 】 (*)^of^ "(W)command of < English >" 』. (In < their cramp consciousness >), (S) < (W)each and every lesson (in < English textbooks >) > (aV) MUST ＼ (aV) be (V) comprehended ／ ((id)then and there), (with < ◎(1){ full } to (2){ high } (*)marks (in < exams >) { to (V) show (O) « their conquest » } >)... *[(S) < which > (V) is]* (C)『 (too) { (foolishly) arrogant } ◎an attitude { (S) < that > (id)(1)(V) comes back to*(= and)* (2)(V) haunt (O) « them » } 』. ((id)So long as (S) < they > (V) are (C)『 (1){ mental } and (2){ social } (id)(*)slaves to < that attitude > 』), (S) < they > (aV) will (id)(V) put (O) « { (^too^) much } stress » on < (id)‡(V) preparing‡ for < the lessons > > 【 (lest (S) < they > [(aV) should] (id)(V) lose (O) « their face » (in < the classroom >)) 】 ^to^ (id)(V) place (O) « { ^enough^ } weight » upon < ‡(V) reviewing‡ (O) « those lessons » > 【 (^to^ (V) secure (O) « their footholds » (in < the world of < English > >)) 】.

(As (S) < this author > ↑ (aV) has (id)(V) pointed out ↑ ((id)at the beginning of < this book >)), (S) < English lessons (in < Japan >) > ＼ (*)(aV) are ^not^ (1)(V) organized ／ (to (V) facilitate (O) « the ‡understanding‡ of < learners > »), ^but^ (2)(arbitrarily) (V) made ((id)for the benefit of < (1)schools and (2)teachers >). (If (S) < learners > (id)(V) tried (desperately) to (V) conquer (O) « everything (in < English >) » ((id)the way { *[(in < which >)]* (S) < teachers > (V) order (O) « them » (C)『 to *[(V) conquer]* 』 })), (S) < they > (id)(V) are (C)『 sure to ＼ (V) get (C)『 stranded 』 ／ (at (quite) an { early } stage of < their ordeals >) 』.

(S) < One (quite) certain point of < shipwreck > > (V) is (C)『 "冠詞(KANSHI: articles)" 』: how (*)to (1)(V) understand and (2)(V) use (O) « "a/an/the" ». (S) < This author > (aV) can (V) assure (O) « you » (O) « [that] (S) < you > (aV) will never (id)be able (*)to (1)(V) comprehend and (2)(V) command (O) « (*){ English } (1){ indefinite }/(2){ definite } (*)articles » ((id)with { relative } freedom) (until (S) < English > ↑ (aV) has (V) become ↑ (C) 〚 your (w)second nature 〛) ». ((id)In other words), (S) < most ◎foreign speakers { with < adequate (w)command of < English > > } > (V) are (still) (C) 〚 awkward (in < their use of < (1)"a/an" and (2)"the" > >) 〛. (aV) Can't (S) < you > (V) believe (O) « it »?... (S) < It >(V) 's (C) 〚 because (S) < you > ↑ (aV) haven't (fully) (V) understood ↑ (O) « the fundamental ˆdifferenceˆ of < English language > ˆfromˆ < ◎the traditional Indo-European languages { like (1)< French > or (2)< Italian > } > » 〛.

- (S) < How (id)tight with < articles > > (V) is (C) 〚 *[◎the point]* { where (S) < English > (id)(V) differs (drastically) from < (id)the rest of < European languages > > } 〛 -

(S) < The French use of < articles(un/une/le/la/les/du/de la/des) > (before < (w)nouns >) > (V) is (C) 〚 the (w)reflective action (for < French natives >) 〛. (In < English >), (however), (S) < (id)lots of < (w)nouns > > ＼ (aV) are (V) used ／ (without < (1)"a/an" or (2)"the" (before < them >) >). (S) < "(S) < Dogs > (V) are (C) 〚 faithful animals 〛" > (V) is (C) 〚 { the most commonplace } English sentence 〛; (S) < (1)"(S) < The dog > (V) is (C) 〚 a faithful animal 〛" or (2)"(S) < A dog > (V) is (C) 〚 a faithful animal 〛" or (3)"(S) < Dogs > (V) are (C) 〚 a faithful animal 〛" > (V) is (C) 〚 ˆtooˆ pedantic (ˆtoˆ (id)(V) sound (C) 〚 like < normal English > 〛) 〛.

(S) < The ˆrelationship betweenˆ < articles > ˆandˆ < (w)nouns > > (V) is (C) 〚 ˆsoˆ airtight (in < French >) 〛 ˆthatˆ (*)(S) < articles(un/une/le/la/les/du/de la/des) > (1)(aV) can and (2)(aV) should ＼ (*)(aV) be (V) taught ／ (at the earliest stage of < French language lessons >). (S) < This > (V) is (C) 〚 (also) (id)true with < most (1){ traditional } (2){ "article-tight" } (3){ Indo-European } (*)languages > 〛.

But (S) < ◎English > (V) is (C) 〚 (w)a black sheep (among < European languages >) 〛, { (S) < which > ↑ (aV) has (totally) (V) abandoned ↑ (O) « the { (meaninglessly) complex } (id)notion of < "(w)gender" of (w)nouns > » }, / (id)with ◎the result {

that (S) < the airtight consciousness of < respective ◎articles >, 〖 (S) < which > (aV) must (id)(V) change (O) « shapes » ((id)according to < (*)the (1)(w)gender and (2)number (*)of < ◎the (w)nouns { †(V) coming†(= (S) < *which* > (V) *come*) (after < them >) } > >) 〗 >, ↑ (aV) has (also) (V) become ↑ (C) 『 unnecessary 』 (in < English >) }. (S) < This freedom > ↑ (aV) has ^(V) liberated^ ↑ (O) « English » ^from^ < ^such^ pedantic sentences ^as^ < "(S) < (1)The/(2)A (*)dog > (V) is (C) 『 a faithful animal 』" > >.

And(= *And yet*), ^(S) < it > (V) is^ (C) 『 this { freewheeling } propensity of < English > 』 ^(S) < that >^ ↑ (aV) has (V) made ↑ (O) « ^it^ » (C) 『 impossible 』 ^for^ (S) < novice learners of < English > > (*)^to^ (1)(V) comprehend and (2)(V) master (*)(O) « "a/an" and "the" »; (S) < the use of < ◎these articles > > (V) is (C) 『 (id)in { (mutually) exclusive } relationship with < the use of < (w)plural forms > > 』, { (S) < the comprehensive ‡understanding‡ of < which > > (*)(V) takes (1)(O) « ^so^ much time », (2)(O) « ^so^ many years of < conscious scrutiny > » and (3)(O) « (id)mountains of < example sentences > » ^that^ (S) < the task > (V) is (C) 『 a total impossibility (for < beginners of < English > >) 』 }. (V) Trust (O) « me », (S) < this > (V) is (C) 『 not (id)peculiar to < Japanese students of < English > > 』; (1){ French }, (2){ Italian } or (3){ Spanish } (*)natives (V) are (C) 『 (also) (id)at < a loss > *[about]* < (O) « what » to (id)(V) do with < English articles > > 』.

- (S) < The { freewheeling } articles of < English > > (aV) can (freely) ＼ (aV) be (V) placed ／ (anywhere (in < English textbooks >)) -

(S) < The problem of < (1){ indefinite }/(2){ definite } (*)articles > > (V) is (C) 『 a handful 』 ((even) for < professional English scholars >, (too)). (There) (V) is (S) < no easy ◎way { to (*)(efficiently) (1)(V) learn or (2)(V) teach (*)(O) « the comprehensive use of < "a/an" and "the" > » } >. But (S) < (w)guidebooks to < English usage > > (aV) must (V) have (O) « articles (about < ◎the (*)article >((1){ indefinite }/(2){ definite })) » (somewhere). (S) < ^It^ > (V) is (C) 『 never possible 』

˘to˘ (V) write (O) « (id)a { superb } piece of < ◎article { to ˘(V) enable˘ (O) « learners » (C) 〚 (*)˘to˘ (1)(V) comprehend and (2)(V) command (*)(O) « English (w)articles » ((id)at a single stroke) 〛 } > ». (S) < ˘It˘ > (V) is, (therefore), (C) 〚 possible 〛 ˘for˘ (S) < writers of < English textbooks > > ˘to˘ (V) place (O) « the article(s) (on < (1){ indefinite }/(2){ definite } (*)articles >) » (anywhere (in < their books >)). ((id)As (S) < it > (V) happens), (S) < { (virtually) all } textbooks (on < traditional Indo-European languages >) 【 ((S) < which > (V) are (all) (C) 〚 (id)tight with < (w)articles > 〛) 】 > (id)(V) begin with < the explanation of < ◎articles > > 【 ([(S) < *which* > (V) *are*] (C) 〚 variable (with < (*)the (1)(w)gender /(2)number (*)of < ◎(w)nouns { †(V) coming†(= (S) < *which* > (V) *come*) (after) } > >) 〛) 】 . (V) Isn't (S) < ˘it˘ > (C) 〚 natural 〛, (then), ˘that˘ (S) < textbooks of ◎< English > 【 ((*)(S) < which > (1)(V) is (C) 〚 (quite) (id)loose with < (w)articles > 〛 but (2)(V) is (still) (C) 〚 "an European language" 〛) 】 > (aV) should (V) ˘(V) start out˘ 【 like (S) < French guidebooks > 】 (˘with˘ < an article on < (w)articles > >), ((C) 〚 however (impossibly) complicated 〛 (S) < it > (aV) may (V) seem (to < beginners >))?... (Now) (S) < you > (aV) must ↑ (aV) have (V) known ↑ (O) « (*)how (1)(C) 〚 unnatural 〛 and (2)(C) 〚 difficult 〛 【 (no, (3)(C) 〚 IMPOSSIBLE 〛!) 】 (S) < ˘it˘ > (V) is ˘for˘ (S) < English learners > ˘to˘ (id)(V) try to (V) master (O) « (1){ indefinite }/(2){ definite } (*)articles » ((id)at the beginning of < their ‡learning‡ career >) ».

- How to (loosely) (V) comprehend (O) « (1){ indefinite }/(2){ definite } (*)articles » -

((id)(S) < Such > †being† (C) 〚 the case 〛), (S) < beginners of < English > > (aV) should not (id)(V) pay (O) « { (too) rigid } attention » to < the problem (*)of < (1)(w)indefinite articles ("a" and "an") and (2)(w)definite article ("the") > >. (S) < ◎The basic knowledge { (O) « [*which*] » (S) < they > (aV) should (V) have (about < these articles >) } > (V) is (simply) (C) 〚 that:

(1)(S) < English (w)articles ("a/an/the") > never (id)(V) change (O) « shapes » ((id)according to < the (w)gender of < ◎(w)nouns { †(V) coming†(= (S) < *which* > (V) *come)* (after < them >) } > > (like (s) < traditional Indo-European languages >)) 【 ((s) < English (w)nouns > (v) have (o) « no such (w)gender ») 】;

(2)(s) < ◎(1)a (w)noun or (2)(w)nouns { [*(s) < which >* ＼ *(*)(av) are*]] (already) (1)(v) talked about or (2)(v) thought about ／ (by < (w)the parties { concerned } >) } > (av) should (v) accompany (o) « (w)the definite article "the" », ((id)regardless of < the number of < ◎(w)nouns { †(v) coming† *(= (s) < which > (v) come)* (after) } > >);

(3)(s) < ◎a (w)singular (w)noun { (id)†(v) coming† up to *(= (s) < which > (v) comes up to)* < the speaker's consciousness > ((id)for the first time) } > (av) should (v) accompany (o) « (w)the indefinite article "a" (eg. "a pen") », ／ (id)with the exception of < (s) < ◎a (w)noun { (id)†(v) beginning† with *(= (s) < which > (v) begins with)* < (w)vowel sounds > } > ‡(v) accompanying‡ (o) « "an" » (eg. "an album", "an FBI intervention") >;

(4)(s) < ◎a (w)noun { [(s) < which > ＼ (av) is] (merely) (id)(v) referred to ／ (as < (id)one of < many possible things > >) } > (av) should (v) accompany (o) « (w)the indefinite article "a" or "an" » (eg. "(s) < I >(v) 'm (c) 『 (just) a passer-by 』");

(5)(s) < ◎(1)a (w)noun or (2)(w)nouns { [*(s) < which >* ＼ ^*(av) are*^]] ^(v) meant as^ ／ < ◎something { special } { [*(s) < that > (v) is*] (c) 『 (id)different from < the rest > 』 } > } > (av) should (v) accompany (o) « (w)the definite article "the" » (eg. "(s) < She > (v) is (c) 『 the witness of < the crime > 』");

(6)(*)(s) < ◎(w)nouns { (s) < which > (av) cannot ＼ (av) be (v) counted ／ ((w)uncountable nouns : eg. "cake") } > (1)(av) can ＼ (id)(av) be (v) accompanied by ／ < (w)the definite article "the" > (eg. "the chalk") but (2)(av) cannot (v) accompany (o) « (w)the indefinite article "a" or "an" » (ng. "~~a chalk~~"), ／ (so) (s) < they > 【 instead 】 (v) accompany (o) « ^such^ expressions ^as^ < "(id)a bulk of / (id)a group of / (id)a lot of / (id)a set of / (id)a sheet of / etc, etc." > » (eg. "(id)a stick of < chalk >");

(7)(s) < ◎(w)nouns { †(v) signifying† *(= (s) < which > (v) signify)* (o) « the name of < a person > » (eg. "John") } > (av) does not (usually) (v) accompany (o) « articles », but (s) < the name of < (id)a group of < persons > > (eg. "the Beatles", "the

Simpsons") > (V) (usually) accompany (O) « (w)the definite article »;

(8)(S) < (1){ indefinite }/(2){ definite } (*)articles("a/an/the") > (1)(id)(V) belong to < (id)(S) < what > ＼ (aV) is (V) called ／ (C) 『 "限定詞(GENTEISHI: ◎(w)determinatives)" 』 >, { (*)(S) < which > (1)(V) modify and (2)(V) determine (O) « the attributes of (*)< ◎(w)nouns { †coming†(= (S) < *which* > (V) *come*) (after < them >) } > », and (2)(aV) cannot ＼ (aV) be (V) used ／ ((id)along with < other (w)determinatives (eg. this, that, my, our, your, his, her, its, their, some, any, every, one, no, etc,etc.) >), ／ { (for < the co-existence of < which > >) ＼ (aV) are (V) used ／ (S) < ^such^ expressions ^as^ < (1)"a friend { of mine } (ng. ~~a my friend~~)" or (2)"this mistake { of his } (ng. ~~this his mistake~~)" or (3)"no business { of yours } / none { of your business } (ng. ~~no your business~~)" > > } };

(9)(in < normal speech >), (S) < (w)nouns > (aV) should (basically) ＼ (aV) be (V) treated ／ (in < the (w)plural >) (eg. "(S) < Men > (V) are (C) 『 mortal 』"), ／ (id)with the exception of < ◎a (w)noun { †(V) requiring†(= (S) < *which* > (V) *requires*) (O) « individual treatment » } (eg."(S) < A man's life > (V) is (C) 『 heavier than (S) < the earth > 』") >. 』

7.^(aV) Let^ (O) « "be" » (C) 『 alone 』, ^and^ (S) < the rest > (aV) will (V) "do" (O) « their job »

- "(w)Be verbs" ((id)as *[(S) < they > ＼ (aV) are]]* (V) opposed to ／ < "(w)do verbs" >) -

(There) (V) are (S) < ◎moments { [when] (S) < words > (V) fail (O) « us », (w)i.e*(= that is)*, { when (S) < we > (aV) cannot (id)(V) hit upon < any suitable ◎words { to (V) utter } > } } >. (At < such moments >), (S) < ordinary English speakers > (V) stammer (O) « "(S) < I >, ah..." », (*[†(V) being†]* (C) 『 (id)at a loss *[about]* < ◎{ what } "(w)do verbs" { to (id)(V) put in } > 』); (S) < ◎Japanese people { *[(S) < who > (V) are]* (C) 『 (id)unacquainted with < English > 』 } > (V) stumble (O) « "(S) < I >(V) 'm (C) 『 a... 』" », ((instinctively) (id)†(V) clinging† to*(= as (S) < they > (instinctively) (id)(V) cling to)* < ◎(id)the very first English (w)sentence pattern { (O) « *[that]* » (S) < they > ＼ (aV) were (V) taught ／ (at < school >) } >).

(S) < I > | (aV) 'm ^not^ (V) saying | (O) « this » (O) « ^to^ (V) show (O) « (C) 『 how shameful 』 (S) < ^it^ > (V) is ^for^ (S) < a Japanese > ^to^ (V) stop (at < "(S) < I >(V) 'm (C) 『 a... 』" >) » 【 (^[as]^ (C) 『 shameful 』 ^as^ (S) < it > (V) is) 】 »; (S) < I > | (aV) 'm (just) (id)(V) pointing out (O) « ◎the fact (1){ that (S) < (1){ "(S) < I > (V) am" } 【 ((more (id)(generally) *[†(V) speaking†]*), (2){ "S+be" }) 】 (*)structure > (V) is (C) 『 (id)one of < the most basic patterns of < English > > 』 }, and (2){ that (S) < ◎anything { (id)other than < { "S+be" } structure > } > (aV) must (invariably) (V) take (O) « the form of < { "S+do" } structure > » } ». ((id)To (V) put (O) « it » (another way)), (if (*)(S) < you > (1)(V) (thoroughly) know (O) « when to (V) use (O) « "(w)be verb" » » and (2)(V) exclude (O) « them » (all)), (S) < all the rest > (aV) can ＼ (aV) be (id)(V) construed as ／ < { "S+do" } structures >. (In { (yet) another } way), (S) < we > (aV) can (aV) let (O) « "be" » (C) 『 (V) EXPROGER (O) « (w)"do" verbs » 』.

- "Be" of < existence > -

(S) < The most fundamental meaning of < "be" > > (V) is (C) 『 "existence" 』, (S) < as

> (aV) can ＼ (aV) be (V) seen ／ (in < ◎sentences { like "(1)(S) < God > (V) is ((S) < God > (V) exists)" or "(2)(V) He (V) is (no more) ((S) < He > | (aV) is ^not^ (V) living | (^any more^))" } >). (S) < This (id)type of < "be" > > (V) is (C) 『 ◎the only case { [where(= *that*)] (*)(S) < the (w)verb "be" > (1)(V) stands (alone) and (2)(V) needs (O) « nothing { else } » (to (V) complete (O) « its meaning ») } 』. ((id)Except for < this case >), (S) < all "be" > (aV) will (V) accompany (O) « ^such^ elements ^as^ < (1)"補語(HOGO: (w)complement)", (2)"現在分詞(GENZAI-BUNSHI: (w)the present participle)" or (3)"過去分詞(KAKO-BUNSHI: (w)the past participle)" » > (to (V) complete (O) « the meaning »).

(S) < The { (id)so-called } { "there+be" } construction > (also) (id)(V) belongs to < this "{ existential } be" >:

eg. "(There) (V) is (S) < a book > (on < the desk >)" (cf: (S) < A book > (V) is (there) (on < the desk >)).

- "Be" of < equation >: type-I((id)along with < (w)subjective complement >) -

(S) < (*)The most (1){ frequent } and (2){ important } (*)function of < "be" > > (V) is (C) 『 "^‡(V) equalizing‡^ (O) « the subject(S) » ^with^ < the (w)complement(C) >" 』; ((id)(mathematically) speaking), (S) < { "(S)=(C)" } (id)type of < equation > > ＼ (id)(aV) is (V) meant by ／ < { "S+be+C" } structure >: (S) < this > (V) is (C) 『 (id)(O) « what » (S) < we > (V) call (C) 『 "(w)sentence pattern #2" 』 』. (S) < This (w)sentence pattern > (V) is (C) 『 ^so^ important 』 ^that^ (S) < most schools > (aV) will ^(V) drill^ (O) « beginners » ^in^ < it >, (†(V) having† (O) « them »(= *as (S) < they > (V) have (O) « them »*) (C) 『 (repeatedly) (V) pronounce (O) « ^such^ sentences ^as^ < "(1)(S) < I >(V) 'm (C) 『 a student 』 / (2)(S) < This > (V) is (C) 『 a pen 』 / (3)(S) < He > (V) is (C) 『 a boy 』 / (4)(S) < She > (V) is (C) 『 a girl 』 / (5)(S) < We > (V) are (C) 『 friends 』 / (6)(S) < You > (V) are (C) 『 beautiful 』 / (7)(S) < They > (V) are (C) 『 kind 』 / (8)(S) < It > (V) is not (C) 『 true 』" > » 』).

(S) < The (C)(w)complement (in < this (w)sentence pattern >) > (aV) can (V) take (O)

« several (id)kinds of < "品詞(HINSHI: (w)parts of speech)" > »:

(1)名詞(MEISHI: (w)noun): eg. (S) < This > (V) is (C)『 my cell-phone 』.

(2)形容詞(KEIYOUSHI: (w)adjective): eg. (S) < That > (V) is (C)『 interesting 』.

(3)副詞(FUKUSHI: (w)adverb): eg. (S) < He > (V) is (C)『 away 』.

(4)前置詞句(ZENCHISHI-KU: (w)prepositional phrase): eg. (S) < She > (V) is (C)『 (id)on the verge of < (w)nervous breakdown > 』.

- "Be" of < equation >: type-II((id)along with < (w)objective complement >) -

(S) < The { equalizing } function of < "be" > > (aV) will (also) ＼ (aV) be (V) seen ／ (in < the "C" part of < (id)(O) « what » (S) < we > (V) call (C)『 "(w)sentence pattern #5": S-V-O-C 』 > >). (S) < The actual usage of < this pattern > >, (however), (V) is (C)『 ^so^ limited 』 ^that^ (S) < ◎all { (O) « *[that]* » (S) < you > (id)have to (V) memorize } > (V) is (C)『 the following two cases 』:

(1)S+consider/regard/deem+O+to be+C:

eg. (S) < He > (V) considered/regarded/deemed (O) « my story » (C)『 to (V) be (C)『 a fiction 』』.

(In < this case >), (S) < the { "to be" } part > (*)(aV) can (1) ＼ (aV) be (id)(V) substituted with ／ < "as" > and (2) ＼ (aV) be (V) written ／ ((id)(S) < as > (V) follows):

eg. (S) < He > ^(V) considered/regarded/deemed^ (O) « my story » (C)『 ^as^ < a fiction > 』.

(2)S+let+O+be+C:

eg. (If (S) < you > (V) say (O) « such a thing »), (S) < you > (aV) will (aV) let (O) « yourself » (C)『 ＼ (aV) be (V) misunderstood ／ 』.

(id)(Traditionally) *[†(V) speaking†]* , (S) < (w)the auxiliary verb "let" > (aV) will (V) accompany (O) « the (w)complement *[of]* " ＼ (aV) be (V) misunderstood ／ " » (without < ‡(V) omitting‡ (O) « the "be" » >); (nowadays), (however), (S) < "misunderstood" { without < "be" > } > (V) is (also) (C)『 allowable (with < "let" >)

』, / (id)so that (S) < you > (aV) could (V) say (O) « "(S) < you > (aV) will (aV) let (O) « yourself » (C) 『 misunderstood 』" » (without < ‡(V) making‡ (O) « yourself » (C) 『 misunderstood 』 >).

- "Be" of < (w)progressive > -

(S) < ◎"Be" (w)verbs { *[(S) < which > ＼ (aV) are]]* (V) followed ／ by < "現在分詞(GENZAI-BUNSHI: (w)the present participle)" > } > (V) mean (O) « "進行形(SHINKOUKEI: (w)the progressive form)" » (in < the following three tenses >):

現在進行形(GENZAI-SHINKOUKEI: (w)the present progressive form):

(S) < He > | (aV) is (V) studying | (O) « English » (now).

過去進行形(KAKO-SHINKOUKEI: (w)the past progressive form):

(S) < He > | (aV) was (V) studying | (O) « English » (ten years ago).

未来進行形(MIRAI-SHINKOUKEI: (w)the future progressive form):

(S) < He > (aV) will (still) | (aV) be (V) studying | (O) « English » (ten years (from < now >)).

- "Be" of < (w)passive > -

(S) < ◎"Be" (w)verbs { *[(S) < which > ＼ (aV) are]]* (V) followed ／ by < "過去分詞(KAKO-BUNSHI: (w)the past participle)" > } > (V) mean (O) « "受動態(JUDOUTAI: (w)the passive voice)" »:

eg. (S) < I > ＼ (aV) was (V) hurt ／ by < his comment >. (cf: (S) < His comment > (V) hurt (O) « me ».)

eg. (S) < This fact > (id) ＼ (aV) is not (V) known to ／ < everyone >. (cf: (S) < Not everyone > (V) knows (O) « this fact ».)

eg. (S) < The garden > (id) ＼ (aV) was (V) covered with ／ < snow >. (cf: (S) < Snow > (V) covered (O) « the garden ».)

eg. (S) < Cider > (id) ＼ (aV) is (*)(V) made (1)from ／ < apples >, not (2)from < grapes

>. (cf: (S) < They > (V) make (O) « cider » (^not^ (1)from < grapes > ^but^ (2)from < apples >).)

eg. (S) < His parents > ＼ (aV) were (V) killed ／ in < a (w)car accident >. (cf: (S) < A (w)car accident > (V) killed (O) « his parents ».)

eg. (S) < I > (id) ＼ (*)(aV) was (1)(V) born and (2)(V) bred ／ (here (in < Tokyo >)).

((S) < As > (aV) can ＼ (aV) be (V) seen ／ from < the examples { above } >), (S) < "動作主(DOUSANUSHI: (w)the agent)" in < (w)the passive voice > > (aV) can ＼ (aV) be (V) shown ／ by < several ◎(w)prepositions 〖 ((1)by, (2)to, (3)with, (4)from, (5)in) 〗 >, { (of < which >) (S) < { (the most frequently) used } one > (V) is (C) 『 "by" 』}.

((id)(Theoretically) [†(V) speaking†]), (S) < "受動態((w)the passive voice)" of < "X is -ed by Y (eg. (S) < You > ＼ (aV) are (V) loved by ／ < her >)" > > (V) is (C) 『 an inverted statement of < "能動態((w)the active voice)" of "Y - X" (eg. (S) < She > (V) loves (O) « you ») > 』. (Actually), (S) < any sentence (in < (w)the passive voice >) > ＼ (id)^(*)(aV) is^ (originally) (1)^(V) meant^ ^to^ ／ (V) be (C) 『 in < (w)the passive voice > 』, and ((id)not exactly) (2) ＼ (V) made ／ (as < "a reflected image 〖 in < a mirror > 〗 " of < (w)the active voice > >). (S) < The last example "(S) < I > ＼ (*)(aV) was (1)(V) born and (2)(V) bred ／ (here (in < Tokyo >))" > (V) is (there) (to (V) prove (O) « it »). (S) < No one > (aV) will ^(w)(V) paraphrase^ (O) « it » ^into^ < (w)the active voice *[of]* "(1)(S) < My mother > (V) bore (O) « me » and (2)(S) < my family > (V) bred (O) « me » (*)(here (in < Tokyo >))" >. (S) < ◎The reason { why (S) < this latter sentence > (V) sounds (C) 『 strange 』} > (V) is (C) 『 [that] (S) < the essential message of < the original { "(w)passive" } sentence > > (V) was (C) 『 "where (S) < I > ＼ (*)(aV) was (1)(V) born and (2)(V) bred ／ " 』 / while (S) < the { "(w)active" } (w)paraphrase > (id)(V) puts (O) « { undue } stress » upon < "(*)(S) < who > (1)(V) bore and (2)(V) bred (*)me" > 』.

(Although (S) < schools > (aV) will ^(V) drill^ (O) « you » ^in^ < "(1)passive/(2)active (*)(w)paraphrase" >), (id)(V) be (C) 『 advised 』 [that] (S) < (id)‡(V) pulling‡ (O) « { such } a stunt » > (V) is (C) 『 (id)not always possible 』. (aV) Let (O) « "(w)passive" » (C) 『 (V) be (C)『 "(w)passive" 』』 and (V) forget about < (id)‡(V) getting‡ back to < "(w)active" > >.

[(Here) (V) is] (S) < ◎One more thing { to (V) consider } >: (in < ^such^ expressions ^as^ < (1)"(id)(V) Be (C)『 advised 』..." or (2)"(S) < I > (V) was (C)『 surprised 』" > >), (S) < (*)the (1){ "be+advised" } and (2){ "be+surprised" } (*)parts > ＼ (aV) are ^not^ (*)(V) considered ／ (1)(C)『 to (V) be (C)『 "be+(w)the past participle" 』』 ^but^ (2)(C)『 as < "be+(w)adjective" combination > 』, ／ (id)with ◎the result { that (S) < they > ＼ (aV) are not (V) deemed ／ (C)『 as < "(w)the passive voice" > 』 }. (There) (V) are (S) < as many such "◎(w)adjectives { [(S) < which > ＼ ^(aV) are^]] ^(V) derived from^ ／ < (w)the past participles > } (eg. amazed, bored, excited, interested, etc,etc.)" as "◎(w)adjectives { (id)†(V) deriving† from < (w)the present participles > } (eg. amazing, boring, exciting, interesting, etc,etc.)" >. (Unless (S) < they > (strongly) (id)(V) point to < the latent (w)agent > (eg. (S) < We > ＼ (aV) were (V) bored ／ by < his long speech >)), (S) < these (w)past participles > (aV) can ＼ (aV) be (V) deemed ／ (C)『 to (*)(V) be (1)(C)『 (w)adjectives 』』, not (2)(id)part of < (w)the passive voice > (eg. (S) < We > (V) were (generally) (C)『 bored 』 (in < the concert >)).

- "Be" of < (w)perfect > -

(Although [(S) < it > (V) is] (C)『 (quite) (id)few (in < number >) 』), (S) < ◎a "be" (w)verb { [(S) < which > ＼ (aV) is]] (V) followed ／ by < "過去分詞(KAKO-BUNSHI: (w)the past participle)" > } > (aV) can (also) (V) mean (O) « "完了形(KANRYOUKEI: (w)the perfect tense)" »:

eg. "(S) < The sun > ↑ (aV) is (V) set ↑ ",

"(S) < I >(aV) 'll ↑ (aV) be (V) gone ↑ ".

(S) < This ◎"be+(w)past participle" > (V) is (C)『 an archaic form of < "have+(w)past participle" > 』, { (S) < which > (aV) can (also) ＼ (aV) be (V) seen ／ in < ◎French language { †(V) using†(= (S) < which > (V) uses) (O) « "être"(be) ((id)instead of <

"avoire"(have) >) (before < (w)the past participle >) » } > }. But (S) < the actual number of < such expressions > > (V) are (C) 『 ^too^ few ^for^ (S) < novice learners of < English > > ^to^ (studiously) (V) remember 』.

((id)Now that (S) < you > ↑ (aV) have (V) seen ↑ (O) « all possible usage of < "(w)be verb" > »), (aV) let (O) « these instances » (C) 『 (V) EXPROGER (O) « the "realm of < (w)do verbs >" » 』... and (V) stop (O) « ‡(V) making‡ (O) « ^such^ awkward { †stammering† } statements ^as^ < "(S) < I >(V) 'm (C) 『 a... 』" > » ».

8.(Always) (V) be (C) 〚 (id)aware of < the duality of < "-ing" >((w)the present participle /(w)gerund) > 〛

- (S) < "-ING" > (aV) does not (V) compose (O) « "(w)the progressive form (alone)" » -

(S) < ◎A bird { *[(S) < which > ＼ (aV) is]]* (newly) (V) born ／ } > ＼ (aV) is (V) said ／ to (V) believe (O) « ◎the first thing { (O) « *[that]* » (S) < it > (V) sees } » (C) 〚 to (V) be (C) 〚 its mother 〛 〛, ((*)(V) be (S) < it >(= ^*whether*^ *(S) < it >* (*)*(V) is)* (1)(C) 〚 a bird 〛 ^or^ (2)(C) 〚 a man 〛, (3)(C) 〚 living 〛 ^or^ (4)(C) 〚 inanimate 〛). (S) < ◎Anyone >, 【 *[^whether^ (S) < it >* (*)*(V) is]* (1)(C) 〚 fowl 〛 ^or^ (2)(C) 〚 human 〛 }, { *[(S) < that > (V) is]* (C) 〚 (id)new to < ◎the world { *[(S) < which > (V) is]* (C) 〚 (totally) unknown 〛 } > 〛 】 (V) is ^so^ (C) 〚 (id)unsure of < it > 〛 ^that^ (S) < ◎anything { (O) « *[that]* » (S) < it/he/she > (aV) can (V) grasp (in < the earliest stage of < the world's exploration > >) } > (*)(V) looks ^so^ (1)(C) 〚 reliable 〛 and (2)(C) 〚 important 〛 ^that^ (*)(S) < beginners > (instinctively) (id)(1)(V) stick to < it >... and (often) (2)(id) ＼ (V) get (C) 〚 stuck ／ in < that blind belief > 〛.

(S) < The English (w)inflection *[of]* "-ing" > (V) is (C) 〚 a typical "chick's mom" (for < English beginners > (in < Japan >)) 〛. (Since (S) < ◎the first lesson { (O) « *[that]* » (S) < they > ＼ (aV) were (V) given ／ (about < "-ing" >) } > (V) taught (O) « them » (O) « [that] (S) < "◎a (w)be verb { *[(S) < which > ＼ (aV) is]]* (V) followed ／ by < -ing((w)the present participle) > } > (V) is (C) 〚 (w)the progressive form 〛" »), (S) < Japanese people { *[(S) < who > (V) are]* (C) 〚 (id)unaccustomed to < English > 〛 } > (instinctively) (V) believe (O) « "-ing" » (C) 〚 to (always) (V) include (O) « some "(w)progressive" nuance (in < it >) » 〛. (S) < This fallacy > (aV) can ((quite) easily) ＼ (aV) be (V) overcome ／ by < ‡(V) enumerating‡ (O) « ◎all possible usage of < "-ing" > (in < English >) » >, { (S) < which > (broadly) (id)(V) divides into < two kinds > — (1)(w)the present participle and (2)(w)a gerund } — { (S) < the detailed explanation of < which > > *[(aV) is]* (id)†(V) coming† up ((id)(S) < as > (V) follows) }:

- ◎"-ING" { *[(s) < which > ＼ (aV) is]]* (V) used ／ as< (w)the present participle > } -

(1)(w)the progressive form of < "-ing" >(complete style) = "be+-ing"

eg. (S) < ^It^ > (V) is (C) 『 evident 』 ^that^ (S) < we > | (aV) are (V) losing | (O) « the battle ».

(S) < This > (V) is (C) 『 ◎the most basic style of < "(w)the progressive form" > 』, { (S) < which > (*)(V) describes (1)(O) « ◎some action { "(id)in the ‡(V) making‡" } »; ((id)in other words), (2)(O) « ◎an action { [(S) < that > ＼ (1)(aV) is] | (aV) being | (V) taken (now) ／ but ＼ (2)(aV) is (1)(V) felt to ／ (V) be (C) 『 "temporary" 』 【 ((id)(2)likely to (V) stop ((id)sooner or later)) 】 } » }; (id)(S) < ^it^ > (V) follows (from < this >) ^that^ (S) < ◎something { [(S) < that > ＼ (*)(aV) is] (1)(V) felt to ／ (V) be (C) 『 "permanent" 』 【 (((id)at least) (2)(C) 『 (id)unlikely to (V) stop ((id)any time soon) 』) 】 } > (aV) can not ＼ (aV) be (V) expressed ／ in < (w)the progressive form >;

ng. "~~(S) < My house > | (aV) is (V) standing | ((id)next to < his >)~~" ((S) < "(S) < My house > (V) stands ((id)next to < his >)" > (V) is (C) 『 the correct expression 』).

(2)(w)the progressive form of < "-ing"((w)adjective style) > = "-ing+(w)noun" / "(w)noun+-ing"

eg. (S) < We > | (aV) are (V) fighting | (O) « a { †losing† } battle ».(cf. ◎a battle { [(O) « which »] (S) < we > | (aV) are (V) losing | })

(S) < ◎Late summer's heat { †(V) waning† ((id)day by day) } > (*)(V) is (1)(C) 『 (id){ sad } news to < the young > 』, (2)(id)good news to < the elderly >.

(cf. ◎late summer's heat { (S) < which > | (aV) is (V) waning | ((id)day by day) })

(S) < ◎This (id)type of < (w)progressive form > > (V) is (C) 『 (relatively) rare 』 (in < English >), (S) < which > (aV) can ＼ (aV) be (V) understood ／ by < ^(w)‡(V) paraphrasing‡^ (O) « that part » ^with^ < ◎"関係代名詞節(KANKEI-DAIMEISHI-SETSU: the (w)relative pronoun clause)" { †(V) including†*(= (S) < which > (V) includes)* (O) « the complete style of < (w)the progressive form > » } > >.

(3)(w)attributive(non-(w)progressive) form of "-ing" = "-ing+(w)noun" / "(w)noun+-+-ing" eg. (S) < I > (V) love (O) « this singer » (for < her { †soothing† } voice >). (cf. ◎her voice { (S) < that > (V) soothes (O) « listeners » }; ng. ~~◎her voice { (S) < that > | (aV) is (V) soothing | (O) « listeners » }~~)

eg. Never (V) be (C) 〖 a { newspaper-swallowing } fool 〗. (cf. ◎a fool { (S) < that > (V) swallows (O) « newspapers » }; ng. ~~◎a fool { (S) < that > | (aV) is (V) swallowing | (O) « newspapers » }~~)

(S) < This (id)type of < (w)present participle > > (aV) does not (V) include (O) « { "(w)progressive" } nuance (in < it >) ». (In < the examples { above } >), (S) < the former ("-ing+(w)noun") > ＼ (aV) is ^so^ (frequently) (V) used ／ ^that^ (S) < most of < the "-ing" (in < this combination >) > > ＼ (aV) are (V) felt ／ to (*)(V) be (1)(C) 〖 "an (w)adjective" 〗 (id)rather than (2)(C) 〖 "(w)the present participle" 〗; (S) < (virtually) nobody (in < the { English-speaking } world >) > (V) feels (O) « "an interesting story" » (C) 〖 to (V) be (C) 〖 a combination of < "an+-ing((w)the present participle)+(w)noun" > 〗 〗; (S) < it > (definitely) (V) feels (C) 〖 to (V) be (C) 〖 "an+(w)adjective+(w)noun" 〗 〗. (Though (S) < (id)not all of < these "-ing"s > > ＼ (aV) are (V) listed ／ (in < the dictionary >) (as < "(w)adjective"s >)), (when (S) < you > (V) see (O) « an "-ing+(w)noun" combination »), (S) < you > (id)had better (V) see (O) « the "-ing" » ((*)as (1)< an "(w)adjective" > (id)rather than (2)< "(w)the present participle" >).

(S) < The latter example(◎"(w)noun+(w)hyphen+-ing" combination) > ＼ (aV) is (usually) (V) used ／ with < "-((w)hyphen)" ^in between^ < the (w)noun > ^and^ < (w)the present participle > >, (in < which >) (S) < the (w)noun > (V) functions (as < the (w)object of < ◎(w)the present participle { †(V) coming†(= (S) < *which* > (V) *comes*) (after < it >) } > >). (In < the { above-mentioned } example *[of]* "a { newspaper-swallowing } fool" >), (there) ＼ (aV) is (V) contained ／ (S) < { "(S)A fool (V)swallows (O)newspapers" } semantic structure >.

(id)(V) Beware of < the "number" of < the (w)noun > >: (in < the { "newspaper-swallowing" } (id)type of < combination > >), (S) < ◎the (w)noun { †(V) preceding†(=

(S) < which > (V) precedes) (O) « (w)the present participle » } > (id)is (always) to ＼ (aV) be (*)(V) used ／ (1)(in < (w)the singular form >), never (2)in < (w)the plural form >. (aV) Do (S) < you > (V) know (O) « why »?... (S) < The reason > (V) is (C) 『 simple 』: (S) < the { "newspaper-swallowing" } unit > (*)(V) is ^not^ (1)(C) 『 a "(w)noun" 』 ^but^ (2)(C) 『 ◎an "(w)adjective" { †(V) modifying†*(= (S) < which > (V) modifies)* (O) « the following (w)noun "fool" » } 』. (S) < ◎The only "品詞(HINSHI: (w)parts of speech)" { (S) < that > (aV) can (V) take (O) « "the (w)plural" » } > (V) are (C) 『 (2)"名詞(MEISHI: (w)nouns)" and (2)"代名詞(DAIMEISHI: (w)pronouns)" 』; ◎(S) < "形容詞(KEIYOUSHI: (w)adjectives)" > (aV) can (never) ＼ (aV) be (V) used ／ (in < the (w)plural >) (in < English >), { (S) < { which } attribute > (automatically) ^(V) reduces^ (O) « "newspapers"((w)plural) » ^to^ (O) « "newspaper"((w)singular) » (in < "a { newspaper-swallowing } fool" >), (just like < in < ^such^ expressions ^as^ < (1)"a { two-lane } street", (2)"a { four-door } car" or (3)"a { six-member } family" > > >) }.

(4)(w)predicative((w)progressive) form of "-ing" = "S+V+O+-ing"

eg. (S) < I > (V) heard (O) « him » (C) 『 †(V) saying† (O) « that » 』. (cf. (S) < He > | (aV) was (V) saying | (O) « that »; (S) < I > (V) heard (O) « it ».)

eg. (S) < I > (aV) can't (V) have (O) « you » (C) 『 †(V) saying† (O) « ◎things { like < that > } » 』. (cf. (S) < You > | (aV) are (V) saying | (O) « ◎things { like < that > } »; (S) < I > (aV) can't (V) leave (O) « it » (C) 『 (id)as (S) < it > (V) is 』.)

(S) < This > (V) is (C) 『 a (rather) complicated style of < (w)progressive form > 』, *[(S) < which > ＼ (aV) is]]* (V) used ／ (in < the { "補語(HOGO: (w)complement)" } part of < S-V-O-C (w)sentence pattern(#5) > >). (S) < The { "(w)progressive" } implication (in < the { "O+-ing" } part >) > (V) is (C) 『 ◎clear { to (V) see } 』 (in < the former example ("(S) < he > | (aV) was (V) saying | (O) « that »") >). While, (in < the latter example >), (S) < the { O-C } part ("(S) < you > †(V) saying† (O) « ◎things { like < that > } »") > ＼ (aV) is ^not^ ^(*)(V) meant^ ／ (1)^as^ < a (1){ "dynamic" } and (2){ "momentary" } (*)(w)progressive form > (ng. "~~(S) < you > | (aV) are (V) saying | (O) « ◎things { like < that > } » (now)~~") ^but^ (2)^as^ < a { "habitual" } action (over < a certain (id)span of < time > >) (cf. "(1)(S) < you > (usually) (V) say (O) « ◎things { like < that > } » / (2)(S) < you > (V) keep (O) « ‡(V) saying‡ (O) « ◎things { like < that > } » » / (3)(S) < you > (V) are (C) 『 (id)in the habit of ‡(V) saying‡ (O) « ◎things { like < that > } » 』") >. (id)(V) Be (C) 『 advised 』 *[that]* (S) < "(w)the progressive form" > (V) contains (O) « such "{ long-span } habits" »;

eg. (S) < He > ＼ (aV) is (always) (V) complaining ／ about < something > 〚 ((id)*[even]* if *[(S) < he > | (aV) is]]* not (V) complaining | ((id)right now)) 〛 .

- ◎"-ING" { *[(S) < which >* ＼ *(aV) is]]* (V) used ／ (as < (w)a gerund >) } -

eg. ◎(S) < (1)‡(V) Doing‡ (O) « publicity » and (2)(forcibly) ‡(V) making‡ (O) « consumers » (C) 『 (id)(V) want to (V) buy (O) « something » 』 > (V) is (C) 『 the main way of < business > 』 (today), { (S) < which > ((almost) completely) (id)(V) takes over < ‡(V) making‡ (O) « ◎good products { [(O) « that »] (S) < consumers > (naturally) (id)want to (V) buy } » > }. (S) < ◎The only way { to (id)(V) get over < this detestable trend > } > (V) is (C) 『 the ‡training‡ of < ◎consumers { *[(S) < who > (V) are]* (C) 『 wise ^enough^ (^not to^ ＼ (id)(V) get (V) carried away ／ (by < obtrusive hypes >) } >) 』 』.

(S) < ◎"動名詞(DOUMEISHI: (w)a gerund)" > (V) is (C) 『 a unique form 』, { [(S) < which > (*)(V) is] (1)^partly^ (C) 『 "(w)verb" 』 and (2)^partly^ (C) 『 "(w)noun" 』 }. (S) < The weight ^between^ < "(w)verb" > ^and^ < "(w)noun" > > (aV) can ^(V) vary (from^ < ^one^ (w)gerund > ^to^ < ^another^ >). (In < the example { above } >), (S) < the { "verbal" } characteristic of < the (w)gerund > > (aV) can ＼ (aV) be (V) seen ／ ((*)in (1)< "(V)‡doing‡ (O)publicity" >, (2)< "(V)‡making‡ (O)people (C)want to buy something" > and (3)< "(V)‡making‡ (O)good products" >): (only) (S) < (w)verbs ((w)transitive) > (aV) can (directly) (V) take (O) « (w)objects(O) » (without < the intervention of < (w)prepositions > >).

((id)On the other hand), (S) < the { "(w)nounal" } characteristic of < the (w)gerund > > (aV) can ＼ (aV) be (V) seen ／ (in < "takes over <making good products>" >): (

only) (S) < (1)(w)nouns 〘 (and (2)(w)pronouns) 〙 > (aV) can (V) be (C) 『 the (w)object of < (w)prepositions > 〘 ((in < this case >), "over") 〙 』. And (S) < { "the training of consumers" } part > (V) is (C) 『 (id)still more "(w)nounal" 』; (only) (S) < (1)(w)nouns and (2)(w)adjectives > (aV) can ＼ (aV) be (V) modified ／ by < (w)the definite article "the" >.

((id)In fact), (S) < ^such^ { (originally) "gerund" } terms ^as^ < (1)"training", (2)"cooking", (3)"hearing" or (4)"living" > > (*)(V) are not so much (1)(C) 『 "verbals" 』 as (2)(C) 『 "(w)nouns" 』, ((even) in < the consciousness of < Japanese people > >). ((id)In short), (S) < a gerund > (V) is (C) 『 ◎a (w)verb { (id)†(V) playing† (O) « the part » of(= (S) < *which* > (V) *plays* (O) « *the part* » *of*) < a (w)noun > } 』, ((sometimes) (id)to the point of < "never (id)‡(V) appearing‡ to ↑ (aV) have (aV) been ↑ (C) 『 a (w)verb 』" >).

\- (S) < (w)Prepositions > (id)(V) call for < (w)gerunds > -

(Whenever (S) < a (w)preposition > (*)(V) takes 〘 as < its (w)object > 〙 ^not^ (1)(O) « a (w)noun » ^but^ (2)(O) « a (w)verb »), (S) < the (w)verb > (aV) must (V) take (O) « the form of < a (w)gerund("-ing") > ». ((id)That is to say), (S) < ◎any "-ing" { [(S) < that > ＼ (aV) is] (V) used ／ ((immediately) after < a (w)preposition >) } > (aV) can ＼ (aV) be (V) deemed ／ (C) 『 (*)as (1)< a (w)gerund >, not (2)< (w)the present participle > 』.

(However), (there) (V) is (S) < ◎one (w)preposition { (S) < which > (V) needs (O) « special attention » } > — ◎"to", { (S) < which > (V) has (O) « two faces »: (1)◎a simple (w)preposition { *[(S) < which > ＼ (aV) is]]* (V) followed ／ by < a (w)gerund ("-ing") > }, and (2)◎an infinitive(不定詞:FUTEISHI) { *[(S) < which > ＼ (aV) is]]* (V) followed ／ by < (w)the root form of < a (w)verb >("-") > } }.

eg. (Although (S) < he > (aV) used to (V) be (C) 『 (rather) awkward (in < English >) 』), (S) < he > | (aV) is ＼ (id)(V) getting (C) 『 used to ／ | < ‡(V) living‡ (in < the States >), (1)(linguistically) or (2)(socially) 』 >.

(In (the example { above })), (*)(S) < the first "to" 〖 (in < "(S) < he > (aV) used to (V) be" >) 〗 > (1) ＼ (aV) is (V) used ／ as < an (w)infinitive > and (2)(V) requires (O) « (w)the root form "be" » (after < it >). (S) < The second "to" 〖 (in < "(S) < he > | (aV) is ＼ (id)(V) getting (C) 『 used to ／ | ‡(V) living‡ 』" >) 〗 > (V) is (C) 『 ◎a simple (w)preposition { †(V) requiring†*(= (S) < which > (V) requires)* (O) « the (w)gerund "living" » (after < it >) } 』.

(Thus), (whenever (S) < you > (V) see (O) « a "to" » (C) 『 ＼ (id)(*)(V) coupled (1)with ／ "動詞型(DOUSHIKEI: (w)verbals)", not (2)with < (w)nouns > 』), (S) < you > (aV) must (V) be (C) 『 careful 』 *[about]* < ◎^whether^ (S) < it > (*)(V) is (1)(C) 『 "a simple (w)preposition" 』 ^or^ (2)(C) 『 "an infinitive" 』 >, { (S) < which > (aV) can ＼ (aV) be (V) determined ／ by < the form of < ◎the verbal { †(V) coming†*(= (S) < which > (V) comes)* (after < "to" >) } > >: (1)"to((w)preposition)+-ing((w)gerund)" or (2)"to((w)infinitive)+-((w)root)" }.

9.(S) < ^It^ > (V) takes (O) « proficiency » ^to^ ^(V) discern^ (O) « (w)the past participle » ^from^ < (w)the past form >

- 述語(JUTSUGO: (w)Predicate) or 後位修飾語(KOUI-SHUUSHOKUGO: (w)qualifier): ◎a tough hurdle { for < (S) < novice learners > > to (id)(V) get over } -

eg. (S) < ◎Old schools { revisited } > (V) felt (all) ^so^ (C) 『 strange 』 (to < me >) ^that^ (S) < I > | (aV) was (id)(V) beginning to | (id)(V) wonder < if (S) < I > ↑ (aV) had (really) (V) passed ↑ (O) « my life » (there) >.

(S) < The { above-mentioned } sentence > (aV) could (hardly) ＼ (aV) be (V) understood ／ by < novice learners of < English > (in < Japan >) >; (S) < they > (id)(aV) couldn't (*)(V) make (1)(O) « head » or (2)(O) « tail » of < { "revisited felt" } part >, (†^(V) thinking† of^ < it >(= *because (S) < they > (id)^(V) think of^ < it >)* ^as^ < "◎two (w)verbs { *[(S) < which > ＼ (aV) are]]* (intangibly) (V) combined ／ in < (w)the past form >" > }).

(Actually), (S) < no two English (w)verbs > (aV) can (ever) ＼ (aV) be (V) used ／ ((id)in tandem): (S) < no English (w)verb > (aV) can (immediately) (V) follow (O) « another (w)verb » 〖 (except (id)in < ^such^ cases ^as^ (S) < "(S) < He > (V) helped (O) « me » (C) 『 *[to]* (V) solve (O) « the problem » 』" > ＼ [‡(aV) being‡] (V) abbreviated ／ into < "(S) < He > (V) helped (C) 『 *[to]* (V) solve (O) « the problem » 』" > >) 〗. (Only) (S) < "助動詞(JODOUSHI: an (w)auxiliary verb)" > (aV) can (V) follow (O) « a (w)verb » (eg. "(S) < Old schools > (aV) do (V) feel (C) 『 strange 』"), ((id)but then again), ◎the (w)verb { *[(S) < which > ＼ (aV) is]]* (V) followed ／ by < (w)an auxiliary verb > } (aV) must (always) (*)(V) take (1)(O) « (w)the root form », never (2)(O) « (w)the past form » or (3)(O) « (w)the past participle » 〖 ((S) < this > (V) is (also) (C) 『 (id)true with < the { above-mentioned } { "(V) help (C) 『 (V) solve (O) « the problem » 』" } (id)type of < structure > > 』, (S) < ◎the (w)verb { †(V) following†*(= (S) < which > (V) follows)* (O) « "help" » } > ＼ [‡(V) being‡] (always) (V) used ／ in < (w)the root form >) 〗.

[(V) Is (S) < it >] (C) 『 ^Too^ complicated (^to^ (V) follow) 』?... OK, (here) (V) comes

(S) < the answer >: (S) < ◎the true structure of < the first example > > (V) is (C) 〚 "(S)<Old schools {revisited}> (V)felt all (C)so strange to me" 〛, { (in < which >) (S) < the { "verbal" } part > (V) is (C) 〚 the second "felt" 〛, and (S) < the first "revisited" > (*)(V) is ^not^ (1)(C) 〚 (w)the past form of < "revisit" > 〛 ^but^ (2)(C) 〚 ◎(w)the past participle { †(V) modifying†(= (S) < which > (V) modifies) (O) « the { preceding } (w)noun "old schools" » } 〛 }. (S) < Such ◎terms { (1)†(V) modifying† 〖 (=†(V) describing†(= (S) < which > (V) describe) (O) « the attribute » (2)of) 〗 (*)(O) « terms » (from < behind >) } > ＼ (aV) are (V) called ／ (C) 〚 "(w)qualifiers: 後位修飾語: KOUI-SHUUSHOKUGO" 〛, ((id)as opposed to < "(w)◎modifiers: 前位修飾語: ZENI-SHUUSHOKUGO" (S) < which > (V) modify (O) « terms » ((immediately) after < them >) >).

(S) < The "<名詞{後位修飾語}述語>:<(w)noun {qualifier} predicate>" structure > (V) is (C) 〚 (id)one of < the most perplexing (in < English sentences >) > 〛, but (here) (V) is (S) < a useful (id)tip for < (id)‡(V) getting‡ over < this puzzle > > >: (whenever (S) < you > (V) see (O) « "an (apparently) (w)past form of < a (w)verb" > » (C) 〚 [(S) < which > ＼ (aV) is]] (V) followed ／ by < "another (w)verb, (whether [(S) < it > (V) is] (C) 〚 in < (*)the (1){ past }/(2){ present }/(3){ future } (*)form > 〛)" > 〛), (id)(V) be (C) 〚 sure 〛 [that] (S) < the first one > (*)(V) is "^not^ (2)(C) 〚 a (w)verb (in < (w)the past form >) 〛, ^but^ (2)(C) 〚 ◎(w)the past participle of < a (w)verb >" { (S) < which > (V) qualifies (O) « ◎the (w)noun { [(S) < which > (V) is] ((immediately) before < it >) } » 〛 }. (S) < This > (V) is (C) 〚 ◎(quite) a powerful info { (S) < which > (aV) will (V) advance (O) « your level of < English > » (^from^ < sheer beginner > ^to^ < intermediate >) } 〛.

But (there) (V) is (S) < ◎one exceptional case { (S) < which > (V) defies (O) « (even) the advanced-class learners of < English > » } >... (*)(aV) Would (S) < you > (1)(id)(V) like to (V) see (O) « it », or (2)(id)(V) hate to (V) see (O) « ◎anything { [(S) < which > (V) is] (C) 〚 (even) more scary 〛 } »?... (Anyway), (S) < I >(aV) 'll (V) show (O) « you », ([^whether^ (S) < you >] (V) like (O) « it » ^or^ not).

- ◎SVOC { †(V) developing† (= (S) < *which* > (V) *develops*) around < (w)verbs of perception >, [with] (S) < O > †(V) coming ((id)in front)† }: *[(S) < which > (V) is]* (C) 『 tough ((id)like hell) (for < (id)all but < the erudite > >) 』 -

eg. (S) < ◎(1)Houses, (2)cars and (3)(even) humans { (O) « *[that]* » (S) < she > (V) saw (C) 『 ＼ (V) washed away ／ by < the Tsunami > 』 } > ^(V) left^ (O) « ^a^ permanent ^impression^ » (^upon^ < her heart >).

(In < this example >), (S) < the { "saw / washed" } part > (*)(V) is ^not^ (C) 『 (1){ "(w)the past participle / (w)the past form" } combination 』 ^but^ (C) 『 (2)"(w)the past form / (w)the past participle" 』... *[(aV) Does (S) < it > (V) feel]* (C) 『 Mind-boggling 』? (S) < It > (sure) (V) is *[(C) 『 mind-boggling 』]*, but (aV) don't (V) be (C) 『 afraid 』, for (S) < the explanation > | (aV) is (soon) (id)(V) coming up |, (after < three more ◎example sentences { †(V) developing† (= (S) < *which* > (V) *develop*) around < the (1){ famous } 【 (or (2){ infamous }?) 】 "知覚動詞(CHIKAKU-DOUSHI: (w)verbs of perception)" > } >).

(S) < ◎(w)Verbs of perception { *[(S) < which > ＼ (aV) are]]* (V) used ／ (in < the (V)verb part (of < SVOC (w)sentence pattern(#5) >) >) } > (V) requires (O) « the following three forms of < verbals > (in < the part of < (C)(w)complement > >) »:

(1)S+知覚動詞((w)perceptional verb)+O+原形不定詞(GENKEI-FUTEISHI: (w)the root infinitive):

eg. (S) < She > (V) heard (O) « people » (C) 『 (V) shout (O) « "Run!" » 』

(2)S+知覚動詞((w)perceptional verb)+O+現在分詞(GENZAI-BUNSHI: (w)the present participle):

eg. (S) < She > (V) saw (O) « the Tsunami » (C) 『 †(V) coming† 』.

(3)S+知覚動詞((w)perceptional verb)+O+過去分詞(KAKO-BUNSHI: (w)the past participle):

eg. (S) < She > (V) saw (O) « (1)houses, (2)cars and (3)(even) humans » (C) 『 ＼ (V) washed away ／ by < the Tsunami > 』.

(Now), (id)(S) < you > (V) see (O) « *[that]* , (S) < the first example sentence > ＼ (id)(aV) is (V) based on ／ < the last one's SVOC (w)sentence pattern >, ([with] (S) < the (w)word order > ＼ *[(aV) being]* (V) inverted ／ into < O-SVC >): (S) < the "(V)saw (C)washed" > (V) was (C) 『 { "(V)(w)the past form (C)(w)the past participle" } combination 』, ([with] (S) < ◎the { "(O)houses, cars and even humans" } part ((S) < which > (aV) ought 【 logically 】 to (V) be (^in between^ < the (V) ^and^ (C) >)) > ＼ *[(aV) being]* (V) placed ／ ((id)at the beginning of < the sentence >) (as < the focus of < attention > >)) ». And (S) < the whole { "O-SVC" } part ("(S)<(o)Houses, cars and even humans {(s)she (v)saw (c)washed away (by the Tsunami)}>") > (V) functions (as < the (S)(w)subject of < "(V)left (O)<a permanent impression (upon her heart)>" > >).

- (There) (V) is (S) < no ^such^ thing ^as^ < (V)(V) (in < English (w)sentence patterns >) > > -

(id)(S) < I >(V) 'm (C) 『 sorry 』 (to ↑ (aV) have ^(V) troubled^ ↑ (O) « your brains » ^with^ < (unrealistically) complicated sentences >). But (S) < those sentences > ＼ (*)(aV) are (actually) (1)(V) used 【 (^not only^ (2)(V) written ^but^ (3)(V) spoken!) 】 ／ (in < the world of < English > >). (S) < My advice < for < you > > > (V) is (C) 『 simple 』: (when (S) < you > (V) see (O) « a (seemingly) (V)(V)(dual-(w)verb) combination »), (S) < the former part > (id)(V) is (C) 『 most likely to (V) be (C) 『 "◎a qualifier { (id)in the form of < (w)the past participle > }" 』 』. (id)◎The odds { [that] (S) < you > (V) encounter (O) « the (*)(far) (1){ rarer } and (2){ tougher } (*)(w)sentence pattern of < "O-SV(a (w)verb of perception)C((w)the past participle)" > » } (V) are (C) 『 less than < 100 to < 1 > > 』!

10.SPAT-5: (S) < five (w)sentence patterns > (V) are

(C) 〚 ◎(id)a { magical } set of < molds > { to (V) comprehend (O) « English » in } 〛 - A (1){ long }, (2){ cynical } (*)failure story of < KATA (in < Japan >) > -

(Since (S) < English > (V) is (C) 〚 a (quite) assimilative language 〛), (S) < it > ↑ (aV) has (V) acquired ↑ (O) « { (id)not a few } words » (from < Japanese >). (S) < "型(カタ:KATA)" > (*)(V) is (1)(C) 〚 (id)one of < them > 〛, and (2)(C) 〚 (quite) a popular one 〛 【 (id)at that 】 , / (probably) because (S) < it > (V) signifies (O) « the { very } ◎notion { (S) < that > 【 (S) < most foreigners > (V) feel 】 (V) is (C) 〚 (symbolically) Japanese 〛 – ◎a pattern, form, mold or structure { (in < which >) (S) < (1)things or (2)actions > ＼ (*)(aV) are (1)(V) created and (2)(V) interpreted ／ } } ».

(In < the world of < English grammar > >), (there) (V) is (S) < ◎(id)a (very) { powerful } set of < KATA > { *[(S) < which > ＼ (aV) is]]* (V) called ／ (C) 〚 "五文型(GOBUNKEI): Five(5) (w)Sentence Patterns of < English >" 〛 } >. (*)(S) < This KATA > ＼ (1)(aV) was (originally) (V) conceived ／ by < a British scholar Charles Talbut Onions > and (2) ↑ (aV) has (long) (V) formed ↑ (O) « the backbone of < traditional ‡teaching‡ of < English > > (in < Japan >) ». ((id)As such), (when (S) < self-styled reformists of < the (miserably) faulty { Japanese } English education > > (V) sought (O) « ◎scapegoats { to ^(V) point^ (O) « their { blaming } ^fingers^ » ^at^ } »), (S) < ◎the traditional ^importance^ { *[(S) < which > ＼ (aV) had (aV) been]]* ^(V) set^ ／ ^upon^ < these (w)Five Sentence Patterns of English > } > ＼ (aV) was (id)(V) made (C) 〚 a target 〛 of ／ , ((id)along with < many other KATA-DORI(型通り:rigidly formal) methodologies >) – (possibly) because (S) < they > ＼ (aV) were (V) felt ／ to (V) be (C) 〚 (too) (symbolically) Japanese 〛.

But (S) < the practical usefulness of < this KATA > (for < English learners (in < Japan >) >) > (V) is ^so^ (C) 〚 great 〛 ^that^ (S) < ^it^ > (V) is (C) 〚 (downright) foolish 〛 ^of^ (S) < some { Japanese } English educators > ^to^ (pervertedly) (id)(V) go against < ‡(V) teaching‡ (O) « it » >. (S) < Their bigoted (id)antipathy to < ◎anything { with < a flavor of < "英文法(EIBUNPOU)" > – English (*){ grammatical } (1)comprehension and (2)‡teaching‡ > } > > — (V) is (C) 〚 the { very } embodiment of < KATA-DORI-NO-NIHONJIN: ◎a typical Japanese { (id)†(V) making† (O) « a villain » of (= (S) < *who* > *(V) makes (O) « a villain » of*) < (1)someone/(2)something (*){ else } > (to (id)(V) play (O) « the role of < Captain Justice > »), (id)only to (V) perpetuate (O) « the problem » (by < (id)‡(V) refusing‡ (*)to (1)(V) seek and (2)(V) solve (*)(O) « the real cause of < (*)the problem > » >) } > 〛.

(When (in < 1982 >) (S) < the Japanese (w)Ministry of Education 〖 (*[(S) < which > ＼ (*)(aV) is]]* (now) (pompously) (1)(V) called ／ (C) 〚 "(w)Ministry of Education, Culture, Sports, Science and Technology" 〛 or (compactly) (2) ＼ (V) dubbed ／ (C) 〚 "(w)MEXT" 〛) 〗 > (id)(V) decided to (V) "abolish" (O) « official censorship of < ◎textbooks { regarding < English grammar > } > »), (S) < ◎their original message { to "^(V) liberate^" (O) « English grammatical education » ^from^ < (unduly) rigid official restriction > } > ＼ (aV) was ^(V) misinterpreted^ ／ 〖 by < too many Japanese > 〗 ^as^ (C) 〚 (w)a "death sentence" to < ‡teaching‡ of < grammar > (at < school >) > 〛. (S) < The result > (V) was (C) 〚 [that] (S) < the level of < English literacy (in < Japan >) > >, (without < systematic grammatical comprehension >), (id)(V) went (even) downward ((id)ever since < the 80s >) 〛. (S) < Too many Japanese, { (1)teachers ^and^ (2)learners ^alike^, ((possibly) including < "MEXT" folks (themselves) (nowadays) >) } >, 〖 by < (id)‡(V) making‡ (O) « a scapegoat » of < English grammar > > 〗 , (id)(V) fell (C) 〚 victims to < ◎their own absurd fallacy { that (S) < grammar > (V) was (C) 〚 not necessary (for < English mastery >) 〛 } > 〛. (S) < They > (V) were (C) 〚 foolish ^enough^ (^to^ (V) believe (O) « [that] (S) < they > ↑ (aV) had (V) been ↑ , 〖 (id)up until the 1980s 〗 , (id)unable to (V) command (O) « English » (BECAUSE (S) < they > ↑ (aV) had (V) been ↑ (C) 〚 (too) (id)conscious of < grammar > 〛) ») 〛. (So), (*)(S) < the Japanese > (bravely) (1)(id)(V) gave up (O) « EIBUNPOU(English grammar) » (altogether) and (2)(V) went (boldly) into < the world (*)of < (1)"総合英語:SOUGOU-EIGO 〖 (?{ GENERAL }?English) 〗 " or (2)"生きた英語:IKITA-EIGO 〖 (English !{ ALIVE }!) 〗 " > >, (id)only to (id)(V) commit (O) « {

collective } suicide » (^(*)on^ < (1){ linguistic } and (2){ logical } (*)^plane^ >). (id)*[(S) < It > (V) is]* Not (C)『 that (S) < grammatical facts > ＼ (aV) were (id)(V) forbidden to ／ ＼ (aV) be (V) taught ／ (in < classrooms >) 』; (id)(S) < it > (V) is (only) (C)『 that (*)(S) < they > (1) ＼ (aV) were (V) provided ／ (as < occasional "useful tips" > (^on^ { "(id)as *[(S) < it > (V) was]* (C)『 necessary 』" } ^basis^)), and (2)(totally) (V) lost (O) « their integrity (as < a collective system of < knowledge > >) » 』. ((id)Ever since < then >), ((id)for lack of < (*){ (consciously) systematic } (1)‡teaching‡ or (2)‡training‡ ((*)in < English education >) >), (S) < (1)systematical comprehension, (2)(*){ comprehensive } (1)thinking and (2)action or (3)responsible coherence (*)(in < any action >) > (V) are (all) (C)『 ◎(quite) rare { to (V) find } 』 (here (in < Japan >)). And (w)(S) < the rest > (V) is (C)『 history 』: decades of < decay of < this { (once) prosperous } nation > >.

(＼ *[(aV) Being]* (id)(Simply) (V) put ／ ,) ^(S) < it >^ (aV) didn't (id)(V) occur to < shallow grammar-haters (in < Japan >) > ^that^ (S) < they > (aV) didn't (V) have (O) « ^that^ privilege of < so many Indo-European learners of < English > > { ^(S) < which >^ ^(V) enabled^ (O) « them » (C)『 ^to^ (V) comprehend (O) « this foreign language » (in { (roughly) the same } grammatical KATA ^as^ < their own >) 』 } ». (S) < English language > (V) is as (1)(C)『 (grammatically) (id)similar (*)to (1)< French > or (2)< Italian > 』 as (2)[(S) < it > (V) is] (C)『 (structurally) (id)alien from < Japanese language > 』. (S) < Native speakers of < Indo-European languages > > (aV) can (id)(V) take (O) « advantage » of < their innate linguistic KATA (as < ◎the mold { (in < which >) to (V) interpret (O) « English » } >) >. (S) < Japanese natives >, ((id)on the other hand), (id)have to ^(V) "migrate"^ ^from^ < their own NIHONGO-NO-KATA > ^into^ < { "(totally) alien" } English grammatical structure >. (S) < (1){ Spanish }, (2){ Italian } or (3)(even) { French } (*)natives > (aV) could (V) become (C)『 speakers of < English > 』, 【 (C)『 however broken*(= no matter how broken)* 』 *[(S) < their English > (aV) might (V) be]* 】 , (by < (randomly) (*)‡(V) memorizing‡ (O) « (1)words and (2)(w)phrases ((*)in < English >) » ((id)without < { much } thought to < grammar > >

) >); (S) < the same random ‡memorizing‡ effort > ^(V) leads^ (O) « Japanese » ^(nowhere)^ { without(= *because* (S) < *they* > (aV) *don't* (V) *have*) < the logical backbone of < { (structurally) similar } grammar > > }.

[(S) < *It* > (V) *is]* (C) 〚 ^Too^ lucidly simple (^to^ (id)(V) point out) 〛, 〖 right 〗 ? (S) < The last thirty years of < this miserable country > > (aV) would (V) be (C) 〚 (id)more than ^enough^ 〛 (^to^ (V) prove (O) « the absurd failure of < ◎^that^ Japanese attitude { (*)^(S) < which >^ (1)(id)(V) made (too) (O) « little » of < logical ‡understanding‡ > and (2)(id)(V) opted (too much) for < (mindlessly) ‡(V) imitating‡ (O) « the success of < ◎others { *[* (S) < *who* > (V) *were]* (C) 〚 (essentially) (id)different from < themselves >, (linguistically (id)or otherwise) 〛 } > » > } > »). (id)(S) < It > (V) is (C) 〚 high time *[that]* (S) < Japan > (id)(V) woke up ^from^ < such { idle } { gainless } sleep > ^into^ < (w)stark reality >: (for (S) < them > to (V) master (O) « English »), (S) < they > (id)(V) have (O) « need » of < KATA, (totally) different linguistic structural ◎molds { to (V) comprehend (O) « English » in } > 〛.

(S) < That > (V) is (C) 〚 *[the point]* where (S) < the (w)Five Sentence Patterns of English > (V) shines ((so) graciously); 〛 (id)so much so that (id)(aV) let (O) « us » (C) 〚 (thankfully) (id)(V) benefit from < it > 〛, (†(V) devising†(= *while* (S) < *we* > (V) *devise)* 〖 ^for^ < it > 〗 (O) « ^a nickname^ *[of]* *SPAT-5, { †(V) meaning†(= (S) < *which* > (V) *means)* (O) « { clear-cut 〖 (!SUPATTO!) 〗 } ‡understanding‡ of < English > (in < five tangible molds >) » } »).

*(id)(V) Be (C) 〚 advised 〛 *[that]* (*)(S) < "SPAT-5" > (1)(V) is (C) 〚 an { (originally) coined } phrase (by < this author Jaugo Noto >) (in < 2012 >) 〛, and (2)(aV) will not ＼ (aV) be (V) understood ／ by < ◎anyone { (S) < who > (aV) doesn't (V) read (O) « this book » } >.

\- The limitation of < SPAT-5 >: (w)five sentence patterns of English -

(Since ^(S) < it > (V) is^ (C) 〚 Japanese folks 〛 ^that^ (S) < this book > ＼ (aV) is (mainly) (V) written ／ for), (S) < I > (aV) must ((id)at first) ^(V) remind^ (O) « you »

^of^ < ^this^ plain ◎fact, 【 [(S) < *which* > (V) *is*] ^too^ (C) 『 plain { ^for^ < most people (in < the world >) > (^to^ (V) explain) } 』】, { ^that^ (S) < the value of < KATA > > (aV) does ^not^ (id)(*)(V) lie (1)in < its perfect (id)application to < everything > > ^but^ (2)in < its special usefulness (in < something >) > } >. (S) < SPAT-5, (w)Five Sentence Patterns of English >, (V) is ^not^ (C) 『 (perfectly) (id)applicable to < ^all^ English sentences > 』. (S) < They > (aV) cannot (id)(V) deal with < (1)"命令文:MEIREIBUN((w)imperative sentences)", (2)"進行形:SHINKOUKEI((w)the progressive form)", (3)"受動態:JUDOUTAI((w)the passive voice)" or (4)"群動詞:GUNDOUSHI((w)group verbs)" ((id)as (S) < they > (V) are) >. (S) < These inapplicable objects > (aV) must ＼ (aV) be (id)(V) changed into ／ < some other manageable forms >:

eg. (S) < (w)imperative "(V) Go" > (*)(aV) must ＼ (1)(aV) be (id)(V) supplemented with ／ < the (w)subject "you" > and ＼ (2)(aV) be (V) treated ／ as < "(S)You (V)go" >;

(S) < "I was sleeping" > (id)is to ＼ (aV) be (id)(V) interpreted as ／ < "(w)the progressive form of < (S)I (V)slept >" >;

(S) < "Caesar was killed by Brutus" > (id)needs to ＼ (aV) be (id)(V) translated into ／ < "(w)the passive voice of < (S)Brutus (V)killed (O)Caesar >" >;

and (S) < "We've (id)done away with the custom" > (aV) should ＼ (aV) be (V) treated ／ as < ◎something { like < "(S)We (V)have abolished(= ↑ (aV) 've (id)(V) done away with ↑) (O)the custom" > } >. (S) < This imperfection of < SPAT-5 > > (aV) may (V) be (C) 『 unacceptable to < "型通りの日本人:KATA-DORI-NO-NIHONJIN", Japanese (id)believers in < the omnipotence of < KATA > > > 』, but ((id)other than < that >), (S) < most reasonable learners > (aV) must (V) find (O) « these molds » (C) 『 (quite) useful (in < ‡(V) comprehending‡ (O) « the (seemingly) endless patterns of < English sentences > » >) 』. ((id)(S) < That > ＼ [*(aV) having (aV) been*] (V) said ／), (id)(aV) let (O) « us » (C) 『 (id)(V) proceed to < the actual forms of < SPAT-5 > > 』.

\- Actual explanation of < SPAT-5: (w)Five Sentence Patterns of < English > > -

<I: SV>... ◎a sentence { †(V) requiring†(= *(S) < which > (V) requires*) (O) « no (1)(w)object (O) or (2)(w)complement (C) » }

eg. (S)I (V)sing.

(S) < This 1st (w)sentence pattern > (V) is (C) 『 the simplest 』, ((id)†(V) consisting† of(= *(S) < which > (V) consists of*) < { (w)subject -(w)verb } combination (only) >, ((*)without (1)< (id)‡(V) referring‡ to < any (w)object > > or (2)< ‡(V) requiring‡ (O) « any (w)complement » > (to (V) complete (O) « the meaning »))).

(S) < ^It^ > (V) is (C) 『 well 』 ^to^ (V) remember (O) « [that] (S) < this (w)sentence pattern (I) > ＼ (aV) is not ((so) often) (V) used ／ as < a simple combination of < S-V > > ». (S) < ◎The reversed style { (id)†(V) beginning† with(= *(S) < which > (V) begins with*) < the (w)adverbs "(1)There" or "(2)Here" > } > ＼ (aV) are (more frequently) (V) used ／ *[than (S) < a simple combination of < S-V > >]* :

eg. There (V)is (S)a book on my desk.

eg. Here (V)is (S)something for you.

(In < both examples { above } >), (S) < ◎the (w)adverbs { *[(S) < which > ＼ (aV) are]]* (V) placed ／ ((id)at the beginning) } > (aV) can ＼ (aV) be (V) moved ／ ((id)deep into < the sentences >) to(= *and*) (*)(V) make (O) « (1)"(S)A book (V)is there on my desk" and (2)"(S)Something (V)is here for you" ».

(S) < ◎The split structure { *[(S) < which > ＼ (aV) is]]* (V) shown ／ (below) } > (also) (id)(V) belongs to < the 1st (w)sentence pattern >:

eg. (S)The fact (V)is that she doesn't really love him.

(Although (S) < many (*){ English } (1)learners/(2)speakers > ^(V) regard^ (O) « the sentence { above } » (C) 『 ^as^ < "(S)The fact (V)is (C)that she doesn't really love him" > 』), (S) < it > (actually) (V) is (C) 『 a modified form of < "(S)The fact that she doesn't really love him (V)is(=exists)" > 』; but (S) < ^it^ > (aV) might (V) be (C) 『 (just) (id)as well 』 ^to^ ^(V) regard^ (O) « it(= *the sentence*) » (C) 『 ^as^ < S-V-C > 』, (if (S) < it > (V) makes (O) « ^it^ » (C) 『 easier 』 ^to^ (V) comprehend (O) « the meaning of < this complicated sentence > »). (S) < Grammar > (V) is (there) (1)(to (V) serve (O) « the

‡understanding‡ »), not (2)(to (V) dictate (O) « how to (V) understand (O) « something » »).

(S) < { ((id)A little) controversial } interpretation of < this 1st (w)sentence pattern > > (aV) can (also) (V) comprehend (O) « ◎sentences { (S) < which > (id)(V) point at < (O)(w)objects > ((id)by way of < (w)prepositions >) } »:

eg. (S)She (V)looked at me.

(In < the sentence { above } >), (since (S) < the (w)verb "look" > (V) is (C) 『 (w)intransitive 』), (S) < it > (aV) cannot (directly) (id)(V) refer to < the (w)object "me" > ((id)in the form of < "~~She looked me~~" >), and (so) (S) < it > (id)(V) has (O) « need » of < the intervention of < the (w)preposition "at" > >. (S) < ^It^ > (V) is (therefore) (C) 『 (structurally) correct 』 ^to^ (V) say (O) « [that] (S) < the sentence { above } > (id)(V) belongs (1)to < S-V(1st) (w)sentence pattern >, not (2)to < S-V-O(3rd) > ». But (S) < ◎the fact > (still) (V) remains { that (S) < the { above-mentioned } sentence > (V) needs (O) « the (w)object *[of]* "me" » (to (V) complete (O) « its meaning »), { (S) < which > (V) makes (O) « ^it^ » (C) 『 (equally) logical 』 ^to^ ^(V) regard^ (O) « it » (C) 『 ^as^ < S-V-O > 』 } }. ^(V) Compare^ (O) « it » ^with^ < the example { below } >:

eg. (S)She (V)looked (O)me in the eye.

(S) < These two sentences > (V) are as (C) 『 (structurally) different 』 as [(S) < they > (V) are] (C) 『 (semantically) similar 』. (In < such cases >), (S) < ^it^ > will (id)(*)(V) do (O) « more (1)harm than (2)good » ^to^ (id)(V) dwell (too much) upon < structural interpretation >. (S) < Meaning > (V) matters (more than (S) < structure >): (*[^whether^ (S) < it > (*)(V) is]* (1)(C) 『 SV 』 ^or^ (2)(C) 『 SVO 』), (S) < "She" > (V) needs (O) « "me" » (as < a target of < her "look" > >); (if (S) < (id)that much > ＼ (aV) is (V) understood ／), (there) ＼ (aV) is (S) < no more (*){ structural } (1)interpretation or (2)definition > (V) needed ／ .

<II: SVC>... ◎a sentence { †(*)(V) requiring†*(= (S) < which > (*)(V) requires)* (1)(O) « a (w)complement »(C) but (2)(O) « no (w)object(O) » }

eg. (S)I (V)am (C)a singer.

(S) < ◎This 2nd one > (V) is (C) 『 (*)the (1){ basic } and (2){ (most frequently) used } (*)(w)sentence pattern of < English > 』, { (S) < the essential meaning of < which > > (V) is (C) 『 (id)equivalent to < the mathematical equation [of] "(S)=(C) >: (S) < (w)subject > (V) equals (O) « (w)complement »" 』, ([with] (S) < (C)(w)complement > (specifically) †(V) defining† (O) « the characteristic of < (S)(w)subject > » ((id)by the aid of < (V)(w)verb >)) }.

(S) < ◎The (w)verb { [(S) < which > ＼ (aV) is]] (most frequently) (V) used ／ (in < this SVC pattern >) } > (V) is (C) 『 (id)(S) < what > ＼ (aV) is (V) called ／ (C) 『 the "(w)be verb" 』, (id)an { English } equivalent for < the mathematical symbol [of] "=(equal)" > 』. But (S) < ˆitˆ > (id)is to ＼ (aV) be (V) noted ／ ˆthatˆ (S) < (id)the { so-called } "(w)do verbs" > (aV) can (also) ＼ (aV) be (V) used ／ (in < this 2nd (w)sentence pattern >), (if (S) < they > 〖 ((even) loosely) 〗 (V) comprehend (O) « the meaning of < "(S) equals (C)" > », (as (in < ◎the examples { [(S) < which > ＼ (aV) are]] (V) shown ／ (below) } >))):

eg. (S)I (V)will become (C)a singer.

(*)(S) < The example { above } > (1)(V) is (C) 『 (virtually) (id)identical with < "(S)I (V)will be (C)a singer" > 』 and (2)(aV) can (naturally) ＼ (aV) be (id)(V) interpreted as ／ < (id)‡(V) belonging‡ to < the 2nd (w)sentence pattern > >.

(In < the next example >), 〖 while [(S) < ˆitˆ > (V) is] (C) 『 (structurally) impossible 』 ˆtoˆ (V) say (O) « < { which } (w)sentence pattern of < SPAT-5 > > (S) < it > (id)(V) belongs to » 〗 , (S) < it > (id)is to ＼ (aV) be (essentially) (id)(V) interpreted as ／ < a form of < S-V-C > >:

eg. (S)I was born (C)a singer.

(S) < The main structure of < the { above-mentioned } sentence > "(S) < I > ＼ (aV) was (V) born ／ " > (V) is (C) 『 in < (w)the passive voice > 』 and, ((id)as such), (S) < it > (V) defies (O) « structural interpretation ((id)according to < SPAT-5 >) »: (S) < the rigid ˆtranslationˆ of < it > ˆintoˆ < "(w)the passive voice of < (S)My mother (V)bore (O)me" > > > (id)(V) makes (O) « ˆnoˆ sense » (ˆ(id)at allˆ). But (there) (V) is (S) < (

certainly) ◎an "equal relationship(S=C)" (^between^ < (S)"I" > ^and^ < (C)"a singer" >) >, { (S) < which > (aV) can ＼ (aV) be (V) certified ／ by < ^‡(V) linking‡^ (O) « them » ^with^ < "(w)be verb" > to (V) make(= and ‡(V) making‡) (O) « "(S)I (V)am (C)a singer" » > }. (Therefore), (S) < SPAT-5 > ^(V) regards^ (O) « it » (C) 『 ^as^ < (w)sentence pattern II: SVC > 』. (Likewise), (S) < the sentences { below } > ＼ (aV) are (also) (V) deemed ／ (C) 『 to (V) be (C) 『 S-V-C 』 』:

eg. (S)She (V)sank (C)crying into the sofa.

eg. (S)I (V)slept (C)naked in the bed.

eg. (S)He (V)came back home (C)a different man.

<III: SVO>... ◎a sentence { †(*)(V) requiring†(= (S) < which > (*)(V) requires) (1)(O) « an (w)object (O) » but (2)(O) « no (w)complement (C) » }

eg. (S)I (V)sing (O)songs.

(S) < This (w)sentence pattern > (*)(V) appears (1)((only) with < (id)the { so-called } "(w)do verbs" >) and (2)((never) with < "(w)be verbs" >), (except < (id)in the case of < (w)the progressive form > >):

eg. (S)I (V)was singing (O)songs.

(S) < The essential ^difference^ ^between^ < S-V-O > ^and^ < S-V-C > > (id)(V) lies in < the ^relationship^ ^between^ < (S)(w)subject > ^and^ < (O)(w)object > >: (S) < they > (V) are (C) 『 (w)two different things 』 【 (except < in ^such^ sentences ^as^ < "(S)She (V)killed (O)herself" >) 】 >, and (S) < the S-V-O sentence > (V) develops (around < the action of < (S)(w)subject > against < (O)(w)object > >). ((id)On the other hand), (in < S-V-C((w)sentence pattern II >)), (S) < (C)(w)complement > (V) is (there) (to (V) specify (O) « the characteristic of < (S)(w)subject > »). ((id)In other words), (S) < (C) > (V) is (C) 『 (id)subordinate to < (S) > 』: (while (S) < (S) > (V) equals (O) « (C) » (in < meaning >)), (S) < (C) > (aV) does ^not^ (*)(V) exist (1)((id)on { equal } terms with < (S) >) ^but^ (2)as < its attribute >. ((id)(Symbolically) speaking), (S) < S-V-C (w)sentence pattern(II) > (V) is (C) 『 a unilateral story of < (S)(w)subject (alone) > 』, ／ while (S) < S-V-O (w)sentence pattern(III) > (V) is (C) 『 an interactive story (

^between^ < (S) > ^and^ < (O) >) 』.

(S) < ◎The (w)verbs { to ＼ (aV) be (V) used ／ in < this S-V-O (w)sentence pattern (III) > } > (V) are (C) 『 "◎(w)transitive" 』, { (S) < which > (V) means (O) « *[that]* (S) < they > (aV) can (id)(V) refer to < (O)(w)object > (without < the intervention of < any (w)preposition > >) » }. But (S) < the same (w)verb > (aV) can (^both^) (*)(V) be (1)(C) 『 "(w)transitive" 』 ^and^ (2)(C) 『 "(w)intransitive" 』, (†(V) making†*(= (S) < which > (V) makes)* (O) « the (w)sentence pattern » (^sometimes^) (1)(C) 『 S-V-O 』 and (^sometimes^) (2)(C) 『 S-V 』):

eg. (S)You (V)must improve (O)your technique more.

eg. (S)You (V)must improve upon your technique more.

(S) < These two sentences >, 【 while *[(S) < they > (V) are]* (C) 『 (structurally) different 』 】 , (V) have (O) « (id)(practically) the same meaning ». (In < such cases >), (S) < the most important thing > (V) is (C) 『 the objective awareness 』 – ◎the realization { that (S) < the (w)verb "improve" > (V) needs (O) « "your technique" » (as < its (w)object >), (^whether^ (S) < it > (id)(*)(V) refers (1)(directly) to < the (w)object > ^or^ (2)(via < some (w)preposition >)) }. (In < that sense >), (S) < the ^relationship^ ^between^ < (V)verb > ^and^ < its (O)(w)object > > (aV) should (always) ＼ (aV) be (V) conceived ／ as < (V)-(O) relationship >, ((id)regardless of < the presence of < (w)prepositions > (between < them >) >).

<IV: SVOO>... ◎a sentence { †(V) requiring†*(= (S) < which > (V) requires)* (O) « two (O)(w)objects – ◎(1)(iO)(w)indirect object and (2)(dO)(w)direct object » – { †(V) signifying†*(= (S) < which > (V) signifies)* (O) « the action (*)of (1)< transfer > or (2)< benevolence > 【 ((sometimes) (3)malevolence) 】 (*)of < (dO)(w)direct object > (from < (S)(w)subject > to < (iO)(w)indirect object >) » } }

eg. (S)He (V)gave (iO)me (dO)some money.

(*)(S) < The sentence { above } > (1)(V) signifies (O) « the transfer of < (dO)"some money" (from < (S)"He" > to < (iO)"me" >) > », and (2)(aV) can ＼ (aV) be (V) written ／ (id)in the form of < S-V-O((w)sentence pattern III) > ((id)(S) < as > (V) follows):

eg. (S)He (V)gave (O)some money to me.

(S) < The "destination" of < the transfer > > ＼ (aV) is (V) shown ／ by < the (w)preposition "to" >. (Although (S) < the act of < "‡(V) giving‡ (O) « me » (O) « some money »" > > (V) has (O) « an element of < "benevolence" > »), (*)(S) < the action > (1)(V) is (essentially) (C) 『 "transfer" 』 and (so) (2)(id)(V) calls for < the vectorial (w)preposition "to" >.

eg. (S)I (V)sing (iO)my baby (dO)a lullaby.

(S) < The sentence { above } > (aV) can (also) ＼ (aV) be (V) written ／ (id)in the form of < S-V-O((w)sentence pattern III) > ((id)(S) < as > (V) follows):

eg. (S)I (V)sing (O)a lullaby for my baby.

(S) < The action of < "‡(V) singing‡ (O) « my baby » (O) « a lullaby »" > > ＼ (aV) is ^not^ (*)(V) made ／ (1)(as < "transfer" >) ^but^ (2)(as < "benevolence" >), (so) (S) < it > (id)(V) calls for < the (w)preposition "for" >.

(S) < ◎The (w)verbs { to ＼ (aV) be (V) used ／ (in < this S-V-O-O((w)sentence pattern IV) >) } > (aV) can (mostly) ＼ (aV) be (V) classified ／ ((id)according to < ◎the (w)preposition 〖 – (1)"to" or (2)"for" – 〗 { *[(S) < which > ＼ (aV) is]]* (V) needed ／ (in < (w)‡(V) paraphrasing‡ (in < S-V-O (w)sentence pattern (III) >) >) } >). But (there) (V) are (S) < ◎some exceptional (w)verbs { †(V) requiring†*(= (S) < which > (V) require)* (O) « ◎(w)prepositions { (id)other than < (1)"to" or (2)"for" > } » } >:

eg. (S)He (V)asked (iO)me (dO)some questions.

(S) < The action of < "‡(V) asking‡ (O) « me » (O) « some questions »" > > ＼ (aV) is (V) made ／ ((id)in order to "(V) get (O) « something » ((id)out of < someone >)"), (so) (S) < it > (V) requires (O) « the (w)preposition "of" » (in < S-V-O(III) ‡(w)paraphrasing‡ >):

eg. (S)He (V)asked (O)some questions of me.

(S) < The (w)verbs (1)"provide" or (2)"supply" > (V) are (C) 『 ^similar^ 〖 in < meaning > 〗 ^to^ < "give" > 』, but (S) < they > (basically) (V) require (O) « ^different^

(w)prepositions ^than^ < "to" > »:

eg. (S)Many foreign countries (V)provide/supply (iO)Japan (dO)oil.

eg. (S)Many foreign countries (V)provide/supply (O)Japan with oil.

eg. (S)Many foreign countries (V)provide/supply (O)oil for Japan.

eg. (S)Many foreign countries (V)provide/supply (O)oil to Japan.

<V: SVOC>... ◎a sentence { (in < which >) (S) < ◎the ^relationship^ ^between^ < (O)(w)object > ^and^ < (C)(w)complement > > (id)is to ＼ (aV) be (id)(V) interpreted as ／ (C) 〚 "a virtual ^interaction^ ^between^ < (S)(w)subject > ^and^ < (V)verb >" 〛, { (^to^ < which >) (S) < "the { structural } S-V ((id)at the beginning of < the sentence >") > ^(V) refers^ (as < an { intervening } factor, ((id)in the capacities of (*)a (1)< (w)third-person >, (2)< observer >, (3)< instigator >, (4)< promoter >, etc,etc.) >) } }

eg. (S)I (V)made (O)her (C)my secretary.

(In < the sentence { above } >), (S) < the first ◎relationship { to (V) consider } > (V) is (C) 〚 "(O)her(=she) (V)is (C)my secretary" 〛. (S) < ◎This virtual S-V relationship > ＼ (aV) is (V) called ／ (C) 〚 "(w)nexus" 〛, { (S) < which > (V) is (C) 〚 the { very } essence of < S-V-O-C((w)sentence pattern V) > 〛 }. (S) < The status of < "(O/S)her/she (V)is (C)my secretary" > > (V) is (C) 〚 ◎something { [(O) « that »] "(S)I (V)made" } 〛, { (in < which >) (S) < ^(w)top priority^ > (id)is to ＼ (aV) be (*)^(V) given^ ／ (1)(^to^ < { "(O)her-(C)my secretary"(virtual (S)she-(V)is (C)my secretary) } relationship >), not (2)(^to^ < "(S)I (V)made" >) }. (V) Remember: (O) « (S) < you > (*)(aV) must (first) (1)(V) interpret (O) « the (w)nexus 〖 (=virtual S-V relation) 〗 (between < (O)-(C) >) » (and then) (2)(V) add (O) « (S)-(V) » (to < it >) (as < an { intervening } supplement >) ».

(S) < S-V-O-C's (id)difference from < { (seemingly) similar } S-V-O-O > > (V) is (C) 〚 (*)the (1)presence/(2)absence (*)of < "(w)nexus 〖 (virtual S-V relationship) 〗 " (*)between < (1)O-C >/< (2)O-O > > 〛:

eg. (S)I (V)made (iO)her (dO)some drink.

((id)^In order to^ (V) prove (O) « [that] (S) < the { above-mentioned } sentence > (aV) does not (V) have (O) « S-V-O-C((w)sentence pattern V) structure » »), (S) < you > ^have only (*)to^(1) (id)(V) pick out (O) « { "(iO)her (dO)some drink" } part » and (2)(id)(V) try to ^(V) interpret^ (O) « them » (C) 『 ^as^ < virtual S-V > 』: (since (S) < ^it^ > (V) is (C) 『 impossible 』 ^to^ ^(V) change^ (O) « it » ^into^ < "(S)She (V)is (C)some drink" >), ◎(there) ＼ (aV) is (S) < no "(w)nexus" > (V) found ／ (^between^ < "(iO)her" > ^and^ < "(dO)some drink" >), { (S) < which > (V) makes (O) « it » (1)(C) 『 SVOO 』 ((id)instead of (2)< (C) 『 SVOC 』 >) }.

(S) < ◎S-V-O-C (w)sentence pattern(V) > (V) is (C) 『 ((id)by far) (*)the most (1){ complicated } and (2){ versatile } (*)structure of < English > 』, { (*)(S) < the mastery of < which > > (certainly) (1)(V) takes (O) « (*){ much } (1)time, (2)effort and (3) ＼ (id)‡(V) getting‡ (C) 『 used to 』 ／ », but (2)(aV) will (surely) (V) make (O) « learners » (C) 『 (id)confident of < their { growing } (w)command of < English > > 』 }. (Although (S) < I > (aV) will not (V) give (O) « (*){ further } (1)explanations or (2)examples (*)of < S-V-O-C > » (here)), (always) (id)(V) remember (1)to (1)(V) check (O) « "O-C" » (first) and (2)(V) confirm (O) « the { lurking } "(w)nexus" (behind < them >) », (2)never to (V) bother (O) « "S-V" » (until (S) < you > ↑ (aV) have (V) grasped ↑ (O) « the "virtual S-V relationship (between < O-C >)" »).

11.Backbone of < English comprehension >: (い)5 (id)kinds of < sentences >, (ろ)6 sentential elements and (は)8 (w)parts of speech

- The (1)importance, or (2)the (id)limitation to < the importance >, (*)of < (w)technical terms > -

(S) < The importance of < "a name" > (as < (id)a key to < ‡(V) grasping‡ (O) « something » > >) > ＼ (aV) is ˆneverˆ (V) felt ／ so (dearly) as (in < ‡(V) playing‡ (O) « music » >). (S) < I > (V) believe (O) « *[that]* (S) < most of < you readers > > (1) ↑ (aV) have (V) heard ↑ and (2)(aV) can (V) remember (*)(O) « the memorable introduction of < "(aV) Let (O) « it » (C) 『 be 』" > (by < the Beatles >) » ». (S) < (id)Not a few of < you > > (aV) could (even) (V) hum (O) « the tune » ((w)a cappella). But (S) < (id)very few of < you > > (aV) could (V) describe (O) « the ‡opening‡ stream of < the music > » ((id)by way of < chords > (like < "C - Am - G - F... C - G - F - C" >)); (C) 『 fewer (still) 』 (V) are (S) < ◎the { (exceptionally) cultured } people { (S) < who > (aV) can (V) write (O) « the sound » (in < notes >) } >. (Without < proper ‡training‡ (in < music >) >), (S) < no one > could (ever) (1)(V) read and (2)(V) play, 【 (id)let alone 】 (3)(V) write, (*)(O) « the notes ».

(S) < You > (aV) can (1)(V) hear, (2)(V) enjoy, and (even) (3)(V) play (*)(O) « music » (without < ‡(V) knowing‡ (O) « anything » ((*)about (1)< chords > or (2)< notes >) >); but (S) < the knowledge of < (O) « { what } chords » (S) < you > | (*)(aV) are (1)(V) hearing or (2)(V) playing (now) | > > (aV) will (certainly) (*)(V) help *[(O) « you »]* (C) 『 *[to]* (1)(V) remember and (2)(V) re-create (*)(O) « the music » ((id)later on) 』. And ((ˆtheˆ more) (S) < you > (V) grasp (O) « the sound » ((*)via (1)< chords > or (2)< notes >)), (ˆtheˆ more deeply) ＼ ˆ(V) ingrainedˆ ˆinˆ < your memory > (S) < the music > (aV) will (V) be ／ .

(S) < The same > (aV) can ＼ (aV) be (V) said ／ about < (id)(S) < what > ＼ (aV) is (V) called ／ (C) 『 "(w)technical terms" of < linguistics > 』 >. (S) < ˆItˆ > (V) is (C) 『 true 』 ˆthatˆ (S) < the knowledge of < (w)technical terms (alone) > > (aV) can (id)(V) take (O) « you » (nowhere), but (once (S) < you > (id)(V) get (somewhere) (in < the world of

< English > >)), (S) < ◎the point { [(S) < that > ＼ (aV) is] (V) reached ／ } > (id)(aV) might as well ＼ (aV) be (V) inscribed ／ in < your memory > (with < some memento >). (S) < (w)Technical terms > ^(V) are^ (^to^ < your comprehension of < English > >) (C) 〚 (C) 〚 ^what^ 〛 (S) < ◎^pictures^ { *[(S) < which > ＼ (aV) are]]* ^(V) taken^ ／ ((id)here and there ((id)on the way)) } > ^(V) are^ (^to^ < your memory of < a trip > >) 〛: ◎the magical keys { (by < which >) to (V) recollect (O) « something » < from < your memory > > }.

But (S) < such keys > (V) are (C) 〚 (totally) meaningless 〛 (to < ◎^those^ { (S) < ^who^ > ↑ (aV) have not (id)(V) made (O) « the trip » ↑ } >). (S) < (Only) ◎^those^ { ^(S) < who >^ ↑ (aV) have (themselves) (id)(V) made (O) « the trip » ↑ } > (aV) can (id)(V) make (O) « use » of < the keys > ((*)in < (1)‡(V) remembering‡ and (2)‡(V) enjoying‡ (*)(O) « their actual memory of < the trip > » >). ((id)In { this } sense), (S) < (id)‡(V) talking‡ about < English > ((id)in terms of < esoteric terminology >) > (V) is (C) 〚 just like < ＼ ‡(aV) being‡ (V) shown ／ (O) « pictures of < ◎a stranger's ^trip^ { (O) « *[which]* » (S) < you > never ^(V) made^ (yourself) } > » > 〛: (S) < ◎^those^ { [^(S) < who >^ | (*)(aV) are] (1)(V) talking or (2)(V) showing | } > (aV) may | (aV) be (V) enjoying | (O) « the experience », but (S) < you > (definitely) (aV) can't *[(V) enjoy (O) « it »]*. (To (V) enjoy (O) « a trip »), (S) < you > (id)have to (id)(V) make (O) « the trip » ((id)for yourself) ((id)at first); (likewise), (to (really) (V) comprehend (O) « English grammar »), (S) < you > (initially) (id)have to (id)(V) make (O) « a trip » (in < the world of < English > >), ^not^ (1)(through < (w)technical terms >) ^but^ (2)((id)by way of < example sentences >). (Once (S) < you > ↑ (aV) have (id)(V) made (O) « the trip » ↑ – when (S) < you > ↑ (aV) have (V) come to ↑ < a full ‡understanding‡ of < a certain pattern of < English > > > (through < some example sentence >)) – (S) < ◎a (w)technical term { *[(S) < which > (V) is]* (C) 〚 (id)fit for < ‡(V) describing‡ (O) « that pattern » > 〛 } > (aV) will (id)(V) make (O) « sense » (as < ◎an anchor { to (V) fix (O) « that particular knowledge » (in < your intellectual reservoir >) } >). (S) < (w)Technical terms > (without < (id)‡(V) making‡ (O) « trips » >(*= unless (S) < you >*

(V) make (O) « trips »)) (simply) (id)(V) make (O) « ^no^ sense » (^(id)at all^): (S) < the authentic knowledge of < English > > (aV) must ＼ (aV) be (V) certified ／ ((id)in the form of < example sentences >), (with (S) < suitable (w)technical terms > ＼ *[(aV) being]* (id)(V) put aside ／ (as < captions >)).

(S) < (O) « What » (S) < I > ↑ (aV) 've (just) (V) written ↑ > (V) is (C) 『 a truism 』 (to < all good linguists >), *[(S) < which > ＼ (aV) is]]* (id)(V) taken (^so^ much) for granted ／ by < them > ^that^ (S) < ^it^ > (*)(V) is (1)(C) 『 needless 』, (even) (2)(C) 『 absurd 』, ^to^ (id)(V) point (O) « it » out ((id)as if (S) < it > (V) were (C) 『 ◎a great truth { to (V) guide (O) « one » (to < some hidden treasure >) } 』). (Still), (S) < I > (id)have to (id)(V) point (O) « it » out (here), (because (S) < I > (V) know 【 from < years of < ‡teaching‡ experience > > 】 (O) « (S) < how many Japanese students of < English > > (V) are (totally) (C) 『 (id)unaware of ^this^ truistic lesson: ^that^ (S) < English >, 【 (*)unlike (1)< music > or (2)< mathematics > 】 , (aV) cannot ＼ (aV) be (id)(V) talked about ／ ((*)via (1)< chords >, (2)< notes >, (3)< symbols > or (4)< formulas > (*)(alone)) 』 »). (S) < (1)Musicians and (2)mathematicians > (aV) can (V) get (C) 『 (id)proficient in < their fields > 』 (by < (id) ＼ ‡(V) getting‡ (C) 『 used to ／ < the world of < ◎abstraction { *[(S) < which > ＼ ^(aV) is^]]* ^(V) composed^ (solely) ^of^ ／ < (w)technical terms > } > > 』 >): (unless (S) < they > (aV) can (V) grasp (O) « the whole picture » (from < (id)a series (*)of (1)< (w)musical notes > or (2)< numerical expressions > >)), (S) < they > ＼ (aV) are not (V) considered ／ (C) 『 *[to (V) be]* (C) 『 proficient ((*)as (1)< musicians > or (2)< mathematicians >) 』 』. (S) < English learners > (id)(aV) cannot (V) get (anywhere) (without < (actually) (id)‡(V) making‡ (O) « trips » (via < ◎countless numbers of < example sentences > { *[(S) < which > ＼ (aV) are]]* (V) inscribed ／ in < their memory > ((id)with the { humble } aid of < (w)technical terms >) } >) >): (unless (S) < you > (aV) can (instantly) (V) recite (O) « ◎some example sentences { (id)†(V) coming† up to *(= (S) < which > (V) come up to)* < your mind > ((id)at the hint of < some (w)technical terms >) } »), (S) < your (w)command of < English > > (V) is (C) 『 (still) immature 』.

((S) < That > ↑ [(aV) having ＼ (aV) been] (V) said ／ ↑), (S) < I > (aV) can (id)(V) feel (C) 〖 free 〗 to ^(V) introduce^ (O) « you readers » ^to^ < the (1){ following }, (2){ (rather) abstract } (id)(*)kind of < ◎knowledge in < English > > >, { (S) < which >, (nevertheless), (aV) will (V) benefit (O) « you » (greatly) }. (Without < the help of (1)< (*)these (1)(w)technical terms and (2)knowledge > >, (2)< ◎the abstract notion { *[(S) < which > ＼ (aV) is]]* (V) made ／ (C) 〖 possible 〗 (by < ‡(V) comprehending‡ (O) « these { (seemingly) esoteric } (id)sets of < terminology > » >) } >), (S) < you > (id)(V) are (C) 〖 sure to ＼ (id)(V) get (C) 〖 lost 〗 ／ (in < the world of < English > >) 〗. (id)^(V) Grope^ (O) « { your } way » ((id)by the aid of < the following >), ^and^ (S) < you >(aV) 'll (V) stumble (much less than (S) < you > (otherwise) (aV) would *[(V) stumble]*). (V) Trust (O) « me »: (S) < I >(V) 'm (C) 〖 ◎(*)no (1)mathematician or (2)magician { (S) < who > (id)(V) tries (*)to (1)(V) fascinate or (2)(V) hypnotize (*)(O) « you » } 〗; (S) < I >(V) 'm (C) 〖 ◎a teacher of < English > { (S) < who > never (V) tells (O) « you » (O) « ◎anything { (O) « *[that]* » (S) < you > (aV) need not (V) know } » } 〗. (S) < (O) « What » (S) < I >(id)'m going to (id)(V) write down (below) > (V) are (all) (C) 〖 ^too^ important (^to^ (V) forget) 〗: ^(V) forget^ (O) « them », ^and^ *[(S) < you > (aV) must]* (V) forget about < ‡(V) mastering‡ (O) « English » >. (S) < They > (V) are (C) 〖 the { very } backbone of < your English comprehension > 〗.

- Five (id)kinds of < sentences > (in < English >) -

((id)From the standpoint of < the purpose of < speech > >), (S) < English sentences > (aV) can ＼ (aV) be (id)(V) divided into ／ < the following five(5) kinds >:

(1)平叙文(HEIJOBUN: (w)declarative sentences): to (V) say (O) « something » ((id)in the affirmative)

eg. (S) < She > (V) is (C) 〖 beautiful 〗.

eg. (S) < She > ↑ (aV) has (V) sung ↑ (beautifully).

eg. (S) < She > (V) sings (beautifully).

eg. (S) < She > (V) sang (beautifully).

(S) < Declarative > (V) is (C) 〖 the most basic form (of < all sentences >) 〗.

(2)否定文(HITEIBUN: (w)negative sentences): to (V) say (O) « something » ((id)in the negative)

eg. (S) < She > (V) is not (C) 〖 beautiful 〗.

eg. (S) < She > ↑ (aV) has not (V) sung ↑ (beautifully).

eg. (S) < She > (aV) does not (V) sing (beautifully).

eg. (S) < She > (aV) did not (V) sing (beautifully).

((id)As for < ◎sentences { †(V) developing†(= (S) < *which* > (V) *develop*) (*)around < (1)"(w)be verb" or (2)"'have' of < (w)the perfect tense >" > } >), (S) < (w)negative sentences > (aV) can ＼ (aV) be (V) made ／ by < (simply) ‡(V) inserting‡ (O) « "not" » ((id)at the end of < the (w)verb (of < (w)declarative sentences >) >) >.

((id)When (S) < it > (V) comes to < ◎sentences { †(V) developing†(= (S) < *which* > (V) *develop*) around < ◎(w)verbs { (id)other than < "(1)be/(2)have" > } > } >), (S) < the process of < ‡(V) making‡ (O) « them » (C) 〖 negative 〗 > > (V) is (C) 〖 threefold 〗:

(I)(if (S) < the sentence > (id)(V) belongs to < (w)the present tense >), ((id)according to < the (w)subject >), ^(V) divide^ (O) « the { "verb" } part » (*)^into^ < (1)"does+verb" (He/She/It: (w)the 3rd person (w)singular = 三単現:SANTANGEN) or (2)"do+verb" (I/We/You/They: (id)other than < (w)the 3rd person (w)singular >) >;

(II)(if (S) < the sentence > (id)(V) belongs to < (w)the past tense >), (id)regardless of < the (w)subject (He/She/It/I/We/You/They) >, ^(V) divide^ (O) « the { "verb" } part » ^into^ < "did+verb" >;

(III)(V) add (O) « "not" » ((id)at the end of < the "do/does/did" >) (to (V) compose (O) « (w)negative sentences »).

(3)疑問文(GIMONBUN: (w)interrogative sentences): to (V) ask (about < something >)

eg. (V) Is (S) < she > (C) 〖 beautiful 〗?

eg. ↑ (aV) Has (S) < she > (V) sung ↑ (beautifully)?

eg. (aV) Does (S) < she > (V) sing (beautifully)?

eg. (aV) Did (S) < she > (V) sing (beautifully)?

((id)As for < ◎sentences { †(V) developing†(= (S) < *which* > (V) *develop*) (*)around < (1)"(w)be verb" or (2)"'have' of < (w)the perfect tense >" > } >), (S) < (w)interrogative sentences > (aV) can ＼ (aV) be (V) made ／ by < (simply) ‡^(V) inverting^‡ (O) « the position of < the (S+be/have/has/had)((w)subject+(w)verb) > » ^to^ < (Be/Have /Has/Had+S)((w)Verb+(w)subject) > >. (S) < No modulation { (id)other than < the (w)word order > } > (V) is (C) 〖 necessary 〗.

((id)When (S) < it > (V) comes to < ◎sentences { †(V) developing†(= (S) < *which* > (V) *develop*) around < ◎(w)verbs { (id)other than < "(1)be/(2)have" > } > } >), (S) < the process of < ‡(V) making‡ (O) « them » (C) 〖 interrogative 〗 > > (V) is (C) 〖 threefold 〗:

(I)(if (S) < the sentence > (id)(V) belongs to < (w)the present tense >), ((id)according to < the (w)subject >), ^(V) divide^ (O) « the { "verb" } part » (*)^into^ < (1)"does+verb" (He/She/It: (w)the 3rd person (w)singular = 三単現:SANTANGEN) or (2)"do+verb" (I/We/You/They: (id)other than < (w)the 3rd person (w)singular >) >;

(II)(if (S) < the sentence > (id)(V) belongs to < (w)the past tense >), ((id)regardless of < the (w)subject (He/She/It/I/We/You/They) >), ^(V) divide^ (O) « the { "verb" } part » ^into^ < "did+verb" >;

(III)^(V) move^ (O) « the "Do/Does/Did" » (^to^ < the beginning of < the sentence > >) (to (V) compose (O) « (w)interrogative sentences »).

(4)感嘆文(KANTANBUN: (w)exclamation sentences): to (V) express (O) « (id)wonder at < something > »

eg. (C) 〖 How beautiful 〗 (S) < she > (V) is!

eg. (C) 〖 { What } a { beautiful } woman 〗 (S) < she > (V) is!

(S) < (w)Exclamation sentences > (V) take (O) « two forms »: (1)(id)‡(V) beginning‡ with < "How" > (when *[(S) < they > | (aV) are]]* †(V) stressing† | (O) « (w)adjectives »(eg. "beautiful")) and (2)(id)‡(V) starting‡ with < "What" > (when *[(S) < they > | (aV) are]]* †(V) stressing† | (O) « (w)nouns »(eg. "a { beautiful } woman")).

(5)命令文(MEIREIBUN: (w)imperative sentences): to (V) tell (O) « someone » (C) 『 to (V) do (O) « something » 』

eg. (V) Be (C) 『 beautiful 』.

eg. (id)(aV) Let(O) « 's » (C) 『 (V) play (O) « some music » 』.

eg. (aV) Let (O) « me » (C) 『 (V) play (O) « the guitar » 』.

eg. (aV) Let (O) « girls » (C) 『 (1)(V) love and (2)(V) be (C) 『 beautiful 』 』.

(S) < (w)Imperative sentences > (id)(V) begin with < (w)the root form of < a (w)verb > >, (without < any (w)subject >). (S) < (w)The imperative sentence > (usually) (V) takes (O) « the form of < ◎an order { for "(S) < you >" to (V) do (O) « something » } > » 〖 ((w)2nd person (w)imperative) 〗 .

(S) < ◎(w)Imperative sentences { (id)†(V) beginning† with(= (S) < which > (V) begin with) < (1)"(id)Let's(=Let us)" or (2)"Let me" > } > (V) are (C) 『 special 』 ((id)in that (*)(S) < they > (V) do ^not^ "(1)tell (O) « you » (C) 『 to (V) do (O) « something » 』" ^but^ "(2)(V) propose (to < you >) (O) « [that] (S) < (1)we/(2)I > [(aV) should] (V) do (O) « something » »"). (S) < This > (aV) may ＼ (aV) be ^(V) regarded^ ／ (C) 『 ^as^ < "a pseudo (w)1st person (w)imperative" > 』.

(By < ‡(V) using‡ (O) « ^such^ (w)auxiliary verbs ^as^ < "(1)let/(2)make/(3)have" > » >), (S) < ^it^ > (V) is (C) 『 possible 』 ^to^ (V) make (O) « ◎"a pseudo (w)3rd person (w)imperative" { (1)†(V) allowing† or (2)†(V) ordering†(= (S) < which > (V) allows or (V) orders) (O) « "him/her/it/them" » (C) 『 to (V) do (O) « something » 』 } », but, ((id)(exactly) speaking), (S) < ◎the one { (*)(S) < who > "(1)(V) lets/(2)(V) makes/(3)(V) has" (*)(O) « "him/her/it/them" » (C) 『 (V) do (O) « something » 』 } > (V) is (still) (C) 『 "you"((w)the 2nd person) 』.

((id)In short), (S) < the { supposed } (w)subject of < an (w)imperative sentence > > (V) is (always) (C) 『 ◎"you" { [(S) < who > (V) are] ((id)in front of < ◎the one { (S) < who > (V) gives (O) « the order » } >) } 』.

((id)Aside from < (w)negative sentences >), (S) < all the ^other^ sentences ^than^ < declarative > > (V) take (O) « { inverted } (w)word order »: (S) < none of < them > >

(id)(V) starts with < (S)(w)subject > ((id)at the beginning). ((id) ＼ [(aV) *Being*] (Simply) (V) put ／), (S) < beginners of < English > > ^(V) have only to^ ＼ (id)(V) get (C) 『 used to ／ < such (w)word order inversion > 』 (^to^ (id)(V) get (O) « the knack » of < English communication >). (S) < You > (aV) ca^n't^ (id)(V) go ^very^ (far) (by < such (w)paraphrasing (only) >), ((id)to be sure), but (S) < you > (id)(aV) can't (V) go (anywhere) (without < (id)‡(V) being‡ (C) 『 able to (instantly) (id)(V) switch between < these five patterns of < English sentences > > > 』).

- Six elements of < the sentence (in < English >) > -

(When (S) < we > ^(V) shift^ (O) « our attention » ^from^ < the purpose of < speech > (of < sentences >) > ^to^ < the function of < words > (within < a single sentence >) >), (S) < we > (aV) can ^(V) divide^ (O) « an English sentence » ^into^ < the following six(6) different elements >:

(1)主語(SHUGO: (w)subject) = (S)

(2)動詞(DOUSHI: (w)verb) = (V)

(3)目的語(MOKUTEKIGO: (w)object) = (O)

(4)補語(HOGO: (w)complement) = (C)

(5)形容詞型修飾語(KEIYOUSHIGATA-SHUUSHOKUGO: (w)adjective (w)modifier) = {ADJ}

(6)副詞型修飾語(FUKUSHIGATA-SHUUSHOKUGO: (w)adverbial (w)modifier) = (ADV)

(S) < (id)Not all sentences > (V) have (O) « all those six elements » (in < them >). (S) < Some sentences > ＼ (id)(aV) are (V) composed of ／ < (V)(w)verb (only) > (eg. (V) Go! (V) Run! (V) Sing!), ／ while (S) < others > (V) comprehend (O) « multiple elements » (inside). (eg. (S)<The singer {(o)whom (s)we (v)heard (c)shouting rock'n'roll (adv)(at the beginning of the concert)}> (V)sang (O)us (O){ADJ.}{a sweet, dreamy} lullaby.)

(S) < The roles of < (1)(S)(w)subject, (2)(V)verb, (3)(O)(w)object and (4)(C) (w)complement > > (V) are (all) ˆsoˆ (C) 〚 (1)essential and (2)important 〛 ˆthatˆ (S) < they > ＼ (aV) are (V) called ／ (C) 〚 the four(4) main elements of < a sentence > 〛. (S) < All textbooks of < English > > (V) give (O) « you » (1)(O) « ◎(*)explanations, (1){ sketchy } or (2){ detailed }, ((*)about < these 4 main elements >) » and (2)(O) « ◎the (w)5 sentence patterns { (O) « *[which]* » (S) < they > (aV) can (V) take 〖 (◎SPAT-5 { (C) 〚 as 〛 (S) < we > (V) call (O) « it » (in < this book >) }) 〗 } ». (S) < These four >, 〖 (S)(V)(O) and (C) 〗 , 〖 since (S) < they > (V) are (C) 〚 the { "main" } elements 〛 〗 , (V) are (C) 〚 ˆ(*)tooˆ (1)clear-cut and (2)◎easy { to (V) understand } 〖 (once (S) < we > (id)(V) make (O) « them » out (C) 〚 to (V) be (C) 〚 (id)as such 〛 〛) 〗 (ˆtoˆ (V) demand (O) « any comment » (here)) 〛.

(S) < The most difficult part of < English interpretation > > (id)(V) lies in < ‡ˆ(V) distinguishingˆ‡ (O) « those four main elements », 〖 (S)(V)(O) and (C) 〗 , ˆfromˆ < the rest > > — ◎the { lengthy }, { misleading } (id)chunks of < words > { [(S) < which > (*)(V) are] ˆnotˆ (1)(C) 〚 essential 〛 ˆbutˆ (merely) (2)(C) 〚 (id)accessory to < the essence of < the sentence > > 〛: (S) < {ADJ: (w)adjective} > †(V) being†(= (S) < *which* > *(V) is*) (C) 〚 (id)accessory (1)to < some particular (w)noun > 〛, and (S) < (ADV: (w)adverb) > *[†(V) being†(= (S) < which > (V) is) (C) 〚accessory]]* (2)to < *[{ some particular }]* (w)verb > 〛 }. (S) < These two superfluities > (V) are (often) ˆsoˆ (C) 〚 bulky 〛 ˆthatˆ (S) < (id)the very length of < them > > (V) is ˆenoughˆ (ˆtoˆ ˆ(V) discourageˆ (O) « beginners » (ˆfromˆ < ‡(V) reading‡ (any further) >)). (Indeed), (S) < the success (*)of < (1)‡(V) reading‡, (2)‡(V) writing‡ or (3)(id)‡(V) listening‡ to (*)(O) « < English > » > > (id)(V) lies in < your (id)skill at < ˆ‡(V) discerning‡ˆ (O) « the essential » ˆfromˆ < the accessory > > >. ◎ˆThoseˆ { ˆ[(S) < who >ˆ (V) are] (id)(C) 〚 poor at < instant detection of < the essence > > 〛 } (V) are (id)(C) 〚 incapable (*)of < (1){ reading } or (2){ listening } (*)comprehension of < English > > 〛.

(S) < The (1)◎ability or (2)◎inability { (*)to (id)ˆ(V) drawˆ out (O) « the essence » ˆfromˆ < (id)floods (*)of (1)< words > or (2)< news > or (3)< voices > > } > (aV) will (*)(V) determine ^not only^ (1) (O) « whether (S) < you > (aV) can (V) use (O) « English » ((id)at your command) » but^ (2) (O) « if (S) < you > (aV) can (effectively) (*)(V) utilize (1)(O) « stimuli (from < the world >) », 〖 (2)(id)if not (O) « the world » (itself) 〗 , ((id)at your command) ».

((id)*[^Whether^ (S) < you >]* (V) Believe (O) « it » ^or^ not), (S) < the world of < English > >, 〖 ◎the (whole) { wide } world { (S) < that > (V) spreads (outside < our { puny } { Japanese-speaking } island >) } 〗 , (V) is not so (C) 『 (1)short and (2)simple 』 as < your { (usually) monosyllabic } { daily } conversation (with < Japanese folks >) >. (To (V) survive (in < the wave after < (id)waves of < { English-speaking } oceans > > >)), (S) < you > (id)have to (*)(V) practice (O) « (1)^‡(V) distinguishing‡^ (O) « the essence » ^from^ < the unessential > », (2)^‡(V) marking‡^ (O) « (w)adjective modifiers 〖 ((S) < which > (V) modify (O) « (w)nouns ») 〗 » ^with^ < (w)curly brackets{...} > and (3)^‡(V) encircling‡^ (O) « (w)adverb modifiers 〖 ((S) < which > (V) modify (O) « (w)verbs ») 〗 » ^with^ < (w)parentheses(...) >. (S) < This practice >, 〖 if *[(S) < it >* ＼ *(aV) is]]* (earnestly) (V) attempted ／ (amid < { (duly) complicated } English sentences >) 〗 , (aV) will ^(V) take^ (O) « beginners (in < Japan >) » (O) « (1){ four } to (2){ five } (*)years of < intensive study > » ^to^ ^(V) enable^ (O) « them » (C) 『 ^to^ (V) swim 〖 (id)with confidence 〗 (through < the rough sea of < English > >) 』.

- Eight (w)parts of speech (in < English >) -

(^In^ (id)‡(V) try^ing^‡ to (id)(V) distinguish among < (id)mountains of < ◎words { (S) < that > (V) compose (O) « English sentences » } > >), (S) < the knowledge of < "品詞 (HINSHI: (w)parts of speech)" > > (V) is (C) 『 (id)of { the utmost } importance 』. (S) < English (w)parts of speech > (id)(V) divide into < the following eight(8) kinds >:

(1)名詞(MEISHI) = (w)noun(n.):

◎a name { to (V) express (O) « (1)someone/(2)something » }

eg. apples, birds, cats, dogs, eggs, fools, girls, hotels, inns, jokes, etc,etc.

(2)代名詞(DAIMEISHI) = (w)pronoun(pron.):

a general (id)substitute for < (*){ any particular } (1)(w)noun or (2)(w)nouns >

eg. I, we, you, they, he, she, it, one, some, none, any, nobody, everybody, etc, etc.

(3)形容詞(KEIYOUSHI) = (w)adjective (adj.):

◎a word { to (V) modify (O) « a (w)noun » }

eg. absurd, beautiful, charming, detestable, erotic, fascinating, good, husky, interesting, jesting, etc, etc.

(4)前置詞(ZENCHISHI) = (w)preposition (prep.):

◎a (w)function word { *[(S) < which > ＼ (aV) is]]* (V) used ／ (before < a (w)noun >) (to (V) show (O) « the ˆrelation ofˆ < the (w)noun > ˆtoˆ < (*){ some other } (1)(w)noun, (2)(w)verb, or (3)(w)adjective > ») }

eg. at, by, for, in, on, to, with, etc, etc.

(5)動詞(DOUSHI) = (w)verb (v.):

◎a word { to (V) express (O) « (1)action, (2)existence, (3)state or (4)occurrence » }

eg. avoid, bathe, come, die, end, fly, grow, have, invite, join, etc, etc.

(6)副詞(FUKUSHI) = (w)adverb (adv.):

◎a word { to (V) modify (O) « (*)a (1)(w)verb, (2)(w)adjective / or (3)another (w)adverb » }

eg. aside, beside, consequently, down, endlessly, forward, gladly, happily, inside, etc, etc.

(7)接続詞(SETSUZOKUSHI) = (w)conjunction (conj.):

◎a word { to (V) connect (O) « (1)words, (2)(w)phrases, (3)(w)clauses or (4)sentences » }

eg. and, although, but, because, so, then, yet, etc, etc.

(8)間投詞(KANTOUSHI) = (w)interjection (int.):

◎a word { to (V) express (O) « emotion » } { (*)(S) < which > (1)(aV) can (V) stand (alone) and (often) (V) (2)(id)(V) stands out (in < the stream of < conversation > >) }

eg. alas, bravo, cheers, damn, er, fuck, goodness, etc, etc.

(S) < { (id)Not a few } English words > (aV) can (V) function ((id)in the capacities of <

several (w)parts of speech >). ((id)For example), (S) < "kid" > (aV) can (V) work (^either^ ((*)as (1)< a (w)noun > (eg. "(S) < Kids > (V) are (C) 『 lovely 』")) ^or^ (2)< a (w)verb > (eg. "(aV) Don't (V) kid^ (O) « yourself » (^into^ < ‡(V) believing‡ (O) « such nonsense » >)")). (S) < Many words > (V) work (in < the same form >) ((*)as < ^both^ (1)an (w)adjective ^and^ (2)an (w)adverb > (eg. "(S) < She > (V) is (C) 『 a { fast } runner 』"; "(S) < She > (V) runs (fast)")). (S) < Beginners > (aV) will (id)(V) have (O) « a hard time [(of < it >)] » (*[in]* ^‡(V) distinguishing‡^ ^between^ < a (w)preposition > ^and^ < an (w)adverb > (eg. "(S) < The games > (aV) will ＼ (aV) be (V) held ／ ((id)over < the weekend >)"; "(S) < The game > (V) is (C) 『 over 』 (now)")). (To (id)(V) distinguish between < these (w)parts of speech >), (S) < you > (id)have to (id)(V) pay { conscious } (O) « attention » to < ◎the function of < them > (in < the sentence >) >, { (S) < which > (aV) will (V) sharpen (O) « your senses of < grammatical comprehension > » }.

- How to (1)(V) memorize and (2)never (id)(V) fail to (V) recollect (*)(O) « eight (w)parts of speech » -

(S) < ◎Things { *[(S) < which > ＼ (aV) are]]* (V) anchored ／ (in < your memory >) (by < meaningful (id)chains of < association > >) } > (aV) will (hardly) ＼ (id)(V) get (C) 『 lost 』 ／. (If (S) < you > (id)(V) lose (O) « hold of < any particular thing > »), (id)^(V) try^ to (id)(V) draw in (O) « ◎the (id)chain of < memory > { *[(S) < which > ＼ (aV) is]]* (V) connected ／ (with < it >) } », ^and^ (S) < something { else } > (aV) will (id)(V) come up (to < your mind >), ((possibly) ＼ *[(aV) being]* (id)(V) accompanied by ／ < ◎the thing { (O) « *[which]* » (S) < you > (id)(V) seem to ↑ (aV) have (V) forgotten ↑ } >). (S) < That > (V) is (C) 『 *[the reason]* why (S) < you > (aV) should NEVER (V) remember (O) « things » ((id)item by item) 』: (S) < you > (aV) MUST (always) (id)(V) try to (V) remember (O) « things » (in < the web of < meaningful association > ((id)along with < some others >) >).

(In < (id)‡(V) trying‡ (*)to (1)(V) comprehend and (2)(V) memorize (*)(O) « the eight (w)parts of speech (in < English >) » >), (S) < the two main keys of < recollection > > (*)(V) are (1)(C) 『 "(w)noun" 』 and (2)(C) 『 "(w)verb" 』.

(id)(aV) Let (O) « us » (C) 『 (id)(V) begin with < the "◎(w)noun" >, { (S) < which > (naturally) ^(V) reminds^ (O) « us » ^of^ < its special version "(w)pronoun" > } 』; (S) < a "(w)noun" > ＼ (aV) is (V) modified ／ by < an "(w)adjective" >; and (S) < a "(w)preposition" > (aV) can (only) (V) have (O) « (*)a "(1)(w)noun /(2)(w)pronoun" » (as < its (w)object >). (Thus) (S) < we > (V) have (O) « (id)a chain of < ◎(w)parts of speech { †(V) centering† *(= (S) < which > (V) centers)* around < the "(w)noun" > } > » ((id)(S) < as > (V) follows):

(1)名詞(MEISHI) = (w)noun (n.)

(2)代名詞(DAIMEISHI) = (w)pronoun (pron.)

(3)形容詞(KEIYOUSHI) = (w)adjective (adj.)

(4)前置詞(ZENCHISHI) = (w)preposition (prep.)

(S) < What > (V) stands ((id)in contrast with < a "(w)noun" >) (V) is (C) 『 a "(w)verb" 』; and (S) < a "(w)verb" > ＼ (aV) is (V) modified ／ by < an "(w)adverb" >. (Here) (V) comes (S) < ◎the simple pair { †(V) centering† *(= (S) < which > (V) centers)* around < the "(w)verb" > } > ((id)(S) < as > (V) follows):

(5)動詞(DOUSHI) = (w)verb (v.)

(6)副詞(FUKUSHI) = (w)adverb (adv.)

◎The word { (S) < that > (aV) can (V) connect (O) « "(1)nouns", "(2)pronouns", "(3)adjectives", "(4)prepositions", "(5)verbs" and "(6)adverbs" » } (V) is (C) 『 a "(w)conjunction" 』:

(7)接続詞(SETSUZOKUSHI) = (w)conjunction (conj.)

And (S) < ◎a word { (S) < which > (id)(V) stands out (solo) ((id)with (absolutely) no regard to < any other word >) } > (V) is (C) 『 an "(w)interjection" 』:

(8)間投詞(KANTOUSHI) = (w)interjection (int.)

◎(S) < Each of < these eight (w)parts of speech > > (V) has (O) « its distinctive characteristics », { (S) < which > (V) makes (O) « ^it^ » (C) 『 imperative 』 ^for^ (S) < learners > ^(*)to^ (1)(V) study and (2)(V) memorize (*)(O) « them » (differently) }. (S) < How to (id)(V) deal with < each (w)part of speech > ((id)in { respective } manners) > (id)is to ＼ (aV) be (V) detailed ／ (in < the following section >).

12.Respective manners of < (1)study and (2)memorization > (*)(for < eight (w)parts of speech > (in < English >))

- (1)(S) < 棒暗記(BOUANKI: Mechanical memorization) > and (2)(S) < { 片言 (KATAKOTO: broken) } English > (*)(V) are (only) (id)(C)〚 good (*)for < (1)(w)nouns, (2)(w)pronouns and (3)(w)adjectives > 〛 -

(Of < all the eight (w)parts of speech >), (C)〚 ((id)by far) (*)the most (1)numerous and (2)useful (in < conversation >) 〛 (*)(V) are (1)(S) < (w)nouns 【 (including < (w)pronouns >) 】 > and (2)(S) < (w)adjectives >. (Indeed), (*[even]* if (S) < you > (V) are (totally) (C)〚 (id)ignorant of < grammar > 〛), (S) < you > (aV) could 【 even then 】 (id)be able to ˆ(V) communicateˆ 【 (id)more or less 】 ˆwithˆ < a foreigner > ((id)in ˆsuchˆ manners ˆasˆ < "(S) < You >... (C)〚 beautiful 〛... (S) < your cooking >... (C)〚 good 〛" >). (S) < This > (V) is (also) (C)〚 (id)true with < any ˆotherˆ language ˆthanˆ < English > > 〛; (in < French >), (S) < "(S) < Vous >... (C)〚 beau 〛... (S) < votre cuisine >... (C)〚 bon 〛" > (aV) should (V) do (O) « something ».

(In < English >), ((id)thanks to < the absence of < "(w)gender" > (in < (w)nouns >) >), (S) < (*){ mechanical } (1)memorization and (2)utilization (*)of < (1)(w)nouns and (2)(w)adjectives > > (V) is (C)〚 (far) easier than *[(S) < it > (V) is]* (in < traditional Indo-European languages >) 〛. (In < French >), (S) < the same (w)adjective (eg. "grand") > (V) varies ((id)according to < (*)the (1)gender and (2)number (*)of < ◎the (w)noun/(w)pronoun { < *[which]* > (S) < it > ＼ (aV) is (V) used ／ with } > >)
(like
< "(S) < Il > (V) est (C)〚 grand 〛((S) < He > (V) is (C)〚 tall 〛) /
(S) < Elle > (V) est (C)〚 grande 〛((S) < She > (V) is (C)〚 tall 〛) /
(S) < Les monsieurs > (V) sont (C)〚 grands 〛((S) < The men > (V) are (C)〚 tall 〛) /
(S) < Les filles > (V) sont (C)〚 grandes 〛((S) < The girls > (V) are (C)〚 tall 〛)") >, /
while (in < English >) (S) < "tall" > (V) is (simply) (C)〚 "tall" 〛 (with < anything >).

(Still), (there) (V) is (S) < ◎something { (O) « *[which]* » (S) < you > (aV) should (id)(V) keep (in < mind >) (when *[(S) < you > (aV) are]* (id)†(V) trying† to (V) memorize (O) « (1)(w)nouns and (2)(w)adjectives » (in < English >)) } >:

(1)(S) < (w)adjectives > (aV) should ＼ (aV) be (V) memorized ／ ((id)in combination with < some suitable (w)nouns >):

eg. "an { amazing } story", "a { beautiful } woman", "a { chilly } winter's day", "a { daunting } task", etc,etc.

(S) < Beginners > (aV) should (normally) (V) memorize (O) « an (w)adjective » (with < a (w)noun { in < (w)the singular form > } >), ((id)in order to ＼ (id)(V) get (C) 〖 used to ／ < (instinctively) ^‡(V) switching‡^ ^between^ < (w)indefinite articles "a" and "an" > ((id)according to (S) < the ‡opening‡ sound of < ◎the (w)noun { †(V) coming† *(= (S) < which > (V) comes)* (before < the (w)adjective >) } > > (*)‡(V) being‡ (1)(C) 〖 (w)consonant 〗 or (2)(C) 〖 (w)vowel 〗 >)) 〗.

(2)(S) < (w)Nouns > (aV) should (always) ＼ (aV) be (V) memorized ／ (in < (*)their (1){ (w)plural } 【 (id)as opposed to (2){ (w)singular } 】 (*)forms >), (1)(with < "s/es" > ((id)at the end)) and (2)(without < "a/an/the" > ((id)at the beginning)):

eg. "angels", "babies", "cuticles", "diaries", etc,etc.

(S) < You > (aV) must never (V) remember (O) « (w)nouns » ("(id)as is"), (id)(S) < that > (V) is (C) 〖 *[to (V) say* , (O) « (in < ◎(w)the singular form > { *[(S) < which > ＼ (aV) is]]* (V) written ／ (on < the dictionary >) } (without < any article("a/an/the") >)) » 〗

(ng. ~~"angel", "baby", "cuticle", "diary"~~).

(3)(S) < (w)Uncountable nouns 【 (◎(w)nouns { (S) < which > (aV) cannot ＼ (aV) be (V) used ／ (in < the (w)plural >) }) 】 > (aV) should ＼ (aV) be (V) memorized ／ (in < (w)the singular form >) (with < (*){ some } (1)(w)determinatives or (2)numerical expressions > (before < them >)):

eg. "(id)a piece of < advice >", "(id)a spoonful of < butter >", "(id)a slice of < cake >", "(id)beads of < dew >", etc,etc.

(If (S) < you > (V) remember (O) « them » ("(id)as is") (ng. ~~"advice", "butter",~~

~~"cake", "dew"~~)), (S) < you > (aV) will (easily) (V) fall into < ^such^ erroneous expressions ^as^ < "ng. ~~too many advices~~, ~~lots of butters~~, ~~some more cakes~~ or ~~morning dews~~" > >.

((id)(Theoretically) [speaking]), (S) < the number of < (w)nouns > > (V) is (C) 〚 infinite 〛: (S) < you > (aV) could (V) invent (O) « any (w)noun » ((id)at will) (without < limitation >). (S) < All the other (w)parts of speech 〖 (pronouns, adjectives, prepositions, verbs, adverbs, conjunctions, interjections) 〗 > (V) are (C) 〚 ((id)more or less) limited (in < their total number >) 〛, but (S) < (w)nouns > (id)(V) have (O) « no limit » to < their possible number >. (S) < You > (aV) should (exactly) (V) remember (O) « all English (w)pronouns », (S) < you > (aV) could (id)(V) attempt to (V) remember (O) « all possible usages in < (1)prepositions, (2)conjunctions or (3)interjections > »; but (S) < you > (id)(aV) couldn't possibly (V) remember (O) « all (w)nouns »; and, ((id)as (*)for (1)< (w)adjectives > and (2)< (w)adverbs >), (S) < their total number > (V) is (practically) (C) 〚 ^too^ large (^to^ (V) remember) 〛.

(S) < (Only) fools > (id)(V) try 〖 (id)in vain 〗 to (V) challenge (O) « the infinity ». Never (id)(V) try to (V) remember (O) « as many (w)nouns { (O) « as » (S) < you > (id)(V) happen to (V) encounter (in < (1)books or (2)conversation >) } ». (Unlike < computers >), (S) < your memory > (aV) may not (V) overflow (with < such useless (id)floods of < data > >), but (S) < your memory > (aV) will (certainly) (V) fail (O) « you »: (S) < human brains > (aV) will (only) (V) remember (O) « useful information », and (S) < (1){ useless } or (2){ harmful } (*)memories of < the past > > (aV) will ＼ (aV) be (magically) (id)(V) drowned out ／ (from < your life >). (S) < Wise selection of < words > >, 〖 (1)◎{ which } one { to (V) remember } and (2)◎{ which } one { to (V) forget } 〗 (V) is (especially) (C) 〚 important 〛 (with < (w)nouns >). (V) Use (O) « your dictionary » (to (V) measure (O) « the relative significance of < ◎a (w)noun { (O) « *[which]* » (S) < you > (id)(V) happened to (V) know (in < (1)books or (2)conversation >) } > »), and (V) decide (O) « ^whether^ (*)to (1)(id)(V) store (O) « it » up (in < your permanent memory >) ^or^ (2)(id)(V) lay (O) « your hand » on < it > ((only) temporarily) ». (S) < Most dictionaries (for < students >) > (aV) will (kindly) ^(V) mark^ (O) « words » ^with^ < some ◎symbols { †(V) signifying†(= (S) < *which* > (V) *signify)* (O) « their relative importance » } >.

(S) < The same > (aV) can ＼ (aV) be (V) said ／ about < (w)verbs >: (S) < you > (aV) may (id)(V) try to (mechanically) (V) remember (O) « all { existing } (w)verbs (in < English >) », 〖 (only) (id)to no avail 〗. (S) < These two (w)parts of speech – (1)(w)nouns and (2)(w)verbs – > (aV) can ^(^only^)^ ＼ (aV) be (*)(wisely) (1)(V) memorized and (2)(V) utilized ／ (^by^ < (*)the (1){ selected } (2) 〖 ({ (consciously) selective }) 〗 (*)few >).

((id)As for < other (w)parts of speech > – pronouns, adjectives, prepositions, adverbs, conjunctions and interjections –) (S) < you > (aV) will (id)(V) lose (O) « nothing » by < (id)‡(V) attempting‡ to (V) remember (O) « ◎anything { [(O) « that »] (S) < you > (id)(V) happen to (V) meet } » >. (1)(S) < Their total number > and (2)(S) < possible (1)usages or (2)meanings > (*)(V) are (C) 〘 ^so^ large 〙 ^that^ (S) < you > (aV) will (naturally) (V) forget (O) « (id)lots of < them > », but ((^the^ more) (S) < you > (id)(V) try to (V) remember), (C) 〘 ^the^ better 〙 *[(S) < it > (V) is]* . ((id)At least), (there) (V) is (S) < ◎nothing 〖 in < these (w)parts of speech > 〗 { [(O) « that »] (S) < you > (aV) should (consciously) (id)(V) try not to (V) keep (in < your permanent memory >) } > (as < (id)in the case of < (1)(w)nouns and (2)(w)verbs > >).

- (S) < (w)Verbs > (aV) must ＼ (aV) be (id)(V) learnt (by heart) ／ (in < example sentences >) -

(S) < Poor linguists > (aV) will (invariably) (id)(V) try to (V) save (O) « intellectual energy », (id)only to (id)(V) commit { logical } (O) « suicide » ((id)in the end). (S) < ◎(*)^Those^ (1){ ^(S) < who >^ (id)(V) try to (V) remember (O) « an English (w)verb » ("(id)as is") } – (2){ ^(S) < who >^ (only) (id)(V) lay (O) « their hands » on < the meanings (in < the dictionary >) (in < ◎the raw form { *[(S) < which > ＼ (aV) is]]* (V) written ／ (on < it >) } >) > } – > | (aV) are (V) wasting | (O) « (*){ their } (1)time and (2)intellectual resources ». (S) < They > (aV) could (id)(V) go (nowhere) (by < such haphazard methods >), not(= (S) < *they* > (aV) *could not* (V) *go (anywhere)*) ((id)at least) (in < the world of < English (w)verbs > >).

(When (S) < you > (id)(V) try (*)to (1)(V) remember and (2)(V) utilize (*)(O) « (w)verbs (in < English >) »), (S) < you > (aV) must (id)(V) stick to < the following principles >:

(1)(Always) (V) remember (O) « a (w)verb » (in < some example sentence >). (S) < A (w)verb > (*)(V) is ^only^ (1)(C) 〚 useful 〛 (^with^ < usage >), (2)(C) 〚 meaningless 〛 (with < meanings (only) >). ((id)For example), (V) remember (O) « ◎the term 【 ((1)(w)verb /(2)(w)noun) 】 { (O) « *[which]* » (S) < we > (V) invented ((id)early on) (in < this book >) } » — EXPROGER: (S) < you > (aV) can't (id)(V) make (O) « use » of < it > (by < ‡(V) remembering‡ (O) « its definition, *[(S) < which > (V) is]* (C) 〚 "to (V) prove (O) « the general rule » (by < the exception(s) >)" 〛 » >). (S) < You > (aV) can (^only^) (V) give (O) « it » (O) « a full life (in < your memory >) » (^by^ (id)‡(V) storing‡ (O) « it » up (in < your brains >) (with < ^such^ example sentences ^as^ < "(S) < (1)The relative ease and (2)the universal popularity (*)of < English > > (V) EXPROGER (O) « ◎the ^difficulty^ { (O) « *[which]* » (S) < foreign learners > ^(V) find^ (^in^ < ^such^ (1){ gender-strict } (2){ Indo-European } (*)languages ^(*)as^ (1)< French >, (2)< Spanish > or (3)< Italian >) } »" > > >)).

(If (S) < you > ↑ (aV) have (id)(V) read through ↑ < the earlier parts of < this book > >), (S) < the meaning of < the { above-mentioned } example sentence > > (aV) must (V) be (C) 〚 clear 〛... ((id)in case (S) < it > (V) isn't (C) 〚 *[clear]* 〛), (S) < I >(aV) 'll (V) explain (O) « *[it]* » ((id)in detail): "(S) < English >, 【 [while] [†(V) being†] (C) 〚 a member of < Indo-European languages > 〛 】 , (V) is (C) 〚 ◎an exceptional tongue { (S) < which > (V) is (totally) (C) 〚 (w)gender-free 〛 } 〛. (S) < That > (V) is (C) 〚 *[the reason]* why (S) < it > (*)(V) is (1)(C) 〚 (relatively) easy (for < beginners >) 〛 and (2)(generally) ＼ (V) spoken ／ ((id)all over the world) 〛. ((id)With the exception of < English >), (S) < ◎Indo-European languages { (*)like (1)< French >, (2)< Spanish > or (3)< Italian > } > (V) have ◎(O) « strict rules (about < the (w)gender of < (w)nouns > >

) », { (S) < which > (V) makes (O) « ^it^ » (C) 〚 difficult 〛 ^for^ (S) < foreign learners > ^to^ (V) master (O) « such languages » }, ((thereby) †(V) making† (O) « them » (C) 〚 less popular than (S) < English > 〛)."

(Now), (id)(S) < you > (V) know (O) « *[that]*, (S) < (w)verbs > (V) are ^only^ (C) 〚 useful 〛 (^when^ *[(S) < they > ＼ (aV) are]]* (V) memorized ／ (with < example sentences >)) ». (S) < (id)‡(V) Trying‡ to (V) remember (O) « (w)verbs » (with < their definitions (only) >) > (aV) will (id)(V) get (O) « you » (nowhere).

(2)(V) Memorize (O) « (w)verbs » (in < ◎the actual (w)sentence pattern(s) 【 ((O) « what » (S) < this book > (V) calls (C) 〚 "SPAT-5" 〛) 】 { (in < which >) (S) < they > (aV) can ＼ (aV) be (V) used ／ } >). (S) < Some (w)verbs > (aV) can ＼ (aV) be (V) used ／ (in < SVOO >(#4: eg. "(S) < She > (V) denied (O) « me » (O) « (id)entrance to < her room > »")) / while (S) < others > (aV) cannot *[(aV) be (V) used (in < SVOO >)]* (ng. "~~She prohibited me entrance to her room~~"; cf: "(S) < She > ^(V) prohibited^ (O) « me » ^from^ < ‡(V) entering‡ (O) « her room » >"). (If (S) < you > (id)(V) are (C) 〚 in the habit of < ‡(V) remembering‡ (O) « (w)verbs » (with < their meanings (only) >) > 〛), (S) < you > (aV) may (id)be able to (V) wade (through < the { (relatively) easier } flows (*)of (1)< SV > or (2)< SVO > >), but (S) < you > (aV) will (soon) ＼ (id)(V) get (C) 〚 stuck ／ in < the narrower channels (*)of (1)< SVOO > or (2)< SVOC > > 〛. ((id)So as not to ＼ (id)(V) get (C) 〚 lost 〛 ／ ((id)later on)), (id)(V) try to (V) remember (O) « (w)verbs » (in < their particular (w)sentence patterns >).

(3)Never (id)(V) try to (V) save (O) « your efforts » (in < (w)^‡(V) paraphrasing‡^ (O) « a particular (w)verb » (*)^with^ (1)< "同意語(DOUIGO: (w)synonyms)" > or (2)< "反意語(HANIGO: (w)antonyms)" > >). (S) < English (w)verbs > (V) have (O) « (*){ ^so^ many } (1)(w)synonyms and (2)(w)antonyms » ^that^ (S) < (id)‡(V) trying‡ to (V) remember (O) « them » ((id)one by one), (without < any logical ◎chain of < association > { to (*)(collectively) (1)(V) grasp and (2)(V) recollect (*)(O) « many (w)verbs » ((id)in a single stroke) } >) >, (V) is (C) 〚 ^too^ arduous (^to^ (V) be (C) 〚 (practically) possible 〛) 〛. (S) < All good linguists > (instinctively) (V) know (C) 〚 (1)(C) 〚 how easier 〛 (S) <

ˆitˆ > (*)(V) is 〖 (although (seemingly) (2)(C) 『 harder 』) 〗 ˆtoˆ (V) remember (O) « many other related words » ((id)along with < any particular term >) 』.

(S) < ˆ(w)‡(V) Paraphrasing‡ˆ (*)ˆwithˆ (1)< synonyms > and (2)< antonyms > > (V) is (also) (C) 『 effective 』 (in < ‡(V) avoiding‡ (O) « wrong usage of < words > » >). ˆ(V) Takeˆ (O) « the { above-mentioned } (w)verb "deny" » (ˆas < an example >ˆ). (As (S) < I > ↑ (aV) 've (already) (V) shown ↑), (S) < it > (aV) can ＼ (aV) be (V) used ／ (in < SVOO (w)sentence pattern >), (unlike < its synonym "prohibit" >). But, (if (S) < you > (V) consult (O) « your dictionary »), (S) < you > (aV) will (V) know (O) « [that] (S) < the (w)verb "forbid" > (aV) can (also) ＼ (aV) be (V) used ／ (in < SVOO >) (eg. "(S) < She > (V) forbade/denied (O) « me » (O) « (id)entrance to < her room > »") ». (Without < such knowledge of < possible usage (in < some particular (w)sentence pattern >) > >), (S) < you > (aV) cannot (id)(V) make { correct } (O) « use » of < English (w)verbs >: (S) < your ◎effort { to (V) memorize (O) « (w)verbs » } > (V) is (C) 『 (practically) powerless 』 (without(= *if (S) < you > (aV) don't (V) memorize*) < such useful example sentences >).

(S) < ◎ˆThoseˆ { ˆ(S) < who >ˆ (V) have (O) « no such knowledge » > } (aV) will (id)(V) try to (V) use (O) « (w)verbs » (in < { "impossible" } (w)sentence patterns >). ((id)As a result), (S) < ◎some (w)verbs { (S) < which > (aV) could not (originally) ＼ (aV) be (V) used ／ (in < a certain (w)sentence pattern >) } > (aV) will (id)(V) come to (V) get (O) « (id)a license to < it > » (after < (w)a lapse of time >) (with < a certain number of < "abusers" > >). (If (S) < you > (V) go ((id)deeper into < your dictionary >)), (S) < you > (aV) may (V) find (O) « ˆsuchˆ example sentences ˆasˆ < "(S) < The Japanese law > (V) forbids (O) « citizens » (C) 『 to (V) carry (O) « guns » 』(*informal='from < ‡(V) carrying‡ (O) « guns » >')" > ». (S) < You > (aV) should (V) know (O) « the reason why »: because (S) < ˆsoˆ many ◎people { [(S) < who > (V) are] (id)in the habit of < not ‡(V) memorizing‡ (O) « a (w)verb » (with < example sentences >) > } > (id)(V) are (C) 『 prone to ˆ(V) associateˆ (O) « the (w)verb "forbid" » ˆwithˆ < its synonym "prohibit" > 』 ˆthatˆ (S) < they > (id)(V) are (C) 『 liable to (V) make (O) « an { (originally) "impossible" } (w)paraphrase *[of]* "(S) < The Japanese law > (V) prohibits(=forbids) (O) « citizens » (from < ‡(V) carrying‡ (O) « guns » >)" » 』. While (S) < the { reversed } version *[of]* "~~(S) < The Japanese law > (V) prohibits (O) « citizens » (C) 『 to (V) carry (O) « guns » 』~~" > ＼ (aV) is (V) forbidden ／ (in < English >). (S) < You > (aV) must (V) know (O) « the reason why »: because (S) < the number of < ◎people { (S) < who > (V) use (O) « "prohibit" » (in < such a wrong SVOC (w)sentence pattern >) } > > (V) is ^so^ (C) 『 small 』 ^that^ (S) < the dictionary > (id)does not have to (V) show (O) « any linguistic (id)respect for < this { "impossible" } usage > ».

(Since (S) < linguistics > ＼ (id)(aV) is (*)(V) based (1)on ／ < popular usage >, not (2)on < { (definitely) fixed } (w)golden rules of < grammar > >), (S) < the (id)increase in < the number of < ◎people { (S) < who > (V) "abuse" (O) « some { "impossible" } usage » } > > > (aV) will ^(V) change^ (*)(O) « "not allowed" » (1)^into^ < "informal" > and (eventually) (2)^into^ < "normal, (id)if not*(= even if (S) < it > (V) is not)* formal" >. But (since (S) < you learners of < English > > (V) are (C) 『 no collectors of < statistical data (in < English usage >) > 』), (S) < ^it^ > (V) is (C) 『 safe 』 ^for^ (S) < you > ^to^ (id)(V) try to (V) remember (O) « English (w)verbs » (in < some { "formal" } ◎example sentences { *[(S) < which > ＼ (aV) are]]* (V) listed ／ (in < the dictionary >) } >).

- (S) < The vast seas of < (w)adverbs > > (aV) should ＼ (aV) be (id)(V) waded through ／ (by < { "(1)where/(2)how/(3)when/(4)why" } distinction >) -

(S) < The number of < English (w)adverbs > > (V) is ^so^ (C) 『 large 』 ^that^ (S) < you > (aV) will (simply) ＼ (id)(V) get (C) 『 lost 』 ／ (if (S) < you > (blindly) (id)(V) try to (V) remember (O) « them » (as (S) < you > (id)(V) happen to (V) meet (O) « them »)). (id)(V) Keep (in < mind >) (O) « the following points » (whenever (S) < you > (V) see (O) « an (w)adverb »):

(1)(S) < { (w)adjective-based } (w)adverbs > (aV) need not ＼ (aV) be (consciously) (V) memorized ／ .

(Although (S) < the name *[of]* "(w)adverb" > (id)(V) derives from < ◎its function { to "(id)(V) add on to < (w)verbs >" } >), (S) < the composition of < most English (w)adverbs > > (V) is (C) 〚 "(w)adjective +ly" 〛. ((id)For example), (S) < ◎a suffix "ly" { *[(S) < which > ＼ (aV) is]]* (id)(V) added on to ／ < the (w)adjective "quick" > } > (aV) will (V) make (O) « an (w)adverb "quickly" ». ((id)Aside from < ^such^ tricky (w)adverbs ^as^ < ◎(1)< "hardly" > or (2)< "supposedly" > >, { (S) < which > (aV) can (hardly) ＼ (aV) be (V) supposed ／ (C) 〚 to (V) be (C) 〚 { "(w)adjective +ly" } (id)versions of (1)< "hard" > or (2)< "supposed" > 〛 〛 } >), (S) < ◎an (w)adverb { *[(S) < which > ＼ (aV) is]]* (simply) (V) made ／ (by < ^‡(V) adding‡^ (O) « "ly" » ^to^ < (w)any given (w)adjective > >) } > (aV) should (basically) ＼ (aV) be (*)(V) remembered ／ (1)(as < an "(w)adjective" >), not (2)(as < an independent "(w)adverb" >). (Just) (V) remember (O) « such (w)adverbs » (as < (w)adjectives >), and (V) add (O) « "ly" » ((id)at the end) (to (V) use (O) « them » (as < (w)adverbs >) ((id)as *[(S) < it > (V) becomes]* (C) 〚 necessary 〛)). (S) < You > (aV) should (V) save (O) « ^such^ meaningless efforts ^as to^ (id)(V) try to (V) remember (O) « these { "add-on" } (id)types of < (w)adverbs > » (respectively) (with < as much respect as *[(S) < you > (V) pay to]* < their "original (w)adjectives" > >) », (as(= *because*) (S) < your conscious memory bank > (V) is (C) 〚 (id)not without < limitation > 〛).

(2)(V) Be (always) (C) 〚 aware 〛 *[about]* < < which (of < "(1)where/(2)how/(3)when /(4)why" >) > (S) < an (w)adverb > (id)(V) belongs to >.

(S) < An (w)adverb > (always) (id)(V) belongs to < (id)one of < the four semantic categories > - (1)where, (2)how, (3)when, and (4)why >. (S) < You > (aV) should (also) (V) remember (O) « [that] (S) < English (w)adverbial expressions > ＼ (aV) are (normally) (V) used ／ ((id)in { that } order(1:where > 2:how > 3:when > 4:why)) », ((O) « as » (S) < you > (aV) can (V) see (in < the following example >)):

eg. (S) < I > (V) went (to my office) (by bicycle) (yesterday) (because (S) < the bus > (V) was (C) 〚 (id)on strike 〛).

(S) < (id)One of < ◎the most effective ways { *[(in < which >)]* (S) < beginners > (aV) can ＼ (id)(V) get (C)『 used to ／ < English > 』} > > (V) is (C)『 to (V) make (O) « "5W1H (w)interrogative sentences », (including < (1)Who, (2)What, (3)Where, (4)How, (5)When, (6)Why >") 』 ((id)out of < ◎EVERY English sentence { (O) « *[that]* » (S) < they > (id)(V) happen to (V) meet } >), (id)such as:

cf. (S) < Who > (V) went (to < the office >) (by < bicycle >) (yesterday)?

cf. (S) < What > (aV) did (S) < you > (V) do (yesterday)?

cf. Where (aV) did (S) < you > (V) go (by < bicycle >) (yesterday)?

cf. How (aV) did (S) < you > (V) go (to < your office >) (yesterday)?

cf. When (aV) did (S) < you > (V) go (to < your office >) (by < bicycle >)?

cf. Why (aV) did (S) < you > (V) go (to < your office >) (by < bicycle >) (yesterday)?

(By < (1)(constantly) and (2)(instantly) (*)‡(V) making‡ (O) « such (w)interrogative sentences » ((id)out of < (w)each and every ◎English sentence { (O) « *[that]* » (S) < they > (V) see (in < textbooks >) } >) >), (S) < beginners > (*)(aV) can (id)(1)(V) get (O) « the knack » of < English composition > and (2)(V) develop (O) « their categorical sense of < (w)adverbs > » (simultaneously). (Whenever (S) < you > ^(V) add^ (O) « an (w)adverb » ^to^ < your memory bank >), (id)(V) be (C)『 sure to ^(V) label^ (O) « it » ^with^ < (id)one of < the four categories > 』: (1)where, (2)how, (3)when and (4)why >.

(S) < This distinctive attitude (in < (w)adverbial categorization >) > (V) is (also) (id)(C)『 essential to < ‡(V) refining‡ (O) « your ability (in < (1)‡(V) reading‡, (2)‡(V) listening‡ or (3)‡(V) writing‡ >) » > 』. (Of < "5W1H" >), (S) < human mind > (*)(aV) will (easily) (1)(V) detect and (2)(id)(V) be (C)『 aware of (*)(O) « < (1)"Who" and (2)"What" > » 』: (*)(S) < they > (1)(V) are (C)『 (rarely) long 』, and (2)(aV) will (usually) ＼ (aV) be (V) used ／ (in < ^such^ conspicuous sentential elements ^as^ < (1)(S)(w)subject, (2)(O)(w)object or (3)(C)(w)complement > >): (S) < who { but < the sloppy > } > (aV) could (ever) (V) miss (O) « them »? ((id)On the other hand), (S) < (w)adverbial parts of < sentences > > (V) are (often) (C)『 (very) long 』, ((sometimes) (id)to the point of < ‡(V) being‡ (C)『 boring 』 >). (S) < They > (V) are (

usually) (C) 『 ◎unessential elements of < sentences >, { [which ＼ ^(aV) are^]] ^(V) meant to^ ／ (V) serve (as < (id)accessories to < some (w)verb > >) } 』, (id)only to (V) serve (as < (w)red-herring (to < beginners >) >). ((id)So as not to ＼ (V) get (V) hypnotized ／ (by < such attention-distracters >)), (S) < (*)a (1){ long }, (2){ boring } or (even) (3){ misleading } (*)(w)adverbial part of < the sentence > > (1)(aV) should (always) ＼ (aV) be (1)^(V) labeled^ ／ ^either^ (*)^as^ < (1)"where(PLACE)" or (2)"how(MANNER)" or (3)"when(TIME)" or (4)"why(REASON)" > and (2) ＼ (V) treated (simply) ／ , ^or^ (2)(aV) should ＼ (aV) be (simply) (id)(V) dismissed as ／ < ◎flabby part { (simply) †(V) making†(= (S) < which > (simply) (V) makes) (O) « the sentence » (C) 『 ◎^too^ fat { ^to^ (V) embrace } 』 } >!... (V) Remember, (O) « ◎the way { ([in < which >]) (S) < you > (V) treat (O) « (w)adverbs » – ◎^that^ bulky element { [(S) < ^which^ > (V) is] (C) 『 ((id)far too) long 』 (for < their unessential role (in < sentences >) >) } – } (aV) will (V) decide (O) « ^whether^ (S) < you > (aV) can (really) (V) enjoy (O) « ‡(V) reading‡ (O) « sentences » », ^or^ (S) < you >(aV) 'll (simply) (id)(V) join in < { reading } sleepers >...zzz » ».

- (1)(S) < (w)Pronouns > and (2)(S) < (w)auxiliary verbs > (id)had better ＼ (aV) be (V) memorized ／ (all) ((id)at once) -

(Unlike < ◎Japanese { (S) < which > (V) has (O) « no definite "代名詞(DAIMEISHI: (w)pronouns)" » } >), (S) < (*)the (1)number and (2)usages (*)of < English (w)pronouns > > (*)(V) are (1)(C) 『 (definitely) fixed 』 and (2)(C) 『 (relatively) few 』. ((id)Aside from < ^such^ (1){ personal }/(2){ impersonal } (*)(w)pronouns ^as^ < "I, we, you, they, he, she, it" > >), (S) < English language > (V) has (O) « ^such^ (w)pronouns ^as^ < "all, any, each, few, none, one, same, some, such, that, this, those, what, when, where, which, who, whom, whose, etc,etc." > ».

(S) < The number of < "助動詞(JODOUSHI: (w)auxiliary verbs)", ◎specialized (id)versions of < English (w)verbs > { (S) < which > (V) serve ((only) to ^(V) add^ (O) « some meaning » (^to^ < other (w)verbs >)) } > >, (*)(V) is (also) (1)(C) 『 fixed 』 and

(2)(C) 『 few 』 — (C) 『 twelve(12) ((id)in all) 』 ((id)to be exact): "(1)be, (2)can, (3)dare, (4)do, (5)have, (6)may, (7)must, (8)need, (9)ought, (10)shall, (11)used, (12)will".

(Although (S) < (*)the (1)number and (2)usages (*)of < (1)(w)pronouns and (2)(w)auxiliary verbs (*)(in < English >) > > (*)(V) are (C) 『 (rather) (1)large and (2)daunting (for < beginners >) 』), (S) < they > (aV) should (still) ＼ (aV) be (V) memorized ／ ((id)in a stroke): ^not^ (1)((id)on { "(id)as necessary" } basis), ^but^ (2)(in < (id)a series of < systematic studies (on < their possible usages >) > >). ((id)In other words), (S) < studies (*)of (1)< (w)pronouns > and (2)< (w)auxiliary verbs > > (aV) ought to ＼ (aV) be (id)(V) dealt with ／ (as < (id)a set of < grammatical knowledge ((id)as opposed to < (id)a part of < random (w)vocabulary building > >) > >).

- (1)(S) < (w)Conjunctions > and (2)(S) < (w)interjections > (*)(aV) could ＼ (aV) be (V) memorized ／ ((id)at a sweep), 【 (only) (id)to little avail 】 -

(Unlike < (id)in the case (*)of (1)< (w)pronouns > and (2)< (w)auxiliary verbs > >), (S) < you > (aV) should not (id)(V) try to (V) remember (O) « (1)(w)conjunctions and (2)(w)interjections » ((id)in a single stroke): (*)(S) < their memorization > (1)(aV) should (V) be (C) 『 (merely) haphazard 』 and (2)(aV) need not (V) be (C) 『 systematic 』. (S) < Their limited number > (aV) may (V) make (O) « ^it^ » (C) 『 possible 』 ^to^ (V) list (O) « them » (all) (in < ◎a small book { for (S) < you > to (mechanically) (V) remember } >), but (S) < (1)their { overlapping } meanings and (2){ minute } differences (in < nuance >) > (aV) will (V) make (O) « such attempts » (C) 『 (practically) futile 』.

((id)For example), (S) < (id)a group of < ◎(w)conjunctions { (S) < that > (V) bind (O) « two (w)clauses » (in < contradictory relationship >) } > > (aV) will (V) contain (O) « ^such^ (1)words or (2)(w)phrases ^as^ < "(1)although, (2)(id)and yet, (3)but, (4)though, (5)whereas, and (6)yet" > ». (S) < To(id)(V) try to (V) remember (O) « them » > (aV) may (V) look (C) 『 fruitful 』, but ((id)in fact), (S) < it >(V) 's (totally) (C) 『 (id)no use 』: (S) < these (w)conjunctions > (V) appear (^so^ many times) (in < English sentences >) ^that^ (S) < you > (id)(V) have (absolutely) (O) « ◎no need { to (consciously) (V) remember (O) « them » } ».

(Besides), (S) < the (w)part of speech "(w)conjunction" > (aV) does not (V) include (O) « ^such^ (1)words and (2)(w)phrases ^as^ < "(1)(id)but then again, (2)conversely, (3)however, (4)nevertheless, (5)notwithstanding, (6)still, (7)while" > » — (S) < these > ＼ (aV) are (all) (V) termed ／ (C) 〖 "(w)adverb" 〗 (while †(V) meaning†(= *(S) < they > (V) mean)* (O) « the same thing as < "(1)although, (2)(id)and yet, (3)but, (4)though, (5)whereas, and (6)yet" > »). (S) < Such terms, 〚 *[^whether^ (S) < they > (V) are]* (C) 〖 (1)(w)conjunction ^or^ (2)(w)adverb 〗 〛 >, (aV) should ＼ (aV) be (naturally) (id)(V) stored up ／ (in < your memory >) (as (S) < you > (V) encounter (O) « them » (in < English sentences >)). (S) < They > (id)(V) stand out (in < the streams of < contexts > >) (^so^ outstandingly) ^that^ (S) < they > (aV) will (easily) (V) stay (in < your linguistic memory >) (1)(without < any conscious effort ((id)on your part) >), or (2)without < ‡(V) having‡ (O) « their obvious roles (in < the sentence >) » (C) 〖 (pompously) ＼ (id)(V) pointed out ／ 〗 (in < (1){ cheap }, (2){ cheeky } textbooks (on < "how to (V) read (O) « English »" >) >) >.

(S) < ◎The only meaningful ^effort^ { (O) « *[that]* » (S) < you > (aV) can ^(V) make^ ((*)regarding (1)< (w)conjunctions > 〚 (or (2)< (w)adverbs >) 〛) } > (V) is (C) 〖 to ^(V) associate^ (O) « { (relatively) rare } words and expressions » ^with^ < some other familiar (1)(w)conjunctions or (2)(w)adverbs > 〗. ((id)For example), (S) < an archaic (w)conjunction "albeit" > (id)had better ＼ (*)(aV) be (1)(V) comprehended and (2)(V) memorized ／ ((id)along with < ^such^ expressions ^as^ < "(V) Be (S) < it > (C) 〖 (ever so) humble 〗, (there)(V) 's (S) < no ◎place { like < home > } > > >) ; (Although (S) < it > (aV) may (V) be (C) 〖 humble 〗), (S) < home > (V) is (C) 〖 the best place (in < the world >) 〗". (S) < Contradictory "and" (eg. "(S) < The commander > (V) knew (O) « *[that]* (S) < we > (aV) couldn't (V) win »; and, (S) < he > (V) ordered (O) « us » (C) 〖 to (id)(V) fight on 〗") > (aV) should ^not^ ＼ (aV) be (V) comprehended ／ (1)(as < a strange usage of < "and" > >) ^but^ (2)(as < an abbreviated form of < "(id)and yet" > >

).

((id)As for < (w)interjections >), (1)(S) < mechanical memorization > and (2)(S) < random exclamation > (*)(V) are (C)〚 (quite) (id)fitting for < this (id)part of speech > 〛. (S) < You > (*)(aV) could (1)(id)(V) store (O) « them » up (in < your vocabulary >) (in < (totally) haphazard ways >) and (2)(id)(V) shout (O) « them » out ((id)from time to time)... 【 (id)at your own risk, 【 (id)that is 】 】. (S) < ^Such^ (w)interjections ^as^ < (1)"Bullshit!", (2)"Fuck!", (3)"Goddamn!", (4)"Holy shit!" or (5)"Holy smoke!" > > (V) are (all) (C)〚 appealing (to < English beginners >) 〛 (because (S) < they > (aV) can ＼ (aV) be (V) used ／ ((id)with (absolutely) no regard (1)to < grammar > 【 (and (2)to < others' feelings >, (too)) 】)). (^For^ < this ^reason^ >), (S) < this author > (V) is (C)〚 (quite) (id)sure of < the popularity of < a short seminar on < "How to (V) draw (O) « attention » (by < simple exclamation of < (w)interjections > >)" > > >, ((especially) among < ◎^those^ { ^(S) < who >^ (miserably) (id)(V) failed to (V) master (O) « English » } >) 〛. But (S) < this author > (*)(V) is (1)(C)〚 ^too^ busy 〛 and (2)(C)〚 ^too^ decent 〛 (^to^ (id)(V) engage in < such vulgar business >). (S) < (w)Interjections > (id)ought 【 simply 】 to ＼ (aV) be (id)(V) learnt (by heart) ／ ((totally) (id)by chance), (as (S) < you > (id)(V) happen (*)to (1)(V) encounter (O) « them » and (2)(V) find (O) « them » (1)(C)〚 interesting 〛 【 (or (2)(C)〚 shocking 〛) 】). (S) < (*){ Systematic } (1)categorization and (2)memorization (*)of < all (w)interjections (in < English >) > >, 【 though *[(S) < it > (V) is]* (C)〚 possible 〛 】, (*)(V) seems *[to (V) be]* (1)(C)〚 (id)anything but < fruitful > 〛 and (2)(C)〚 (downright) absurd 〛. (*)(S) < You > (1)(aV) may (V) cry (O) « "Eureka!" » (at < the idea >) ((id)at first), but (2)(aV) will (soon) (V) shout (O) « "Enough!" » (after (S) < you > (actually) (V) practice (O) « ‡(V) chanting‡ (1)(O) « "Alas!" », (2)(O) « "Bravo!" », (3)(O) « "Cheers!" » or (4)(O) « "Boo!" » »)

- (S) < (w)Prepositions > (aV) could never ＼ (aV) be (V) learnt ／ ((id)at a sweep); (id)^(V) learn^ (O) « (w)idioms » (by heart), ^and^ (S) < (w)prepositional comprehension > (aV) will (naturally) (V) come (with < them >) -

(Of < all English (w)parts of speech >), (S) < ((id)by far) ◎the most difficult { to (V) master } > (V) is (C) 『 the (w)preposition 』. (S) < It > (V) is (C) 『 difficult 』 (for < Japanese learners >) (^for^ < three ^reasons^ >).

(1)(S) < Japanese language > (V) has (O) « no (id)equivalent of < (w)prepositions > ». (S) < The ^nearest^ 【 in < Japanese > 】 ^to^ < English (w)prepositions > > (V) are (C) 『 "助詞(JOSHI: (w)postpositional particles)" (id)such as < (1)"て(TE), (2)に(NI), (3)を(WO), (4)は(WA)" > 』. (S) < They > (V) are (C) 『 (id)not unlike < English (w)prepositions > ((*)in (1)< simplicity (in < form >) > and (2)< multiplicity (in < meaning >) >) 』, but (S) < (*)their (1)position (in < the sentence >) and (2)actual usage > (V) are (C) 『 ^too^ different (^to^ ＼ (aV) be (V) deemed ／ (C) 『 as < equivalents >) 』 』. (S) < English (w)prepositions > (V) are (C) 『 (id)a { total } stranger to < Japanese learners > 』, †(V) making† *(= (S) < which > (V) makes)* (O) « them » (C) 『 ◎the toughest hurdle { to (id)(V) get over } (in < all English words >) 』.

(2)(S) < A (w)preposition > (id)(V) belongs to < (id)(S) < what > ＼ (aV) is (V) called ／ (C) 『 "a (w)function word" 』, 【 *[(S) < which > (*)(V) is]* (1)(id)(C) 『 devoid of < meaning > ((id)in itself) 』 and (2)(C) 『 (^only^) meaningful (^(id)in relation to^ < some other words >) 』 】 >, (thereby) †(V) making† (O) « ^it^ » (1)(C) 『 ◎difficult 』 or (2)(C) 『 (even) ◎impossible 』 (*){ ^to^ (V) comprehend ("(id)as is") }, ◎†(V) making† *(= (S) < which > (V) makes)* (O) « ^it^ » (C) 『 imperative 』 ^to^ (V) remember (O) « it » (in < some example sentence >), { (S) < which > (V) makes (O) « it » (C) 『 ◎harder (still) { for (S) < ◎Japanese learners > to (V) conquer } { (S) < who > (V) are *(= because (S) < they > (V) are)* (C) 『 (id)in the habit (*)of "(just) (1)‡(V) seeing‡, not (2)‡(V) speaking‡" (*)(O) « English » ((id)without any regard to < ^such^ (1){ minute } and (2){ (seemingly) meaningless } (*)words ^as^ < (w)prepositions > >) 』 } 』 }.

(S) < You > (*)(aV) could (1)(V) remember (O) « nouns, pronouns, adjectives, adverbs, conjunctions and interjections » (◎the way { *[in < which >]* (S) < they > ＼ (aV) are (V) presented ／ (in < the dictionary >) }) and (id)(2)(V) put (O) « them » (to { practical } use) ((id)more or less); but (S) < you > (simply) (aV) couldn't (V) do

(O) « that » ((*)with (1)< (w)verbs > and (2)< (w)prepositions >). ◎(S) < They > ^(V) need^ (O) « ‡(V) remember^ing^‡ (in < example sentences >) », { (S) < which > (V) makes (O) « them » (C) 『 ◎(1)◎harder 【 ((indeed) (2)◎impossible) 】 (*){ to (V) master (for (S) < ◎Japanese learners > } { (*)(S) < who >(= *because (S) < they >*) (id)(1)(V) like (1)to (V) study (C) « abstractions » and (2)to (V) absorb (O) « fragmentary information » but (positively) (id)(2)(V) hate to (1)(V) read (aloud), (2)(id)(V) type in and (correctly) (3)(V) recite (*)(O) « sentences » }) 』 }.

(3)(*)(S) < Most (w)prepositions > (1)(V) have (O) « multiple usages » and ＼ (2)(aV) are (also) (V) used ／ ((id)in the capacities of < other (w)parts of speech > (in < the same form >)). (id)(V) Take (O) « your time » and (id)(V) look up 【 in < the dictionary > 】 (O) « ^such^ (w)prepositions ^as^ < (1)"as", (2)"for", (3)"of" > »... (S) < the number of < their (respectively) categorized usages > — *[(S) < which > ＼ (aV) are]]* (V) labeled ／ (C) 『 (1)"(w)conjunction", (2)"(w)adverb", (3)"(w)pronoun" and (4)"(w)preposition" 』 ((id)like < so many floors (in < (w)a department store > >)) — > (V) is (C) 『 daunting 』 (enough), and (S) < the (id)floods of < example sentences > ((id)in the form of < idiomatic expressions >) > (aV) will (id)(V) drown out (O) « your ◎will { to (id)(V) swim through < their semantic streams > } ». How could (S) < you > (ever) (V) conquer (O) « such (impossibly) diverse seas of < meanings > »?

(S) < The answer > (V) is (C) 『 (1)simple and (2)sober 』: (S) < ^it^ > (aV) will (V) take (O) « you » (O) « years of < ‡(V) memorizing‡ (O) « (w)idiom after < (w)idiom > » > » (^to^ (id)(V) come to < practical ‡understanding‡ of < English (w)prepositions > >). (S) < Each (w)preposition > (V) has (O) « its own manners (*)of (1)< connection > or (2)< arrangement > ((id)in relation to < other words >) »; (S) < (1)(w)verbs and (2)(w)nouns > (V) have (O) « ◎some particular (w)prepositions { (^with^ < which >) (S) < they > (aV) can ^(V) combine^ (to (V) compose (O) « some particular meaning ») } ». (S) < Such formal relationship 【 (*[(S) < which > ＼ (aV) is]]* (V) called ／ (C) 『 "(w)collocation" 』) 】 > (V) is (C) 『 (definitely) fixed 』 (in < English >), { (without < the knowledge of < which > >) (S) < you > couldn't (V) get (C) 『 (id)proficient in < this language > 』}.

((id)With < the help of < (really) good guidebooks > >), (S) < you > could (V) master (O) « the whole realm of < English grammar > » (in < (id)a couple of years >); but (S) < you > could (ˆonlyˆ) (V) get (C) 『 (reasonably) (id)proficient in < English (w)collocation > 』 ((*)ˆin (1)< a decade >)ˆ, 【 (id)if not (2)(id)a couple of < decades > 】. Never (id)(V) attempt 【 (id)in vain 】 to (V) conquer (O) « English (w)prepositions » (◎the way { ([*in < which >*]) (S) < you > (id)(V) try to (V) master (O) « other (w)parts of speech » }). (S) < (*){ Some } (1)books, (2)schools or (3)teachers > (aV) may (V) prompt (O) « you » (C) 『 to ˆ(V) makeˆ (O) « that futile ˆattemptˆ » 』, but (aV) don't (id)(V) kid (O) « yourself » into ‡(V) believing‡ (O) « [that] (S) < such a stunt > (V) is (C) 『 (practically) possible 』 »: (S) < they > (simply) (V) make (O) « you » (C) 『 (V) remember (O) « something » 』 (1)((just) (id)in order that (S) < they > (aV) can (V) test (O) « your performance (in < ‡(V) remembering‡ (O) « something » >) »), (not (2)(id)in order ˆforˆ (S) < you > ˆtoˆ (V) master (O) « everything »). (S) < To (id)(V) attempt to (systematically) (V) master (O) « everything (in < (w)prepositions >) » ((w)via < ◎lessons { [*(S) < which > ＼ (aV) are*]] (V) given ／ (by < (*){ your } (1)schools or (2)teachers >) } >) > (V) is (C) 『 ◎(*)the most (1){ daunting } yet (2){ futile } thing { < [*that*] > (S) < this author > (aV) can (ever) (V) think of } 』: (*)(S) < they > (1)(aV) may (V) help ((id)to some extent), but (2)(aV) will (V) leave (O) « you » (C) 『 (1)helpless and (2)powerless 』 ((id)in the end). (S) < ◎The only teacher { (S) < that > ˆ(V) enablesˆ (O) « you » (C) 『 ˆtoˆ (really) (V) master (O) « (w)prepositions » 』 } > (V) is (C) 『 (w)idiomatic expressions 』: to (id)(V) learn (O) « them » (by heart) ((id)in the form of < ◎innumerable example sentences { (S) < which > (aV) will (id)(V) come up to < { your } memory > (whenever [*(S) < they > ＼ (aV) are*]] (V) inspired ／ by < some particular (w)preposition >) } >).

((id)For example), (S) < the meaning of < "(1)derivation/(2)deprivation" > (in < the (w)preposition "of" >) > (aV) should ＼ (aV) be (id)(V) stored up ／ (in < your brains >) ˆnotˆ (1)(as < an abstract item of < knowledge > >) ˆbutˆ (2)(in < ˆsuchˆ concrete forms ^as^ < (1)"^(V) Clear^ (O) « the street » ^of^ < snow >", (2)"(w)(aV) May (S) < I > (V) ask (O) « a favor » (of < you >)?", (3)"(S) < She > (id)(V) comes of < a noble family >" or (4)"(S) < You > ^(V) expect^ (O) « too much » ^of^ < me >" > >). (1)^(V) Be^ (C) 『 ((id)a little more) imaginative 』 and (2)^(V) add^ (O) « "f" » (^to^ < "of" >), ^and^ (S) < you > (aV) will (V) get (O) « ◎"off" », { (S) < which > (aV) will ^(V) remind^ (O) « you » ^of^ < the handy expression *[of]* 'spin-off", *[(S) < which > (V) is]* ◎a thing { (id)†(V) coming†(*= (S) < that > (V) comes*) out from < ◎something { (^with^ < which >) (S) < it > ＼ (aV) was (originally) (id)^(V) bound^ (together) ／ } > } > }. (Now), (S) < you > (id)(V) get (O) « the knack » of < "of" of < (1)derivation/(2)deprivation > >.

(S) < I > ^(*)(aV) cannot (1)(V) emphasize^ and (2)(V) repeat (O) « ^this^ » (often ^enough^): ^that^ (S) < the knowledge of < English (w)prepositions > > (aV) will (id)(V) grow up (with < your (id)store (*)of (1)< (w)idioms > and (2)< (w)collocations > (in < your brains >) >). (id)(V) Take (O) « your time »; (w)(S) < haste > (only) (V) makes (O) « waste ».

- (S) < (1)Noun/(2)verb/(3)adjective/(4)adverb > (all) (V) combine (together) (to(= *and)* (V) count (as < one word >)) -

((id)With the exception of < ◎(1)(w)pronouns, (2)(w)prepositions, (3)(w)conjunctions and (4)(w)interjections { (S) < { whose } forms > (*)(V) are (1)(C) 『 fixed 』 and (2)(C) 『 unchangeable 』 } >), (S) < all the other English (w)parts of speech > (V) are (id)interchangeable with < other (w)parts of speech >. (S) < ^It^ >(V) 's (C) 『 a good idea 』 ^to^ (V) comprehend (O) « all these (w)parts of speech » (as < one single entity >).

(Just) (V) imagine (O) « yourself » (C) 『 (id)†(V) trying† to (V) remember (O) « "(1)image", "(2)imagery", "(3)imagination", "(4)imagist", "(5)imagine", "(6)imaginable", "(7)imaginal", "(8)imaginary", "(9)imaginative", "(10)imaginably", "(11)imaginarily" and "(12)imaginatively" » (respectively), ((id)as though (S) < they > (V) were (C) 『 ◎twelve different words { *[(S) < which > ＼ (aV) were]]* (C) 『

(id)unrelated with ／ < (id)one another > 』} 』) 』. (id)^(V) Try^ to (V) remember (O) « them » (all) ((id)in a single stroke), ^and^ (S) < your effort > (aV) will (V) be (id){ twelve } times less than (if (S) < you > (id)(V) tried to (V) remember (O) « them » ((id)one by one)). (S) < ◎The apparent ^difficulty^ { (O) « [*which*] » (S) < you > ^(V) find^ (^in^ ‡(V) comprehending‡ (O) « all these twelve » ((id)at a time) ((id)for the first time)) } > (aV) may (V) seem [*to (V) be*] (C) 『 ^too^ ◎forbidding { ^to^ (V) tackle } 』, but (S) < (w)the end result > (V) is (C) 『 (well) { worth } (O) « the effort » 』: (S) < the { minute } ^difference between^ "(1)imaginable", "(2)imaginal", "(3)imaginary" and "(4)imaginative" > (aV) can (best) ＼ (aV) be (V) understood ／ (*)by (1)(id)‡(V) dealing‡ with < them > ((id)at a time) and (2)(always) (id)‡(V) trying‡ to (V) think of < any one (w)adjective > ((id)in { conscious } contrast with < the others >).

(V) Trust (O) « me »: ((^the^ more) (S) < you > (V) remember), (C) 『 ^the^ less ^likely^ 』 (S) < you > (V) are ^to^ (V) forget — (S) < that > (V) is (C) 『 the paradoxical truth of < (w)vocabulary building > 』. ◎^Those^ { ^(S) < who >^ (id)(V) try to (V) remember (O) « the least » } (V) are (quite) (C) 『 (id)likely to (V) forget (O) « the most » 』.

(S) < Many (w)nouns > ＼ (aV) are (V) used ／ (as < (w)verbs >) (in < the same form >) (eg. (1)"(id)How about < a drive >?" ; (2)"(id)(aV) Would (S) < you > (V) like to (V) drive (O) « my car »?"), and (S) < (w)any given verb > (aV) can (generally) (V) take (O) « the form of < a (w)noun > » (by < ‡(V) adding‡ (O) « some suffix » >) (eg. (1)"How (aV) can (S) < you > (V) treat (O) « me » ((so) bad)?" ; (2)"(S) < I > (V) protest (O) « your cruel treatment »") or (by < ‡(V) changing‡ (O) « (id)a part of < it > » > (eg. (1)"(S) < You > (id)never (V) fail to (V) please (O) « me »" ; (2)"(w)(S) < The pleasure > (V) is (C) 『 mine 』")). (S) < Most (w)adjectives > (aV) can ＼ (aV) be (V) used ／ (as < (w)adverbs >) (by < the simple addition of < the suffix "ly" > > ((id)at the end)), ／ while (S) < some > (aV) can ＼ (aV) be (V) used ／ ^both^ ((w)adjectively) ^and^ ((w)adverbially) (in < the same form >) (eg. (1)"(S) < I >(V) 'm (C) 『 a { slow } reader 』" ; (2)"(V) Speak (((id)a little more) slowly)" ; (3)"(S) < You > (V) drive (too slow)"). (S) < These (1){ (1)(w)noun/(2)(w)verb } and (2){

(1)(w)adjective/(2)(w)adverb } (*)interchangeability > (aV) should ＼ (aV) be (naturally) (V) acquired ／ ((id)in the process of < your (w)vocabulary building >), ((id)never to ＼ (aV) be (V) learnt ／ (as < ◎an academic fact { *[(S) < which > ＼ (aV) is]]* (V) taught ／ (in < some particular section of < an English guidebook > >) } >)); (S) < such knowledge > (aV) will (id)(V) get (O) « you » (nowhere), (for (S) < they > ＼ (aV) are (^only^) (V) written ／ (^as^ < a scholar's notebook >)). Never (id)(V) try to (V) read and (V) learn(= *(V) learn at the same time as (S) < you > (V) read)*: (S) < you > (simply) (aV) can't *[(V) read and (V) learn]* . (V) Remember and (V) learn(= *(V) Learn (O) « things » (by < ‡(V) remembering‡ (O) « them » >)).*

- (S) < English vocabulary { without < ＼ (id)‡(aV) being‡ (V) braced (*)with ／ < (1)(w)synonyms and (2)(w)antonyms > > } > (V) is (C) 『 a mere (w)castle in the air 』 -

(S) < The abundance of < (1)(w)synonyms and (2)(w)antonyms > > (V) is (C) 『 (id)one of < the most { outstanding } characteristics of < English language > > 』. ((id)In contrast), (S) < ◎Japanese language, { (S) < { whose } (1)words and (2)(w)phrases > ＼ (aV) are (basically) (V) composed ／ as < combinations of < several "漢字(KANJI: (w)Chinese characters)" > } > >, (V) is (relatively) (C) 『 (id)poor (*)in < (1)(w)synonyms and (2)(w)antonyms > 』. ((id)Or rather), (S) < (*){ (w)any given } (1)word or (2)expression ((*)in < Japanese >) > (V) has (O) « (*){ its particular } (1){ synonymous } and (2){ antonymous } (*)expressions » (C) 『 ＼ (strictly) fixed ／ (in < the consciousness of < Japanese people > >) 』. (Since (S) < the number of < (w)Chinese characters > > (V) is (C) 『 (strictly) limited 』 【 – ◎a Japanese { with < average education > } (id)(V) is (C) 『 supposed to (V) know (O) « (id)as few as 1,945 KANJI » 』 (to (V) lead (O) « a (decently) intellectual life » (in < Japanese language >))) – 】 (S) < (1){ synonymous } or (2){ antonymous } (*)expressions (in < Japanese >) > (aV) can never ＼ (aV) be (V) expected to ／ (V) grow (much) (in < number >).

(S) < That > (V) is (C) 『 *[the reason]* { why (S) < Japanese learners of < English > > (

rarely) (id)(V) try to (V) remember (O) « (w)any given English word » ((id)in { conscious } connection with < (*)its (1)(w)synonyms or (2)(w)antonyms >) } 』. (S) < They > (V) are (therefore) (C) 『 ^too^ (id)prone to (V) use (O) « (*){ the same } (1)word or (2)expression » ((id)again and again) (^to^ ＼ (aV) be (V) deemed ／ (C) 『 as < ◎intelligent speakers of < English > { with(= *(S) < who > (V) have*) < adequate vocabulary > } > 』) 』. (S) < ^It^ > (V) is (C) 『 not enough 』 ^to^ (id)(V) store up (O) « words » (in < your memory bank >) (◎the way { (*[in < which >]*) (S) < you > ^(V) feed^ (O) « computers » (^with^ < data after < data > >) }); ^(S) < it > (V) is^ (C) 『 the associated connection of < (*){ different } (1)words and (2)(w)phrases > – (1)(w)synonyms, (2)(w)antonyms and (3)(w)paraphrases – 』 ^(S) < that >^ (V) makes (O) « you » (C) 『 (id)rich in < your linguistic resources > 』.

^(V) Save^ (O) « your efforts ((id)with relation (*)to (1)< (w)synonyms >, (2)< (w)antonyms > and (3)< (w)paraphrases >) »... ^and^ (S) < you > (id)(V) are (C) 『 sure (1)to (first) (id)(V) lose (O) « your face » (as < an intellectual >) and (eventually) (2)to (V) lose (O) « your vocabulary » ((id)for lack of < relevant linguistic association >) 』. (id)(*)(V) Save (1)(O) « your face » and (2)(O) « memory » (by < ‡(V) buying‡ (O) « the effort of < ^‡(V) binding‡^ (O) « (*){ (id)lots of } (1)words and (2)(w)phrases » (^together^) > » > (whenever (S) < you > (id)(V) try to (V) remember (O) « (*){ any particular } (1)word or (2)(w)phrase »)). (S) < ◎Vocabulary { *[(S) < which >* ＼ *(aV) is]]* (thus) (V) enriched ／ } > (aV) will (id)(V) bear (O) « interest » (at < ◎some point >), ／ { where(= *and, there*) (S) < you > (V) feel (O) « ^it^ » (C) 『 much more interesting 』 ^to^ (V) say (O) « one thing » (in < many different ways >) ((id)by way of < ◎ample alternatives { *[(S) < which >* ＼ *(aV) are]]* (id)(V) stored up ／ (in < your brains >) } { [(S) < that > (V) are] (id)ready to (V) come into < your mouth > ((id)at { your } command) }) } >. (Once (S) < you > (V) get (C) 『 (that) (id)rich (*)in (1)< your vocabulary > and (2)< joy of < English > > 』), (S) < your success > ＼ (V) is (C) 『 (fully) (V) guaranteed 』 ／ : (S) < you > ＼ (id)(aV) are (V) guaranteed to ／ (V) be (C) 『 an authentic master of < English > 』.

13.(V) Be (always) (C) 〖 aware [of] < (O) « what » (S) < you > | (aV) are (V) studying | > 〗

– (1)terms (vocabulary), (2)idioms (collocations), (3)sentence patterns (SPAT-5), (4)constructions, (5)grammar, or (6)anatomical interpretation of < English sentences >

- ◎^Those^{ ^(S) < who >^ (V) succeed } (always) (V) know (O) « (O) « what » (S) < they > | (aV) are (V) doing | »; ◎^those^ { ^(S) < who >^ (aV) don't (V) [succeed] } (aV) don't (V) know (O) « (O) « what » (S) < they > ＼ (aV) are | (aV) being | (V) made ／ to (V) do » -

(id)(aV) Let (O) « us » (C) 〖 ^(V) begin^ (O) « this section » ^with^ < ◎a question { [(S) < *which* > ＼ (aV) *is*]] (typically) (V) found ／ (in < Japanese (w)college entrance examination >) } > 〗, (†(V) featuring†(= (S) < *which* > (V) *features*) (O) « ◎(abnormally) faulty English sentences { [(S) < *which* > ＼ (aV) *are*]] (artificially) (V) made ／ (C) 〖 so 〗 (by < the examiner >) { to ＼ (aV) be (V) corrected ／ by < examinees > } } »).

(V) Correct (O) « errors » 【 ((id)if [(*there*) (V) *are*] (S) < any [*errors*] >) 】 (in < the following English sentences >):

One of Japanese Anime-character that is popular for all the world is Tezuka Osamu's "鉄腕アトム(TETSUWAN ATOM)", translating into English in "Astroboy". The fact was interesting that his original name is not literarily translated as an "Iron-armed Atom" but to the "Astroboy". While this sounds futuristic and tinged with the optimistic hope in future, but the former wouldn't simply, for that remind us of a inhuman robot powered on inside nuclear reactor, who feels rather danger to Japanese after that terrible unclear powerplant disaster of 2011.

...(S) < The following > (V) is (C) 〖 the (correctly) modified English 〗, (with (S) < ◎respective parts { †(*)(V) needing†(= (S) < *which* > (*)(V) *need*) (1)(O) « correction », (2)(O) « insertion » or (3)(O) « deletion » } > ＼ (*)(aV) being (1)(V) numbered and (2)(V) highlighted ／ with < 【 ((id)as many as 31!) 】 [(w)square brackets] >):

(S) < (id)One of < ◎(1)[the] Japanese Anime-character(2)[s] { (S) < that > (V) (3)[~~is~~→are] (C) 『 popular 』 ((4)[~~for all the world~~→(id)all over the world]) } > > (V) is (C) 『 Tezuka Osamu's "鉄腕アトム(TETSUWAN ATOM)" 』, { *[(S) < which > ＼ (aV) is]*] ((5)[~~translating~~→^(V) translated^] ／ (6)[~~into~~→in] < English >) ((7)[~~in~~→^into/to^] < "Astroboy" >) }. (S) < The fact > (8)[~~was~~→(V) is] (C) 『 interesting 』 { that (S) < (9)[~~his~~→its/the] original name > ＼ (10)[~~is~~→(aV) was] ^not^ ((11)[~~literarily~~→literally]) (id)(V) translated (12)[~~as~~→into/to] ／ (13)[~~an~~...to be deleted] < "Iron-armed Atom" > ^but^ to (14)[~~the~~...to be deleted] < "Astroboy" > }. (While (*)(S) < ^this^ > (1)(V) sounds (C) 『 futuristic 』 and (2)(15) [~~tinged~~→ ＼ (id)(aV) is (V) tinged] with ／ (16)[~~the~~...to be deleted, or to be replaced with "an"] optimistic hope ((17)[~~in~~→for] future)), (18)[~~but~~...to be deleted] (19)[~~the former~~→(S) < ^that^ >] (20)[~~wouldn't simply~~→(simply) (aV) wouldn't *[(V) sound (C) 『 futuristic 』 or (aV) be (V) tinged with < optimistic hope for future >]*],

／ for (21)[~~that~~→(S) < it >] (22)[~~remind~~→^(V) reminds^] (O) « us » ^of^ < ◎(23)[~~a~~→an] inhuman robot { (24)[~~powered on~~→(V) powered by / (V) working on] (25)[~~inside nuclear reactor~~→< a (W)nuclear reactor (inside) / an { inner } (W)nuclear reactor >] } >, { (26)[~~who~~→(S) < which >] (V) feels (C) 『 (rather) (27)[~~danger~~→dangerous] 』 (to (28)[~~Japanese~~→< the Japanese / Japanese people >] (after < that terrible (29)[~~unclear~~→nuclear] (30)[~~powerplant~~→(W)power plant] disaster (31)[~~of~~→in] < 2011 >)) > }.

(S) < ◎A nightmarish treasure of < faults > { like < the sentences { above } > } > (aV) may (V) appear (C) 『 *[to (V) be]* ^too^ (C) 『 surreal 』 (to < Europeans >) (^to^ ＼ (aV) be (actually) (V) found ／ (in < English compositions >)) 』; (here (in < Japan >)), (however), (W)(S) < anything > (V) goes — (among < ◎^those^ { ^(S) < who >^ (*)(aV) don't (V) know (1)(O) « where (S) < they > | (aV) are (V) going | » and (2)(O) « (O) « what » (S) < they > | (aV) are (V) doing | » } >)... ／ although (S) < 31 mistakes (in < 3 consecutive sentences >) > (V) are (C) 『 ^too^ gorgeous (^not to^ (V) be (C) 『 artificial 』) 』.

(Since ◎(s) < such { (elaborately) mistake-ridden } sentences (in < English >) { for (s) < examinees > to (v) correct } > (v) are (among < the favorite repertoires of < examiners (in < Japan >) > >)), (s) < students > (id)have to (v) be (c)『 (id)proficient in < (1)‡(v) detecting‡ and (2)‡(v) correcting‡ (*)(o) « errors » (in < such { (artificially) incorrect } English >) > 』. ((id)To tell you the { blunt } truth), (however), (with < this (id)type of { detect-and-correct } question >), (s) < practice > never (v) makes [(o) « you »] (c)『 perfect 』: (s) < (only) ◎analytical intelligence { *[(s) < which >* ＼ ^*(aV) is*^ *]]* ^(v) based^ ^on^ ／ < comprehensive ‡understanding‡ of < English > > } > does(= *(v) makes (o) « you » (c)『perfect 』*). (^For^ < that ^purpose^ >), (s) < (blindly) ‡(v) devouring‡ (o) « knowledge » > (v) is (c)『 never enough 』: (s) < ‡(v) knowing‡ (o) « (o) « what » (s) < you > | (aV) are (v) devouring | » > (w)(v) is (c)『 the name of < the game > 』. ((id)In other words), (s) < intelligence > (v) matters (more than (s) < diligence >). (s) < You > (aV) must not (simply) (v) memorize (o) « (o) « what » (s) < you > ＼ (aV) are | (aV) being | (v) taught ／ »: (s) < lesson contents > ^(v) need^ (1)(first) (o) « ‡(v) categoriz^ing^‡ ((id)according to < the nature of < the (w)subject > >) » (2)(and then) (o) « (id)‡(v) stor^ing^‡ up (in < your memory >) ((id)according to < their respective categories >) » (3)(and (1)finally and (2)most importantly) (o) « ‡(v) review^ing^‡ (as many times as (*)(1)(s) < their priority > and (2)(s) < your mental capacity > (1)(v) demand and (2)(v) warrant) ». (If (s) < your memory > (v) is (c)『 short 』), (v) study ((1)long and (2)often); (c)『 ^the^ shorter 』 (s) < your memory > (v) *[is]*, (^the^ (1)longer and (2)oftener) *[(s) < you > (aV) must (v) study]* . (s) < A subject { (id)of top priority } > ^(v) needs^ (o) « ‡(v) study^ing^‡ ((1)repeatedly and (2)systematically) » (to ^(v) keep^ (o) « it » (c)『 ^out of^ < idle oblivion > 』); (s) < a matter { (id)of lesser priority } > (aV) need (only) ＼ (aV) be (v) learnt ／ ((rather) (1)occasionally and (2)randomly).

- Six analytical categories (in < systematic studies of < English > >) -

((id)In order to (v) be (c)『 (analytically) selective (in < your studies >) 』), (s) <

◎everything { (O) « *[that]* » (S) < you > (V) learn (about < English >) } > (aV) must ＼ (aV) be (intelligently) (id)(V) divided into ／ < the following six(6) categories >:

I)English terms (vocabulary);

II)English idioms (collocations);

III)English sentence patterns (SPAT-5);

IV)English constructions;

V)English grammar;

VI)anatomical interpretation of < English sentences >.

(S) < I > (V) believe (O) « *[that]* (1)"terms (vocabulary)", (2)"(w)idioms ((w)collocations)" and (3)"(w)sentence patterns (SPAT-5)" (*)(aV) need not ＼ (aV) be (V) clarified ／ (here) », but (S) < most of < you > > (aV) will | (aV) be (V) wondering | *[about]* < (O) « what » (S) < "(w)constructions" > (V) mean >. (S) < A "(w)construction" > (V) is (C) 〖 ◎(id)a group of < "KATA(form)" > { *[(S) < which > ＼ (aV) is]]* (V) categorized ／ ((1)by < meaning >), not ((2)by < ◎structural characteristics { like (w)the five sentence patterns of English 【 ((O) « what » (S) < this book > (V) calls (C) 〖 "SPAT-5" 〗) 】 } >) }, { (S) < which >, 【 (id)according to < the actual lessons (in < English >) (by < this author >) > 】, (id)(V) divides into < the following twelve(12) categories > }:

(1)不定詞(FUTEISHI: INFINITIVE)

(2)動名詞(DOUMEISHI: GERUND)

(3)分詞(BUNSHI: PARTICIPLE)

(4)比較(HIKAKU: COMPARISON)

(5)関係詞(KANKEISHI: RELATIVES)

(6)否定(HITEI: NEGATION)

(7)仮定法(KATEIHOU: SUBJUNCTIVE)

(8)倒置・語順(TOUCHI・GOJUN: INVERSION)

(9)省略(SHOURYAKU: ELLIPSIS)

(10)共通関係(KYOUTSUU-KANKEI: COMMON-RELATION)

(11)挿入(SOUNYUU: PARENTHESIS)

(12)同格(DOUKAKU: APPOSITIVE)

』

(S) < I > (1)(aV) will not 【 ((S) < I > (2)(aV) CANNOT!) 】 (*)(V) give (O) « detailed explanations of < these twelve "(w)semantic constructions" of < English > > » ((id)here and now), and (S) < those categories > (*)(V) are (1)(C) 『 (definitely) not fixed 』 and (2)(C) 『 not (even) authoritative ones 』; ((id)in fact), (S) < this author > (himself) (aV) would (sometimes) (V) add (O) « one more (w)construction category », (13)名詞構文(MEISHI-KOUBUN: NOUN CONSTRUCTION), ((id)in the form of < a brief seminar (about (five days) long 【 (three hours (each)) 】) >). ((id)In short), (S) < any pattern of < ◎English composition { *[(S) < that > ＼ (aV) is]]* (semantically) (V) grouped (together) ／ } > { (*)(S) < which > (1)(V) requires and (2)(V) is (id)(C) 『 fit for (*)(O) « < (*){ systematic } (1)comprehension and (2)memorization > » } > (aV) can ＼ (aV) be (V) called ／ (C) 『 "a (w)construction" 』.

(^By^ < "grammar" >) ＼ ^(aV) is (V) meant^ ／ (here) 【 ((rather) loosely) 】 (S) < ◎any particular rule of < English > { (S) < that > (aV) does not (id)(V) belong to < (*)the { above-mentioned } "(1)terms", "(2)(w)idioms", "(3)SPAT-5" and "(4)(w)constructions" > } >.

(S) < (O) « What » (S) < "anatomical interpretation of < English sentences >" > (V) means > (V) is (C) 『 ◎the (*){ practical } (1)method and (2)‡training‡ { *[(S) < which > ＼ (aV) are]]* (V) needed ／ (to (V) comprehend (O) « the meaning of < (rather) complicated sentences > ») } 』. (V) Take 【 (id)for example 】 (O) « the ‡opening‡ headline of < this (id)series of < paragraphs > >, "◎^Those^ { ^(S) < who >^ (V) succeed } (always) (V) know (O) « (O) « what » (S) < they > | (aV) are (V) doing | »; ◎^those^ { ^(S) < who >^ (aV) don't } (aV) don't (V) know (O) « (O) « what » (S) < they > ＼ (aV) are | (aV) being | (V) made ／ to (V) do »" ». (S) < Novice learners > (aV) may (V) be (C) 『 (id)at a loss *[about]* < (O) « what » to ^(V) make^ ^of^ < { "◎^those^ { ^(S) < who >^ (aV) don't } (aV) don't (V) know' } part > > 』, (id)†(V) wondering† if(= *as* (S) < *they* > (V) *wonder if)* (S) < the "don't don't" > (V) isn't (C) 『 ◎a sloppy duplication { *[(S) < which >* ＼ *(aV) was]]* (V) committed ／ (by < some { absent-minded } author >) } 』. ◎^Those^ { [^(S) < who >^ (V) are] (C) 『 (id)adept at < "省略(SHOURYAKU: ELLIPSIS)" (w)construction > 』 } (aV) will (instantly) ^(V) interpret^ (O) « it » ^as^ < an abbreviation from < "<those who don't [succeed]> don't know" > >. (S) < This > (V) is ◎(C) 『 the anatomical interpretation of < English > 』, { (S) < which > ((id)of course) (id)(V) calls for < comprehensive knowledge (*)of < "(1)terms" >, < "(2)(w)idioms" >, < "(3)(w)sentence patterns" >, < "(4)(w)constructions" > and < "(5)grammar" > > }. (S) < "Anatomy" > (V) is (^only^) (C) 『 possible 』 (^after^ (S) < you > ↑ (aV) have (perfectly) (id)(V) acquainted (O) « yourself » (*)with ↑ < ^both^ (1)"atoms 【 (< (1)terms >, < (2)(w)idioms > and < (3)grammar >) 】 " ^and^ (2)"cosmos 【 (< (1)(w)sentence patterns > and < (2)(w)semantic constructions >) 】 " >).

\- (*){ Actual } (1)categorization and (2)interpretation -

(Well), (id)(S) < it >(V) 's (about) (C) 『 time *[that]* (S) < we > (id)(V) went into < details > 』. (S) < ◎The (artificially) faulty English sentences { *[(S) < which >* ＼ *(*)(aV) are]]* (already) (1)(V) corrected (above) and (2)(V) numbered ((1) through (31)) ／ } > (aV) can (each) ＼ (aV) be (V) categorized ／ into < the following groups >:

questions (about):

I)terms (vocabulary)

(11)[literarily→literally]... ^confusion^ of < "literally = (id)to the letter" > ^with^ < "literarily = ^in^ < ◎^manners^ { *[(S) < which > (V) are]* (id)(C) 『 suitable for < literature > 』 > }" >, ◎an awkward ^mistake^ { (O) « *[which]* » (S) < ◎persons { ^of^ < authentic literary ^taste^ > } > (aV) would never ^(V) make^ }

(16)[the...to (aV) be (V) deleted, or to (id)(aV) be (V) replaced with < "an" >]... (S) < the (w)noun "hope" (in < this context >) > (V) is (C) 『 ^too^ vague (^to^ (V) require (O) « the (w)definite article "the" ») 』

(20)[wouldn't simply→(simply) (aV) wouldn't]... (S) < the (w)adverb "simply" >

(id)is to ＼ (aV) be (V) placed ／ ((id)prior to < a (1)(w)verb /(2)(w)auxiliary verb >) (^for^ < emphatic ^purposes^ >)

(25)[inside nuclear reactor->◎a (w)nuclear reactor (inside) / an { inner } (w)nuclear reactor]... ((id)in addition to < the omission of < "an" > >), (S) < the term "inside" > ＼ (aV) is (more often) (V) used ／ ((1)as < an (w)adverb 【 ([(S) < which > ＼ (aV) is]] (V) placed ／ (after < ◎the term { (O) « [which] » (S) < it > (V) qualifies } >)) 】 >) than ((2)as < (w)an attributive adjective 【 ([(S) < which > ＼ (aV) is]] (V) placed ／ (before < ◎the term { (O) « [which] » (S) < it > (V) modifies } >)) 】 >); (S) < a more suitable (w)attributive adjective (in < this context >) > (aV) should (V) be (C) 『 "inner" 』... (if (S) < you > (still) (id)(V) insist on ‡(V) using‡ (O) « "an <inside> (w)nuclear reactor" »), (S) < you >(aV) 'll | (aV) be (V) declaring | (O) « "(S) < I >(V) 'm (C) 『 an <outside> speaker of < English > (from < abroad >) 』" »

(28)[Japanese→the Japanese / Japanese people]... (S) < the term "Japanese" { [(S) < which > ＼ (aV) is]] (V) used ／ (without < (w)articles >) } > (V) means (O) « "Japanese language" »; (V) add (O) « "the" » (to (V) make (O) « it » (C) 『 "people (in < Japan >)" 』)

(29)[unclear→nuclear]... a (1){ typical } 【 though (2)not { comical } 】 (*)(w)typo (=typographical error) ((id)in view of < the Fukushima (w)nuclear meltdown (in < 2011 >) >)

【 (*(actually), (there) (V) is (S) < no ^such^ term ^as^ < "unclear" > > (in < English >)) 】

(30)[powerplant→(w)power plant]... (S) < { separating } space > ＼ (aV) [is] (V) needed ／ (^between^ < 'power" > ^and^ < "plant" >)

II)idioms (collocations)

(4)[(id)for all the world→(id)all over the world]... (*)(S) < "(id)for all the world" > (1)(V) means (O) « "never" » and (2) ＼ (aV) is (V) used ／ (in < ◎a negative context { (id)such as < "(S) < She > (aV) won't (id)(V) listen to < my pleas > ((id)for all the world)" > } >)

(12)[as→into/to]... (S) < "(id)(V) translate (O) « A » as < B >" > (V) is (C) 『 ◎a (1){ semantic } 〖 ((id)as opposed to (2){ linguistic }) 〗 (*)expression { [(S) < which > (V) is] (id)(C) 『 similar to < "(id)(V) interpret/understand/deem/regard/think of/consider (O) « < A > » as < B >" > 』 } 』, { (S) < which > (V) is (id)(C) 『 unsuitable for < ◎this { "linguistic translation" } context { †(V) requiring†(= (S) < which > (V) requires) (O) « the (w)preposition "into/to" » ((id)instead of < "as" >) } > } 』

(17)[in→for]... (S) < "(id)in future" > (V) means (O) « "(*)sometime (1)((id)in the future), not (2)(now)" »; (S) < this context > (V) requires 〖 instead 〗 (O) « "◎ˆhopeˆ 〖 [(O) « [which] » (S) < we > (now) (V) have] 〗 (ˆforˆ < future >)" »

(24)[powered on→(V) powered by / (V) working on]... (S) < the (w)preposition "on" > (V) means (O) « "◎a basis { (ˆonˆ < which >) (S) < something > ˆ(V) reliesˆ }" »; (S) < "a (w)power source" > (aV) should ＼ (aV) be (V) expressed ／ (by < "by" >)

(31)[of→in]... ◎the year { (in < which >) (S) < something > (V) happens } ＼ (aV) is (V) expressed ／ ((id)in the form of < (1)"in XXXX", not (2)"◎of XXXX" >), { (S) < which > (V) is (C) 『 a typical ◎Japanese error 』, { (in < whom >) (S) < their postpositional particle(助詞) "の" > ＼ (aV) is (instinctively) (id)(V) associated with ／ < the English (w)preposition "of" > } }

III)sentence patterns (SPAT-5)

...NONE...

IV)constructions

(1)[the](RELATIVES)... (S) < "先行詞(the (w)antecedent)" of < a (w)relative pronoun clause > > (usually) (V) requires (O) « ＼ ‡(aV) being‡ (V) modified ／ by < the (w)definite article "the" > »

(5)[translating→(V) translated](PARTICIPLE)... (S) < this context > (V) requires (O) « (w)the passive voice "translated" »

(15)[tinged→(aV) is (V) tinged](COMMON-RELATION)... (while [(S) < both > |

(aV) *are]]* (id)(V) pointing to | < the same (w)subject "this" >), ◎(S) < the first verbal part *[of]* "sounds futuristic" > (aV) does not (V) accompany (O) « "(w)be verb" », { (S) < which > (V) makes (O) « ^it^ » (C) 『 necessary 』 ^to^ (newly) (V) introduce (O) « "is" » (before ◎the second verbal part *[of]* "tinged with" { (S) < which > (V) is*(= because (S) < it > (V) is)* (C) 『 in < (w)the passive voice > 』 }) }

(26)[who→(S) < which >](RELATIVES)... (if (S) < the ^(w)antecedent^ ^to^ < this (w)relative clause > > (V) were (C) 『 "鉄腕アトム(Astroboy)" 』), (S) < ◎the (w)relative pronoun { to ＼ (aV) be (V) used ／ (here) } > (aV) should (V) be (C) 『 personal "who" 』; ((id)in fact), ◎(S) < the actual (w)antecedent (here) > (V) is (C) 『 the (w)impersonal content "that an inhuman robot is powered by a nuclear reactor inside" 』, { (S) < which > (V) requires (O) « the (w)relative pronoun "which" ((id)instead of < "who" >) » }

V)grammar ((id)in general)

Anime-character(2)[s]... (since (S) < "one of < one >(=$^1/_1$)" > (V) is (C) 『 (practically) meaningless 』), (S) < the expression "(id)one of < A >" > (always) (V) requires (O) « the (w)plural form of < "A" > »; (S) < the mistake of < ‡(V) using‡ (O) « this expression » (with (S) < the { "A" } part > *[†(V) being†]* (C) 『 in < the (w)singular > 』) > > ＼ (id)(aV) is (V) triggered by ／ ◎< the sound "one" >, { (S) < which > (naturally) (V) suggests (O) « "a single one" » }

(3)[is→(V) are]... (as *[(S) < it > ＼ (aV) was]]* (V) explained ／ (above)), (S) < the { "A" } part of < "(id)one of < A >" > > (*)^(V) is^ (1)(always) (C) 『 (w)plural 』, (2)(never ^to^ ＼ (aV) be (V) used ／ (in < (w)the singular form >)), (†(*)(V) requiring†*(= (S) < which > (*)(V) requires)* (O) « the (w)verb (1)"are" ((id)instead of < (2)"is" >) »)

(8)[was→(V) is]... (although (S) < "鉄腕アトム/Astroboy" > (V) is (C) 『 a classical work of < Tezuka > 【 (April 7, 1951 - 1968) 】 』), ◎(S) < ◎the time { [when] (S) < this author > (V) feels (O) « "the fact" » (C) 『 [to (V) be] (C) 『 "interesting" 』 』 } > (V) is (definitely) (C) 『 "the present", 』 (†(*)(V) requiring†*(= (S) < which > (*)(V) requires)*

(therefore) (O) « (1)"is" ((id)instead of < (2)"was" >) »)

(9)[his→its/the]... ◎(S) < the author > | (aV) is (*)^(V) referring^ | ^not^ ((1)^to^ < "アトム/Astroboy" (as < a person >) >) ^but^ (2)^to^ < the work (itself) >, { (S) < which > (*)(V) requires (1)(O) « the (w)impersonal (w)determinative "its" » or (2)(O) « the (w)definite article "the" » }

(10)[is→(aV) was]... (S) < the act of < ^translation from^ < "鉄腕アトム" > ^to^ < "Astroboy" > > > (*)^(V) belongs^ ^not^ (1)^to^ < { the present } ^but^ (2)^to^ { the past } (*)tense >, (†(*)(V) requiring†(= (S) < *which* > (*)(V) *requires)* (O) « (1)"was" ((id)instead of < (2)"is" >) »)

(13)[an...to be deleted]... (S) < this (w)indefinite article "an" > (*)(V) is (1)(C) 『 strange 』 and (2)(C) 『 misleading 』 (because (S) < it > (id)(V) seems to (V) suggest (O) « *[that]* ◎(S) < this title "Iron-armed Atom" > (V) is (C) 『 (id)one of < many possible { (literally) translated } titles > 』, { (S) < which > (V) is (definitely) (C) 『 (id)not the case 』 (here) } »)

(14)[the...to be deleted]... (S) < this (w)definite article "the" > (V) is (C) 『 (totally) meaningless 』 (because (S) < the { (actually) translated } title "Astroboy" > (aV) does not (V) accompany (O) « any (w)article » (with < it >)); (S) < ◎the only possible meaning { (O) « *[that]* » (S) < this "the" > (aV) can (V) have } > (V) is (C) 『 ◎that*(= the meaning)* of < emphasis > 』, { (S) < which >, (nevertheless), (aV) should ＼ (aV) be (V) expressed ／ (in < a more emphatic expression *[of]* 'that "Astroboy"' >) }, (†(V) making†(= (S) < *which* > (V) *makes)* (O) « this "the" » (C) 『 meaningless 』 (anyway))

(21)[that→(S) < it >]... (S) < ◎the most usual (w)impersonal pronoun { (S) < which > (id)(V) points to < something > } > (*)(V) is (C) 『 (1)"it" 』, ((id)instead of < (2)"that" >), ／ for (S) < this 【 (=the latter expression "that") 】 > ＼ (aV) is (often) (V) used ／ ((id)in { special } combination with < ◎some other terms { (id)such as < "which" > } >(eg. "(S) < Tastes > ^(V) vary^ (^from^ < person > ^to^ < person >). ◎^That^ (aV) can (V) be (C) 『 distasteful 』 (to < others >) { ^(S) < which >^ (V) is (quite) (C) 『 tasty 』 (for

< you >) }.")), / while (S) < that 〘 (=the former expression "it") 〙 > (V) is (id)(C) 〚 free from < such coordinated ^association with^ < other terms > > 〛, ((id)except for < (1)"that" and (2)"to" >(eg. (1)"(S) < ^It^ > (V) is (C) 〚 strange 〛 ^that^ (S) < he > (aV) doesn't (V) know (O) « the fact »." / (2)"(S) < ^It^ > (*)(V) is (1)(C) 〚 painful 〛 but (2)(C) 〚 not shameful 〛 ^to^ (V) admit (O) « faults »."))

(22)[remind→(V) reminds]... ◎a sloppy omission of < "s/es" > { *[(S) < which > (V) is]* (id)(C) 〚 typical of < (*){ Japanese } (1)speakers/(2)writers (*)of < English > > 〛 }

(23)[a→an]... ◎an unthinkable ^mistake^ 〘 ({ *[(S) < which > ^(V) is^]* (only) ^to^ ＼ (aV) be ^(V) made^ ／ by < foreign speakers of < English > > }) 〙 { *[of]* (*)‡(V) using‡ (O) « (1)"a" ((id)instead of < (2)"an" >) » (before < a (w)vowel >) }

(27)[danger→(C) 〚 dangerous 〛]... ◎a (*)(typically) (1){ foreign } 〘 (and (2){ novice }) 〙 (*)mistake { ^†(V) confusing^† *(= (S) < which > ^(V) confuses^)* (O) « a (w)noun » ^with^ < an (w)adjective > }

VI)anatomical interpretation of < sentences >

(6)[into→in]/(7)[in→into/to]... (S) < the object of < the action "(id)(V) translate (O) « A » into/to < B >" > > (*)(V) is (1)(C) 〚 'into/to < "Astroboy" >' 〛, not (2)(C) 〚 'into/to < English >' 〛; (S) < 'in < English >' > ＼ (aV) is (simply) (V) inserted ／ (in < '^(V) translate^ "鉄腕アトム" ^into^ < "Astroboy" >' >)... *[(S) < this > (V) is]* (C) 〚 ◎a short-sighted mistake { [(S) < which > (V) is] (C) 〚 ◎(quite) hard { to (V) detect } 〛 } 〛, (†(V) making† *(= (S) < which > (V) makes)* (O) « it » (C) 〚 favorite of < favorites > 〛 (for < { hard-core } examiners of < Waseda University > >))

(18)[but...to be deleted]... (*)(S) < the ‡opening‡ (w)conjunction "while" > (1)(V) implies (O) « contradiction » ((id)in itself) and (thus) (2)(V) repels (O) « the use of < "but" > ((id)at the beginning of < the contrasted (w)clause >) », (just as (S) < "While (S) < she > (V) is (C) 〚 tall 〛, (S) < her husband > (V) is (C) 〚 short 〛" > ＼ (id)is (never) to (aV) be (V) written ／ as < "While she is tall, ~~but~~ her husband is short" >); (S) < a (too) lengthy { "while..." } part > (aV) will (often) (V) invite ◎(O) « this (id)type of <

error > », { (S) < which > (aV) can (hardly) ＼ (aV) be (V) detected ／ (by < persons { of < short (w)attention span > } > })

(19)[the former→(S) < that >]... (id)(V) Pay (O) « attention » to < the ‡opening‡ words of < the sentence >, "While this sounds futuristic" >; (in < this context >), (S) < ◎{ that } "this" > (V) means (O) « "{ the latter } one (of < the { two } ◎things { (id)in question } >)" », { ＼ (V) used ((id)in contrast to < which >) (aV) is ／ (S) < "that" > }; (S) < the expression "the former", 〖 though †(V) meaning†(= (S) < *it* > (V) *means*) (O) « the same thing » 〗 >, (aV) must ＼ (aV) be (V) used ／ (＼ (aV) *[being]* (id)(V) coupled with ／ < "the latter" >)... (since (S) < the use of (O) « "(1)that" and "(2)this" » ((id)in { this } sense) > (V) is (C) 『 (quite) rare 』), (S) < ◎the intentional abuse of < it > { for (S) < examinees > to (V) correct } > (V) is (C) 『 ˆtooˆ difficult (ˆtoˆ (id)(V) make (O) « sense » ((even) as < a trick question (by < an ill-intentioned examiner >) >)) 』

- (S) < Vocabulary > (V) is (C) 『 an { (*)endless } (1)riddle and (2)struggle 』 -

(Well), (id)(O) « what » (aV) do (S) < you > (V) say to < that >? While (S) < 31 questionable points > (aV) might ↑ (aV) have (V) been ↑ (C) 『 ˆtooˆ much (ˆforˆ (S) < you > ˆtoˆ (V) correct) 』, / (1)(S) < the 31 explanations >, 〖 ((id)at least) (2)(S) < many of < them > > 〗 , (*)(aV) should not (V) be (C) 『 ˆtooˆ much (ˆtoˆ (V) understand) 』. But (S) < whether (S) < you > (V) understood (O) « them » (all) ((id)here and now) > (aV) does ˆnotˆ ˆreallyˆ (V) matter 〖 ((S) < you > (certainly) (aV) will *[(V) understand (O) « them » (all)]* ((id)in time) (if (S) < you > (id)(V) keep on ‡(V) studying‡ (O) « English »)) 〗 ; (S) < (S) < what > (aV) does (V) matter > (C) 『 is 』 (C) 『 if (S) < you > (V) became (id)(C) 『 aware of < the ˆdivisionˆ of < those thirty-one questions > ˆintoˆ < five different categories > > 〖 ([with] (S) < "(w)sentence pattern SPAT-5" > ＼ [†(aV) being†] (V) excluded ／ (herein)) 〗 ((id)according to < the nature of < ◎(w)each and every mistake { *[(S) < that > ＼ (aV) was]]* (V) committed ／ (*[in order]* to ＼ (aV) be (V) corrected ／) } > >) 』 』.

((O) « As » (S) < you > (aV) must ↑ (aV) have (V) seen ↑), (S) < the { "term" } category > (V) is (C) 〚 the fuzziest part of < { detect-and-correct } (id)type of < questions > > 〛. (S) < Each English word > (V) has (O) « ◎its distinctive character (1){ (S) < that > (V) defies (O) « generalization » } », (2){ (S) < which > ＼ (id)has to (aV) be (respectively) (V) remembered ／ ((id)in the process of < (w)◎vocabulary building >), { (S) < which > (literally) (V) has (O) « ^no^ goal » (^(id)at all^) (until (1)(S) < one > 〖 (or (2)(S) < one's linguistic aspiration >) 〗 (*)(V) dies) } }. (S) < (1)[Even] The most { learned } student 〖 (((id)in fact), (2)(even) (S) < the examiners > (themselves)!) 〗 > (*)(aV) could not (id)(V) hope to (V) get (O) « (w)full marks » (in < "terminology quiz" >) (without < the aid (*)of (1)< dictionaries > or (2)< (w)reference books > >). (S) < ^It^ > (V) is (therefore) (C) 〚 illogical 〛 ^to^ (id)(V) aspire for < (w)full marks > (in < this (id)type of < endless riddle > >): (S) < you > (id)have only to (id)(V) try and *(= (V) try to)* (V) get (O) « as many points { ^(O) « as »^ (S) < your terminological memory > (V) permits } ». (S) < ◎{ How many } "term" points { (O) « *[which]* » (S) < you > (aV) can (V) get (in < (w)any given exam >) } > (largely) (id)(V) depends on < luck >. (S) < That > (V) is (C) 〚 *[the reason]* why (S) < a (really) excellent examiner > (V) avoids (O) « "◎terminology overdose" » 〛, { (S) < which >*(= because (S) < it >)* (invariably) (V) degrades (O) « the quality of < ◎the exam ((id)as a whole) { *[(S) < that > ＼ (aV) is]]* (too much) (V) influenced ／ by < (C) 〚 how (1)lucky/(2)unlucky 〛 (S) < each examinee > (id)(V) happens to (V) be > } > » }... ／ although (there) (aV) do (V) exist (S) < ◎^such^ universities { (S) < ^as^ > (aV) will (intentionally) (aV) let (O) « luck » (C) 〚 (id)(V) play (O) « a part » (in < ‡(V) making‡ (O) « ^it^ » (C) 〚 harder 〛 ^for^ (S) < { super-intelligent } students > ^to^ (V) get (O) « ◎"(w)reserved seats" » ((id)at the exclusion of < candidates { of lesser intelligence } >), (*[(S) < which > ^(V) are^]* (id)only ^to^ ＼ (aV) be (id)(V) thrown away ／ (when (S) < they > (V) pass (O) « (w)exams to { higher grade } universities »)) >) 〛 } >... ／ (id)except for < such (intentionally) sloppy ones >, (S) < ◎examiners { *[(S) < who > (V) are]* (C) 〚 too (id)prone to < "word quiz" > 〛 } > (V) are (C) 〚 ^too^ low (in < English literacy >) (ˆtoˆ (id)(V) be (C) 〚 entitled to (V) be (C) 〚 examiners 〛 〛) 〛 〘 (although (S) < Japan > (id)(V) is (C) 〚 teeming with < such "problem makers" > 〛) 〙 .

((id)In any case), (S) < ˆitˆ > (V) is (C) 〚 (downright) foolish 〛 ˆtoˆ (id)(V) hope (*)for < (1){ perfect } or (2)(even) { good } (*)marks (in < "haphazard terminology quiz" >) >. ((id)Of course), (S) < you > (id)have to (id)(V) do (O) « your utmost » (*[in]* (id)‡(V) trying‡ (*)to (1)(V) enlarge and (2)(V) enrich (*)(O) « your vocabulary »), but (S) < { however great } a vocabulary > never (V) warrants (O) « your success (in < (purely) terminological questions >) »... (id)(V) do (O) « your best » and (id)(V) prepare for < the worst >. (S) < ◎Any point { (O) « *[that]* » (S) < you > (V) get (in < "word quiz" >) } > (aV) should ＼ (aV) be (V) considered ／ (C) 〚 *[to (V) be]* (C) 〚 a "bonus" 〛 〛; (S) < high points (in < exams >) > (id)had best ＼ (aV) be (V) acquired ／ (somewhere { else }) ("(id)as *[(S) < they > ＼ (aV) are]]* (V) planned ／ ").

- Tangible patterns (in < questions (*)on (1)< (w)idioms > and (2)< (w)collocations > >) -

((id)*[When (S) < it > ＼ (aV) is]]* (V) Compared with ／ < (largely) haphazard { "terminological" } questions >), (S) < "(1)idiom/(2)(w)collocation" (*)category > (V) is (C) 〚 *[the point]* where (S) < the (really) excellent student > (aV) can (id)(V) hope to (id)(V) get (C) 〚 ahead of < their rivals > 〛 〛.

(Firstly), (S) < English (w)idioms >, 〘 though *[(S) < they > (V) are]* (C) 〚 numerous 〛 〙 , (V) are (C) 〚 much fewer than (S) < English words > 〛. (While (S) < vocabulary > (V) is (C) 〚 (w)a bottomless pit 〛), (there) (V) is (S) < (w)a { practical } ceiling on < how far (S) < you > (aV) must (V) go (in < the world of < (w)idiomatic expressions > >) > >; (S) < diligent students { with < moderate intelligence > } > (aV) can (V) reach (O) « that ceiling » (while *[(S) < they > (V) are]* (in < (w)high school >)) ((id)with the help from < reasonably { well-written } books (on < English (w)idioms > for < (w)college-bound students >) >).

(Secondly), (*)(S) < questions (on < (w)idioms >) > (1)(V) develop (around < the { (

(id)more or less) generalized } usage of < "(w)prepositions" > >) and (2) ＼ (id)(aV) are not (V) meant as ／ < "(id)trivia on < (*){ particular } (1)terms or (2)expressions > >". ((id)Of course), ((id)in the hands (*)of < (1){ (intolerably) bad } 〖 (or (2){ (intentionally) malicious }) 〗 (*)examiners >), (there) (aV) can (V) be (S) < ◎^such^ a nonsense quiz { (S) < ^as^ > (aV) will (V) ask (O) « you » (C) 『 to (V) fill (O) « the blank » (in < "(aV) Don't (V) carry (O) « (???) » (to < Newcastle >)" >, { †(V) meaning†(= (S) < *which* > *(V) means)* (O) « "(aV) Don't (V) do (O) « (O) « what » (S) < you > (id)don't have to *[(V) do]* »" » }) 』 > }. (S) < (Only) luck > (aV) will (V) decide (O) « if (S) < you > (aV) can (id)(V) hit upon < "coals" > »; (*)(S) < "(1)oil" or "(2)ships" > (1)(V) sounds (C) 『 as fine *[as (S) < "coal" >]* 』 but (2)(aV) doesn't (id)(V) ring (O) « the bell »; (S) < { even } "coal" > (id)(aV) won't (V) do (because (S) < this (w)noun > (V) is (C) 『 (w)countable 』)... oh, (C) 『 what a (*)(profoundly) (1){ deep }, (2){ esoteric } and (3){ abysmal } (*)question 』 (S) < it > (aV) could (V) be! (Besides < ‡(V) testing‡ (O) « the examinee's historical knowledge of < the industrial structure of < a certain local town > (on < the small island of < Britain > >) > » >), (S) < it > (aV) can (also) (V) test (O) « ◎(*)the (1)(w)singular /(2)(w)plural (*)consciousness { *[(S) < which > (V) is]* (C) 『 ^enough^ (^to^ (V) add (O) « "s" » ((id)at the end of < ◎the (w)countable noun "coal", { (S) < which >, 〖 though *[(S) < it > (V) is]* (C) 『 (id)similar to < (*)the (1){ material } and (2){ uncountable } (*)(w)noun "chalk" > 』 〗 , (still) (V) retains (O) « its individual countability » (just like < (id)a plate of < "slate" > >) } >)) } 』 »! (S) < (id)None but < (*)the (1)erudite 〖 (or (2)lucky!) 〗 > > (*)(aV) could (ever) (correctly) (V) answer (O) « this wondrous riddle »... But (S) < such (lethally) stupid questions > (V) are (C) 『 (quite) ◎(1)rare 〖 (though (2)not impossible) 〗 { (*)to (V) find } (among < "(w)idiomatic questions" (in < Japanese (w)college entrance examinations >) >) 』. (^If^ *[(S) < the question > ＼ (aV) were]]* (V) asked ／ ((id)as such*(= as < an "(w)idiomatic question" >))* (^(id)at all^)), (S) < the expression "Don't carry coals to Newcastle" > (aV) should ＼ (aV) be ^(V) changed^ ^into^ ／ < ◎"Don't carry coals (???) Newcastle" { †(V) requiring†*(= (S) < which > (V) requires)* (O) « the suitable (w)preposition "to" » (to (id)(V) fill in < the blank >) } >. (S) < To (V) ask *[(O) « examinees »]* (C) 〚 to (V) complete (O) « "Don't carry (???) to Newcastle" » 〛 > (V) is as (C) 〚 foolish 〛 as (S) < ‡^(V) presenting^‡ (O) « examinees » ^with^ < "Don't carry coals to (???)castle" > >. (S) < You > (aV) could (V) get (O) « it » (C) 〚 right 〛 (if (S) < you > (only) (V) knew (O) « "Newcastle United F.C." »), but how (else) *[could (S) < you > (V) get (O) « it » (C) 〚right 〛]* ?

(S) < Such silly trivia > (*)(V) say (1)(O) « "YES" » ((only) to < ◎^those^ { (S) < ^who^ > (V) know } >), (2)(O) « "NO!" » (to < ◎^those^ { (S) < who > (aV) don't (V) *[know]* } >). (C) 〚 Such 〛 (V) is (S) < the evil of < { addle-brained } esotericism > >. (S) < ◎Universities { (S) < which > ↑ (aV) have (V) shown ↑ (O) « themselves » (C) 〚 (hopelessly) (id) ＼ (V) tainted with ／ < it > 〛 ((w)via < "haphazard questions" (*)on < (1)words or (2)(w)idioms > >) } > (id)(aV) might (just) as well ＼ (aV) be (V) avoided ／ (by < examinees >). (S) < The choice > (V) is (C) 〚 yours 〛 (while [(S) < you > (V) are] (C) 〚 a mere candidate 〛)... (S) < you >(id)(aV) 'll (V) have (O) « no choice » but to ＼ (id)(aV) be (V) tainted with ／ < their (*)(intolerably) (1){ foolish } and (2){ arrogant } (*)esotericism > (once (S) < you > (V) get (inside < their (w)ivory tower >), (†(V) spending†(= *and (V) spend)* (O) « (*)^too^ much (1)time and (2)money » (^to^ (id)(V) walk away from < it >))).

◎"Idiomatic questions" { *[(S) < which > (V) are]* (1)healthy and (2)reasonable } (id)never (V) fail to (V) test (O) « your knowledge of < (1)"(w)prepositions" and (2)◎their (id)relationship with < particular (1)(w)verbs and (2)(w)nouns >, { *[(S) < which > ＼ (aV) are]]* (V) known ／ as < "(w)collocations" > } > ». ((id)As such), (*)(S) < they > (1)(aV) can ＼ (aV) be (id)(V) dealt with ／ (as < (id)a { systematic } set of < knowledge > >) and (2)(aV) can (therefore) (V) be (C) 〚 (id)a { truer } test of < your English literacy > than (S) < (aimlessly) random (id)"trivia on < words >" > 〛. ((aV) Would (S) < you > (V) be(= *If (S) < you > (aV) would [(V) like to] (V) be)* (C) 〚 (w)a smart aleck 〛), (just) (V) devour (O) « words » (as (S) < pigs > (V) do(= *(V) devour)* (in < their sty >)); (if (S) < you > (aV) would (really) (id)(V) belong in < the ranks of < the intelligentsia > >), (id)(V) learn (by heart) (O) « (w)idioms » (wisely) and (V) conquer < the world of < (w)collocations > >.

- (There) (V) is (S) < (1)a limited size and (2)assured success ((*)in < ◎English grammar >) >, { (in < which >) (id)(V) stand out (S) < the two paramount mountains: (1)the handy molds of < SPAT-5 > and (2)semantic (id)varieties of < (w)constructions > > } -

(Unlike < ◎(1)"words" and (2)"(w)idioms" { (S) < which > (id)have to ＼ (aV) be (respectively) (1)(V) remembered and (2)(id)(V) dealt with ／ (as < { ((id)more or less) individual } (id)pieces of < knowledge > >) } >), (S) < "grammatical questions" > (V) are (C) 『 ◎easier { to (id)(V) deal with } 』 (because (S) < they > (V) are more (1)(C) 『 questions of < logic > 』 than (2)(C) 『 tests of < sheer memory > 』) — (S) < you > (id)don't have to (V) remember, (S) < you > (*)(id)have only to (1)(V) use (O) « your brains » and (2)(V) think. ((id)So long as (S) < you > ↑ (aV) have (V) established ↑ 【 in < your brains > 】 (O) « how to (V) think (grammatically) »), (S) < you > (aV) can (assuredly) (id)(V) hope for < (w)full marks (in < grammatical questions >) >. (S) < { (Authentically) learned } masters of < English > > (id)don't (even) have to (V) think — (S) < they > (*)(aV) can (instinctively) (1)(V) detect and (2)(V) correct (*)(O) « grammatical faults » ((id)at a glance): (unless (S) < they > (aV) can *[(instinctively) (V) detect and (V) correct (*)(O) « grammatical faults » ((id)at a glance)]*), (S) < they > (aV) can ^(V) make^ (O) « the same ^mistakes^ » (themselves)... (*)(S) < a true commander of < English > > (1)(V) detects and (2)(V) avoids (*)(O) « possible errors » ((even) before (*)(S) < they > (1)(V) speak or (2)(V) write) — (S) < that >(V) 's (C) 『 (id)(C) 『 what 』 (S) < ^it^ > (V) is ^to^ (V) command (O) « English » 』.

(Though (S) < (id)not all learners of < English > > ＼ (aV) are (V) required ／ to (V) be (C) 『 the authentic masters of < this language > 』), (S) < a certain level of < grammatical comprehension > > ＼ (aV) is (id)(V) demanded of ／ < all (w)college-bound students > (because (S) < it > (V) is (C) 『 the { very } essence of <

the (w)command of < English > > 』). (*)(S) < Examiners (in < Japan >) > (1)(aV) can and (often) (2)(aV) do (*)(V) make (O) « { silly }, { nonsensical } trivia » ((id)as regards < "(1)terms" and "(2)(w)idioms" >), but (S) < they > (aV) can (hardly) (V) do (O) « the same » (with < "grammar" >). (*)(S) < Grammar > (1)(V) is (C) 『 (id)a set of < established principles of < speech > > 』 and, ((id)as such), (2)(V) is (C) 『 much more (1)tangible and (2)manageable (*)than (1)(S) < the (w)bottomless pit of < English terms > > or (2)(S) < (seemingly) endless world of < (1)(w)idioms and (2)(w)collocations > > 』. ((id)In order (*)to (1)(V) get (O) « high marks (in < English >) » and (2)(V) pass (O) « exams »), (S) < you > (id)have to (V) be (C) 『 (adequately) (id)proficient in < English grammar > 』. (S) < You > (aV) need ^not^ (V) be (C) 『 ^very^ (id)rich in < English terminology > 』, (S) < you > (id)don't have to (V) be (C) 『 (perfectly) (id)sure of < ◎the world of < English (w)collocations > > 【 { (^with^ < which >) (S) < you > (V) become (C) 『 (vaguely) ^familiar^ 』 (through < (id)‡(V) learning‡ (O) « (w)idioms » (by heart) >) } 】 』, but (S) < you > (aV) must (V) be (C) 『 (fairly) (id)certain of < your systematic knowledge of < grammar > > 』 (1)(to (V) avoid (O) « ‡(V) getting‡ (O) « (w)poor marks » (in < English exams >) ») and (2)(to (V) be (C) 『 (really) (id)proficient in < the use of < English > > 』).

((S) < As > ↑ (aV) have ＼ (aV) been (V) shown ／ ↑ (above)), (S) < ◎(even) the (abnormally) rich (id)treasure of < faulty English sentences > { (O) « *[which]* » (S) < this author > (elaborately) (V) created } > (aV) does not (V) include (O) « any ◎errors { regarding < "(w)five sentence patterns of < English > 【 (SPAT-5) 】 " > } », ／ ^^for^^ < the very simple ^^reason^^ { that (S) < they > (V) are (C) 『 ^so^ (1)basic and (2)easy 』 ^that^ (S) < ◎mistakes { *[(S) < which > ＼ (aV) are]]* (id)(V) related with ／ < them > } > (V) are (C) 『 too ◎hard { to forge } 』 } >; (S) < no { self-respecting } speaker of < English > > (aV) could (V) make (O) « ^such^ an (artificially) erroneous sentence ^as^ < "~~(S) < I > (V) gave (O) « it » (O) « him »~~" > » ((even) (id)in jest). (id)(V) Be (C) 『 advised 』 *[that]* (S) < the (*){ perfect } (1)‡understanding‡ and (2)manipulation (*)of < SPAT-5 > > (V) is more (1)(C) 『 requisites 』 than (2)(C) 『

assets 』 (in < the world of < (w)college entrance examination > >); (*)(S) < examiners > (1)(aV) may (V) test (O) « how fast (S) < you > (aV) can (V) run », but (2)(aV) will not (id)(V) check to(= *and*) (V) see (O) « if (S) < you > (V) have (O) « ◎two legs { to (V) run on } » ».

((1)Beyond 〖 (but (mostly) (2)upon) 〗 (*)< the (w)foundation stones of < English (w)sentence patterns 〖 (SPAT-5) 〗 > >) (V) stand (S) < the magnificent edifices of < ◎(w)semantic constructions { (id)such as < INFINITIVE >, < COMPARISON >, < RELATIVES > or < SUBJUNCTIVE > } > >. ^(S) < It > (V) is^ (in < the realms of < these (w)constructions > >) ^that^ (S) < the main ^battle^ (*)for (1)< the command of < English > > 〖 (and (2)(w)entrance to < college >) 〗 > (*) ＼ (aV) is ^(V) engaged^ ／ . (Unless (S) < you > (id)(aV) are (well-)(V) armed with < knowledge in < respective fields of < these (w)semantic constructions > > >), (S) < the battle > ＼ (aV) is (V) lost ／ , (^whether^ (1)(in < the narrow straits of < (w)college entrance exams > >) ^or^ (2)(in < the broader world of < { (actually) spoken } English > >)).

(S) < The world of < English grammar > > (V) is (C) 『 ^so^ large 』 ^that^ (S) < you > (aV) will (V) be (C) 『 (id)at a loss *[about]* < how (*)to (1)(V) traverse 〖 (id)let alone (2)(V) conquer 〗 (*)(O) « it » > 』 (unless (S) < you > ^(V) divide^ (O) « it » (^into^ < three tangible spheres of < (1)"(w)sentence patterns", (2)"(w)constructions" and (3)"the rest" > >)). (S) < (O) « What » (S) < "the rest" > (V) contains > (*)(V) is (1)(C) 『 (still) large 』, but (2)(C) 『 not ^too^ large (^to^ (V) comprehend) 』 (after (S) < you > ↑ (aV) have (V) subtracted ↑ (O) « (*)the (1){ structural } 〖 (SPAT-5) 〗 and (2){ semantic } 〖 ((w)construction) 〗 (*)patterns » from < the whole picture of < English grammar > >).

- (S) < "(id)Back to < the basics >" > (V) is (C) 『 (w)a lost cause 』 (in < linguistics >) -

(Among < (id)"the rest" of < grammar > >) ＼ (aV) are (V) contained ／ (S) < ^such^ basic principles (*)^as^ (1)< (w)tense >, (2)< (w)conjugation >, or (3)< (w)parts of speech > >. (S) < ^It^ > (V) is (C) 『 true 』 ^that^ (S) < you > (aV) can (id)(V) go (nowhere) (

without < these basic principles (in < English >) >), but (S) < ˆitˆ > (V) is (C) 〚 (also) true 〛 ˆthatˆ (S) < those principles > (aV) can ＼ (aV) be (V) learnt ／ (anywhere) (because (S) < they > (V) are (C) 〚 "basic" 〛).

(S) < ◎ˆThoseˆ { ˆ(S) < who >ˆ (id) ＼ (V) get (C) 〚 stuck ／ in < (relatively) early stages of < English studies > > 〛 — (*)after (1)< ＼ ‡(V) being‡ (id)(V) introduced to ／ < "SPAT-5" > and (2)< (id)‡(V) starting‡ to ＼ (id)(aV) be (V) perplexed at ／ < the complexities of < "(w)semantic constructions" > > > — } > (simply) (*)(aV) don't (V) know (1)(O) « where (S) < they > | (aV) are (V) standing | » or (2)(O) « (1)where and (2)how far (S) < they > (id)have to (V) go ». (Not †(V) knowing†*(= Because (S) < they > (aV) don't (V) know)* (O) « their destination »), (S) < they > (aV) will (invariably) (id)(V) try 〖 (id)in vain 〗 to "(id)(V) go back to < the basics of < English > >"... ／ (when(*= and then*)) (S) < their destiny > ＼ (aV) is (V) determined ／ . (S) < They > (*)(aV) will (1)(V) start (from < (1)(id)‡(V) writing‡ down and (2)‡(V) pronouncing‡ (*)(O) « the alphabet » ((id)once again) >), (studiously) (2)(V) practice (O) « (w)ˆ‡(V) paraphrasing‡ˆ (O) « sentences » (ˆwithˆ (*){ various } (1)< (w)subjects >, (2)< (w)objects > or (3)< (w)tenses >) », or (3)(V) sharpen (O) « their ◎ability { to (V) construe (O) « sentences » ((id)according to < the five structural molds 〖 (SPAT-5) 〗 >) } » and... ／ (id)(S) < that > (V) is (C) 〚 all 〛; (S) < they > (aV) can (V) go (no further). (Beyond < the "basic" realm of < English > >), (S) < they > (aV) don't (V) know (O) « (1)where or (2)how (*)to (V) go ».

(id)(S) < The fact > (V) is { *[that],* (S) < all those basics > (aV) can ＼ (aV) be (V) learnt ／ (in < (id)a matter (*)of (1)< MONTHS >, not (2)< YEARS > >) }. (S) < ˆItˆ > (aV) will (V) take (O) « years of < practice > » ˆtoˆ ＼ (id)(V) get (perfectly) (C) 〚 used to ／ < the basics > 〛, but (S) < those ‡practicing‡ years > (id)had best ＼ (aV) be (id)(V) spent on ／ < (1)‡(V) studying‡ and (2)‡(V) conquering‡ (*)(O) « the paramount summits of "(w)semantic constructions" » >. (V) Remember — (O) « (S) < basics > (aV) can ＼ (aV) be (V) learnt ／ (anywhere), (at < (*)the (1)foot, (2)ridge or (3)top (*)of < the mountains > >) ». (*)(S) < ◎ˆThoseˆ { ˆ(S) < who >ˆ (id)(V) stick to < the basic

‡training‡ > (in < the (w)base camp ((id)at the foot of < the mountains >) >) } > (1)(aV) will never (V) start (O) « ‡(V) climbing‡ », and (2)(aV) will (eventually) (id)(V) give up (O) « ◎their wish { to (V) command (O) « English » } ». [(S) < It > (V) is] (C) 〚 (id)not that (S) < they > (V) are (C) 〚 (mentally) (id)disabled from < ‡(V) going‡ (any higher) > 〛 〛. [(S) < It > (V) is] (C) 〚 (simply) that (S) < they > (aV) don't (V) know (O) « how to (*)^(V) categorize^ (1)(O) « the world of < English > », (2) 【 (especially) the realm of < grammar > 】 (^into^ < three different levels (*)of (1)"(w)sentence patterns", (2)"(w)semantic constructions" and (3)"the rest" >) » 〛.

(S) < Each (w)semantic construction (INFINITIVE, GERUND, PARTICIPLE, COMPARISON, RELATIVES, NEGATION, SUBJUNCTIVE, etc,etc.) > (id)had best ＼ (aV) be (V) studied ／ ((id)in a single stroke), ((C) 〚 however (1)tough and (2)long 〛 (S) < the task > (aV) may (V) seem ((id)at first)). (Since (S) < they > (aV) can never ＼ (aV) be (V) learnt ／ (without < (1){ arduous } and (2){ repetitive } (*)reviews >)), (S) < ^it^ > (aV) does not (V) matter (C) 〚 ^how^ tough 〛 (S) < the first attempt > (V) is (for < novice learners >): (S) < it > (*)(aV) will (V) get (1)(C) 〚 ^the^ less tough 〛 and (2)(C) 〚 ^the^ more (lucidly) understood 〛 ((^the^ more) (S) < they > (id)(V) run over < it >). (While (S) < they > (id)(V) go over < it >), (S) < they > (aV) can (naturally) (*)(V) review (1)(O) « "SPAT-5" » and (2)(O) « (id)"the rest" of < grammar > » ((id)over and over [again]). (*)(S) < English "basics" > (1)(aV) need not 【 ((id)in fact, (2)(aV) MUST NOT) 】 (*) ＼ (aV) be (V) learnt ／ (by < ‡(V) getting‡ (backward) >): (just) (id)^(V) go^ forward (in < your (id)struggle with < "(w)semantic constructions" > >), ^and^ (S) < the conquest of < "basics" > > (aV) will ＼ (aV) be (V) achieved ／ (((id)pretty much) (id)as a matter of course).

(S) < ◎All { (S) < who > (id)(V) succeed in < anything, { academic (id)or otherwise } > } >, (V) know (O) « ◎the fact { that ◎things { *[(S) < which > (V) are]* (apparently) (C) 〚 hard 〛 ((id)at first) } (aV) will (V) look (C) 〚 easier 〛 (as (S) < they > (id)(V) proceed to (id)(V) take on < ◎things { *[(S) < which > (V) are]* (C) 〚 more (progressively) difficult 〛 } >) } ». (S) < ◎People { (S) < who > (V) achieve (O) « { (seemingly) impossible } feats » } >, ((id)in fact), (id)(V) have (O) « a way » of < ^‡(V) overcharging‡^ (O) « themselves » ^with^ < ◎tasks { [(S) < which > (V) are] (C) 『 beyond < their current capacity > 』 } > >. (S) < They > (simply) (aV) won't (V) sit (†(V) practicing†(= while (S) < they > (V) practice) (O) « "basics" » ((id)along with < other (w)low achievers >)): (S) < they > (aV) will (id)(V) lose (O) « no time » [in] < (id)‡(V) stepping‡ up to < ◎"intermediate" level > >, { where (S) < they > (*)(aV) will ^at once^ (1)(id)(V) struggle with < harder tasks > ^and^ (2)(id)(V) take (O) « their time » [in] < ‡(V) taming‡ (O) « ◎easier things { (O) « [which] » (S) < they > (aV) didn't (V) have (O) « much time » ([in] < ‡(V) practicing‡ >) (in < (*)the (1){ long }, (2){ tedious } ◎(*)lessons of "basics" { < [which] > (S) < they > (promptly) (id)(V) turned (O) « their backs » on }) } > > » }. (Thus), (S) < they > (aV) will (V) gain (O) « a footing (in < basics >) » (while (S) < they > (id)(V) jump up (for < something { higher } >)). ◎^Those^ { ^(S) < who >^ (id)(V) stick to < something { lower } > (until (S) < they > (V) are (C) 『 sure [that] (S) < they > ↑ (aV) have (perfectly) (V) gained ↑ (O) « a footing (in < basics >) » 』) } (aV) will never (V) achieve (O) « anything { (really) great } ».

((id)As (S) < it > (V) happens), (S) < Japanese folks > (V) are (C) 『 (id)notorious for < (id)‡(V) making‡ (O) « too much » of < "基本(KIHON: basics)" > (without < (id)‡(V) aspiring‡ for < anything { (1)higher 〚 (or (2)irregular) 〛 } > >) > 』. ((id)In fact), (S) < most Japanese 〚 ((1)learners ^and^ (2)teachers ^alike^) 〛 > (simply) (id)(V) have (O) « no notion » of < < what > (S) < { "上級(JOUKYUU: advanced)" } realm of < English > > ＼ (id)(aV) is (V) made of ／ >... [(S) < ^it^ > (V) is] (C) 『 (id)no wonder 』 [^that^] (S) < (id)very few of < them > > (aV) could ever (V) achieve (O) « something » (in < their (painfully) vain (id)struggle for < (w)command of < English > > >). (S) < ◎They > | (aV) are (only) (V) swimming | (in < the shallows of < English bay > >), { (to < whom >) (S) < the epic odyssey (to < the { (1)12 〚 ((2)13, (3)fourteen, (id)(you) (V) name (O) « it ») 〛 } (*)semantic seas of < constructions > >) > (V) is (C) 『 ◎a myth { (O) « [which] » (S) < (only) idle dreamers > (aV) will ever (id)(V) take (seriously) } 』 }.

(Learners), never (V) spend (O) « too much time » ([in] (1)‡(V) playing‡ 〚 ((id)or rather, (2)‡(V) consoling‡ (O) « yourselves ») 】 (*)with < "basics" (alone) >): (just) (id)(V) step (forward) and (V) learn (O) « basics » ((id)on the way). ((1)(^The^ higher) (S) < you > (V) go and (2)(C) 『 ^the^ tougher 』 (S) < the task > (V) gets), ◎(^the^ more) (S) < you > (aV) can (id)(V) familiarize (O) « yourself » with < (really) basic matters >, { (S) < { which } familiarity > (aV) will (confidently) (V) encourage (O) « you » (in < your (id)struggle with < ◎something { *[(S) < which > (V) is]* ◎much tougher { to (V) master } } > >) }. (S) < (1)Difficulty and (2)confidence > (id)(V) go (by < comparison >). ((id)In order to (V) tame (O) « ◎something { (O) « *[which]* » (S) < you > (V) find (O) « ^it^ » (initially) (C) 『 ◎difficult { ^to^ (V) master } 』 } »), (just) ^(V) challenge^ (O) « something { *[(S) < which > (V) is]* (C) 『 ◎harder (still) { to (V) tame } 』 } », ^and^ (S) < the initial difficulty > (V) seems (C) 『 *[to (V) be]* (id)(C) 『 nothing 』 *[as ＼ compared ／]* to < the new { daring } challenge > 』, (†(V) giving† *(= (S) < which > (V) gives)* (O) « you » (O) « an emotional conquest of < (*)the (1){ first } (2){ easier } (*)challenge > »); (S) < the conquest > (aV) may (V) be (merely) (C) 『 emotional 』, but (S) < the imagined conquest > (V) is (C) 『 (far) better than < the feeling of < defeat > > 』. (^As^ (1)(S) < ability > and (2)(S) < effort > (*)(V) are (C) 『 the wheels of < achievement > 』), ^so^ (V) is (S) < confidence > (C) 『 (id)fuel for < success > 』. (S) < That >(V) 's (C) 『 (w)the name of the game (in < ‡(V) conquering‡ (O) « anything { (really) great } » >) 』. (S) < ◎The realm { where (S) < you > (aV) can (really) (V) achieve (O) « something » (in < your pursuit of < the (w)command of < English > > >) } > (V) lies (beyond < (1)"SPAT-5" and (2)(id)"the rest" of < grammar > >) — (V) learn (O) « them » (retrospectively) (while (S) < you > (id)(V) struggle with < { mcuh harder } "(w)semantic constructions" of < English > >).

- ^(V) Learn^ (O) « (w)semantic constructions of < English > », ^and^ (S) < anatomical interpretation of < English sentences > > (aV) will (naturally) (V) follow -

(While (S) < you > ＼ (aV) are | (aV) being | (V) taught ／ (O) « "basic" things » (in < Japanese classrooms >)), (S) < you > (aV) will (V) encounter (O) « ◎(virtually) no

English sentences { *[(S) < which > (V) are]* (C) 〚 complicated ^enough^ (^to^ (V) require (O) « (1){ anatomical } 〖 (id)as opposed to (2){ mechanical } 〗 (*)interpretation ») 〛 } ». ((id)In order to (V) get (C) 〚 (id)proficient in < anatomical interpretation of < English > > 〛), (S) < you > (naturally) (id)have to (V) walk into < (*)the (1){ thick } (2){ semantic } (*)forests of < "(w)constructions" > >.

(id)(S) < ◎The sad truth > (V) is { *[that]*, (S) < most Japanese students > ＼ (id)(aV) are (V) introduced to ／ < (impossibly) (1){ small } (2){ fragmented } and (*)(seemingly) (3){ isolated } and (4){ unrelated } (*)portions of < the real world of < English (w)constructions > > > }. (S) < (O) « What » (S) < (*){ Japanese } (1)schools or (2)teachers > (V) show (O) « you » (regarding < ^such^ constructions ^as^ < INFINITIVE, GERUND, PARTICIPLE, COMPARISON, RELATIVES, NEGATION or SUBJUNCTIVE > >) > (V) are (all) (C) 〚 (*)^too^ (1)small and (2)separated (^to^ (V) be (C) 〚 (actually) useful 〛) 〛; (S) < they > (*)(V) are (1)(C) 〚 fragmented (id)pieces of < info > 〛 (id)rather than (2)(C) 〚 systematic knowledge of < grammar > 〛. ((id)As for < more (highly) specialized (id)groups of < (w)constructions > { ^such as^ < INVERSION, ELLIPSIS, COMMON-RELATION, PARENTHESIS or APPOSITIVE > } >), (S) < (practically) (*)no (1)time or (2)thought > ＼ (aV) is (V) given ／ (O) « them » (in < (*)ordinary { Japanese } (1)schools or (2)books >).

(S) < The ^reason^ ^for^ < this piteous situation (in < Japan >) > > (V) is (C) 〚 (1)simple but (2)hopeless 〛 — (S) < ^both^ (1)teachers ^and^ (2)writers (*)of < English textbooks > 〖 ((id)at least most of < them >) 〗 > (V) are (themselves) (C) 〚 (totally) (id)ignorant of < these (w)constructions > (as < "(id)a { systematic } set of < knowledge >" >) 〛. (S) < These (w)constructions > (V) exist (in < the heads of < most (*){ Japanese } (1)teachers or (2)writers > >) (as < mere fragments of < ◎(O) « what » 〖 (S) < they > (V) feel 〗 (1)(S) < they > (V) know 〖 (or (even) (2)"(S) < they > ↑ (aV) have (V) seen ↑ (somewhere)") 〗 > >, { (O) « which » (S) < they > (V) need (O) « some (w)reference books » (to (1)(V) confirm or (even) (2)(V) understand) }). (S) < No one > (aV) can (V) give (O) « others » (O) « systematic comprehension of < (id)a group of < ◎things { (O) « [which] » (S) < they > (themselves) (only) (V) know ((id)in parts), (

without < any idea of < the whole picture > >) } > > »... (w)tough luck for < ◎ˆthoseˆ { ˆ(S) < who >ˆ (V) have (O) « the misfortune of < ＼ (aV) being (V) taught ／ (O) « English » (by < such teachers >) > » } >.

- ˆ(V) Beˆ (C) 『 aware 』 *[about]* < where (S) < you > | (aV) are (V) going | >, ˆorˆ *[(S) < you > (aV) will]* (id) ＼ (*)(V) get (C) 『 (1)stuck ／ 』 and (2)(C) 『 dead 』 (*[at the point]* where (S) < you > (V) are) -

(id)(S) < ◎The good news > (V) is { *[that]*, (S) < the author of < this book > > (aV) can (V) give (O) « you » (O) « (*){ comprehensive } (1)‡understanding‡ and (2)‡training‡ (*)of < 12 (w)semantic constructions of < English > > » ((id)in the form of < ◎WEB lessons > { *[(S) < which > ＼ ˆ(aV) areˆ]]* ˆ(V) composed ofˆ ／ < (*){ ample } (1)example sentences and (2)explanations > }, ((id)along with < enough numbers (*)of (1)< grammatical questions > and (2)< answers > >)) }. (For < more details >), (V) check (O) « the url { below } »:

http://furu-house.com/sample

(If (S) < you > (id)(V) aspire to (V) achieve (O) « something { authentic } »), (id)(V) be (C) 『 my guest 』. (Just) (V) ignore (O) « my invitation » (if (S) < you > (aV) can (V) rest (C) 『 ＼ (id)(V) satisfied with ／ < several years of < ◎(painfully) vain "basic" ‡trainings‡ { (O) « *[which]* » (S) < (*){ your } (1)schools or (2)teachers > ˆ(V) forceˆ (ˆuponˆ < you >) } > > 』). (S) < ◎The ˆchoiceˆ > (V) is (C) 『 yours { to ˆ(V) makeˆ } 』, but (please) (V) remember (O) « — (S) < I > (aV) didˆn'tˆ (V) write (O) « this (id)series of < principles > » (ˆ(just) (id)in order toˆ (V) invite (O) « you » (to < my WEB lessons >)): (S) < I > (V) created (O) « my WEB lessons » ((id)according to < those principles >) ».

(ˆWhetherˆ (S) < you > (V) take (O) « my WEB lessons » ˆor notˆ), (id)(V) take (O) « my word » for < ˆitˆ > [ˆthatˆ] (without < the distinctive consciousness of < (O) « what » (S) < you > | (aV) are (V) studying | > — (1)terms (vocabulary), (2)(w)idioms ((w)collocations), (3)(w)sentence patterns 【 (SPAT-5) 】 , (4)(w)semantic constructions, (5)(id)the rest of < grammar >, or (6)anatomical interpretation of < English sentences > — >) (S) < you > (id)(V) are (C) 〚 sure (*)to (1)(id) ＼ (V) get (C) 〚 stuck 〛 ／ and (eventually) (2)(id)(V) give up (O) « (1)‡(V) studying‡ and (2)‡(V) mastering‡ (*)(O) « English » » 〛. (V) Be (always) (C) 〚 aware 〛 *[about]* < (O) « what » (S) < you > | (aV) are (V) doing | >: (S) < ◎ˆthoseˆ { ˆ(S) < who >ˆ (V) do (O) « (O) « what » (S) < they > (V) do » (because (S) < they > ＼ (aV) are (V) told ／ to (V) do (so)) } > (aV) can never (V) do (O) « anything { (really) great } ».

14.E-to-J translation vs. English interpretation, /

(w)literal translation vs. (w)paraphrasing: /

(V) learn (O) « their difference » (through < anatomical interpretation >)

- ◎Anatomical interpretation { [(S) < *which* > ＼ (aV) *is*]] (V) explained ／ [*(id)in { more } detail than (in < the previous section >)]* } -

((O) « As » (S) < this author > ↑ (aV) has (V) written ↑ (in < the previous section >)), (S) < anatomical interpretation of < English > > (V) is (C) 『 ◎the final product { [(S) < *which* > ＼ (aV) *is*]] (V) made ／ (C) 『 possible 』 (by (id)‡(V) putting‡ (together) (O) « all the skill (*)in "< (1)terms >", "< (2)(w)idioms >", "< (3)(w)sentence patterns >", "< (4)(w)constructions >" and "< (5)grammar >" ») } 』.

(Although (S) < it >(V) s (C) 『 final 』), (*)(S) < the anatomical task > (1)(V) begins 【 (and (2)(aV) should (V) begin) 】 (*)(in < the initial stages of < ‡(V) learning‡ (O) « English » > >). (Although (S) < the ultimate stage of < English comprehension > > never (V) needs (O) « the intervention of < anatomical interpretation > » 【 – ＼ (aV) [*being*] (almost) (instinctively) (V) understood ／ (without < ＼ (*)‡(aV) being‡ (consciously) (1)(V) interpreted or (2)(V) translated ／ >) – 】) (S) < that ultimate stage > (aV) can (^only^) ＼ (aV) be (V) reached ／ (^after^ < years of < practice after < { innumerable } practice > (in < anatomical interpretation of < English > >) > >).

(id)(aV) Let (O) « us » (C) 『 (V) see (O) « the illustrated example of < anatomical interpretation > » (in < the following sentence >) 』:

In the global conflict known as World War II, Germany, Italy and Japan were collectively called the Axis Powers as opposed to the Allied Powers consisting of such eventually victorious nations as Britain, Russia and the United States.

...(S) < which >, (after < ＼ ‡(aV) being‡ (V) anatomized ／ >), (aV) will (id)(V) look like < this >:

(In the global conflict {[which is] known as <World War II>}), <Germany, Italy

and Japan> were (collectively) called <the Axis Powers> (as opposed to ≪the Allied Powers {consisting of(=which consisted of) such {eventually victorious} nations as <Britain, Russia and the United States>} ≫).

(S) < The above > (V) is (C) 『 ◎the way [(in < which >)] (S) < a sentence > ＼ (aV) is (semantically) (V) grasped ／ (in < (w)the mind's eye of < (*)the { expert } (1)reader/(2)listener (*)of < English > > >) 』. (S) < Sentences > ＼ (aV) are ^not^ (V) comprehended ／ (1)(in < a single stream of < (1)words or (2)sounds > >), ^but^ (2)(as < (id)a body of < (mutually) related (id)blocks of < meaning > > >). (S) < To (visually) ^(V) illustrate^ (O) « the sentence » (^with^ < conspicuous signs >) > (aV) will (V) help (O) « learners » (C) 『 [to] (V) understand (O) « the mutual (id)relationship between < ‡composing‡ units of < the sentence > > » 』. (With < this visual guide (in < semantic composition of < the sentence > >) >), (S) < learners > ＼ (aV) are (id)(V) liberated from ／ < the (1){ arduous } 〖 though (2){ (mostly) meaningless } 〗 (*)task of < ‡^(V) translating^‡ (O) « English » (^into^ < their (w)native language >) > >. (S) < "(V) Understand (as (*)(S) < you > (1)(V) look or (2)(V) hear)" > (V) is (C) 『 the common goal of < all learners of < English > > 』, ((id)to be sure), but ((id)aside from < ◎"(w)Howdy English" { [(S) < which > (V) is] (C) 『 ^too^ simple (^to^ (V) require (O) « interpretation ») 』 } >), ◎sentences { [(S) < which > (V) are] (C) 『 { (well) ^worth^ } (O) « ‡(V) read^ing^‡ » 』 } (naturally) (V) demand (O) « anatomical interpretation of < the semantic relationship of < their ‡composing‡ units > > ».

(V) Use (O) « ◎the signs { [(S) < which > ＼ (aV) are]] (V) shown ／ (below) } » (to (semantically) (V) clarify (O) « ◎the English sentence { (O) « [which] » (S) < you > (V) meet } »):

＊<実詞(JISSHI: (w)SUBSTANTIVES)>

(S) < The following substantive units (1)(S:(w)subject),(2)(O:(w)object) and (3)(C:(w)complement) > (id)are to ＼ (aV) be (V) grouped (together) ／ (in < (id)a pair of (1)< (w)angle brackets = "<(1)山括弧(YAMA-KAKKO) or (2)(w)chevrons > or (3)< an lt & gt((1)less-than/(2)greater-than) (*)pair >>" >); (if (S) < { more than one } unit of < (w)substantives > > ＼ (aV) are (V) found ／ (in < the same sentence >)), (S) < the following signs > (aV) can (also) ＼ (aV) be (V) used ／ – (id)a pair of < (w)corner brackets or (w)half brackets = "「鉤括弧(KAGI-KAKKO)」"; (w)black lenticular brackets = "【墨付き括弧(SUMI-TSUKI-KAKKO)】"; (w)double guillemets = "≪二重山括弧(NIJUU-YAMA-KAKKO)≫" >

＜主語(SHUGO: (w)SUBJECT:S)＞

＜動詞の目的語(DOUSHI NO MOKUTEKIGO: (w)VERBAL OBJECT:O)＞

＜前置詞の目的語(ZENCHISHI NO MOKUTEKIGO: (w)PREPOSITIONAL OBJECT)＞

＜補語(HOGO: (w)COMPLEMENT:C)＞

(S) < ◎The units { *[(S) < which > ＼ (aV) are]]* (id)(V) contrasted to ／ "(w)SUBSTANTIVES" } > (V) are (C) 『 "(w)VERBALS" 』:

*動詞／動詞型(DOUSHI/DOUSHI-KEI: (w)verb/(w)VERBALS:V)

(S) < Verbal units > (V) include (O) « the following expressions »:

*熟語(JUKUGO: (w)idioms)

*相関語句(SOUKAN-GOKU: (w)CORRELATIVES)

(S) < (1){ Idiomatic } or (2){ (w)correlative } (*)expressions > ＼ (id)(aV) are (V) composed of ／ < ◎(id)a group of < words > { *[(S) < which > (*)(V) are]* (1)(often) (in < { separated } positions (in < the sentence >) >) } – (2)(sometimes) (^too^ much) ＼ scattered ／ ^for^ (S) < beginners > ^to^ (V) comprehend (as < an integral semantic unit >) >. ((id)So as not to (id)(V) lose (O) « sight » of < these pivotal entities >), (S) < learners > (aV) should ^(V) mark^ (O) « them » ^with^ < ◎something { (visually) outstanding } >, { (id)such as < the use (*)of (1)< underlines > or (2)< colorful (w)marker pens > > }.

(S) < One (very) important (id)part of < the anatomical illustration > > (V) is (C) 『 [省略(SHOURYAKU: (w)ELLIPSIS)] – ◎something { (*)(S) < which > (1)(aV) does not (V) exist (in < the sentence >) but (2)(aV) should ＼ (aV) be (V) complemented ／ }, or (conversely), ◎something { (*)(S) < that > (1)(V) exists (in < the sentence >) but

(2)(id)(aV) might as well ＼ (aV) be (V) omitted ／ } 』

*[省略可能成分(SHOURYAKU-KANOU SEIBUN: OMISSIBLE ELEMENTS)／被省略成文(HI-SHOURYAKU SEIBUN: OMITTED ELEMENTS)]

(Since (S) < English language > (id)(V) makes (O) « much » of < brevity >), (S) < (1)writers/(2)speakers (*)of < English > > (often) (id)(V) cut off (O) « (S) < what > (aV) should 〖 grammatically 〗 (V) exist (in < the sentence >) ». (S) < They > (V) know (O) « (O) « what » (S) < they > | (aV) are (V) saying | », and (S) < the (*){ authentic } (1)readers/(2)listeners (*)of < English > > (also) (V) know (O) « (S) < what > ＼ (aV) is | (aV) being | (V) said ／ » (by < ‡(V) supplementing‡ (O) « the unseen ELLIPSIS » >), but (S) < novice learners of < English > > (id)rarely or never (aV) can *[(V) know (O) « (S) < what > ＼ (aV) is | (aV) being | (V) said ／ »]*. (S) < ^It^ > (V) is (therefore) (C) 『 imperative 』 ^that^ (S) < beginners > (aV) should (id)(V) make { conscious } (O) « ◎efforts { (*)to (1)(V) imagine (O) « (S) < what > ＼ (aV) is (V) omitted ／ » 〖 (if [(S) < it > (V) is] (C) 『 not (personally) impossible 』) 〗 and (2)(V) omit (O) « (S) < what > (aV) can ＼ (aV) be (id)(V) cut off ／ » 〖 (if *[(S) < it > (V) is]* (C) 『 not (grammatically) impossible 』) 〗 } ». (S) < Such (w)ELLIPSIS elements > (aV) should ＼ (aV) be ^(V) marked^ ／ ^with^ < (w)square brackets = "[(1)大括弧(DAI-KAKKO) or (2)角括弧(KAKU-KAKKO)]" >.

＼ (V) Used ((id)in { close } association with < (w)SUBSTANTIVES >) (aV) are ／ ◎(w)adjective ELEMENTS { †(V) modifying† *(= (S) < which > (V) modify)* (O) « (w)nouns » (^either^ (*)from (1)< (id)in front of > ^or^ (2)< behind > (*)the (w)nouns) }, { (S) < which > (aV) should ＼ (aV) be ^(V) marked^ ／ ^with^ < (w)curly brackets = "{中括弧(CHU-KAKKO) or 波括弧(NAMI-KAKKO)}" > }.

*{形容詞(KEIYOUSHI: (w)ADJECTIVES : ADJ.)}

(S) < ◎A single (w)adjective { †(V) modifying† *(= (S) < which > (V) modifies)* (O) « a (w)noun » (from < ahead >) } (eg. (S) < She > (V) is (C) 『 a beautiful woman 』) > (aV) need not ＼ (aV) be (meticulously) (V) marked ／ , but (S) < (1) ◎(id)a group of <

(w)adjective modifiers { †(V) qualifying†(= (S) < which > (V) qualifies) (O) « a (w)noun » (from < behind >) } > (eg. (S) < She > (V) is ◎a woman {beautiful and intelligent}) or (2)◎a single (w)adjective { (S) < which > (V) qualifies (O) « a (w)noun » { [(S) < which > (V) is] ((immediately) before < it >) } } (eg. (S) < He > (V) is (C) 『 a man {alone} 』) > (aV) should ＼ (aV) be (visibly) ^(V) illustrated^ ／ ^with^ < {(w)curly brackets} (^for^ ‡differentiating‡ ^purposes^) >.

(S) < (1){ The most bulky } and (2){ (usually) unessential } 〘 (and (3){ (often) misleading }) 〙 (*)element of < the sentence > > (V) is (C) 『 ◎the (w)adverb part 』, { (S) < which > (aV) should ＼ (aV) be (V) excluded ／ from < (*)the (1){ main }, (2){ essential } (*)(id)parts of < the sentence > > (by < ^‡(V) marking‡^ (O) « it » ^with^ < (w)round brackets > = "((1)小括弧(SHOU-KAKKO) or (2)丸括弧(MARU-KAKKO))") > }.

*（副詞(FUKUSHI: (w)ADVERBS : ADV.)）

(As (S) < its name > (V) implies), (S) < the "(w)adverb" > ＼ (aV) is (V) used ／ ((id)in connection with < the "(w)verb" >). (S) < This > (V) is (C) 『 (1){ (quite) a basic } but (2){ weighty } (*)(id)piece of < knowledge > 』 — (S) < "(w)adverbs" > ＼ (aV) are (id)(V) added on to ／ < "(w)verbs" > / while (S) < "(w)adjectives" > (V) decorate (O) « "(w)nouns" ».

- [(There) (V) needs to (V) be] (S) < (w)No sweat > (with(= if (there) (V) are) < no frills >) -

(S) < The { (id)first and foremost } task of < anatomical interpretation > > (id)(V) starts from < ^(V) separating^ "(w)SUBSTANTIVE (=nounal)" units ((id)along with < (w)ADJECTIVES >) > ^from^ < "(w)◎VERBAL" units { [(S) < which > ＼ (aV) are]] (V) accompanied by ／ < (w)ADVERBS > } >, ((in < which >) (S) < the former >(= (w)substantive units ((id)along with < (w)adjectives >)) (*)(V) are (often) (1)(C) 『 essential 』, (2)(C) 『 brief 』 and (3)(C) 『 ◎easier { to (V) comprehend } 』, / while (S) < the latter >(= (w)verbal units { (V) accompanied by < (w)adverbs > }) (*)(V) are (

usually) (1)(C) 〚 longer 〛 and (2)(C) 〚 ◎tougher { to (id)(V) deal with } 〛).

((id)In other words), (S) < English sentences > (aV) can ＼ (aV) be (1)(simply) and (2)(clearly) (V) understood ／ (when (S) < you > (V) tighten (O) « them » ((*)by (1)< ‡(V) marking‡ (O) « (w)adverbial "flab" » > and (2)< (mentally) ‡(V) deleting‡ (O) « it » (from < your consciousness >) > (for < initial comprehension >)))... (after (S) < you > ↑ (aV) have (V) grasped ↑ (O) « ◎the "essential" components of < the sentence > » 【 ([*(S) < which > ＼ (aV) are]]* (id)(V) made (mostly) of ／ < (1)(w)substantives and (2)(w)adjectives >) 】), (S) < you > (aV) can (V) taste (O) « the "flab" » ((id)at { your } leisure). (id)(V) Make (O) « { wise } use » of < (w)round brackets "( )" > (as < "†{ pending }†" marks (for < { (id)less than essential } (w)adverbial elements >) >). ^(V) Strip^ (O) « a sentence » ^of^ < frills >, ^and^ (S) < the essence > (*)(V) is (always) (1)(C) 〚 simple 〛 and (2)(C) 〚 ◎clear { to (V) see } 〛.

- (S) < ‡(V) Seeing‡ ((id)for yourself) > (V) is (C) 〚 ^one thing^ 〛; (S) < ‡(V) having‡ (O) « others » (C) 〚 (V) see (O) « (O) « what » (S) < you > (V) see » 〛 > (V) is (C) 〚 ^another^ 〛; ‡(V) making‡ (O) « students » (C) 〚 (V) write (O) « ◎all { [(O) « that »] (S) < they > (V) see } » 〛?... (please) (V) (w)(aV) don't (V) bother -

(In < mathematics >), (S) < a formula > (V) speaks (O) « everything ». (S) < Good ‡understanding‡ > ＼ (aV) is (V) proved ／ by < a (flawlessly) written formula >, ／ while (S) < a faulty one > (V) disproves (O) « ◎your claim { that (S) < you > ↑ (aV) have (V) understood ↑ (O) « something » } ». (Although (S) < English > (V) is (C) 〚 no mathematics 〛), (S) < the { above-mentioned } anatomical interpretation signs > (aV) can (V) talk ((nearly) as much as (S) < mathematical formulae > (aV) do*(= (V) talk)*). (Still), (since (S) < English > (V) is (C) 〚 a human speech 〛), (there) (V) are (S) < ◎times { [when] (S) < you > (id)have to (V) speak ((id)(*)in (1)< { human } terms > ((id)instead of (2)< anatomical signs >)) } > — ／ ((especially) if (S) < you > (id)happen to (V) study (O) « English » (in < Japanese schools >)): (S) < (too) many

{ Japanese } English teachers > (id)(V) think (too much) of < ‡^(V) translating^‡ (O) « English » ^into^ < their native Japanese > >. But, (if (S) < you > (really) (id)(V) want to (id)(V) excel in < English >), NEVER (id)(V) write down (O) « ◎everything { (O) « *[that]* » (S) < you > (V) understood } »: (id)(V) make (O) « { wise } { personal } selection » (*)of (1)< (O) « what » { to (id)(V) write down } > and (2)< (O) « what » { to (V) ignore } >, ((id)regardless of < (O) « what » (S) < your teacher > (V) says >).

(S) < Many { Japanese } teachers of < English > > (simply) (V) tell (O) « students » (C) 〚 (*)to (1)(V) translate (O) « ◎every English sentence { (O) « *[that]* » (S) < they > (V) see (on < textbooks >) } » and (2)(id)(V) write down (O) « ◎every (id)piece of < info > { *[(S) < that > ＼ (aV) is]]* (graciously) (V) given ／ (in < lessons >) } » 〛 ((mostly) because (S) < they > (V) want (O) « their students » (C) 〚 [to (V) be] ^too^ busy (^to^ (V) wonder *[about]* < whether (S) < they > | (*)(aV) are (really) (1)(V) doing | 【 ((id)or rather, ＼ | (aV) being | (V) made ／ to (2)(V) do) 】 (*)(O) « the right thing » >) 〛). (When (S) < hands > (V) are (C) 〚 busy 〛), (S) < brains > (V) lie (C) 〚 idle 〛. (S) < ◎(*)The (1){ easiest } and (2){ sliest } way { to (V) conceal (O) « flaws of < fruitless lessons > » } > (V) is (C) 〚 to (V) deny (O) « brains » (O) « ◎a chance { to (V) think } » (by < ‡(V) making‡ (C) 〚 busy 〛 (1)(O) « hands », (2)(O) « eyes » and (3)(O) « ears » (in < the constant flow of < ◎(unilaterally) transmitted info > { ((id)in the midst of < which >) (S) < students > (simply) (id)(V) have ◎no time { to (1)(V) stop and (2)(V) think (intelligently) } } >) >) 〛. (S) < This > (V) is (C) 〚 the most efficient method of < ‡(V) producing‡ (O) « (id)a horde of (1)< (1){ meek }, (2){ unthinking }, (3){ manageable } (*)◎citizens { [(S) < that > (*)(V) are] (1)(C) 〚 (id)no good (as < (w){ thinking } weeds >) 〛 (yet) (2)(C) 〚 (id)not bad (as < stable (w){ founding } stones of < a nation > >) 〛 } > and (2)< ◎gullible customers { ^for^ (1)(S) < big companies > and (2)(S) < industries > ^to^ (easily) (V) exploit } > » > 〛.

(In < ◎(w)any given lesson { †^(V) enabling^† *(= (S) < which > ^(V) enables^)* (O) « students » (C) 〚 ^to^ (really) (id)(V) grow in < intelligence > 〛 } >), (there) (V) is (S) < ◎fruitful void of < voice > { (id)†(V) making† *(= (S) < which > (V) makes)* (O) « room »

{ for (S) < brains > to (V) think } } >; (S) < ◎(1)lessons or (2)teachers { (S) < that > (aV) will (id)(V) take (O) « you » (nowhere) } > (simply) (id)(V) try to (V) make (O) « you » (C) 〚 busy 〛 ((id)on ˆsomeˆ pretext or ˆotherˆ) (to (V) give (O) « plausible substance » (to < empty lessons >)). (S) < ◎ˆSuchˆ teachers { ˆ(S) < as >ˆ (aV) will (V) order (O) « you » (1)(C) 〚 to (V) buy (O) « some particular English book » 〛 and (2)(C) 〚 to (V) translate (O) « (w)each and every sentence (in < it >) » (on < your notebook >) 〛 } > (V) are (C) 〚 (id)one of < the worst enemies { of yours } (in < your (id)road to < intelligence > >) > 〛. (S) < They > (just) (V) want (O) « you » (C) 〚 to (V) be (C) 〚 an { unthinking } slave 〛 〛. (If (S) < you > (aV) can (V) stand (O) « ‡(V) being‡ (C) 〚 a slave 〛 »), (just) (V) do (as (S) < they > (V) tell (O) « you »); (otherwise), (V) think (wisely) and (id)(V) see through < the shallow intentions of < such silly (id)bullies of < teachers > > > (to (V) avoid (O) « (id)‡(V) falling‡ (C) 〚 a victim to < their whims > 〛 »).

((id)Sad to (V) say), (S) < ˆsoˆ many Japanese students > ＼ (id)(aV) are (V) imprisoned in ／ < ◎schools { [(S) < which > (V) are] (C) 〚 (id)teeming with < ◎teachers { †(V) wanting†(= (S) < who > (V) want) (O) « students » (C) 〚 to (*)(V) be (1)(C) 〚 meek slaves 〛, not (2)(C) 〚 { thinking } intelligentsia 〛 〛 } > } 〛 >, ˆthatˆ (S) < this author > (id)has to (V) stress 〖 (id)once again 〗 (O) « ◎the need { ˆforˆ (S) < you > ˆtoˆ (id)(V) make (O) « wise selection » ˆbetweenˆ < ◎(O) « { what } English sentence » { (S) < you > (id)have to (consciously) (V) translate } > ˆandˆ < (O) « what » (S) < you > (*)(aV) can (1)(just) (V) interpret and (2)(id)(aV) let (C) 〚 (V) go 〛 > } ».

(S) < Some students > (aV) might (V) think (O) « [that] (S) < the same advice > (aV) should ＼ (aV) be (V) given ／ to < their teachers > ((id)as well) », but (S) < this author > (aV) would not (V) do (O) « that » (because (S) < he > (V) knows 〖 too well 〗 (O) « [that] (S) < { (simply) inferior } teachers > (id)(V) have (O) « no other way » than to (id)(V) drown out (O) « the doubts of < students > » (with ◎< (*){ endless } (1)voices, (2)orders and (3)homework { [(S) < which > ＼ (aV) are]] (id)(V) pressed upon ／ < them > (with < authority >) } >) »). (If (S) < you > (id)(V) happen to (V) find (O) « yourself » (C) 『 (id)under the curse of < such adverse teachers > 』), (V) be (C) 『 wise ^enough^ (^not to^ (V) invite (O) « ◎their wrath ») 【 ((S) < which > (aV) can (V) be (C) 『 (quite) nasty 』 (for ‡(V) being‡(= *because (S) < it > (aV) is)* (id)(V) empowered with < authority >)) 】 / while †(V) being†(= *(S) < you > (aV) should (V) be)* (C) 『 ((1)secretly) and ((2)wisely) (*)selective (in (1)< ◎{ what } tasks { to (V) perform } > and (2)◎< { what } orders { to (V) ignore } >) 』 』.

- (When *[(S) < you >* ＼ *^(aV) are^]]* ^(V) tempted to^ ／ (anatomically) (V) interpret), ^(1)(V) illustrate^ (O) « a sentence » ^with^ < anatomical signs > and (2)^(V) try^(O) « ‡(V) translat^ing^‡ (O) « it » (in < your head >) »; (otherwise), (just) (1)(V) look and (2)(V) see (O) « the meaning » (*)(without ‡(V) translating‡) -

(S) < The act of < ‡(V) writing‡ > > (V) is (C) 『 final 』: (once (S) < you > (V) write (O) « something », (^whether^ ((1)in < your notebook >) ^or^ ((2)on < (w)the NET >))), (*)(S) < ◎the words { (O) « *[which]* » (S) < you > (id)(V) gave out } > (1)(V) start (O) « (id)‡(V) standing‡ (on < their own feet >) » and (2)(*)(V) deny (1)(O) « correction » or (2)(O) « deletion » (*)(afterwards). (S) < That > (V) is (C) 『 *[the reason]* why (S) < you > (id)have to (V) be (C) 『 (very) careful (in < your ^distinction^ ^between^ (1)< (O) « what » (S) < you > (^only^) (V) think (^in^ < your head >) > ^and^ (2)< (O) « what » (S) < you > (actually) (V) express ((*)in < (1)voice > or < (2)letters >) > >) 』 』.

(O) « (O) « What » (S) < you > (id)don't have to (V) write — ◎things { *[(S) < which > (*)(V) are]* (1)(C) 『 (too) easy (for < yourself >) 』 or (2)(C) 『 (too much) (id)talked about (by < others >) 』 } — » (just) (aV) don't (V) write / and ^(V) remind^ (O) « yourself » ^of^ < their commonness >. (S) < ‡(V) Being‡ (C) 『 common 』 > (often) (V) means (O) « (*)‡(V) being‡ (1)(C) 『 popular 』 and (2)(C) 『 (commercially) valuable 』 (*)(on < (w)the NET >) », but (in < the study of < English > >), (S) < ‡(V) being‡ (C) 『 common 』 (for < you >) > ^(V) translates^ (straight) ^into^ < ‡(V) being‡ (C) 『 (id)unworthy of < translation > 』 >: ◎(S) < you > (aV) can (V) interpret (O) « them » (without < (id)translation into < your (w)native language > >), { (S) < which > (V) means (O) « *[that]* (S) < you > ↑ (aV) have (already) (V) mastered ↑ (O) « them » ([in] ◎the same way { as (S) < (w)native speakers > ↑ (aV) have (V) mastered ↑ (O) « them » }) » }. (S) < ◎The only time { [that] (S) < you > (id)have to (V) translate (O) « them » } > (V) is (C) 『 *[◎the time]* { when (S) < (1)teachers or (2)exams > (V) ask (O) « you » (C) 『 to ^(V) translate^ (O) « them » (^into^ Japanese) 』 (to (V) prove (O) « [that] (S) < you > ↑ (aV) have (really) (V) mastered ↑ (O) « them » ») } 』. (C) 『 ^The^ more ^proficient^ 』 (S) < you > (V) become (^in^ < English >), (^the^ less) (S) < you > (id)(V) need (*)to (1)(V) illustrate or (2)(V) interpret, 【 (id)let alone (3)(V) translate 】 (*)(O) « a sentence », ／ for (S) < it > ＼ (aV) is (V) understood ／ (◎(id)*[at]* the moment { *[that]* (*)(S) < you > (1)(V) see or (2)(V) hear (*)(O) « it » }). (S) < Your ultimate goal > (V) is (C) 『 to (V) reach (O) « ◎a point { [where] (S) < you > (V) need (O) « no conscious efforts » ((*)in (1)< interpretation > or (2)< translation >) ((id)in order to (V) understand (O) « English ») } » 』.

- (S) < (id)Too much of < something > > (V) is (C) 『 worse than < nothing > 』 -

(S) < Some teachers > (aV) may (still) (id)(V) insist upon < ‡(V) having‡ (O) « students » (C) 『 (V) make (O) « translations of < (O) « whatever » (S) < they > (V) see > » 』 >, ((id)on the { supposed } ◎ground { that (S) < students > (aV) cannot (id)(V) improve upon < their (id)skill in < translation > > (without < (actually) (id)(V) writing down (O) « Japanese sentences » >) }). (S) < It > (aV) may (V) sound (C) 『 reassuring 』, but (S) < the argument > (V) is (C) 『 (practically) powerless 』. (When *[(S) < they > ＼ ^(aV) are^]]* ^(V) forced to^ ／ (V) translate (O) « sentence after < sentence > »), (S) < students > (id)(V) start to (V) stop (O) « (id)‡(V) paying‡ (O) « attention » (*)to (1)< the meaning of < each sentence > >, (2)< its (id)relation with < other sentences > > and (3)< its relative weight (in < the whole context >) > »; (S) < the task of < ‡(V) making‡ (O) « translations » > > (V) becomes (C) 『 (w)an end ((id)in itself) 』 and (S) < everything { else } > ＼ (id)(V) gets (C) 『 lost 』 ／ (until (S) < the students > (V) finish (O) « ‡(V) translating‡ (O) « them » (all) »). (S) < (Too) many Japanese students > ^(V) spend^ (O) « (*)too much (1)time and (2)effort » (^on^ < lessons of < English > >) 【 (completely) (id)in vain 】 , (mainly) because (1)(S) < they > (V) are 【 (or (2)(S) < their teachers > (V) are) 】 (*)(C) 『 (totally) indiscriminate (in < their blind (id)passion for < translation > >) 』.

(S) < The act of < ‡(V) writing‡ (with < a pen >) (on < paper >) > > (V) takes (O) « (*)^so^ much (1)time and (2)physical effort » ^that^ (S) < it > (aV) will (actually) (V) spoil (O) « linguistic studies ». (S) < ‡(V) Writing‡ (too much) > (id)never (V) fails to (V) make (O) « your handwriting » (C) 『 dirty 』, (never (id)†(V) leading† to(= *(S)* < *which* > *never (V) leads to*) < better penmanship >). (S) < (id)‡(V) Writing‡ down (O) « (id)a { particular } version of < translation > » > (aV) will ^(V) prevent^ (O) « you » ^from^ < (id)‡(V) thinking‡ about < any other (id)alternative to < ◎the "final manuscript" { [(O) « which »] (S) < ^it^ > (V) took (O) « you » (O) « so much trouble » ^to^ (V) write (with < your own hand >) } > > >. And, (when (S) < you > (id)(V) are (finally) (C) 『 ^through^ < ‡(V) writ^ing^‡ ◎so many Japanese sentences { *[(S)* < *which* > ＼ *(aV) are]]* (V) translated ／ (from < English >) } > 』), (S) < you > (aV) must (V) heave (O) « a heavy sigh of < ◎contentment { that (S) < you > ↑ (aV) have (V) achieved ↑ (O) « something { great } » > } »... 【 (actually) (id)to no purpose, 【 unfortunately 】 】 . ^Never^ (V) be (C) 『 such a diligent fool 』, ^but^ (id)(V) aspire to (V) be ◎(C) 『 an intelligent idler 』, { (S) < who > (id)(V) makes (O) « much more » (1)of (1)(anatomically) ‡(V) illustrating‡ and (2)‡(V) reading‡ (aloud) (*)(O) « the original English sentences » than (2)of < (id)‡(V) writing‡ down (O) « { quick-and-dirty } Japanese translations » 【 (only) (id)to your { empty } satisfaction 】 > }.

- (S) < ‡Writing‡ > (V) is (C) 『 ^one thing^ 』, (S) < ‡typing‡ > (V) is (C) 『 (quite) ^another^ 』 -

(S) < The { only } (id)exception to < ◎the principle { *[(S)* < *which* > ＼ *(aV) was]]* (V) stated ／ (above) } > > (V) is (C) 『 *[◎the time]* { when (S) < you > (1)"(V) type" 【

(id)instead of (2)"‡(V) writing‡" 】 (*)(O) « your translation » } 』. (S) < ‡(V) Making‡ (O) « your notebook » (C) 『 dirty 』 (by < your handwriting >) > (aV) will (id)(*)(V) do (O) « you » more (1)(O) « { linguistic } harm » than (2)(O) « good »; (*)(S) < ‡(V) making‡ (O) « your fingers » (C) 『 (rhythmically) busy *[in]* < (id)(V) typing in (O) « letter after < letter > » > (from < the keyboard of < your computer > >) 』 > (1)(hardly) (V) tortures (O) « you » (physically) (*)(†(V) taking†*(= because (S) < it > (V) takes)* (1)(O) « (far) less time » and (2)(O) « (almost) no conscious effort ((id)on the part of < your fingers >) ») and (2)(id)never (V) fails to (V) advance ◎(O) « your typing skill », { (S) < which > (V) is (C) 『 a great asset 』 (for < anyone (in ◎a society { where (S) < (w)computer literacy > (V) talks (so much) }) >) }.

((id)But then again), (S) < indiscriminate translation practice (on < the keyboard >) > (aV) will (merely) (V) benefit (O) « you » (by < ‡^(V) making^‡ (O) « a better typist » (^of^ < you >) >); (aV) don't (V) expect (O) « it » (C) 『 to (V) make (O) « you » (C) 『 a better translator 』 』.

- (S) < The authentic translation > (V) is (C) 『 (*)an act (1)of < creation >, not (2)of < transplantation > 』 -

(S) < All good translators > (V) are (C) 『 excellent ^choosers^ ^between^ (1)◎sentences { *[(S) < which > (V) are]* (C) 『 (well) { ^worth^ } (O) « translat^ing^ » 』 } ^and^ (2)◎those { (S) < which > (*)(V) merit (1)(O) « (only) interpretation » and (2)(O) « no translation » } 』. And (*)(S) < they > (rarely) (1)(id)(V) write down or (2)(id)(V) type in (*)(O) « the translated sentences » (except when *[(S) < they > ＼ (aV) are]]* (V) required to ／ (V) do (so) 【 ((1)for < ‡(V) getting‡ (O) « marks » (in < exams >) > or (2)(for (id)‡(V) making‡ (O) « money » (as < translators >))) 】). (When (S) < they > (V) detect (O) « ◎a sentence { *[(S) < which > (V) is]* (C) 『 (id)worthy of < translation > 』 } »,) (first) (*)(S) < they > (1)(V) make (O) « anatomical interpretation (of < it >) » and (2)(V) grasp (O) « the meaning », (and then) (3)(V) make (O) « Japanese sentences (of < ◎the meaning { (O) « *[which]* » (S) < they > (V) have (in < their mind >) } >) ». (V) Note (O) « [that] (S) < they > (aV) do ^not^ (V) make (O) « a Japanese translation (of < the original English sentence >) », ^but^ (S) < they > (V) create (O) « ◎a (wholly) new Japanese sentence { *[(S) < which > (V) is]* (id)(C) 〖 suitable for < ◎the idea (1){ (O) « *[which]* » (S) < they > (V) have (in < their head >) } (2){ *[(S) < that > ＼ (aV) is]]* (V) inspired ／ by < the original English sentence > } } > 〗 » ». (S) < They > | (*)(aV) are (1)(V) creating (id)rather than (2)(V) translating | (*)(O) « sentences ». (S) < This creative (id)type of < ‡translating‡ skill > > (aV) will (^only^) (V) develop (^if^ (S) < you > (id)(V) stick to < ◎two principles >); (W)namely,

(1){ that (S) < you > (aV) must (V) grasp (O) « the meaning of < English sentences > » (1)((id)by way of < anatomical interpretation >), not (2)(through < Japanese translation >) }

and

(2){ that (S) < you > (aV) will (always) (V) keep (O) « (id)‡(V) thinking‡ about < ◎various ways { (in < which >) to (V) express (O) « the meaning of < ◎(W)any given English { (O) « *[that]* » (S) < you > (id)(V) happen to (V) meet } > » } > » (without < (id)‡(V) holding‡ on to < (id)any { particular } version of < Japanese translation > > > ((id)as though (S) < it > (V) were (C) 〖 the only authoritative one 〗)) }.

(^For^ this ^purpose^), (S) < { translated } sentences (in < Japanese >) > (aV) should ＼ (aV) be (*)(V) inscribed ／ (1)in < your head >, not (2)in < your notebooks >. (Once (S) < you > (id)(V) write down (O) « some translation »), (S) < you > (id)(V) are (C) 〖 prone to ＼ (aV) be (V) bound ／ by ◎< (id)that { particular } version of < translation > > 〗, { (S) < which > (aV) will ^(V) hinder^ (O) « you » ^from^ < (id)‡(V) hitting‡ upon < (1){ any other } 【 ((2)(possibly) { better }) 】 (*)translation > > }. (S) < ◎Any particular answer { *[(S) < which > ＼ (aV) is]]* (id)(V) written in ／ } > (aV) will ^(V) stop^ (O) « you » ^from^ < ‡(V) thinking‡ (any more) >. (S) < The only purpose of < ‡(V) writing‡ (O) « an answer » > > (V) is (C) 〖 to (id)(V) check to*(= and)* (V) see ◎(O) « if (S) < you > (id)(V) happen to (V) be (C) 〖 correct 〗 (at ◎the { very } moment { [that

] (S) < you > (id)(V) hit upon < the answer > }) » 』, { (S) < which >, 【 naturally 】, (V) is (C) 『 (w)none of your business 』 (afterwards) }. (aV) Don't (V) make (O) « (*){ your } (1)notebooks or (2)textbooks » (C) 『 dirty (with < such personal memoirs >) 』, / unless (S) < ˆitˆ > (V) is (C) 『 your main business 』 ˆtoˆ (V) cherish (O) « nostalgic memories of < your past struggle > » (many years later), / when(= *and then*) (S) < you > (id)(V) are (more) (C) 『 likely to ↑ (aV) have (V) failed ↑ in < ◎your original desire { to (V) master (O) « English » } > 』 than (if (S) < you > (id)(aV) had (V) made (O) « much less » of < such (memorably) wasteful efforts >).

((id)In summary), (1)(S) < interpretation > and (2)(S) < translation > (*)(V) are (C) 『 ◎(w)two different things 』, { (in < which >) (S) < the former > (V) is (C) 『 much more important 』 than (S) < the latter > }. (S) < ◎ˆThatˆ (id)kind of < students > ˆ(S) < who >ˆ (id)(V) find (O) « satisfaction » in ‡(V) making‡ (O) « (id)heaps of < translations > » > (id)(V) are (quite) (C) 『 likely to (V) fail (in < ◎their efforts { to (V) master (O) « English » } >) 』. (If (S) < you > (V) have (O) « ◎time { ˆenoughˆ (ˆtoˆ (id)(V) write down (O) « English-to-Japanese translations ») } »), (id)(V) make (O) « { (far) better } use » of < it > (by < (1)(repeatedly) ‡(V) reciting‡ and (2)‡(V) inscribing‡ 【 in < your mind > 】 (*)(O) « ◎the English sentences { (O) « *[which]* » (S) < you > (V) find (C) 『 { ˆworthˆ } (O) « translatˆingˆ » 』 } » >). ˆ(S) < It > (V) isˆ (1)(C) 『 the accumulated memories of < English > (in < your head >) 』, not (2)(C) 『 the (id)mountains of < ◎dirty notebooks { (O) « *[which]* » (S) < you > (painstakingly) (V) produced } > 』, ˆ(S) < that >ˆ (aV) will ˆ(V) enableˆ (O) « you » (C) 『 ˆtoˆ (V) command (O) « English » ((id)in the end) 』. Never (id)(V) indulge in < ◎disoriented diligence >, { (S) < which > (V) is (C) 『 (*)the (1){ worst } (2){ suicidal } (*)cause of < linguistic impasse > 』 }.

- (S) < The (id)delight in (id)‡(V) getting‡ over < the boundary of < (w)word-for-word translation > > (by < ‡(w)paraphrasing‡ >) >... (aV) ought not to ＼ (aV) be (V) enjoyed ／ (too much) -

(S) < (id)One of < ◎the questions { (O) « *[which]* » (S) < many Japanese (w)college-bound students > (V) have } (regarding < the ways of < translation > >) > > (V) is (C) 『 ◎"(S) < Which > (V) is (C) 『 better 』, (1)'直訳(CHOKUYAKU: (w)a literal translation)' or (2)'意訳(IYAKU: (w)a paraphrase)'" 』, { (to < which >) (S) < the answer > (V) is (C) 『 simple 』: "(O) « (O) « What » (S) < you > (V) find (O) « ^it^ » (C) 『 impossible 』 ^to^ (V) translate ((id)word for word) », (S) < you > (aV) must (w)(V) paraphrase, (otherwise), (id)(V) try to (V) make as (1){ literal } and (2){ meaningful } (*)a translation as (S) < you > (aV) can *[(V) make]* ((id)out of < the original English expression >)" }.

((id)For example), (when (S) < you > (V) see (O) « "an { enticing } woman" »), (S) < you > (aV) should (*)(V) write (1)(O) « "魅力的な女性(MIRYOKUTEKI NA JOSEI)" » ((id)instead of (2)< "イケてる女(IKETERU ONNNA)" >), ((id)in order to (V) avoid (O) « (id)‡(V) making‡ ◎an impression { that (S) < you > (V) escaped into < the vague expression *[of]* "イケてる(IKETERU)" > ((just) because (S) < you > (id)(V) happened to (id)(V) be (C) 『 ignorant of < the exact meaning of < "◎enticing" > { †(V) meaning†(= *(S)* < *which* > *(V) means*) (O) « "attractive, charming, enchanting" » } > 』) } »). (V) Remember (O) « [that] (1)(S) < teachers > and (2)(S) < examiners > (*)(V) are (always) (1)(C) 『 (id)doubtful of < ◎your ability { to (exactly) (V) understand (O) « English » } > 』 and (2)(C) 『 (id)suspicious of < your (id)motive for < (id)‡(V) trying‡ to (id)(V) get away with it (by < equivocation >) > > 』 ». (When (S) < you > ↑ (aV) have (clearly) (V) understood ↑ (O) « something »), (V) make (O) « your wording » (C) 『 as clear as (S) < your head > 』: (when (S) < you > ↑ (aV) haven't *[(clearly) (V) understood]* ↑), (just) (V) equivocate and (V) hope (O) « *[that]* (S) < others > (aV) will (V) misunderstand (O) « you » ((id)for the better) ».

((id)On the other hand), (there) (V) are (S) < ◎many English expressions { (S) < which > (V) defy (O) « { (w)word-for-word } (id)translation into < Japanese > » } >. (S) < ^Such^ ones ^as^ < "(id)Many thanks" > > (1)(aV) should ^not^ ((id)of course) ＼ (aV) be (1)(literally) (id)(V) translated into ／ < "いくつもいくつもありがとう(IKUTSU MO

IKUTSU MO ARIGATOU)" > or (2) ＼ ^(V) rendered^ ／ 【(id)as though *[(S) < it > (V) were]* (C) 『 Chinese 』】 ^into^ < "多謝(TASHA)" > ^but^ (2)(aV) ought to (V) be (C) 『 "ほんと、どうもありがとう(HONTO, DOUMO ARIGATOU)" 』. (Since (S) < it > (V) is (C) 『 { (id)(less than) formal } (as < a way of < ‡(V) expressing‡ (O) « gratitude » > >) 』,) (S) < it > (aV) must not ＼ (aV) be (V) rendered ／ (too courteously) (like < "幾重にも御礼申し上げます(IKUE NIMO ONREI MOUSHIAGEMASU)" >). But (S) < this "(id)Many thanks" > (V) is (C) 『 nothing { difficult } 』, (since ◎the term "thanks" (V) is (C) 『 eloquent (enough) (in < ‡(V) telling‡ (O) « Japanese » (O) « *[that]* (S) < it > (V) is (C) 『 (id)an { emphatic } version of < "(id)Thank you" > 』 » >) 』).

(S) < (S) < What > (definitely) (V) requires (O) « ‡(w)paraphrasing‡ » > (V) is ◎English expressions { (for < which >) (*)(S) < suitable Japanese > (1)(aV) do (V) exist but (2)(aV) will never (id)(V) come out of < literal ‡translating‡ efforts > }. (V) Take (O) « a glimpse at < the following English dialogues > » (to (V) detect ◎expressions { *[(S) < which > ＼ ^are^] never ^to^ (aV) be (literally) (V) translated ／* }) / and (id)(V) see (O) « if (S) < you > (aV) can (instantly) (id)(V) hit upon < their Japanese equivalents > »:

*(FATHER)"Hey, son, (S) < you > (aV) must (V) study (as (hard) as (S) < you > (aV) can) (while [(S) < you > (V) are] (C) 『 a student 』)." –
(MOTHER)"(V) Look (O) « (S) < who > | (aV) 's (V) talking | »!"

*(A FOREIGNER)"(id)(S) < I > (V) wonder < why (S) < the Japanese > (V) are (C) 『 (so) (laughably) (id)inept at < ‡(V) speaking‡ (O) « English » > 』 >... *[(S) < I > (id)mean to ^(V) give^]* ^No offense^." –
(A JAPANESE)"None*(= No ^offense^) ＼ [(aV) was]* ^(V) taken^ *[by < me > ^at^ < your comment >] ／* ."

*(MAN A)"(S) < I > (V) heard (O) « *[that]* (S) < Jack > (id)(V) had (O) « a crush » on < Betty > »." –
(MAN B)"(id)^(V) Speak^ of < the devil >...*[^and^ (S) < he > (aV) will (V) appear]* "

*(THE COMMANDER)"(There) (aV) will (V) be (S) < no attack (from < the enemy >) > (in < this rough weather >)." –
(A WARRIOR)"(id)With < all due respect >, sir, (S) < I > (V) believe (O) « *[that]* (S) < we > (aV) must (V) be (C)『 more careful 』»."

(WIFE)"[(aV) Does (S) < it > (V) tell (O) « us » to]* (V) Take (O) « the highway »? Hey, (S) < this nav system > (id)(V) has (O) « no idea » *[about]* < (C)『 how congested 』(S) < it > (aV) can (V) be ((id)at this time of day) >! (S) < Bypath > (V) is (C)『 ((id)by far) the fastest way 』, 【 (id)(C) « what » (aV) do (S) < you > (V) say *[to < my plan >]* ? 】" – (HUSBAND)"(S) < You > (V) are (C)『 the teacher 』."

*(WIFE)"(S) < ^It^ > (V) seems *[^that^]* (S) < we > ↑ (aV) 've ＼ (id)(V) got (C)『 lost 』／ ↑ . (S) < The nav map > (V) says (O) « *[that]* (S) < we > (V) are ((w)in the middle of nowhere) ». (S) < I > (V) believe (O) « *[that]* (S) < we > (id)have to (id)(V) go back (◎the way { (*[in < which >]*) (S) < we > (V) came (here) }) ». (aV) Do (S) < you > (id)(V) have (O) « any { better } idea » *[than (S) < mine >]* ?" –
(HUSBAND)"(S) < Your guess > (V) is (C)『 as good as (S) < mine > 』."

(S) < The following > (V) are (C)『 the (id)answers to < (S) < { what } expressions > (*)(V) require (1)(O) « ‡(w)(V) paraphrasing‡ » ((id)instead of (2)(O) « ◎literal translations », { (S) < which > (V) sound (C)『 (totally) absurd 』(in < those contexts >) } > 』):

*"(V) Look (O) « (S) < who > | (aV) 's (V) talking | »!:あらまぁ、よく言うわねぇ、自分の子供時代は棚上げにして・・・" ng.~~誰が喋っているのか見てごらんなさい~~

*"(S) < No (id)offense [against < you > > ＼ (aV) is (V) intended ／ by < my comment >].:気い悪くしないでね" ng.~~これは攻撃ではない~~ – "(S) < None(=^No offense^) > ＼ [(aV) was] ^(V) taken^ ／ [by < me > (^at^ < your comment >)].:べつに気にしてないさ" ng.~~何も取られたものはない~~

*"(id)^(V) Speak^ of < the devil > [^and^ (S) < he > (aV) will (V) appear]...:おやおゃ、噂をすれば影、ご当人がおいでなすったよ" ng.~~悪魔の話をしなさい~~

*"(id)With < all due respect >:お言葉を返すようですが" ng.~~十分な敬意の全てを伴いつつ~~

*"(S) < You > (V) are (C)『 the teacher 』.:わかったよ、君の言う通りにするよ" ng.~~あなたは先生です~~

*"(S) < Your guess > (V) is (C)『 as good as (S) < mine > 』.:俺に聞かれてもわかるもんか" ng.~~あなたの推量は私の推量と同じぐらい正しい~~

(S) < (S) < What > (V) is (C)『 (id)troublesome with < the { above-mentioned } expressions > 』> (V) is (C)『 [that] (there) (id)(V) seems to (V) be (S) < ◎nothing { (id)out of the ordinary (about < them >) } >, but (when *[(S) < they > ＼ (aV) are]]* (literally) (V) translated ／), (S) < they > (aV) will (V) fail (O) « you » (miserably) 』. (S) < ◎A sentence { like < "(S) < Jack > (id)(V) had (O) « a crush » on < Betty >" > } > (V) is (C)『 ◎impossible { to (V) translate } 』(until (S) < one > ↑ (aV) has (V) consulted ↑ (O) « a dictionary » (to ^(V) confirm^ (O) « the meaning of < the (w)idiom "to (id)have a crush on someone" > » (^as^ < "to (id)(V) fall (desperately) in love with < someone >) 【 ((often) †(V) meaning†*(= (S) < which > (often) (V) means)* (O) « ◎a (w)one-sided love { (id) | (V) ending | up*(= (S) < which > (V) ends up)* (C)『 broken-hearted 』} ») 】 ") >). (S) < Such (apparently) strange (id)combination of < words > > (V) are (C)『 all ^the^ less troublesome 』(^for^ ‡(V) looking‡ (C)『 suspicious 』): (S) < (id)none but < the novice > > (aV) will (id)(*)(V) fail (1)to (V) detect (O) « the (w)idiom (inside) » and (2)to (id)(V) come up with < the correct translation > ((id)with the help of < a dictionary >). (S) < ^It^ > (V) takes (O) « (id)nothing but < diligence > (in < ‡(V) consulting‡ (O) « a dictionary » >) » ^to^ (id)(V) deal with < such (obviously) (w)idiomatic expressions >, ／ while (S) < ^it^ > (V) takes (O) « much more sensitivity » (*)^to^ (1)(V) see (O) « (id)something strange with < ◎{ (seemingly) plain } expressions { like < "You are the teacher" > } > » and (2)(id)(V) hit upon < ◎suitable Japanese expressions { (S) < which > (*)(V) are (1)(C)『 (totally) different (in < form >) 』but (2)(C)『 similar (in < meaning >) 』} >.

(Here) (V) is (S) < a warning > (to < Japanese learners of < English > >) (

regarding < ^such^ expressions (*)^as^ (1)< "You're the teacher" > or (2)< "Look who's talking" > >): (*)never (-)(id)(V) take (O) « pride » in < your knowledge of < them > > or (2)(id)(V) try to (V) employ (O) « those expressions » (to (V) prove (O) « your (id)superiority to < ◎^those^ { ^(S) < who >^ (id)(V) happen to (V) be (id)ignorant of < them > } > »). (S) < (id)One of < (*)the most (1){ laughable } 〖 ((indeed), (2){ abominable }!) 〗 (*)propensities of < ◎the Japanese { [(S) < who > (V) are] (C) 『 (actually) illiterate (in < English language >) 』 } > > > (V) is (C) 『 to (id)(V) try to (V) look (C) 『 much smarter than (S) < their linguistic ability > (aV) should (V) warrant 』 (by < (id)‡(V) referring‡ to < ◎(*){ foreign } (1)terms and (2)expressions { [(S) < which > (V) are] (supposedly) (C) 『 (id)beyond comprehension of < other Japanese > 』 } > >) 』. ((id)Rather than (id)(V) try to (V) increase (O) « the (id)store of < such "esoteric" expressions > »), ^(V) make^ (1){ much more painful } yet (2){ fruitful } ^◎efforts { to^ (id)(V) acquaint (O) « yourself » with < the usage of < (w)prepositions > > ((id)by way of < ‡(V) enriching‡ (O) « "normal" (id)stocks of < (*){ English } (1)(w)idioms and (2)(w)collocations > » >) }; ＼ (aV) be (S) < ^it^ > (also) (V) remembered(= *(aV) let (O) « it » (aV) be (also) (V) remembered*) ／ ^that^ (S) < you > (aV) can't (id)(V) hope to (V) be (C) 『 wiser 』 (by < (id)‡(V) making‡ (O) « fools » of < others > >).

(Well), (w)(S) < that >(V) 's (C) 『 about < it > 』. (id)(V) Stick to < (w)literal translation > (whenever (S) < you > (aV) can). (Although (S) < (w)‡(V) paraphrasing‡ > (V) looks (C) 『 enticing 』 (to < ◎^those^ { ^(S) < who >^ (id)(V) want to (V) look (C) 『 smart 』 } >)), (S) < they >(aV) 'll (just) ^(V) make^ (O) « smart ^asses^ » (^of^ ^< themselves >^) (by < the abuse of < it > >).

15.Input (before < output >)

– 英借文:EI"SHAKU"BUN ((id)rather than < 英作文:EI"SAKU"BUN >);

English recitation ((id)rather than < J-to-E translation >)

- (S) < Good output > (V) is (^only^) (C) 『 possible 』 (^through^ (*){ considerable } (1)amount and (2)quality (*)of < input >) -

(S) < (w)The Internet > ↑ (aV) has (id)(V) brought about ↑ (O) « "information explosion" ». (Until < the middle of < the 1990s > >), (S) < ◎the detestable flow of < worthless information > { †(V) prevailing†(= (S) < *which* > (V) *prevailed*) (in < the world >) (through < (w)mass media >) } > ↑ (aV) had ＼ (aV) been (id)(V) lamented upon ／ ↑ (with < a (1){ disdainful } 〖 though (2){ manageable } 〗 (*)phrase [of] "(id)floods of < information >" >). ((id)Now that (S) < computer technology > ↑ (aV) has (V) made ↑ (O) « ^it^ » (C) 『 possible 』 ^for^ (S) < ◎everyone { with < (id)access to < (w)the Internet > > } > ^to^ (id)(V) play (O) « the role » of < "personal media" >), (S) < the amount of < ◎information { †(V) drowning†(= (S) < *which* > (V) *drowns*) (O) « (w)the Net » } > > ↑ (aV) has (lethally) (V) increased ↑ , ／ while (S) < the overall quality of < ◎info { *[(S) < which > ＼ (aV) is]]* (thus) (id)(V) thrust upon ／ < mankind > } > > ↑ (aV) has (even more murderously) (id)(V) degraded to ↑ < the level of < a global farce > >.

(S) < The most abominable thing (about < (1){ numberless } 〖 (and (2){ worthless }) 〗 (*)"personal" media >) > (V) is (C) 『 ◎the way { (*[in < which >]*) (S) < they > (V) "output" (O) « (O) « whatever » (S) < they > (V) "input" » ((*)without (1)< due process (*)of (1)< consideration > or (2)< accumulation > >, (id)let alone (2)< any (w)added value { (id)of their own } >) } 』. ((id)(Simply) †(V) speaking†), (S) < they > (*)(V) are ◎(1)(C) 『 { mere } echoes of < someone { else } > 』 and (2)(C) 『 harmful noises 』 { to ＼ (aV) be (consciously) (V) avoided ／ (^for^ (S) < intelligent humans > ^to^ (id)(V) filter out (O) « something { (really) important } ») }. (If (S) < the truth > (aV) were (V) told), (S) < such worthless things > (id)(aV) might as well ^not^ (V) exist (^(id)at all^): (S) < they > (V) are (C) 『 (absolutely) (w)no good 』 (except (1)for < the mediocrity's vain self-satisfaction of < ‡(V) making‡ (O) « their presence » (C) 『 felt 』

【((possibly) (to < the world >)!) 】 > > and (2)for (S) < { profit-pursuing } vultures > to (id)(V) take (O) « easy advantage » of < (w)the riffle effect (in < the { echoing } mouths of < such { noisy } { omnipresent } folks > >) > ((id)in order to (V) promote (O) « their sales »)).

(Still), (*)(S) < explosive amount of < { worthless } and { shameless } words > > (1)(aV) do (V) exist and (2)(V) surround (O) « humans » (on < (w)the Net >)... (S) < such > (V) is (C) 『 the reality of < this planet > ((id)at the beginning of < the twenty-first century >) 』. ((id)In order to (V) survive (in < this { (mostly) useless } info-explosion >)), (S) < you > (aV) must (V) avoid (O) « "direct output of < input >" » (^both^ (*)as (1)< a reader > ^and^ (2)< a writer >). (As < a reader >), (S) < you > (aV) should (id)(V) see through < the shallowness of < ◎others { (*)(S) < who > (just) (1)(V) do or (2)(V) say (*)(O) « ◎things { (O) « *[which]* » (S) < they > (V) see (O) « others » (C) 『 (1)(V) do or (2)(V) say 』 } » } > >. (S) < Such worthless echoes > (V) are (C) 『 (quite) ◎easy { to (1)(V) see and (2)(V) avoid } 』 (since (*)(S) < they > (all) (V) look (1)(C) 『 (essentially) the same 』 and (2)(C) 『 no different 』, and (consequently), (3)(C) 『 nothing { worth } 』). (S) < ◎Words { *[(S) < which > (V) are]* (C) 『 (id)worthy to ＼ (aV) be (V) read ／ 』 } > (V) have (O) « ◎their own weight { *[(S) < which > ＼ (aV) is]]* (V) born ／ ((id)in the process of (1)< ‡(V) pondering‡ about < the original input > > and (2)< ‡(V) assimilating‡ (O) « it » to(= *and*) (V) form (O) « a (wholly) new output { (id)of their own } ») > } ». (S) < This added value > (V) is (C) 『 (S) < what > (V) makes (O) « you » (C) 「 a uniquely worthy writer 』 ((id)in { eloquent } contrast to < (id)swarms of < (1){ worthless } echoes and (2)noises > >) 』.

(S) < The { above-mentioned } opinion of < this author > > (id)(V) refers (mainly) to < (1)contents 【 (or (2)lack of contents) 】 (*)of < the output > >, but (S) < the same thing > (aV) can (also) ＼ (aV) be (V) said ／ about < the form of < the output > >: (S) < good output 【 ({ well-written } sentences { (id)of your own }) 】 > (V) is (^only^) (C) 『 possible 』 (^after^ (S) < you > ↑ (aV) have (1)(V) absorbed and (2)(V) assimilated ↑ (*)(O) « (id){ considerable } amount of < good input > 【 (example sentences) 】 »). (S)

< ◎Easy output { [*(S)* < *which* > ＼ *(aV) is*]] (id)(V) given away ／ (as < (*)an (1){ instant }, (2){ (poorly) digested } (*)imitation of < some input > >) } > (*)(V) is (1)(C) 〚 (id)lacking in < beauty (in < shape >) > 〛 (id)as well as (2)(C) 〚 (id)devoid of < (*){ unique } (1)value or (2)personality > 〛.

((id)After all), (S) < people { (id)of { authentic } taste } > (aV) will (simply) (V) ignore (O) « (linguistically) distasteful sentences », ((C) 〚 (*)however (1){ unique } or (2){ charming } 〛 (S) < their authors > (aV) may (V) believe (O) « themselves » (C) 〚 to (V) be 〛). (S) < (1)Uniqueness or (2)charm > (aV) can (^only^) (id)(V) stand out (^(id)on the basis of^ < good language >). (S) < (id)No amount of < (poorly) written English (on < (w)the Net >) > > (aV) will (V) make (O) « bad English » (C) 〚 any less distasteful 〛. (In < this global explosion of < { less-than-fascinating } English > >), (*)(S) < your ◎chance { to (id)(V) stand out (with < well-written English >) (as (S) < a beautiful swan > ((id)in the midst of < (forever) (w)ugly ducklings >)) } > (1)(V) is (C) 〚 all-time-high (in < the history of < this language > >) 〛 and (2)(aV) will (ever) (V) be (C) 〚 (id)on the rise 〛 (as (S) < noisy echoes > (ever) (V) increase (on < (w)the Net >)). (S) < You > (aV) should ^not only^ (id)(V) try to (V) read (O) « English » ((id)with freedom)^;^ (S) < you > (id)(aV) might as well (id)(V) aspire (*)to (1)(V) speak and (2)(V) write (*)(O) « English » ((id)with ◎finesse { ^enough^ ^for^ (S) < others > ^to^ (id)(V) want to (id)(V) take (O) « notice of < you > » }).

(S) < - EISAKUBUN – English composition (by < Japanese students >) > (aV) must ^not^ ＼ (aV) be (*)(V) made ／ ((1)as < a translation >) ^but^ ((2)as < a rendition >): (V) create (O) « ◎English { (id)of your own } { [*(S)* < *which* > ＼ *(aV) is*]] (V) inspired ／ by < the original Japanese sentences > } » -

((id)As regards < EISAKUBUN(English composition) (by < Japanese learners >) >), (S) < this author > (V) feels (O) « [*that*] (S) < he > (id)(aV) cannot (V) overemphasize (O) « the danger of < ‡(V) jumping‡ to < poor output > (before < ＼ ‡(aV) being‡ (V) enriched ／ with < good input > >) > » ». (S) < The author > ↑ (aV) has (V) said ↑

〖in < the previous section >〗 (O) « that (S) < a good ^translation^ ^from^ < English > ^into^ < Japanese > > ＼ (*)(aV) is ^not^ "^(V) transplanted^ ／ (literally) (^from^ < the original sentence >)" ^but^ ＼ "(V) created ／ ((id)out of < ◎the mind's image of < the translator > { [(S) < which > ＼ (aV) is]] (V) inspired ／ by < the original sentence > } >)" »: (1)(S) < the same > or (2)(S) < (even) more > (*)(aV) can ＼ (aV) be (V) said ／ (about < Japanese-to-English translation >).

(S) < You > (aV) must not (id)(V) try to (V) make (O) « English composition » (◎the way { ([in < which >]) (S) < you > (aV) will (V) make (O) « a model plane » }), ((id)†(V) putting† together (= as (S) < you > (V) put (together)) (O) « ◎small parts { [(S) < which > ＼ (aV) are]] (V) made ／ (to (V) resemble (O) « the original airplane ») » })... (S) < you > (aV) can't (id)(V) hope to (V) fly (that way) (in < the skies of < English > >). (Instead), (S) < you > (*)(aV) should (1)(id)(V) picture (to < yourself >) (O) « < what > (S) < the airplane > (V) is (C) 『 like 』 », ((1)†(V) grasping† and (2)†(V) re-modeling† (= while (S) < you > (V) grasp and (V) re-model) (O) « the essence of < the original > » (in < your mental image >)), (and then) (finally) (2)(V) give (O) « shape » (to < your idea of < the original > >) ((id)in terms of < English >). (S) < You > (aV) must not (simply) ^(V) transplant^ (O) « the original Japanese » ^to^ < { corresponding } terms (in < English >) >. (id)(V) Catch (O) « hold of < the whole idea of < ◎the original Japanese » 〖({ (O) « which » (S) < someone { else } > ↑ (aV) has (V) written ↑ ^for^ (S) < you > ^to^ (V) translate })〗 > >, and (id)(V) try to (V) make (O) « that idea » (C) 『 (id) ＼ (V) known to ／ < others > 』 (in < your own words > (in < English >)), ((id)as if (S) < the idea > (id)(V) sprang up (from < within < yourself > >)).

(^In^ (id)‡(V) try^ing^‡ to (V) perform (O) « ◎that (id)kind of < "creative" J-to-E translation > », { (S) < which > ↑ (aV) has ＼ (aV) been 〖wittedly〗 (V) called ／ ↑ (C) 『 "英借文(EISHAKUBUN: ^borrowed^ expressions ^from^ < English >)" ((id)as opposed to < "英作文(EISAKUBUN: forged English)" >) 』 }), (S) < you > (id)(V) have (O) « need » of < abundant (id)stores of (1)< (*){ English } (1)terms and (2)expressions

>, (id)to (V) say (O) « nothing » of (2)< perfect grammatical knowledge > >. (Without < such good input >), (S) < good output > (V) is (C) 『 impossible 』. (S) < Bad output > (aV) might (V) be (C) 『 (w)better than < none > 』, ((id)to be sure), but why (aV) should (S) < you > (V) rest (C) 『 (id) ＼ (V) contented with ／ < bad output > 』 (when (S) < good output > ＼ (aV) is (V) guaranteed ／ by < (id)a { certain } amount of < (*)(systematically) (1){ accumulated } & (2){ assimilated } (*)input > >)?

- (V) Recite (before *[(S) < you >]* (V) write) -

(S) < The practical advice (for < learners (in < Japan >) >) > (V) is, (C) 『 "while *[(S) < you > (V) are]* (C) 『 a novice 』, (id)(V) make (O) « { ˆnoˆ } attempt at < English composition >, ˆbutˆ (simply) (id)(V) stick to < English recitation >" » 』. (There) (V) are (S) < ˆsoˆ (*){ many } "(1)terms" and "(2)(w)idioms" (in < the world of < English > >) > ˆthatˆ (S) < you > (aV) cannot (V) wait (until (S) < the input > (V) is (C) 『 ripe 』 (within < you >) (regarding < these two realms >)). (S) < (*){ Unknown } (1)words or (2)(w)idiomatic expressions > (aV) can ＼ (aV) be (id)(V) found out ／ ((simply) by < (id)‡(V) looking‡ (O) « them » up (in < the dictionary >) >); (besides), (S) < English language > (V) is ˆsoˆ (C) 『 (id)rich in < synonymous expressions > 』 ˆthatˆ (S) < you > (id)(V) are (C) 『 sure to (id)(V) come up with < some (*){ suitable } (1)terms or (2)(w)idioms > (by < ‡(V) consulting‡ (O) « ◎a good dictionary { with < reasonable { (w)Thesaurus 〖 (lists of < (w)synonyms >) 〗 } assistance > } » >) 』. (S) < ◎The realms { (in < which >) (1)(S) < patience > 〖 (and (2)(S) < perfection >!) 〗 ＼ (*)(aV) is (V) required ／ (until (S) < you > (V) get (C) 『 (sufficiently) (id)rich in < input > 』) } > (*)(V) are (1)(C) 『 "(w)sentence patterns 〖 (SPAT-5) 〗 " 』, (2)(C) 『 "(w)semantic constructions" 』 and (3)(C) 『 "grammar" 』. (S) < (1)Words and (2)(w)idioms > (aV) can ＼ (aV) be (rather awkwardly) (V) used ／ ((*)without (1)< much practical (id)hindrance to < the meaning > > or (2)< serious (id)harm to < your honor > >), but (1)(S) < grammatical errors > and (2)(S) < structural shortcomings > (*)(aV) cannot (V) escape (C) 『 ＼ unpunished ／ 』 (in < the severe eyes of < (w){ self-respecting } citizens of < the { English-speaking } world > > >).

(S) < The desirable (id)kind of < "英借文(borrowed English)" practice > > (aV) should (V) develop (around < ◎some particular "カタ(KATA: form)" { as < a focus of < creative attention > > } >). ((id)In other words), (S) < it > (aV) must (V) function (as < ◎a test { to (V) see (O) « whether (S) < some particular pattern (*)of (1)< "SPAT-5" >, (2)< "(w)semantic construction" > or (3)< "grammar" > > ↑ (aV) has ＼ (aV) been (successfully) (V) mastered ／ ↑ (by < a student >) » } >). (S) < The following > (V) are (C) 『 examples of < such dual function questions of < "EISHAKUBUN" > > 』:

SPAT-5-I:

"あなた、クサイわよ(ANATA, KUSAIWAYO)"

– "汗、そうとう掻いたからなぁ(ASE, SOUTOU KAITA KARANAA)"

"(S) < You > (V) stink."

– "(S) < I > (V) sweated (so much)."

SPAT-5-II & COMPARISON & ELLIPSIS:

"あれ、僕、遅刻した？(ARE, BOKU, CHIKOKU SHITA?)"

– "いいえ、私が5分早かったの(IIE, WATASHI GA GOFUN HAYAKATTA NO)"

"(Well), (V) am (S) < I > (C) 『 late 』?"

– "No, (S) < I > (V) was (C) 『 (five minutes) earlier [than < the appointed time >] 』."

SPAT-5-III:

"イタメシ好き？(ITAMESHI SUKI?)"

– "大好物よ(DAI-KOUBUTSU YO)"

"(aV) Do (S) < you > (V) like (O) « Italian food »?"

– "Yes, (S) < I > (V) love (O) « it » (very much)."

SPAT-5-IV & GRAMMAR(TAG-QUESTION):

"おっと、ピザ食うとオナラが出るなぁ(OTTO, PIZA KUU TO ONARA GA

DERUNAA)"

– "ちょっと、いい加減にしてくれる？(CHOTTO, IIKAGEN NI SHITE KURERU?)"

"Oops! (S) < Pizza > (V) gives (O) « me » (O) « farts »."

– "(id)(V) Give (O) « me » (O) « a break », (id)(aV) will (S) < you > ?"

SPAT-5-V:

"君といると緊張するよ(KIMI TO IRUTO KINCHOU SURUYO)"

– "あなたと一緒だと、私、恥ずかしいわ(ANATA TO ISSHO DATO WATASHI HAZUKASHIIWA)"

"(S) < You > (V) make (O) « me » (C) 『 nervous 』."

– "(S) < You > (V) make (O) « me » (C) 『 ashamed 』."

((1)Fortunately or (2)unfortunately), (there) (V) are (S) < ^so^ many ◎English example sentences { to (id)(V) learn (by heart) (before < ‡(V) conquering‡ the (relatively) limited ^spheres^ 【 ((id)[as] compared (*)to (1)< "words" > and (2)< "(w)idioms" >, 【 (id)that is 】) 】 (*)^of^ (1)< "(w)sentence patterns" >, (2)< "(w)semantic constructions" > and (3)< "grammar" > >) } > ^that^ (S) < novice learners > (aV) will never (id)(V) be (C) 『 in want of < good input > 』 (before (S) < they > (V) are (finally) (C) 『 (id)at liberty to (id)(V) turn out (O) « their own output » 』). (Since (S) < ^such^ input { ^(O) « as »^ (S) < they > (V) find (in < English textbooks >) (^for^ (S) < them > ^to^ (V) master (O) « ◎something { *[(S) < which > (V) is]* (C) 『 (grammatically) important 』 } ») } > (V) are (C) 『 more (id)likely to (V) be (1){ good } (*)English than (2){ bad } 』), (S) < (*){ systematic } (1)accumulation and (2)assimilation (*)of < such good input > > (aV) will (hardly) (id)(V) fail to ^(V) enable^ (O) « them » (C) 『 ^to^ (V) produce (O) « good output » 』... / after < several years of < intensive ‡memorizing‡ process > >.

Never (id)(V) make (O) « haste ». (While [(S) < you > (V) are] (C) 『 in < such an "input" period > 』), (aV) don't (you) (ever) (id)(V) try to (V) say (O) « anything » ("in < your own words >"): (S) < ◎anything { *[(S) < that > \ (aV) is]]* (V) said ／ (in < your own words >) } > (V) are (C) 『 most (id)likely to (V) be (C) 『 ^too^ bad 』 (^to^

(id)(V) make (O) « any sense » (in < English >)) 』. (Instead), (id)(V) try to (V) say (O) « anything » ("in < someone { else }'s words >"): (S) < you > (aV) must (id)(V) attempt (*)to (1)(V) memorize and (exactly) (2)(V) recite (*)(O) « as many good English sentences as possible^ ». (aV) Don't (you) (id)(V) take (O) « it » ((too) easy), for (S) < 100% accuracy (in < ‡(V) reciting‡ (O) « those sentences » >) > ＼ (aV) is (V) required ／ ^for^ (S) < you > ^to^ (id)(V) be (finally) (C) 『 able to (V) produce (O) « good output of < (O) « what » (S) < you > ↑ (aV) have (id)(V) stored up ↑ (in < your memory >) > » (as < the final result of < such intensive input > >) 』. ((id)In the end), (S) < you > (aV) will (id)be able to (V) express (O) « your own idea » (in < ◎"someone { else }'s words" { (S) < which > ↑ (aV) have ＼ (aV) been ^so^ (completely) (V) assimilated ／ ↑ (^as to^ ＼ (aV) be 【 safely 】 (V) called ／ (C) 『 "your own words" 』) } >) — (S) < that >(V) 's (C) 『 the idea of < "英借文(EISHAKUBUN)" { (id)as opposed to < "英作文(EISAKUBUN)", mechanical ^transplant^ of < Japanese terms > ^into^ < English > > } > 』.

- (S) < Incorrect pronunciation > (V) disrupts (O) « your English » -

◎(S) < English > (V) is ◎a language { [(S) < which > ＼ (*)^(aV) is^]] ^(V) meant ／ to^ (1) ＼ (aV) be (V) spoken ／ , not ^to^ (2) ＼ (aV) be (V) read ／ ((id)in silence) }, { (S) < which > ^(V) differentiates^ (O) « it » (drastically) ^from^ < ◎Japanese language { [(S) < which > ＼ ^(aV) is^]] ^(V) composed^ (mostly) ^of^ ／ < "漢字(KANJI: (w)Chinese characters)" > } > }. (S) < A (w)Chinese character > (V) is (C) 『 ◎an ideogram { †(V) signifying†(= (S) < which > (V) signifies) (O) « something » (by < its figure >) } 』, { (S) < the meaning of < which > > (V) is (C) 『 ^so^ clear (to < the eye >) 【 (just like < icons (on < the computer screen >) >) 】 』 ^that^ (S) < Japanese people > (id)(V) are (C) 『 inclined toward < { silent } (1)‡reading‡ 【 ((id)or rather (2)‡viewing‡) 】 (*)of < sentences > (without < ‡(V) reading‡ (aloud) >) > 』 }: (S) < they > (id)(V) tend to (id)(V) depend on < (1){ visual } 【 (id)rather than (2){ audible } 】 (*)(id)clues to < ‡understanding‡ > >. ((id)On the other hand), (S) < English > ＼

(id)(aV) is (V) composed of ／ ◎phonograms { [(S) < *which* > ＼ (aV) *are*]] (V) called ／ (C) 『 "alphabets" 』 } (1){ †(V) meaning†(= (S) < *which* > (V) *mean*) (O) « (id)nothing but < sound > » ((id)in themselves) }, (2){ (S) < each of < which > > (id)has to (id)(V) combine with < some other > ((id)in order to (V) convey (O) « any meaning ») } 【 ((id)except for < ^such^ terms ^as^ (1)< "a = (w)an indefinite article" >, (2)< "I = a (w)singular (w)pronoun (in < (w)the first person >)" >, (3)< "o = an (w)exclamation" > >) 】. (S) < Comprehension (through < silent ‡reading‡ >) > (V) is (also) (C) 『 possible 』 (with < English >), ((id)of course), but (S) < (1)‡memorization‡ and (2)‡appreciation‡ (*)of < English > > (*)(V) is (1)(C) 『 (hardly) possible 』, (2)(C) 『 ((id)at least)imperfect 』, (*)(without < ‡(V) reading‡ (aloud) >).

(S) < (S) < What > (V) is (C) 『 (uniquely) strange (about < Japanese language >) 』 > (V) is (C) 『 its (id)lack of (1)< attention > or (2)< respect > (*)to (1)< spoken sound > or (2)< (*){ traditional } (1)usage and (2)meaning > (*)of < (w)any given term > 』. (There) (V) are (S) < ^so^ many ◎Japanese words { [(S) < *which* > ＼ (aV) *are*]] (V) written ／ in < "(uniquely) strange combination" of < (w)Chinese characters > > } > ^that^ (S) < ^it^ > (V) is (C) 『 (practically) impossible 』 ^to^ (V) (correctly) read (O) « them » (aloud) (unless (S) < you > ^(V) ask^ (O) « ◎someone { (S) < who > (V) uses (O) « them » (eg. "大和") } » ^for^ < the correct pronunciation > (eg. (1)"やまと:YAMATO" or (2)"だいわ:DAIWA")). (S) < The same term > (aV) can ＼ (aV) be (V) pronounced ／ (differently) ((id)as (S) < the case > (aV) may (V) be), and (there) (V) is (S) < (absolutely) no general rule of < their correct pronunciation > >: (S) < that (there) (V) is (S) < no general rule > > (V) is (C) 『 the only (w)golden rule of < Japanese pronunciation > 』. ◎(Since (S) < (id)very few Japanese > (id)(V) pay (O) « homage » to < { "(traditionally) correct" } pronunciations > (eg. "CHOUFUKU" for < "重複" >)), (S) < { "(formerly) incorrect" } ones (eg. "重複" { [(S) < *which* > ＼ (aV) *is*]] (V) read ／ as < "JUUFUKU" > }) > (aV) will (id)(V) come to (V) claim (O) « their place » (in < the { (practically) lawless } world of < Japanese pronunciation > >), { (S) < which > (V) makes (O) « ^it^ » (C) 『 (id)more and more difficult 』 ^for^ (S) < anyone >

^to^ "(correctly) (V) read (aloud)" (O) « Japanese sentences » }. And, (V) remember (O) « – ◎Japanese sentences { [(S) < which > ＼ ^(aV) are^]] ^(V) composed^ (mostly) ^of^ ／ (visually) comprehensible (w)Chinese characters } (V) are (C) 〚 (quite) (id)fit for < silent reading > (without < ‡(V) pronouncing‡ (O) « anything » >) 〛... ((id)as a result), (S) < Japanese learners of < English > >, 【 just like < in < (w)their mother tongue > > 】, (id)(V) make (O) « (^too^) little » of < English pronunciation > (^for^ (S) < them > (1)^to^ (id)be able to (correctly) (V) speak (O) « English », (2)^to^ (V) appreciate (O) « English » (as (S) < they > (V) read (aloud)), and (3)^to^ (V) memorize (O) « English sentences » (as < ◎phonetic entities { [(S) < which > ＼ (aV) are]](V) stored ／ (in < their memory >) ((id)in the form of < { (actually) spoken } language >) } >)) ». ((id)In { logical } consequence), (S) < the Japanese { (id)in general } > (V) are (C) 〚 (lethally) (id)poor at < ‡(V) remembering‡ (O) « English sentences » > 〛, (†(V) meaning†(= (S) < which > (V) means), 【 (id)of course 】, (O) « [that] (S) < they > (aV) can never (id)(V) hope to (V) master (O) « ◎this language », { (S) < which >(= because (S) < it >) ＼ (aV) is (*)(V) made ／ (1)to ＼ (aV) be (V) spoken ／ , not (2)to ＼ (aV) be (V) seen ／ } »).

(w)(aV) Let (O) « ^this^ » (C) 〚 (V) be (C) 〚 a sermon 〛 〛, (Japanese fellows), ^that^ (S) < (silently) (id)‡(V) looking‡ at < English > > (aV) will (id)(V) take (O) « you » (nowhere) – ^(1)(V) read^ (aloud) and ^(2)(V) memorize^ (*)(O) « ^as many^ good English sentences ^as^ (S) < you > (aV) can », ^and^ (S) < ◎the sound of < { living } English > { †(V) reviving†(= (S) < which > (V) revives) (from < your memory >) } > (aV) will (V) guide (O) « you » ((id)in { the right } direction), (†^(V) enabling^†(= (S) < which > (aV) will ^(V) enable^) (O) « you » (C) 〚 ^to^ (V) speak (in < ◎"someone else's words" { (O) « [which] » (S) < you > ↑ (aV) have (securely) (V) made ↑ (C) 〚 "your own" 〛 ((*)through (1)< years of < practice > > and (2)< innumerable recitation >) } >) 〛). (If (S) < you > (still) (id)(V) insist on < English composition ("in < your words >") > ((even) before (S) < you > (V) are (sufficiently) (C) 〚 (id)rich in < mental (id)stores of < good example sentences > > 〛)), (id)(V) do (O) « me » (O) « a favor » and ^(V) try^ (O) «

‡(V) read^ing^‡ (O) « ◎the English { (O) « *[which]* » (S) < you > (V) wrote (in < "your own words" >) } » (aloud) »... *[(aV) do (S) < you > (V) feel (S) < it >]* (V) sounds (C) 〚 good 〛? (w)Congratulations 【 (though (S) < I > (V) doubt (O) « it ») 】 ! *[(aV) Do (S) < you > (V) feel (O) « [that]] (S) < it >]* (V) Sounds (C) 〚 terrible 〛 »? (id)(V) Have (O) « second thoughts » about < (id)‡(V) rushing‡ into < bad output > (before < adequate input >) >. (S) < You > (aV) may ＼ (id)(aV) be (V) allowed to ／ (V) compose (O) « Japanese sentences » (◎any way { *[that]* (S) < you > (V) want } ((id)without regard to < general rules of < correctness (*)in (1)< sound > or (2)< usage > >) >), but (S) < English > (V) is (C) 〚 much more rigid *[than (S) < Japanese >]* 〛 ((id)in { that } regard). (aV) Don't (V) forget (O) « [that] (S) < (id)(w)the test of < good English > > (V) is in < the ‡(V) read^ing^‡ (aloud) > »; (S) < ◎^those^ { ^(S) < who >^ > (aV) won't (even) (id)(V) think about ‡(V) reading‡ (aloud) } (aV) will never (V) pass (O) « any test ». (S) < ◎Good input of < English > { *[(S) < which > ＼ (aV) is]]* (V) kept ／ (C) 〚 alive 〛 (in < your head >) ((*)by (1)< good pronunciation > and (2)< vivid memory >) } > (aV) will (id)never (V) fail to (V) make (O) « you » (C) 〚 a (*){ good } (1)reader/(2)writer/(3)speaker/(4)listener of < English > 〛.

16.(S) < To (V) consult (O) « a portable electric dictionary » >

(V) is (C) 『 ^too^ tentative 』 (^to^ (V) be (C) 『 meaningful 』):

(id)(V) make (O) « { wise } use » of < a { PC-based } electric dictionary >

((id)along with < its ‡consulting‡ log >)

- ^(There) (V) is (S) < { no }^^ *[way of]* < ‡(V) argu^ing^‡ (against < the usefulness of < (1){ electric } 〖 (id)as opposed to (2){ paper } 〗 (*)dictionaries > >) > > -

(S) < This >, 〖 the (1){ first } to (2){ second } (*)decade of < the twenty-first century > 〗 , (V) is (C) 『 ◎(w)a ‡turning‡ point (in < human history >) { where*(= at < which >)* (S) < paper > (id)(V) is (C) 『 about to ＼ (id)(aV) be (V) replaced by ／ < electric (id)means of < record > > 』 } 』. ((id)Regardless of < (S) < what > ＼ (aV) is | (aV) being | (V) said ／ by < ◎people { (id)†(V) sticking† to*(= (S) < who > (V) stick to)* < "traditional" (id)means (*)of (1)< record > and (2)< reference > > } > >), (S) < (1)the { overwhelming } usefulness of < "new" media > 〖 (and (2)(id)consideration for < the { dwindling } resources of < (w)paper pulp > (on < this planet >) >) 〗 > (*)(aV) will (soon) (V) replace (O) « (id)all but < { "(luxuriously) elaborate" } ◎books { (id)such as (1)< photo albums of < famous stars > > or (2)< { (privately) published } memoirs of < rich old folks > > } > ».

(In < Japan >), (there) (still) (V) exists 〖 ((id)and that ((id)in abundance)) 〗 (S) < ◎^that^ (id)kind of < people > { ^(S) < who >^ (id)(V) disagree to < the ^use^ 〖 by < the novice > 〗 ^of^ < electric dictionaries > > } >, but (S) < their argument > (id)(V) seems to (V) be more (1)^(C) 『 sentimental 』 than (2)(C) 『 logical 』, (3)(C) 『 ^too^ personal (^to^ (V) be (C) 『 reasonable 』) 』. (S) < ^It^ > (V) seems [^that^] (S) < they > ↑ (aV) have never (V) had ↑ (O) « the experience of < ‡(V) using‡ (O) « electric (id)versions of < dictionaries > » > » (while *[(S) < they > | (aV) were]]* (V) studying | (O) « English » (as < beginners >)). (S) < Their early memories of < arduous studies > > ＼ (aV) are (inseparably) (id)(V) associated with ／ < ◎the image of < (S) < themselves > (id)‡(V) turning‡ over (O) « the pages of < paper dictionaries > » > >, { (S) < the emotional value of < which > > (id)(V) seems to (V) induce (O) « them » (C) 『 to (id)(V) make (O) « much less » of < the possible merits of < electric dictionaries > > 』 }.

- A (w)human touch and a mechanical dream -

(Since (S) < this author > ↑ (*)(aV) had (1)(V) learnt and (2)(V) mastered ↑ (*)(O) « English » (before < the advent of < ^such^ handy gadgets ^as^ (1)< a pocket electric dictionary > or (2)< a (w)personal computer > > >)), (S) < he > (V) knows (very well) (O) « (*)(O) « what » (1)(S) < a paper dictionary > (V) has and (2)(S) < an electric one > (V) has not » — tactile tangibility.

(S) < One > (*)(aV) can (1)(V) (physically) touch (O) « a paper dictionary », (2)(id)(V) turn over (O) « the pages » and (3)^(V) point^ (O) « a finger » (^at^ ◎the meaning of < a word > { (O) « *[which]* » (S) < one > (V) wants }) and (4)(V) give (O) « a mental shout "(w)Eureka!" » (1)(S) < The relative position of < a certain term (on < a certain page >) > >, (2)(S) < the relative position of < that page (in < the whole dictionary >) > >, (3)(S) < (1)specks or (2)creases (*)(on < a particular page >) >, (4)(S) < (even) the (1)smell or (2)touch (*)of < the paper > >, (all) (*)(V) combine to(= *and*) (V) make (O) « the experience of < (id)‡(V) looking‡ up (O) « a word » (in < a paper dictionary >) > » (C) 〚 (*)(personally) (1)significant and (2)memorable 〛. (S) < ◎Any additional time { (*[that]*) (S) < one > (id)(V) looks up (O) « the same term » } > (aV) will (id)(V) add to < the (strangely) nostalgic emotion (just like < ‡(V) meeting‡ (O) « (*)an (1){ old } (2){ familiar } (*)friend » (in < an (w)alumni association >) >) >. (S) < One > (V) feels (O) « *[that]* (S) < one > ＼ (id)(V) gets (C) 〚 used to ／ < a certain term > 〛 (by < (repeatedly) ‡(V) attending‡ (O) « such "(w)old-pal reunions" » >) ».

(S) < That (id)kind of < feeling >, ◎something (1){ solid } (2){ (directly) †(V) appealing† (*)to(= *(S) < which > (directly) (V) appeals (*)to*) (1)< the physical senses > and (even) (2)< nostalgia > (*)of < the dictionary user > } > (id)(V) is (strangely) (C) 〚 lacking (in < an electric dictionary >) 〛. (S) < ‡(V) Consulting‡ (O) « an electric dictionary » > (V) is (C) 〚 less (*)like (1)< ‡(V) finding‡ (O) « a place » (by < ‡(V) walking‡ (through < a town >) >) > than (2)< (id)‡(V) making‡ (O) « an inquiry » of < a policeman > (about < some address >) (on < a map >) > 〛. (S) < It > (hardly) (V) excites (O) « (1){ physical } 〖 ((id)let alone (2){ emotional }) 〗 (*)^reaction^ » (^from^ <

the inquirer >): (S) < it > (just) (id)(V) talks (coolly) to < the intelligent spheres of < the brains > > (without < any tactile tangibility >).

(S) < You > (aV) can (V) find (O) « a term » ((*)much more (1)easily and (2)quickly) (by < (id)‡(V) typing‡ in (O) « its spelling » (from < the keyboard >) >) than (by < (physically) (id)‡(V) turning‡ over (O) « the paper pages of < a (w)good old bulky dictionary > » >). ([Even] if (S) < you > (aV) can't (V) spell (O) « it » (correctly)), (S) < the powerful search function of < the electric dictionary > > (*)(aV) will (1)(V) suggest (O) « it » and (2)^(V) guide^ (O) « you » ((straight) ^to^ < the correct answer >). (S) < Many electric dictionaries > ＼ (id)(aV) are (V) equipped with ／ < ◎audio function { to (V) show (O) « you » (O) « the correct pronunciation of < a certain word > » (without < (S) < your > ‡(id)‡(V) having‡ to (V) interpret‡ (O) « the intangible phonetic signs » 〖 ((w)Hepburn's Roman Alphabets) 〗 >) } >. (S) < You > (aV) can (V) jump ^from^ < one term > ^to^ < (*)its (1)(w)synonyms or (2)(w)antonyms > (to (V) check (O) « their differences ») (with < a single click >). (*)(S) < All these dream-like capabilities > ＼ (1)(aV) are (V) performed ／ ((id)at your fingertips)!... and(= *and yet*) (2)(V) are (C) 『 (strangely) NOT memorable (like < experiences (in < a dream >) > ((id)due to < (id)lack of < any physical touch > >)) 』. (After (S) < you > (id)(V) wake up), (S) < your dream > ↑ (aV) is (V) gone ↑ and ＼ (C) 『 so(= *(V) gone*) 』 (aV) is ／ (S) < your memory of < it > >. (There) (V) is (S) < ◎nothing { *[(S) < which > ＼ (aV) is]]* (physically) (V) left ／ (of < the dream >) } >... (id)except for < the bed >. (S) < An electric dictionary > (V) is (C) 『 like < ◎a bed { (in < which >) (S) < you > (aV) can (V) have (O) « a dream » } > 』: (S) < a paper dictionary > (V) is ^not^ (1)(C) 『 a bed 』 ^but^ (2)(C) 『 (id)a bunch of < ◎(1)dreams 〖 ((2)nightmares (for < some *[people]* >), (w)maybe) 〗 { *[(S) < which > ＼ (aV) are]]* (physically) (id)(V) left over ／ ^for^ (S) < you > ^to^ (V) revisit (whenever (S) < you > (id)(V) want (*)to (1)(V) touch and (2)(V) feel (*)(O) « it ») } > 』.

- (1)(S) < Reference > and (2)(S) < memorization > (*)(V) are (C) 『 (w)two different things 』-

(S) < The above > (V) is (C) 『 ◎the reason { [why] (S) < many of < the users of < (w)good old paper dictionaries > > > (id)(V) advocate for < the use of < them > > ((id)instead of < their electric counterparts >) } 』. (To (id)(V) sum (O) « it » up), (S) < an electric dictionary > (*)(V) is (1)(C) 『 good 』 ((id)when (S) < it > (V) comes to < (casually) ‡(V) checking‡ (O) « the meaning of < a word > » >) but (2)(C) 『 no good 』 (as < (*)a (1){ constant } and (2){ permanent } (*)◎guide { ˆforˆ (S) < students > ˆtoˆ (id)(V) familiarize (O) « themselves » with < words > } >). (S) < This argument > (aV) may (V) seem (C) 『 reasonable 』 (1)(to < most Japanese >), but not (2)(to < this author >), ／ for (S) < he > (id)(V) knows better than to ˆ(V) confuseˆ (O) « (1)consultation » ˆwithˆ < (2)memorization > (*)of < an English word >.

(S) < Students > (aV) do not (V) memorize (O) « English words » (through < dictionaries >): (S) < they > (V) do (so) (with < much smaller ◎wordbooks, { *[ˆwhetherˆ (S) < they > ＼ (V) are]]* (1)(commercially) published ˆorˆ (2)(personally) hand-written ／ } >). (S) < A dictionary > (V) is (C) 『 ◎a book (1){ for < casual reference > }, not (2){ for < permanent memory > } 』, (just as (S) < (w)a telephone book > (id)(V) is not (C) 『 supposed to ＼ (aV) be (V) remembered ／ 』). (S) < A wordbook > (V) is (C) 『 a list of < ◎things { to (V) remember } >, { *[(S) < which >* ＼ *ˆ(aV) isˆ]]* ˆ(V) meant toˆ ／ (V) be more (1)(C) 『 a (w)mnemonic aid 』 than (2)(C) 『 a (w)reference book 』 } 』. (S) < It > (id)does not have to (V) list (O) « all possible definitions of < a certain term > ». (S) < It > (id)(V) tends to (V) contain (O) « ˆlessˆ information ˆthanˆ (S) < a dictionary > »; ((id)in a way), (O) « the less *[information* » (S) < it > (V) contains, *]* (C) 『 the better 』 *[(S) < it > (V) is]* , ／ for (S) < it > (V) makes (O) « it(= *the wordbook)* » (C) 『 ◎easier { to (V) memorize } 』.

(S) < ˆItˆ > (V) is (therefore) (C) 『 wrong 』 ˆtoˆ (id)(V) argue against < the electric dictionary > (for < its (id)lack of < tactile tangibility > >) — (S) < no serious student > (really) ˆ(V) demandsˆ (O) « it » (ˆofˆ < a dictionary >) 【 (though *[(S) < it > (V) is]* (C) 『 (personally) significant 』 ((id)in retrospect) (years afterwards)) 】. (S) < A dictionary > (id)has only to (V) be (C) 『 a good (w)reference book 』; (S) < it > (id)doesn't have to (V) be (C) 『 ◎a good reminder { (C) 『 as 』 (S) < a wordbook > (id)(V) is (C) 『 supposed to (V) be 』 } 』. (1)(S) < The tactile tangibility > and (2)(S) < the nostalgic feel of < (w)human touch > of < (w)good old paper dictionaries > > (1)(V) are (certainly) (C) 『 good 』 (as < a memento of < studious olden times > >), but (2)(V) are (C) 『 too weak (as < ◎a reason { to (id)(V) advocate against < the use of < { much more efficient } electric dictionaries > > } >) 』.

- (1)^From^ < albums > ^to^ < songs >, (2)^from^ < pages > ^to^ < terms > — (S) < (id)lack of < background > > (V) is (C) 『 the trend (id)of the day 』 -

(S) < The { dwindling } status of < the traditional paper dictionary > > (V) is (C) 『 (id)not unlike < the fate of < (*){ (w)good old } (1)(w)LP records or (2)CDs > (in < the music world >) > 』. (S) < Songs > (aV) used to ＼ (aV) be (V) sold ／ ((id)in ◎a bundle { *[(S) < which > ＼ (aV) was]]* (V) called ／ (C) 『 "◎an album" 』 { (usually) (id)†(V) consisting† of*(= (S) < which > (usually) (V) consisted of)* (1){ ten } to (2){ fourteen } (*)songs } }). (Today), (S) < a song > ＼ (aV) is (V) purchased ／ (on < (w)the Net >) (1)(as < a single commodity >), not (2)(in < albums >). (S) < Such individual purchase of < a particular song > > (V) is (C) 『 not bad 』 ((id)when (S) < it > (V) comes to < ‡(V) consuming‡ (O) < popular songs { by ◎artists { (S) < who > (*)(V) have (1)(O) « ◎(only) a single good song { to (V) offer } » and (2)(O) « nothing { else } » } } » >). ((id)On the other hand), (there) (V) are (S) < ◎songs { (S) < which > (id)have to ＼ (aV) be (V) appreciated ／ (in < the context of < a certain album > >) } >. (S) < "Sgt. Pepper's Lonely Hearts Club Band" (by < the Beatles >) 〖 (1967) 〗 > (id)(*)is (1)to ＼ (aV) be (V) appreciated ／ (as < the ‡opening‡ number of < ◎the album { of < the same title > } > >), (2)not to ＼ (aV) be (id)(V) listened to ／ (as < ◎an individual piece { *[(S) < which > ＼ (aV) is]]* (id)(V) cut out from ／ < the background of < "Sgt. Pepper album" > > } >); (C) 『 so 』 (*)(V) are (1)(S) < "Lucy in the sky with diamonds" > and (2)(S) < "A day in the life" >. (S) < They > (*)(aV) could (1)(V) stand (alone) and

(2)(id)(V) stand out (brightly), but (S) < they > (V) shine (all ^the^ more brilliantly) (^in^ < the ambient atmosphere of < the "Pepper" > >).

(S) < (id)‡(V) Looking‡ up (O) « a word » (in < an electric dictionary >) > (V) is (somewhat) (C) 〚 (id)similar to < ‡(V) purchasing‡ (O) « a single song » (on < (w)the Net >) > 〛: (S) < it > (V) is (C) 〚 ◎a { stand-alone } experience { *[(S) < which > (V) is]* (C) 〚 (totally) (id)devoid (*)of (1)< context > or (2)< ◎ambient atmosphere { *[(S) < which > (V) is]* (id)peculiar (*)to (1)< (id)‡(V) listening‡ to < a whole album > > or (2)< (id)‡(V) turning‡ over (O) « the pages of < a paper dictionary > » > } > 〛 } 〛. (S) < Some people > (aV) will (V) lament (O) « it », but (S) < the trend of < the twenty-first century > > (V) is (C) 〚 (progressively) (*)against (1)< albums > or (2)< paper dictionaries > 〛. (S) < The ^lack^ 〖 in them 〗 ^of^ < contextual meaning > >, (therefore), (id)has to ＼ (aV) be (V) supplemented ／ by < (*){ individual } (1)listeners or (2)learners > (through < some (personally) meaningful efforts >).

- (w)"Relativity" theory of < the dictionary > — (S) < the ◎position of < a term > { (id)relative to < { surrounding } ones > } > (V) gives (O) « it » (O) « a special place (in < one's memory >) »; ^(aV) let^ (O) « a term » (C) 〚 (V) stand alone 〛, ^and^ (S) < it >(aV) 'll (always) (V) be (C) 〚 (*)(strangely) (1)novel and (2)immemorable 〛 -

([To] (V) come to (V) think of < it >), (S) < (*)our (1)memory 〖 (or (even) (2)(w)likes and dislikes) 〗 (*)of < a particular song > > ＼ (id)(aV) is (usually) (V) associated with ／ < ◎some personal circumstances { (in < which >) (S) < we > (V) heard (O) « it » } >. (1)(S) < The "Sgt. Pepper album" > and (2)(S) < the psychedelic atmosphere of < 1967 > > (*)(V) are (C) 〚 the powerful backgrounds for < ◎{ (otherwise) flat } ◎songs 〖 (^in^ this author^'s^ personal ^opinion^) 〗 { (*)like (1)"Fixing a hole" or (2)"Being for the benefit of Mister Kite!" } > 〛. (S) < The experience of (1)< (id)‡(V) listening‡ to < a song > (in < the context of < an album > >) > or (2)< (id)‡(V) looking‡ up (O) « a term » (in < a thick paper dictionary >) > > (V) offers (O) « us » (O) « ◎the background { (against < which >) (S) < (1)the song or (2)the term > (id)(V) stands out (vividly) (in < our memory >) } ».

(S) < ◎(1)A term or (2)a song { [(S) < *which* > ＼ (aV) *is*]] (electrically) (1)(V) consulted or (2)(V) downloaded ／ } > (V) is 【 (id)by default 】 (C) 『 (id)devoid of < that (id)kind of < memorable background > > 』. (Unless (S) < we > (V) give (O) « such backgrounds » (to < ◎(1)songs or (2)terms { (S) < which > (id)(V) tend to (V) stand (alone) ((id)out of context) } >)), (S) < ◎they > (aV) will (V) remain (C) 『 (*)(totally) (1)alone and (2)immemorable 』, { (S) < which > (aV) will ^not^ (V) stay (in < our mind >) (^for long^) }. ((id)In fact), (S) < (id)lots of < ◎songs { [(S) < *which* > ＼ (aV) *were*]] (casually) (V) downloaded ／ > } > ＼ (*)(aV) are (thus) (1)(V) forgotten and (2)(V) left (C) 『 unnoticed 』 ／ (deep inside < the HDD((w)hard disk drive) of < your computer > >). ((id)On the other hand), (S) < ◎a song { [(S) < *which* > ＼ (*)(aV) *is*]] (id)(1)(V) incorporated into ／ < some (personally) created "album" > and (2)(V) played and (3)(V) enjoyed (*)(in < the context of < that custom program { of yours } > >) } > (V) are (C) 『 less (id)likely to ＼ (aV) be (V) forgotten ／ 』.

(S) < The (id)necessity for < such customized ◎(w)play lists > – { (1)official, (2)personal or (3)automatic } – > ↑ (aV) has | (aV) been (V) increasing | ↑ (greatly) ((id)ever since (S) < songs > (id)(V) began to ＼ (aV) be (V) downloaded ／ ((id)one by one ((id)instead of < ＼ ‡(V) being‡ (V) published ／ (in < an album >) >)))). (S) < ◎Music players 【 ([^*whether*^ (S) < *they* > (*)(V) *are*] (1)(C) 『 hardware 』 ^or^ (2)(C) 『 software 』) 】 { without < ◎the ability { to (V) offer (O) « listeners » (O) « (1){ easy } and (2){ fascinating } (*)programs of < downloaded songs > » } > } > (aV) will (V) find (O) « themselves » (C) 『 (id)at a { dire } disadvantage 』. (*)(S) < (w)The test of < a really excellent music storage > > (1)(V) is ^not^ 【 (((id)at least) (2)(aV) will not (V) be) 】 (1)(C) 『 (O) « how many songs » (S) < it > (aV) can (V) hold 』 ^but^ (2)(C) 『 how (S) < it > ^(V) presents^ (O) « the listener » ^with^ < them > ((id)according to < (*)the (1)mood or (2)circumstances (*)of < the moment > >) 』.

(S) < The same > (id)(V) goes for < the electric dictionary >. (S) < (Quickly) ‡(V) showing‡ (O) « the definition of < a term > » ((id)on demand) > (V) is (C) 『 good (

enough) 』 (today), but (^in^ < { ((id)not so) distant } ^future^ >), (S) < it > (aV) will (id)(V) leave (O) « (so) ◎much { to ＼ (aV) be (V) desired ／ } »: (S) < (1){ pre-programmed } and (2){ (personally) customizable } (*)repertoire of (1)< words >, (2)< (w)idioms > or (3)< grammatical information > > (aV) will ＼ (aV) be (V) featured ／ (as < the strong (w)‡selling‡ point of < an electric dictionary > >). (Unfortunately for < English learners { of < today > } >), (however), (S) < ◎electric dictionaries { with < such strong ‡programming‡ features > } > (V) are (C) 『 not (id)in existence 』 (in < the real world >), (nor) (V) is (S) < ^it^ > (C) 『 clear 』 ^whether^ (S) < it > (V) exists (in < the (w)to-do list of < dictionary makers > >).

(S) < (S) < What > (aV) does not (V) exist > (id)has to ＼ (aV) be (V) created ／ ((id)on your own)... but how *[(aV) can (S) < you > (V) create (O) « it »]* ?

- How to (id)(V) make (O) « the best » of < an electric dictionary > -

(S) < ◎The first thing { (O) « *[that]* » (S) < you > (V) need } > (V) is (C) 『 ◎an electric dictionary { (S) < which > (*)(aV) can (1)(V) copy (O) « ◎the (1)terms and (2)definitions { (O) « *[which]* » (S) < you > ↑ (aV) have (V) consulted ↑ } » and (2)(V) paste (O) « them » (onto < a single file >) 〖 ((1)(id)in the form of < "(w)plain text" >, not ((2)in < some ◎specialized formats { *[(S) < which > (V) are]* (C) 『 (id)incompatible with < anything { else } > 』 } >)) 〗 } 』. ((id)In other words), (S) < you > (id)are going to (V) make (O) « "a personal wordbook" of < ◎the words { (O) « *[which]* » (S) < you > (id)(V) looked up (in < the electric dictionary >) } > ». ((id)From { this } standpoint), (S) < most portable electric dictionaries > (V) are (C) 『 (id)out of the question 』, ((id)for lack of < ◎capability { to (V) make (O) « such ‡consulting‡ logs » 〖 ((id)and that in < "◎(w)plain text format" > { (S) < which > (aV) can ＼ (aV) be (V) processed ／ (on < any computer >) }) 〗 } >). (S) < The (1){ simple } 〖 (and (practically) the (2){ single }) 〗 (id)(*)solution to < the problem > > (V) is(C) 『 : (just) (V) forget (O) « your pocket electric dictionary », and (V) consult (O) « a dictionary software (on < your (w)personal computer >) ((id)along (*)with (1)< some (w)editor >

) 〘 (or (2)< (w)word-processor >) 〙 » (to (V) process (O) « a log file ») 』.

(Since (S) < ◎‡consulting‡ logs { [(S) < *which* > ＼ (aV) *are*]] (V) produced ／ by < most electric dictionaries > } > (^only^) (V) show (O) « you » (1)(O) « ^"terms"^ » and (2)(O) « no "definitions" »), (S) < the process of < ‡(V) creating‡ (O) « your own "wordbook" » > > (V) is (rather) (C) 『 (1)rough and (2)arduous 』. (S) < It > (*)(V) is (1)(C) 『 (id)anything but < automatic > 』 and (2)(C) 『 (hardly) systematic 』 〘 ((3)(C) 『 (wildly) random 』, (id)in fact) 〙 but (4)(C) 『 (quite) (fruitfully) personal 』 ((id)in the end). (Once (S) < you > (V) know (O) « its enormous merits »), ^(there) (V) is (S) < no^^ *[way of]* < ‡(V) return^ing^‡ to < a paper dictionary > > >. (V) Follow (O) « ◎the steps { [(S) < *which* > ＼ (aV) *are*]] (V) shown ／ (below) } » (to (id)(V) benefit from < the use of < a (1){ computer-based } 〘 ((id)as opposed to (2){ a portable }) 〙 (*)electric dictionary > >):

(1)(V) Start (O) « (1)an (w)editor 〘 (or (2)a (w)word-processor) 〙 » (on < your computer >) and (V) make (O) « a new file » (in < (w)any given name >) (eg. ◎"engwb001.txt", { (S) < which > (id)(V) stands for < English Wordbook No.1 { with < the (w)extension *[of]* "txt" > } > });

(2)(Whenever (S) < you > (V) meet (O) « ◎a term { [< which >] 〘 (S) < you > (V) believe 〙 (S) < you > (aV) should (id)(V) pay { special } attention to } »), (V) copy (O) « ◎(1)the term and (2)the definition 〘 (or (even) (3)the whole definitions!) 〙 { [(O) « that »] (S) < you > (V) believe (C) 『 to (V) be (C) 『 important 』 』 } », and (V) paste (O) « them » (onto < your personal electric wordbook 〘 (in < the case { above } >, "engwb001.txt") 〙 >);

(3)((id)In order to (V) jump (between < terms >) ((id)by way of < search function of < (*)the (1)(w)editor/(2)(w)word-processor > >)), (aV) don't (id)(V) forget to (V) insert (O) « ◎some { separating } sign » ((id)at the top of ◎< each term > { (O) « *[that]* » (S) < you > ↑ (aV) have (just) (V) pasted ↑ } { (S) < which > NEVER (V) appears (in < the definitions of < any terms > >) (eg. (1)"%%", (2)"^^", (3)"______", etc,etc.) }). (V) Avoid (O) « ‡(V) using‡ (O) « (1)"--" or (2)"■" or (3)"●" or (4)such marks » », /

for (S) < some (w)word-processors 〖 ((id)such as < Microsoft Word >) 〗 > (aV) will (V) do (O) « the kind job of < (automatically) ^‡(V) converting‡^ (O) « them » 〖 (at < their (w)default settings >) 〗 ^into^ (1)< "—" > or (2)< (w)serial numbers (1, 2, 3, 4, ... n) > > », (†(V) making†(= (S) < *which* > (aV) *will* (V) *make*) (O) « them » (C) 〚 (totally) useless (as < { separating } signs >) 〛);

(4)(aV) Don't (V) be (C) 〚 (too much) selective ((*)in < (O) « what » to (V) (1)(V) copy/(2)(V) paste > and (2)< (O) « what » to (V) ignore >) 〛. (If (S) < you > (id)(V) come across < ◎a term { (^with^ < which >) (S) < you > (V) are (C) 〚 (id)not completely ^familiar^ 〛 } >), (just) (id)(V) look (O) « it » up and (V) enter (O) « it » (onto < your personal wordbook >). ([Even] if (S) < a single wordbook > (V) includes (O) « (*)the same (1)term/(2)definition » ((id)more than once)), (just) (V) leave (O) « them » (C) 〚 (id)as (S) < they > (V) are 〛 and never (id)(V) try to (V) delete (O) « them » (to (V) make (O) « the wordbook » (C) 〚 (V) look (C) 〚 (w)neat and clean 〛 〛): (S) < it > (V) is (C) 〚 counter-productive 〛. (S) < Such redundant entries > (V) are (C) 〚 the proof of < (C) 〚 how important 〛 〖 (S) < you > (V) believed 〗 (S) < (*){ those } (1)terms/(2)definitions > (V) were (at < the moment of < the consultation > >) > 〛. (S) < Such { (seemingly) awkward } redundancy > (aV) will (V) make (O) « meaningful "backgrounds" (to < that particular term >) ». (When (later) (*)(S) < you > (1)(id)(V) open up (O) « your wordbook » and (2)(V) find (O) « ◎the term "awkward" » (C) 〚 ＼ (V) entered ／ ((id)over and over [again]) 〛 and (3) ＼ (aV) are (V) faced with ／ < (w)the same old definition > (often enough)), (id)(S) < ◎chances > (V) are *[{ that]*, (S) < you >(aV) 'll never (id)have to (1)(id)(V) look up 〖 ((id)let alone (2)(w)(V) copy and (V) paste) 〗 (O) « ◎the term "awkward" » (again) }. (S) < That >(V) 's (C) 〚 the beauty of < (id)‡(V) building‡ up (O) « your vocabulary » (by < the ugly means of < (electrically) ◎‡(V) repeating‡ (O) « the same thing » ((id)to the level of < (*)‡(V) being‡ (1)(C) 〚 awkward 〛 〖 (or (2)(C) 〚 (even) crazy 〛!) 〗 >) > >) > 〛, { (S) < which > (V) is (C) 〚 never possible 〛 (by < the traditional means of < (physically) (id)‡(V) writing‡ down (on (id)a sheet of < paper >) > >) };

(5)(V) Avoid (O) « (*)‡(V) entering‡ (1)(O) « "(w)pronouns(代名詞:DAIMEISHI)" », (2)(O) « "(w)conjunctions(接続詞:SETSUZOKUSHI)" » and (3)(O) « "(w)prepositions(前置詞:ZENCHISHI)" » » — (S) < they > (V) are (C) 『 (*)the stuff (1)for < "grammar" >, not (2)for < "(w)vocabulary building" > 』;

(6)(aV) Don't (id)(V) try to (V) make "(O) « (id)(*)a (1){ single } (2){ complete } version" of < wordbook > ». (Just) (V) make (O) « as many wordbooks as < the number (*)of (1)< your lessons (at < school >) > or (2)< the chapters of < ◎a book { (O) « *[which]* » (S) < you > | (aV) are (V) reading | } > > > ». (V) Remember — (O) « (S) < a wordbook > (V) is (C) 『 ◎a list of < ◎words and definitions { to (V) remember } > 』, { [(S) < which > (V) is] (C) 『 useless 』 (if (S) < it > ^(V) disinclines^ (O) « you » (C) 『 (*)^to^ (1)(V) remember 【 (or (even) (2)(V) read!) 】 ((id)due to < its { daunting } length >)) } » 』;

(7)NEVER (id)(V) print out (O) « your electric wordbook » (on < paper >). (id)(V) Grow out of < your ^dependence on^ < tactile tangibility > ^for^ < comprehension > >. (S) < (w)The { authentic } test of < the intelligentsia { of < the 21st century > } > > (V) is (C) 『 ^whether or not^ to (id)be able to (V) understand (in < an abstract manner >) ((id)without recourse to < ◎physical aid { (*)like (1)< ‡(V) writing‡ (by < hand >) > or (2)< ‡(V) reading‡ (on < paper >) > } >) 』. (O) « ◎Anything { (O) « *[that]* » (S) < you > (V) see (on < a computer screen >) } », (just) ^(V) comprehend^ ((id)then and there), ^or^ *(= (S) < you > (aV) will)* ＼ (*)(aV) be (1)(id)(V) left behind and (2)(id)(V) frowned upon ／ (by ◎^those^ { (S) < ^{ whose }^ ‡understanding‡ > (V) needs (O) « no tactile intervention » }).

(S) < This author > (id)(V) refrains from < ‡(V) recommending‡ (O) « (*){ any particular } (1){ computer-based } dictionary and (2)(w)editor 【 (or (3)(w)word-processor) 】 (*)software » >, (id)for fear of < ‡(V) sounding‡ (C) 『 (nostalgically) (id)out of date 』 > (when (S) < you > (V) read (O) « this » (years later)). (Just) ^(V) search^ 【 on < (w)the Net > 】 ^for^ < ◎anything { with { (*)(reasonably) adequate (1)copy/(2)paste } capability } >, or (V) ask (O) « ◎someone (around < you >) { (S) < who > ↑ (aV) has (V) taken ↑ (O) « the right step » (in < this electric enlightenment >) } ».

(S) < Many of < ◎"wondrous technologies" { [(S) < which > ＼ (aV) are]] (proudly) (V) advocated ／ (by < evangelists >) } > > (V) are (C) 『 (id)good for nothing (in < the world of < linguistics > >) 』, but (S) < ◎the ^method^ 【 { [(S) < which > ＼ (V) was]] (V) shown ／ (above) } 】 ^of^ < "‡(V) creating‡ (O) « your own personal wordbooks » ((w)via < { computer-based } software)" > > > (V) is (C) 『 ^so^ (really) powerful 』 ^that^ (S) < you > (id)(V) are (C) 『 sure to ＼ (id)(aV) be (V) left (hopelessly) behind ／ by < ◎^those^ { ^(*)(S) < who >^ (1)(V) believe and (2)(V) prove (*)(O) « it » (by < (actually) (id)‡(V) improving‡ upon < their vocabulary > (that way) >) } > 』. (id)(V) Take (O) « my word » for < ^it^ > ^that^ (S) < you > (aV) should ^(V) go^ (C) 『 electric 』... ^or^ [(S) < you > (aV) will] (V) go (C) 『 (elaborately) awry 』.

17.(On < ‡(V) entering‡ (O) « (w)a junior high school » >),

(V) acquire (O) « (w)touch-typing skill »:

(id)(V) learn to (V) type (O) « English » (without < ‡(V) seeing‡ (O) « the keyboard » >)

- ‡Typing‡ (in < Japan >) ((w)yesterday and today) -

(Before < the 1990s >), (S) < few people > (id)were able to (V) type (here (in < Japan >)). (S) < They > (V) had (O) « ^no other^ ◎way { to (V) write } ^than^ < handwriting > ». (S) < They > (V) imagined (O) « ‡typing‡ » (C) 〚 to (V) be ◎a special skill (1){ [(S) < which > (V) was] (id)(C) 〚 peculiar to < (*){ professional } (1)typists or (2)writers > }, (2){ [(S) < that > (V) was] (id)(C) 〚 alien to < ◎normal people { (S) < who > (V) had (O) « ◎their own hands { to (V) write with } » } > } 〛 〛 〛. ((id)Towards the end of < the twentieth century >), (however), (S) < ‡typing‡ skill > (id)(V) came to (V) become (C) 〚 "(w)a must" 〛 ((even) in < Japan >) ((id)due (*)to (1)< the explosive spread of < (w)personal computers > > and (2)< the (rapidly) { growing } network of < WWW((1)(w)World Wide Web or (2)(w)the Internet) > >).

(S) < The general ‡typing‡ (1)skill 【 (or (2)method) 】 of < Japanese people > (today) >, (however), (id)(V) leaves (O) « ◎(^too^) much { to ＼ (aV) be (V) desired ／ } » (^to^ ＼ (aV) be (V) deemed ／ (C) 〚 as < (id)a sort of < (w)computer literacy > > 〛). (*)(S) < ^So^ many Japanese > (1)(id)(V) are (C) 〚 engaged 〛 (mostly) in < KEITAI 【 (cell-phone) 】 mail > and (2)(rarely) (V) write (on < computer keyboards >) ^that^ (S) < their typing > (aV) can (hardly) (id)(V) grow out of < "chopstick dancing" > — *[(there) (V) is]* (S) < too much stress (on < forefingers >) > (while (S) < others > (V) remain (C) 〚 idle 〛). ((id)As for < ◎most Japanese youngsters { *[(S) < who > | (aV) are] (busily) (V) writing* | (O) « mail » (on < KEITAI >) } >), (S) < their act > (V) is (C) 〚 (even) ^too^ strange (^to^ ＼ (aV) be (V) called ／ (C) 〚 "typing" 〛) 〛... (S) < it > (aV) should (more appropriately) ＼ (aV) be (V) called ／ (1)(C) 〚 "pecking" 〛 *[than (2)(C) 〚 "typing" 〛]* , (†(V) using†*(= (S) < which > (V) uses)* (O) « (only) the thumb » (to (id)(V) tap on < (w)ten-keys > (on < the cell-phone >) (to (V) weave (O) « short sentences »))). (While (in < (id)the rest of < the world > >), (S) < the thumb (on < the right hand >) > (V) does (O) « (id)nothing but < ‡(V) hitting‡ (O) « (w)the space key » > »), (S) < it > (V) does (O) « everything » (in < the KEITAI ‡pecking‡ >). (S) < It > (V) is (C) 『 (uniquely) Japanese 』, ((id)to be sure), but (like < many other Japanese originals >), (S) < it > (V) is (C) 『 ^too^ (uniquely) Japanese (^to^ (V) survive (in < the global society >)) 』. (S) < Thumb-‡pecking‡-tap-dance > (id)(V) belongs more (1)to < (w)parlor tricks > than (2)to < ‡typing‡ skill >.

((id)By any standard), (S) < Japanese people { (id)in general } > (V) are (C) 『 (id)anything but < good typists > 』.

- The fundamental ◎reason { [why] (*)(S) < most Japanese > (1)(V) type and (2)(V) write (*)(so poorly) } -

(S) < (w)Word-‡processing‡ (through < thumb-‡pecking‡ >) > (V) seems (C) 『 ^too^ arduous (^to^ (V) be (C) 『 realistic 』) 』 ((id)in the eyes of < foreigners >), but ((even) with < nine fingers 〖 (minus < the left thumb >) 〗 >), (S) < ‡(V) weaving‡ (O) « Japanese sentences » (on < the computer >) > (*)(V) is (1)(C) 『 a hard task 』, (2)(C) 『 (hardly) rhythmical { with < ^too^ many stops ^for^ (S) < typists > ^to^ (pleasantly) (V) ride (on < the stream of < ‡writing‡ > >) > } 』.

(S) < What >, (then), (V) makes (O) « you » (C) 『 (V) stop 』 (in < ‡(V) typing‡ (O) « Japanese » >)? Yes, ((id)of course), (S) < you > (V) know – *[(S) < it > (V) is]* "かな漢字変換(KANA-KANJI HENKAN: the ^conversion^ of < KANA > ^into^ < (w)Chinese character >)", *[(S) < which > (V) is]* archenemy (*)of (1)< rhythm >, (2)< speed > and (3)< accuracy > (*)(in < { (electrically) processed } Japanese >).

((id)For example), (if (S) < you > (id)(V) want to (V) type (O) « "漢字" »), (S) < you > (id)have to (id)(V) go through < two steps >:

(STEP-1) (id)(V) Type in (from < keyboards >) (O) « "k" "a" "n" "j" "i" – "かんじ" » – (in < KANA(Japanese (w)syllabic ‡writing‡ system) >). (If *[(S) < you > (V) type]* not (in < (w)Roman alphabet conversion style >)), (S) < it > (V) is (C) 『 "T" "Y" "D"

"@" 』... *[(V) is (S) < it >]* (C)『 confusing 』(already)? (V) Be (C)『 prepared 』*[because]* (S) < it > (aV) can (V) be (C)『 (much more) so 』(hereafter);

(STEP-2) (From < ◎the many candidates of < "kanji" > { *[(S) < which >* ＼ *(aV) are]]* (V) shown ／ (on < the computer screen >) } (1)("感じ", (2)"幹事", (3)"監事", (4)"完治", (5)"官寺", (6)"患児", etc,etc.) >) (1)(V) find and (2)(id)(V) decide on (O) « < "漢字" > » (to (correctly) (V) complete (O) « the conversion »).

(When (id)every time { *[that]* (S) < you > (id)(V) want to (id)(V) type in (O) « (w)any given KANJI » }, (S) < you > ＼ (id)(aV) are (V) forced (*)to ／ (1)(V) stop, (2)(V) find and (3)(id)(V) decide on (O) « < the right candidate of < the "漢字" > > »), ／ how (aV) can (S) < you > (rhythmically) (V) type (O) « Japanese »? (S) < ‡Typing‡ (in < Japanese >) > (V) is (C)『 ◎such a stressful task { *[(S) < which > (V) is]* (^so^ much) (id)full of < GO/STOP, GO/STOP > } 』 ^that^ (S) < ‡writing‡ speed > ＼ (id)(aV) is (V) compromised for ／ < accuracy > or, (*[(S) < what > (V) is]* (C)『 (id)worse still 』), (w)vice versa *(= (S) < accuracy > (aV) is (V) compromised for < ‡writing‡ speed >)*. (If (S) < you > (id)(V) hate (*)to (1)(V) stop and (2)(V) check (O) « conversion errors 〖 (like ◎"かんじ" { *[‡(V) being‡]* ^(V) converted into^ (1)< "幹事" > and not (2)< "漢字" > }) 〗 » ((id)in the process of < ‡(V) writing‡ (fluently) >)), (S) < your sentences > (aV) will (V) be (C)『 (id)full of < ^such^ absurd Japanese ^as^ (1)< "内臓メモリー(NAIZOU MEMORY: (w)built-in memory = 内蔵メモリー *[‡(V) being‡]* (incorrectly) ^(V) converted into^ < (w)internal organ memory >)" >, (2)< "深いな経験(FUKAI NA KEIKEN: a { disgusting } experience = 不快な経験 *[‡(V) being‡]* (suggestively) ^(V) converted into^ < a profound experience >)" > or (3)< "指摘会話(SHITEKI KAIWA: a personal conversation = 私的会話 *[‡(V) being‡]* (critically) ^(V) converted into^ < (id)‡(V) pointing‡ out conversation >)" > > 』.

(S) < Such ◎structural hindrance { *[(S) < which > (V) is]* (C)『 (id)inherent in < Japanese ‡writing‡ system > 』 } > (id)never (V) fails to (V) thwart (O) « the Japanese » (in < their (*)‡typing‡ (1)speed and (2)accuracy >). But (S) < the saddest truth (of < all >) > (V) is (C)『 ^this^ 』^:^ (S) < the Japanese > (themselves), (most of < them >

), (aV) do not (V) know (O) « the sad truth of < their ‡writing‡ handicap > » ((id)because of < their ◎^inability^ { (*)^to^ (1)(V) compose and (2)(V) type (*)(O) « English » } >). ◎^Those^ { ^(S) < who >^ (V) have (O) « no ◎mirror { to (V) reflect (O) « themselves » (in) } » } (id)(V) have no { true } notion of < themselves > ((id)in the eyes of < others >). (S) < ◎Japanese self-image { *[(S) < which > ＼ (aV) is]]* (V) drawn ／ (in < the void of < objective perspective > >) } > (V) is (often) (C) 〚 ^too^ (id)larger than life (^to^ ＼ (aV) be (*)^(V) taken^ ／ (1)^(C) 〚 serious[ly] 〛^ or (2)(C) 〚 (even) ^humorous[ly]^ 〛) 〛.

(V) Avoid (O) « ‡(V) becoming‡ (C) 〚 such a { self-crowned } clown 〛 » (by < ‡(V) acquiring‡ (O) « ◎some reliable standpoint { to ^(V) enable^ (O) « you » (C) 〚 ^to^ (V) see (O) « yourself » (objectively) 〛 } » >). (S) < (id)‡(V) Typing‡ in (O) « English » > (aV) will (V) be (C) 〚 a desirable (w)‡starting‡ point 〛. (S) < You > (aV) should (V) start (as early as possible^), ／ although (S) < this author > (aV) will (id)(V) refrain from < ‡(V) saying‡ (O) « "(w)the sooner the better" »*(= (^the^ sooner) (S) < you > (V) start, (C) 〚 ^the^ better 〛 (S) < it > (V) is)* >: (S) < too soon > (aV) will (V) be (C) 〚 too much 〛 (in < something >). (S) < The ^time^ > (V) is (C) 〚 (well) ripe ^for^ < (id)‡(V) starting‡ to (V) type (O) « English » > 〛 (when (*)(S) < you > (1) ↑ (aV) have (id)(V) graduated from ↑ < (w)◎primary school > 【 (where (S) < you > ↑ (aV) should (aV) have (V) acquired ↑ (O) « an adequate vocabulary of < KANJI > ») 】 and (2)(id)are about to (V) start (O) « ‡(V) learning‡ (O) « English » » ((id)in earnest)).

- (S) < Japanese students > (aV) should (V) learn (O) « typing » (1)(through < English >), not (2)(through < their native Japanese >) -

(Since (S) < this > (V) is (C) 〚 the 21st century 〛), (S) < you > (aV) will (invariably) (id)(V) try to (V) master (O) « ‡typing‡ » (1)(through < some { computer-based } ‡tutoring‡ system >), not (2)by < the traditional method of < (id)‡(V) typing‡ in (O) « (O) « { whatever } sentences » (S) < you > (V) find (on < paper textbooks >) » > >. (

(id)To (V) tell (O) « you » (O) « the truth »), (however), (there) (V) is (S) < no fundamental ^difference^ ^between^ (1){ computerized } ^and^ (2){ paper-based } (*)practices (in < typing >) >, (once (S) < you > (*) ↑ (aV) have (V) mastered ↑ (1)(O) « the positions of < the keys > » and (2)(O) « ◎{ what } keys { to (V) hit } (by < { which } fingers { of yours } >) »).

(S) < The ^advantage^ of < computerized lessons > ^over^ < paper ‡typing‡ practice > > (V) is (C) 『 (1)not (id)‡(V) having‡ to (V) prepare (O) « physical forms of < textbooks > », and (2)(id)‡(V) being‡ able to (V) check (O) « the accuracy level of < your ‡typing‡ > » (by < ^‡(V) comparing‡^ (O) « the original sentences » ^with^ < (O) « what » (S) < you > (actually) (id)(V) typed in > >) 』. ((id)In the hand of < capable programmers >), (S) < computerized ‡typing‡ lessons > (aV) can (V) be (C) 『 a great fun 』 ((id)in addition to < ‡(V) being‡ (C) 『 instructive 』 >). (S) < Inept programmers > (*)(aV) will (1)(id)(V) try to (V) make (O) « it » (C) 『 all fun 』, and (2)(id)(V) end in < (id)a bunch of < ◎shit { *[(S) < which > (V) is]* (C) 『 ^neither^ (1)interesting ^nor^ (2)instructive 』 } > >. ((id)In order to (V) avoid (O) « such ◎shitty ‡typing‡ ‡tutoring‡ programs { (1)†(V) crowding†*(= (S) < which > (V) crowd)* 【 (and (2)†(V) clouding†*(= and (aV) are (V) clouding))* 】 (*)(O) « the Japanese market » } »), (S) < you > (simply) (id)have to (V) obey (O) « two rules »:

(1)(V) avoid (O) « { Japanese-oriented } programs » and (V) choose (O) « { English-based } ones »... never (V) forget (O) « [that] (S) < the interruption of < KANA-KANJI conversion > > (V) is (C) 『 the archenemy of < ‡typing‡ > 』 »!;

(2)(V) avoid (O) « ◎programs { (proudly) †(V) featuring†*(= (S) < which > (proudly) (V) feature)* (O) « "(id)LOTS OF < FUN >" » } »... ((id)more often than not), (S) < (S) < what > (V) is (C) 『 fun 』 (to < the programmer >) > (V) is (C) 『 (1)none 【 (or (2)dung!) 】 』(to < the learner >).

((id)In short), (V) choose (1)(O) « "{ ◎English-oriented } software { *[(S) < which > ＼ (aV) is]]* (V) designed ／ to ^(V) make^ (O) « a good typist » (^of^ < you >) }" », and

NEVER (2)(O) « "◎Japanese { fun-oriented } software { [(S) < which > ＼ (aV) is]] (V) designed ／ to (id)(V) make money (by < (id)‡(V) making‡ (O) « a fool » of < you > } >)" ». (Unless (S) < you > (id)(V) turn (O) « your back » on < Japanese > (as(= when) [(S) < you > (V) are] < a novice >)), (S) < you > (aV) can't (id)(V) hope to (V) be (C) 〚 a great typist 〛. (S) < ^It^ > (V) is (C) 〚 not necessary 〛 ^to^ (totally) (V) exclude (O) « Japanese language » (from < ‡typing‡ lessons >), but (S) < any (id)attempt at < (w)KANA/KANJI transfer > (in < ‡typing‡ ‡tutoring‡ programs >) > (aV) will (id)(*)(V) do more (O) « (1)harm » than (O) « (2)good ». (From < this author's personal experience >), (S) < most of < ◎the ‡typing‡ lesson programs { [(S) < which > ＼ (aV) are]] (V) made ／ (in (aV) Japan) } > > (V) are (C) 〚 (totally) (id)out of the question 〛 ((id)due to < (id)the { obvious } lack of < (w)command of < English > > ((id)on the part of < the programmers >) >): (S) < they > ^(V) belong^ ^more^ ^to^ < the genre of < (1){ "‡gaming‡" > } ^than^ ^to^ (2){ "education" } (*)software >... ／ and(= and yet) ／ [(S) < they > (V) are] (C) 〚 (id)^not^ much fun 〛, (^either^).

\- (aV) Don't (V) think: (just) (V) type! -

(S) < Some of < you > > may (id)(V) be (C) 〚 afraid to (id)(V) step into < ◎the world of < typing > { [(S) < which > ＼ ^(aV) is^]] ^(V) composed^ (solely) ^of^ ／ < English sentences > } > 〛, ((id)†(V) wondering† if(= as (S) < you > (V) wonder if) (S) < you > (aV) can (V) (really) understand (O) « their meaning » (while [(S) < you > | (aV) are]] (V) typing |)). (Well), (S) < this author > (aV) will (V) tell (O) « you » (O) « ◎^this^ secret », 【 [(S) < which > (id)(V) is] (C) 〚 unknown to < (id)all but < ◎the exceptional Japanese { (S) < who > (*)(aV) can (1)(V) type, (2)(V) read, (3)(V) write and (4)(V) understand (*)(O) « English » ((id)with { perfect } freedom) > 〛 } > 【 (†(V) meaning†(= (S) < which > (V) means) (O) « "◎the truth (about < ‡typing‡ >) { [(S) < which > (V) is] (C) 〚 (virtually) unknown 〛 (in < Japan >) }" ») 】 】 — ^that^ (S) < an English ‡typing‡ lesson > (*)(V) is (1)(C) 〚 possible 〛 【 ((even) (2)(C) 〚 desirable 〛) 】 (by < ◎^those^ { ^(S) < who >^ (id)(aV) can't (*)(V) make (1)(O) « head » or (2)(O) «

tail » of < English sentences > } >).

(S) < The goal of < typing > > (V) is ^not^ (1)(C) 『 to (V) understand (as (S) < you > (V) type) 』 ^but^ (2)(C) 『 to (V) type ((*)without (1)< ‡(V) thinking‡ > or (2)< ‡(V) understanding‡ >) 』. (S) < ‡Typing‡ (by < experts >) > (V) is (C) 『 a (totally) spontaneous act 』: (S) < they > (aV) may | (aV) be (V) thinking | , but (S) < their fingers > | (aV) are not *[(V) thinking]* | . (^Between^ < (O) « what » (S) < they > (V) see > ^and^ < (O) « what » (S) < they > (V) type >), (there) (aV) should never (V) be (S) < an interruption (by < any conscious thought >) >; (S) < ‡thinking‡ > (*)(aV) will (only) (V) spoil (1)(O) « speed » and (even) (2)(O) « accuracy » (*)(in < typing >). (S) < (aV) DON'T (V) THINK (JUST) (V) HIT (O) « THE KEY » > (V) is (C) 『 ◎the way { to (V) go } 』.

((id)In { this } regard), (S) < English natives > (aV) will (V) find (O) « themselves » (C) 『 (id)at < a disadvantage > 』 (because (*)(S) < they > (1)(aV) can 【 (and (2)(aV) WILL) 】 (*)(V) understand (O) « (O) « what » (S) < they > | (aV) are (V) typing | »). (S) < ◎Japanese folks { (*)(S) < who > (1)(aV) can (V) see (O) « alphabets » but (2)(aV) don't (V) know (O) « ◎(O) « what » { to ^(V) make^ ^of^ < them > } » } > (aV) will (naturally) (id)(V) gain (*)in (1)< speed > and (2)< accuracy > (*)(in < English ‡typing‡ >) (because (S) < their brains > (V) are (C) 『 (id)free from < unnecessary ‡thinking‡ process > 』). (S) < They > (aV) can ^(V) make^ (O) « desirable "automatic ‡typing‡ machines" » (^of^ < themselves >)!

(After < years of < practice > (^both^ (*)in (1)< ‡typing‡ > ^and^ (2)< English itself >) >), (S) < Japanese typists > (aV) will (naturally) (id)(V) come (*)to (1)(id)(V) think about and (2)(V) understand (*)(O) « the meaning of < texts > » (while [(S) < they > | (aV) are] (V) typing |). (S) < Bliss of < innocence > > (aV) will not (V) last (forever), but (V) enjoy (O) « it » (while (S) < you > (aV) can). (While (S) < your "(w)beginner's luck" > (V) is (C) 『 (still) active 』), (id)^(V) learn^ to (V) type (without < ‡(V) thinking‡ >), ^(aV) let^ (O) « your fingers » (spontaneously) (id)(V) type in (O) « (O) « whatever »

(S) < you > (V) see » (◎(id)the moment { [(that)] (S) < you > (V) see (O) « it » }), ^(V) make^ (O) « typing » (C) 〖 as instinctive as (1)(S) < speaking > or (2)(S) < walking > 〗... ^and^ (S) < (*){ your } (1)typing and (2)(w)command of < English > > (aV) will ＼ (aV) be (greatly) (id)(V) improved upon ／ ; ((id)along with < it >), [(aV) will ＼ (aV) be (V) improved] ／(3)(S) < your status (in < ◎the world { [(S) < which > ＼ (aV) is]] (V) connected ／ (by < (w)the Net >) } >) >, { where (S) < (excellently) typed English { of yours } > (id)never (V) fails to (id)(V) stand out (among < self-complacent gibberish >) }.

- ◎(O) « What » { to (id)(V) keep (in mind) } (^in^ < (id)‡(V) try^ing^‡ to (V) master (O) « ‡typing‡ skill » >) -

([If (S) < it > ＼ (aV) is]] (V) Pursued ／ (in < the correct way >)), (S) < ‡typing‡ skill > (aV) can ＼ (aV) be (V) mastered ／ (in < less than < (id)a couple of < months > > >): (S) < you > (aV) won't (V) need (O) « half a year » ((id)at the longest). (After < that >), (1)(S) < speed > and (2)(S) < accuracy > (*)(aV) will (progressively) (V) increase / until(= and then) (S) < they > (id)(V) hit (O) « the roof » 〖 ((probably) (1)in < some years >, not (2)in < decades >) 〗. ((*)To (1)(V) minimize (O) « the (1)time and (2)effort » and (2)(V) maximize (O) « the accomplishment »), (id)(V) keep (in mind) (O) « the following principles » and (V) keep (O) « ‡(V) moving‡ (in < the right path >) » 〖 ((aV) don't ^(V) waste^ (O) « your energy » (^in^ < (*){ questionable } (1)methods or (2)software >)) 〗 :

(1)(S) < ◎The first skill { to (V) acquire } > (V) is (C) 〖 to (V) type ((*)without < (*)‡(V) seeing‡ (1)(O) « the keyboard » or (2)(O) « the positions of < your fingers > » >) 〗. (S) < Your eyes > (aV) should ＼ (aV) be (V) fixed (*)on ／ (1)< the computer screen > 〖 (or (2)< paper texts (for < typing >) >) 〗 (without < ‡(V) running‡ ((id)up and down) (nervously) >). (S) < This "(w)touch-typing" skill > (aV) will (greatly) (V) reduce (O) « the physical pressure ((*)on < your (1)eyes, (2)neck and (3)shoulders >) (while [(S)

< *you* > | *(aV) are]]* (V) working | (on < computers >)) ».

(2)(S) < Primary ^attention^ > (aV) should ＼ (aV) be ^(V) paid^ ^to^ ／ < ‡(V) acquiring‡ (O) « ◎the skill { (1)to (V) type (at < high speed >) (with < constant rhythm >) and (2)never to (V) stop ((id)here and there) ((*)for (1)< confirmation > and (2)< correction >) } » >. ((id)In { this } regard), (S) < ◎Japanese sentences { *[(S) < which > (V) are]* (C) 〖 (id)full of < GO/STOP ‡converting‡ process of < KANA/KANJI > > 〗 } > (V) are (C) 〖 (totally) (id)out of the question 〗 (in < ‡typing‡ lessons >). (V) Forget (O) « all { about < Japanese > } » (while [(S) < you > (V) are] (C) 〖 a novice typist 〗)... ／ unless (S) < you > | (aV) are (just) (*)(id)(V) typing in | (1)(O) « "ひらがな" » and (2)(O) « ^no^ '漢字" » (^(id)at all^).

(3)(*)(S) < ‡Typing‡ accuracy > (1)(aV) should ＼ (aV) be (id)(V) given (O) « a back seat » ／ and (2)(aV) should ＼ ^NEVER^ (aV) be (V) practiced ／ (1)(in < { long } { tiresome } sentences >) ^but^ (2)(in ◎< { short } { snappy } ones { like (1)< newspaper headlines > or (2)< famous adages > } >). (S) < Accuracy > (aV) should ＼ (*)(aV) be (1)(V) tested and (2)(V) acquired ／ (1)(in < ◎sentences { (in < which >) (S) < one > (id)(V) feels (C) 〖 inclined to (V) be (C) 〖 accurate 〗 〗 } >), not (2)(where(= *in ◎something (in < which >))* (S) < one > (aV) can (V) be (C) 〖 【 reasonably 】 sloppy 〗).

(4)(S) < ◎Sentences { to ＼ (aV) be (V) used ／ (for < ‡typing‡ practice >) } > (aV) should (V) be (C) 〖 customizable 〗: ((id)in addition to < ◎{ (w)built-in } texts { *[(S) < which >* ＼ *(aV) are]]* (V) prepared ／ by < the programmer > } >), (S) < learners > (aV) should ＼ (aV) be (V) given ／ (O) « ◎the freedom { to (V) use (O) « ◎any sentences { (O) « *[that]* » (S) < they > (id)(V) want to (V) type (in < the program >) } » } ». (S) < The { boring } disadvantage (of < ‡(V) using‡ (O) « the same sentences (for < typing practice >) » ((id)over and over [again]) >) > (aV) should ＼ (aV) be (id)(V) turned to < { great } advantage > ／ (by < (id)‡(V) making‡ (O) « use » of < ◎(personally) selected sentences { (O) « which » (S) < one > (id)(V) wants to (1)(id)(V) learn (by heart) 【 (not (merely) (2)(id)(V) learn to (V) type) 】 } >, { (id)such as <

(1)favorite lyrics of < popular artists >, (2)◎example sentences { [(S) < which > ＼ (aV) are]] (V) quoted ／ (from < wordbooks >) }, or (3)(even) ◎the whole sentences { [(S) < that > ＼ (aV) are]] (V) copied ／ (from < ◎English textbooks { [(O) « which »] (S) < one > (aV) must (V) memorize (to (id)(V) prepare for < the exam >) } >) } > } >). (S) < { Tech-minded } folks > (aV) should (*)(V) use (1)(O) « ‡programming‡ terms » or (2)(O) « (even) a whole functional program » (as < ◎example sentences (1){ to (id)(V) type in } and (2){ to (naturally) (V) memorize (through < fingers >) } >).

- Gospel of < typing > (for < Japanese learners of < English > >) -

(S) < Typing > (aV) will (really) (V) replace (O) « handwriting » (once (S) < you > ↑ (aV) have (V) mastered ↑ (O) « "(W)touch-typing" » 〖 ([(S) < which > (V) is] a { (W)politically-correct } (W)paraphrase of < the traditional appellation of < "(W)blind touch" > > ((id)in view of < the feelings of < ◎those { [(S) < who > (V) are] (C) 『 (physically) handicapped (in < their eyes >) 』 } > >)) 〗). (Once (S) < you > (V) enter (O) « ◎a phase of < English study > { where(= in < which >) (S) < you > (*)(aV) can (1)(V) write and (2)(V) store (O) « ◎anything { (O) « [that] » (*)(S) < you > (1)(V) see or (2)(V) think } » (by < ‡(V) typing‡ (on < keyboards >) >) } »), (S) < you > ＼ (aV) 'll (id)(aV) be (V) blessed with ／ < the following benefits >.

(benefit 1)

(S) < You > (aV) can (V) type (((id)tens of times) faster than (S) < you > (V) write) (without < ‡(V) falling‡ into < (illegibly) dirty handwriting > >). (Indeed), (S) < "(1)quick and (2)legible" > (V) is (C) 『 ◎the primary reason { why (*)(S) < English natives > (1)(usually) (V) type and (2)(rarely) (V) write (*)(O) « their documents » } 』. (S) < { Hand-written } English > (aV) can (*)(V) be (1)(C) 『 a great ordeal (for < the reader >) 』 〖 ([because (S) < it > (V) is] (C) 『 illegible 』!) 〗 (id)as well as (2)(C) 『 a unique identifier of < the writer > 〖 ([because (S) < it > (V) is] (C) 『 characteristic 』!) 〗 { just like < a fingerprint > } 』.

(benefit 2)

(When (S) < you > (V) become (C) 〚 ^proficient^ (enough) ^both^ (*)^in^ (1)< ‡typing‡ > ^and^ (2)< English > 〛), (S) < your ‡typing‡ skill > (aV) will (V) give (O) « you » (O) « an enormous advantage (^in^ < ‡(V) practic^ing^‡ (O) « "英作文(EISAKUBUN: English composition)" » >) ». (S) < ◎The speed { (at < which >) (S) < you > (manually) (V) write } > (V) is (C) 〚 (^so^ much) slower than < ◎the speed { (at < which >) (S) < you > (V) speak } > 〛 ^that^ (S) < the act of < ‡(V) writing‡ (O) « English » > > (aV) will never (V) help [(O) « you »] (C) 〚 *[to]* (V) become (C) 〚 fluent (in < (*){ English } (1)speech or (2)thinking >) 〛 〛. ((id)On the other hand), (S) < you > (aV) can (V) type (O) « English » ((nearly) as fast as (*)(S) < you > (1)(V) speak or (2)(id)(V) think of (*)(O) « < it > »), (†(V) making† *(= (S) < which > (V) makes)* (O) « ^it^ » (C) 〚 possible 〛 ^to^ (V) ride (on < the flow of < ◎the sentence { (id)of { your } own making } > >), while (1)†(V) detecting† and (2)†(V) correcting† *(= (S) < you > (V) detect and (V) correct)* (*)(O) « errors » (on < the computer screen >)). (S) < (O) « What » (S) < you > (id)(V) write down (on < (id)a sheet of < paper > >) > (id)(V) tends to (V) become (C) 〚 "final" 〛 (in < your consciousness >), (†(V) making† *(= (S) < which > (V) makes)* (O) « ^it^ » (C) 〚 difficult 〛 (*)^to^ (1)(V) re-examine and (2)(V) correct (*)(O) « its contents » (after (S) < you > ↑ (aV) have (V) finished ↑ (O) « ‡(V) writing‡ (O) « it » »)). (S) < (O) « What » (S) < you > (id)(V) type in (on < a computer >) > (*)(V) is (1)(C) 〚 (always) "(id)in the making" 〛 and (2)(C) 〚 (id)open (*)to (1)< correction > or (2)< alteration > 〛, (†(V) giving† *(= (S) < which > (V) gives)* (O) « you » (1)(O) « much more perfection » and (2)(O) « possibility for < improvement > »). (S) < ◎^Those^ { ^(S) < who >^ (V) compose (O) « English » ((only) (1)on < paper >) 〖 (or (2)on < their tongues > or (even) (3)in < their heads > (alone)) 〗 } > (V) are (C) 〚 much ^less^ (id)likely to (id)(V) improve upon < their ‡writing‡ > than if (S) < they > (id)(V) made (O) « a point » of < ‡(V) typing‡ (O) « their sentences » (on < computers >) > 〛.

〖 (warning (*)about < (1)‡(V) writing‡/(2)‡(V) typing‡ (for < memorization >) >) 〗

(If (S) < you > (V) are (C) 〚 a novice learner of < English > 〛), (S) < you > (aV) should (id)(V) make (O) « much more » of < (1)‡(V) reading‡ (aloud)< and (2)< ‡(V) memorizing‡ > than (3)‡(V) typing‡ (*)(O) « English ». (If (S) < you > (V) have (O) « ◎time { enough for < ‡(V) typing‡ (O) « a { ready-made } sentence » > } »), (id)(V) make (O) « better use » of < the time > (by < (repeatedly) ‡(V) reading‡ (O) « it » (aloud) >). (Although (S) < you > (aV) can (V) type (much faster than [(S) < you > (aV) can] (V) write)), never ^(V) try^ (O) « ‡(V) typ^ing^‡ (O) « the whole English sentences (from < your textbooks >) » » —(= *because*) (S) < it > (V) is (C) 〚 (simply) meaningless 〛 (except < as < a ‡typing‡ practice > >). (^If^ (S) < you > ^(V) try^ (O) « ‡(V) typ^ing^‡ (O) « sentences » » (^(id)at all^)), (V) try (O) « it » (with < ◎the sentences { (O) « *[which]* » (S) < you > ↑ (*)(aV) have (1)(id)(V) learnt (by heart) and (2)(V) stored (in < your memory >) ↑ } >) (to (id)(1)(V) check and*(= to)* (2)(V) see (O) « if (S) < you > ↑ (aV) have (V) memorized ↑ (O) « them » (all) ((id)to the letter) »).

(S) < Japanese learners of < English > > (id)(V) have (O) « a way » of < (id)‡(V) writing‡ down (O) « (*){ English } (1)words 【 (or (even) (2)(w)idioms or (3)sentences!) 】 » ((id)over and over [again]) (on < paper >) ((id)†(V) trying† to*(= as (S) < they > (V) try to)* ^(V) inscribe^ (O) « them » (^on^ < their memory >))... 【 (id)to (absolutely) no avail >. (S) < They > (V) are (C) 〚 (totally) illogical 〛 ((id)in that (S) < they > (V) ignore (O) « the structural ^difference^ ^between^ < (w)phonograms 【 (English words) 】 > ^and^ < (w)ideograms 【 (漢字:KANJI = (w)Chinese characters) 】 > »).

((id)In essence), (S) < a (w)Chinese character > (V) is (C) 〚 ◎a "picture" { (S) < { whose } "figure" > (id)(V) stands for < a certain meaning > } 〛: (S) < you > (aV) can (V) know (O) « its meaning » (by < ‡(V) seeing‡ (O) « it » >), but (S) < you > (aV) must (V) practice (O) « "‡(V) drawing‡ (O) « the picture »" (with < your own hand >) » (to (id)be able to (V) write (O) « the KANJI » (*[for]* yourself)). (S) < Practice (in < ‡(V) writing‡ (O) « KANJI » >) > (V) is (C) 〚 more a lesson (1)(in < art >) than (2)(in < linguistics >) 〛. (If (S) < you > (V) doubt (O) « me »), (id)(V) think about < the status of < "書道(SHODOU:(w)Japanese calligraphy)" > ((id)in the eyes of < { English speaking } people >) > — (V) isn't (S) < it > (C) 〚 (id)a kind of < ◎visual art { (*)like (1)<

painting > or (2)< photography > } > 』?

(Unlike < KANJI >), (s) < English words > (v) are (c) 『 no pictures 』: (s) < you > (id)don't have to (v) practice (o) « "‡(v) drawing‡" (o) « them » », (s) < you > (just) (id)have to ◎(v) memorize (o) « the combination of < ◎the alphabets { †(v) composing†(= (s) < *which* > (v) *compose*) (o) « them » } > », { (^for^ < { which } ^purpose^ >) (s) < "(id)‡(v) writing‡ (o) « them » down" > (v) is (c) 『 (absolutely) unnecessary 』 }. (If (s) < you > (v) are (c) 『 (id)uncertain of < the spelling > 』), (just) ^(v) try^ (o) « ‡(v) typ^ing^‡ (o) « a term » (about ten times (id)or so) », ^and^ (s) < your fingers > (av) will (v) remember (o) « it » (for < you >). (s) < ‡(v) Typing‡ (o) « "薔薇 (BARA: a rose)" » ((id)dozens of < times >) (from < keyboards >) > (av) will never ^(v) enable^ (o) « you » (c) 『 ^to^ (v) write (o) « this KANJI » (on < paper >) (with < your own hand >) 』, but (s) < ‡(v) typing‡ (o) « "rose, rose, rose" » > (av) will (v) be (c) 『 more than ^enough^ ^for^ (s) < you > ^to^ (*)(correctly) (1)(v) remember and (2)(v) spell (*)(o) « this English term » ((id)ever afterwards) 』.

(benefit 3)

(If (s) < you > (v) type (o) « English sentences » (on < computers >)), (s) < you > (av) will (v) enjoy (o) « the helpful benefit of < ‡(v) having‡ (o) « your sentences » (c) 『 ^(v) checked^ 』 【 by < computer programs > 】 (^for^ < (*)‡(v) correcting‡ (o) « (1){ ‡spelling‡ } or (2){ grammatical } (*)errors > ») > ». ((id)As of < today >), (s) < such computerized grammatical correction programs > (v) are (c) 『 (id)far from < perfect > 』... but (s) < something > (v) is (c) 『 better than < nothing > 』. ((id)On the other hand), (s) < a ‡spelling‡ checker program (in < English >) > (*)(v) is (1)(c) 『 { (nearly) 100% } (1)accurate and (2)reliable 』; ((id)at least) (2)(c) 『 much more so than (s) < human scrutiny > 』. (s) < Their benefits (for < novice learners >) > (v) are (c) 『 ^so^ enormous 』 ^that^ (s) < (id)‡(v) making‡ (o) « no use » of < them > > (v) is (c) 『 (simply) illogical 』: (s) < the logical choice > (v) is (c) 『 (^only^) (id)open to < ◎^those^ { ^(s) < who >^ (v) type ((id)instead of < ‡(v) writing‡ >) } > 』.

(benefit 4)

(Finally), ^(s) < it > (v) is^ (c) 『 (also) ◎^those^ { (s) < ^who^ > (v) type } (^only^) 』 ^(s)

< that >^ (aV) can (V) make (O) « their sentences » (C) 〖 available (on < (w)the Net >) 〗. (By < ‡(V) making‡ (O) « your sentences » (1)(C) 〖 available 〗 and (2)(C) 〖 processable 〗 (for < your teacher >) >), (S) < you > (aV) can (V) have (O) « them » (C) 〖 (1)(V) checked, (2)(V) corrected and (3)(V) evaluated (*)(by < { scrutinizing } eyes of < the examiner > >) 〗. (S) < ◎^Those^ { ^(S) < who >^ (still) (id)(V) insist on < a { hand-written } answer sheet > } > (aV) will (id)have to (id)(V) resort to < the archaic means of < FAX(facsimile) > — ◎(visually) (1)‡(V) copying‡ and (2)‡(V) transmitting‡ (*)(O) « "a document" » ((id)in the form of < "a picture" >) >... { (S) < which > (V) is (C) 〖 an unbearable burden 〗 (^both^ (*)for (1)< the sender > ^and^ (2)< the receiver >) }. (S) < This author > (simply) (id)(aV) cannot (V) bring (O) « himself » to (V) accept (O) « such { (hardly) legible } "pictorial" documents »; (S) < (1)‡(V) checking‡ (O) « them » (for < errors >) and (2)(id)‡(V) referring‡ to and (3)‡(V) correcting‡ (*)(O) « < them > » (by < ‡(V) making‡ (O) « (wholly) new electrical documents » ((id)for myself) >) > (V) is (C) 〖 (simply) (id)out of the question 〗. (If (S) < you > (id)(V) hate to ＼ (aV) be (V) excluded ／ from < any activity (on < (w)the Net >) >), (S) < you > (just) (id)have to (id)(V) learn to (V) type.

- (1)ローマ字((w)Roman alphabets) or (2)かな(KANA), (S) < that > (V) is (C) 〖 the question 〗?...No, (there)(V) 's (S) < ^no^ question > (^(id)at all^): (S) < the answer > (*)(V) is (1)(C) 〖 { just } ROMAN 〗, (2)(C) 〖 no KANA 〗 -

[(Here) (V) is] (S) < ◎{ One more } advice { *[(S) < which > ＼ (aV) is]]* ^(V) meant^ (solely) ^for^ ／ < Japanese learners of < typing > > } >. (As < (*)the (1)input/(2)conversion (*)method >), (S) < you > (*)(aV) MUST (1)(V) choose (O) « "ローマ字変換:ROUMAJI HENKAN = (w)Roman alphabet conversion" » and (2)NEVER (V) choose (O) « "かな変換:KANA HENKAN = KANA conversion" »! (There) (V) is (S) < no question (about < it >) >:「かな変換は絶対に選ぶな！:(Just) (V) say (O) « NO »! (to < KANA conversion >)」. (S) < Even ◎^those^ { ^(S) < who >^ ↑ (aV) have (already) (V) chosen ↑ (O) « "KANA" » } > (id)(aV) would (aV) be (C) 〖 well-advised 〗 (to (id)(V) convert to < "ROUMAJI" >)... ／ ^if^ (S) < they > (V) want (O) « English literacy » (^(id)at all^), 〚 (id)that is 〛. (If (S) < you > (aV) can (V) rest (C) 〖 (id) ＼

satisfied ／ with < the status of < TOTAL ENGLISH ILLITERATE > > 』), (just) (id)(V) go ahead and (id)(V) keep on (O) « ‡(V) typing‡ (O) « KANA keys » ». (Otherwise), (just) (id)(V) KILL OFF (O) « KANA keys » and (V) GO (C) 『 ROMAN 』. (If (S) < you > (id)(V) happen to ↑ (aV) have (V) chosen ↑ (O) « the wrong way »), (id)(aV) don't (V) take (O) « it » (personally); (just) (V) take (O) « it » (logically) and (id)(V) convert to < Roman conversion >... (W)better late than never (= (S) < ^it^ > (V) is (C) 『 better 』 ^to^ (id)(V) convert to < Roman conversion > (late) than ^never^ ^to^ (V) do (so) (^(id)at all^)).

(id)(There) (V) is (absolutely) (S) < no sense > in < (*)‡(V) forcing‡ (1)(O) « your brains » and (2)(O) « fingers » (1)(C) 『 to (V) remember (O) « { two (totally) different } arrangements of < keys > » 』 and (2)(C) 『 to (id)(V) switch between < them > 』 >. (While (S) < (*)an { (1)English/(2)Japanese } (*)bilingual > (V) is (C) 『 (W)◎a dream { [(S) < which > ↑ (aV) has]] come ↑ (C) 『 true 』 } { for < many Japanese > } 』), (S) < (1){ "かな変換日本語(Japanese terms (W)via < KANA conversion >) }／(2){ アルファベット打ち英単語(English terms (W)via < alphabets >) } (*)bilingualism" > (V) is (C) 『 a nightmarish redundancy 』.

(S) < { (1)The greatest } 【 ((indeed) (2){ the only }) 】 (*)◎point { [(S) < which > (V) is] (C) 『 (id)in favor of < KANA conversion > 』 } > (V) is (C) 『 ◎{ the (relatively) fewer } steps { [(S) < which > ＼ (aV) are]] (V) needed ／ (to (id)(V) type in (O) « (W)any given sound (in < Japanese >) ») } 』. ((id)For example), (when (S) < you > (id)(V) want to (id)(V) type in (O) « "かな変換" »), (S) < it > (V) takes (O) « ten(10) steps (k-a-n-a-h-e-n-k-a-n) » ((W)via < (W)Roman alphabet conversion >), ／ while (S) < it > (V) takes (O) « (only) six(6) steps (T-U-^-Y-T-Y) » (through < KANA conversion >). (S) < { 40% } reduction > (id)(V) appears to (V) be (C) 『 a great advantage 』 [(aV) do (S) < you > (V) think] ?... (Well), ↑ (aV) haven't (S) < you > (V) forgotten ↑ (about < something >)? (S) < (id)‡(V) Typing‡ in (O) « Japanese » > (V) is (C) 『 ◎a (structurally) stressful act { [(S) < which > (V) is] (id)full of < GO/STOP > (◎(id)every time { [(that)] (S) < you > (aV) must ^(V) convert^ (O) « KANA » ^into^ <

KANJI > }) } 』. (Since (S) < KANA-KANJI conversion > (aV) must (V) spoil (O) « your speed » (anyway)), why [(aV) should (S) < you >] (id)(V) bother to (V) gain (O) « negligible speed » (by < ‡(V) burdening‡ (O) « (*){ your } (1)brains and (2)fingers » (by < (w)double standards (*)of (1)< "かな文字(KANA characters)" > and (2)< "アルファベット((w)alphabets)" > >) >)?

((id)(S) < Such > †(V) being† (C) 『 the case 』), (*)(S) < ◎{ (practically) all } companies (in < Japan >) { [(S) < which > (V) are] (C) 『 (reasonably) international 』 } > ＼ (1)(aV) are 〖 (and (2)(aV) should (aV) be) 〗 (id)(*)(V) equipped with ／ < ◎computers { (*)working (1)on < "ローマ字変換:(w)Roman alphabet conversion" >, not (2)on < "かな変換:KANA conversion" > } >. ((id)In order to (V) avoid (O) « ‡(V) being‡ (C) 『 (w)a black sheep ((id)in the middle of < Roman folks > 』) »), (V) start (O) « ‡(V) learning‡ (O) « typing » ((id)by way of < (w)Roman alphabet conversion >) » and (JUST) (V) SAY (O) « NO » (TO < KANA CONVERSION >). (If (S) < you > (still) (*)^(V) prefer^ (1)(O) « Japanese » ^to^ < logic >, or (2)(O) « the haphazard choice { of yours } » ^to^ < the sensible choice { of others } >), (id)(so) (V) be (S) < it >... 〖 (id)at your own risk 〗 .

(Anyway), ([^whether^ (S) < you > (V) choose] (1)(O) « Roman » ^or^ (2)(O) « KANA »), ^(V) make^ (O) « a good typist » (^of^ < you >), ^and^ (S) < (w)the road to < English mastery > > (aV) will (V) be (C) 『 (*)(incredibly) (1)smoother, (2)broader and (3)brighter [than (when (S) < you > (V) remain (C) 『a poor typist 』)] 』.

18.(S) < English > (aV) ought to ＼ (*)(aV) be (1)(V) spoken, not (2)(V) written ／ : (S) < (1)minimum memos, (2)maximum memory & (3)no notebook (4m2n) > (V) is (C) 〖 the way ^for^ (S) < 'em(= *them*) > ^to^ < English mastery > 〗 - (S) < ◎^Those^ ^(S) < who >^ (id)(V) make (O) « efforts » ((id)for show) > (aV) will (id)(V) make (O) « no { real } progress » -

((*)With (1)< English > or (2)< anything { else } >), (S) < ◎^those^ ^(S) < who >^ (id)(V) make (O) « { the greatest } efforts » > (V) are (C) 〖 least (id)likely to (V) succeed 〗. (((C) 〖 Paradoxical 〗 as(= *though*) (S) < it > (aV) may (V) sound), (S) < this > (V) is (C) 〖 true 〗:(= *because*) (S) < efforts > (*)(V) are (1)(C) 〖 ◎energy { wasted } 〗 and (2)(C) 〖 (id)hindrance to < anything { (really) great } > 〗. (*)(S) < Efforts > (1)(V) are (C) 〖 (consciously) painful 〗, and (2)(aV) will (id)(V) come to (V) mean (O) « much more than (S) < it > (aV) should *[(V) mean]* » ((id)due (*)to (1)< the weight of < the pain > > and (2)< ◎the time { *[(S) < which > ＼ (aV) was]]* (V) spent ／ (*[in]* < ‡(V) enduring‡ (O) « it » >) } >). ((id)In the end), (*)(S) < efforts > (1)(aV) will (V) become (C) 〖 (w)an end ((id)in itself) 〗 and (2) ＼ (aV) are (proudly) (id)(V) shown off ／ ... / when(= *and then*) (S) < success > (aV) will 【 naturally 】 (id)(V) fly away. (S) < Too many Japanese > ＼ (aV) are (V) wasting ／ (O) « (id)too much of < everything > », (1)< time >, (2)< energy >, (3)< money > or (4)< patience > (^both^ (1){ of themselves } ^and^ (2){ of others }) ((just) (id)in order to (V) give (O) « unwarranted value » (to < their meaningless efforts >)).

(S) < ◎^Those^ { ^(S) < who >^ (really) (V) succeed } > (id)(V) make (O) « ^no^ efforts » (^(id)at all^): (S) < they > (just) (V) do (O) « (*)(O) « (S) < what > » 【 (S) < they > (V) are (C) 〖 sure 〗 】 (1)(S) < they > (aV) must (V) do and (2)(aV) will (V) benefit (O) « them » ((id)in the end) ». ◎(S) < They > (V) do (O) « it » ((id)with all their might), { (S) < which > (aV) may ^(V) seem^ 【 to < others > 】 (C) 〖 [^to^ (V) be] (really) painful efforts 〗 }, but (S) < they > (actually) (V) feel (O) « no pain »: (S) < they > | (aV) are (just) (V) feeling | (O) « the weight of < ◎success { to (V) come } > ». (S) < The weight of <

(id)a pair of < dumbbells > > > (V) are (C) 〚 a tangible (id)guarantee for < future muscles > 〛 (in < the consciousness of < body-builders > >), / while †(V) being†(= (S) < it > (V) is) (simply) (C) 〚 (painfully) heavy 〛 (to < idle viewers >). (S) < Pain > (V) is (C) 〚 no pain 〛 (when (S) < you > (aV) can (id)(V) take (O) « pleasure » in < it >), ^nor^ (*)(V) is (S) < an effort > (1)(C) 〚 any effort 〛 ^but^ (2)(C) 〚 (simply) fun 〛 (when (S) < you > (V) are (C) 〚 sure 〛 *[that]* (S) < you > | (*)(aV) are (1)(V) doing | (O) « something { meaningful } » | , not (just) (2) | (V) enduring (O) « something { painful } »).

(Just) (id)(V) look at (O) « yourself » (C) 〚 | (V) studying | (O) « English » 〛 – (*)(V) is (S) < it > (1)(C) 〚 fun 〛, or (2)(C) 〚 pain 〛 ((*)for < you >)? (If *[(S) < it > (V) is]* (C) 〚 painful 〛), (aV) should (S) < you > (V) feel*(= if (S) < you > (aV) should (V) feel)* (O) « *[that]* (S) < you > | (aV) are (id)(V) making { conscious } efforts | ((id)with perseverance) », (id)(S) < ◎chances > (V) are { [that] (id)(S) < something > (*)(V) is (1)(C) 〚 ^wrong^ 〛, (2)(C) 〚 (terribly) ^wrong^ 〛 (*)^with^ < (O) « what » (S) < you > | (aV) are (V) doing | ((id)in the name of < ‡(V) studying‡ (O) « English » >) > }. ^(S) < It > (*)(V) is^ ^not^ (1)(C) 〚 effort 〛 ^but^ (2)(C) 〚 ◎energy { *[(S) < which >* ＼ *(aV) is]]* (id)(V) coupled with ／ < pleasurable enthusiasm > } 〛 ^(S) < that >^ ＼ (aV) is (V) needed ／ (^in^ < ‡(V) master^ing^‡ (O) « English » >). ◎(S) < ◎Painful consciousness { *[(S) < which > (V) is]* (C) 〚 (id)inherent in < efforts > 〛 } > (aV) will (*)(V) spoil (1)(O) « pleasure » and (2)(O) « enthusiasm » / to*(= and (aV) will)* (id)(V) result in < a flop >, { (S) < which > (V) is (C) 〚 (painfully) evident 〛 (from < the countless examples of < Japanese failures (in < English >) > >) }.

- (S) < (V) Write and learn*(= (V) Learn (by < ‡(V) writing‡ >))* > (V) is (C) 〚 the Japanese way 〛: (S) < (1)(V) recite, (2)(V) memorize and (3)(V) replicate > (V) is (C) 〚 the way of < English > 〛 -

(S) < { (*)The most (1)common and (2)foolish } ◎^mistake^ { (O) « *[that]* » (S) < {

Japanese } English learners > ^(v) make^ } > (v) is (c) 『 (id)‡(v) trying‡ to (v) master (o) « English » (◎the way { (*[in < which >]*) (s) < they > (v) mastered (o) « their native Japanese » }: ‡(v) learning‡ (by < (*)(id)‡(v) writing‡ down (1)(o) « words », (2)(o) « (w)idioms », (3)(o) « sentences » and (4)(o) « translations » >)), 【 (id)to (1){ little } or (2){ no } avail 】 』. (s) < ◎The ^fault^ { to ＼ (av) be ^(v) found^ ／ (^with^ < this method >) — 【 vainly 】 (id)‡(v) trying‡ to (v) master (o) « (w)phonograms » (by < ‡(v) making‡ (o) « them » (c) 『 (visually) tangible { (c) 『 as 』 (s) < (w)ideograms > (id)(v) are (c) 『 supposed to (v) be 』 } 』 >) — } > ↑ (av) has (already) ＼ (av) been (id)(v) pointed out ／ ↑ (in < this book >). (Still), (s) < so many Japanese > (id)(v) stick to < ‡(v) writing and (v) learning‡*(= ‡(v) learning‡ by ‡(v) writing‡)* (o) « English » 【 to < pre-destined failure > 】 > (^for^ < one simple ^reason^ >) — (s) < they > (positively) (id)(v) hate to (v) read (o) « English » (aloud)... / ^for^ < several ^reasons^ >:

(1)(s) < they > (av) don't (v) know (o) « how to (v) intone*(= (v) read (aloud) (o) « a sentence » with < correct (w)intonation >)* »;

(2)(s) < they > (av) don't (v) know (o) « how to (v) accentuate*(= (v) speak (o) « a word » with < correct accent >)* »;

(3)(s) < they > (av) can't (v) be (c) 『 sure 』 if (s) < they > | (av) are (v) pronouncing (correctly) | ;

(4)(s) < they > (id) ＼ (v) get (c) 『 stuck 』 ／ (at < ◎every word { < *[that]* > (s) < they > (v) are (c) 『 ((id)not completely) (id)familiar with 』 } >).

... (s) < These > (v) are ◎minor hurdles { < *[which]* > (s) < you > (av) can (id)(v) get over ((simply) (*)by (1)< diligence > and (2)< practice >) }, / while (s) < the next one > (v) is (c) 『 (really) troublesome 』:

(5)(s) < They > ＼ (av) are (id)(v) presented (*)with ／ < (1)^too^ many English sentences 【 (or (2){ ^too^ boring } ones) 】 { ^for^ (s) < them > ^to^ (id)(v) feel (c) 『 inclined (*)to (1)(v) read (aloud), (id)let alone (2)(id)(v) learn (by heart) 』 } >. ... (s) <

This > (V) is (C) 『 ◎{ the most (seriously) damaging } reason { [why] (S) < most Japanese students > (*)(positively) (id)(V) hate to (1)(V) read (aloud) and (2)(V) memorize (*)(O) « English sentences », ((thereby) †(V) making† (O) « themselves » (C) 『 (virtually) illiterate (in < English >) 』) } 』.

(1)(S) < Schools > and (2)(S) < teachers > (aV) should (V) choose (O) « (only) ◎ˆsuchˆ texts { (O) « ˆasˆ » (*)(S) < their students > (1)(aV) can and (2)(aV) will (*)(id)(V) try to (1)(V) read (aloud) and (2)(V) memorize } ». (S) < They > (id)have to (V) be (1)(C) 『 (id)not too long 』, (2)(C) 『 (grammatically) meaningful 』 and (3)(C) 『 【 preferably 】 ◎fun { to (V) read } 』... (Fun element (aside)(= (id)*Aside from* < *fun element* >)), (S) < selection of < (grammatically) meaningful short sentences > > (V) is (C) 『 (id)one of < the most important tasks ((id)on the part (*)of (1)< teachers >, (2)< schools > and (3)< textbooks >) > 』 (to (*)ˆ(V) enableˆ (O) « (1)students, 【 (especially) (2)beginners 】 », (C) 『 (*)ˆtoˆ (V) acquire the good habit of < ‡(1)(V) memorizing‡ 【 as (S) < they > (2)(V) read (aloud) 】 (*)(O) « English sentences » > 』)... (id)(S) < ◎The { sad } truth > (V) is *[{ that]* , (S) < (*)too many { Japanese } (1)schools, (2)teachers, or (3)(even) textbooks > (*)(V) are (id)(1)neglectful 【 ((even) (2)unaware!) 】 (*)of < their ◎duty { to (V) be (C) 『 selective about < (O) « what » to ˆ(V) presentˆ (O) « students » ˆwithˆ > 』 } > }.

(id)(S) < ˆItˆ > (V) follows (from < this >) ˆthatˆ (S) < you, students >, (id)have to (V) be (C) 『 (very, very) selective (*)in (1)< (O) « what » to (1)(V) read (aloud) and (2)(V) remember > and (2)< (O) « what » to (just) (id)(1)(V) browse through and (2)(V) forget > 』. (If (S) < (O) « what » (S) < your school > (V) gives (O) « you » > (V) are (all) (C) 『 (id)unworthy of < memorization > 』), (S) < you > (aV) will (id)have (*)to (1)(V) seek and (2)(V) find ((id)for yourself) (O) « (*)some ◎worthy textbooks { *[(S) < which > (V) are]* (id)full of < ◎(meaningfully) memorable sentences >, { (O) « which » (S) < you > (*)(aV) must (1)(V) read (aloud) and (2)(V) remember }, (while (id)†(V) dealing†*(= (S) < you > (V) deal)* (half-heartedly) with < ◎immemorable stuff { (O) « *[which]* » (S) < your school > (V) thrusts (upon < you >) } >) } ».

(aV) Do not (id)(V) kid (O) « yourself » into < ‡(V) believing‡ (O) « [that] (S) < you > (aV) can (V) neglect (O) « (O) « whatever » (S) < you > (V) find (C) 〚 uninteresting 〛 » » >: (< your feelings > notwithstanding(= *notwithstanding < your feelings >*)), (S) < (S) < what > ＼ (id)(aV) is (V) meant to ／＼ (aV) be (V) memorized ／ 〖 ((id)such as (1)< example sentences (in < your "grammar" textbooks >) > or (2)< ◎tasteless English { (O) « *[which]* » (S) < you > (V) find (in < "reader" >) } >) 〗 > (aV) must ＼ (aV) be (V) memorized ／ , ((C) 〚 ((id)no matter how(= *however*)) terrible 〛 (S) < you > (V) (personally) find (O) « them » *[(C) 〚to (V) be 〛]*). (S) < (O) « What » (S) < you > (*)can (1) 〖 rightly 〗 and (2)(lightly) (*)(V) browse (1)(for < tentative interpretation >) and not (2)(for < permanent memorization >) > (V) is (C) 〚 ◎stuff { like (1)< ◎a whole book (of < some novelist >) { (O) « *[which]* » (S) < your teacher > (V) orders (O) « you » (C) 〚 (*)to (1)(V) buy and (2)(V) read 〖 (and (even) (3)(V) translate!) 〗 〛 (as < homework (during < (w)summer vacation >) >) } >, or (2)< ◎{ (casually) quoted } newspaper articles { *[(S) < which > ＼ ^(aV) are^]]* ^(V) meant to^ ／ ^(V) introduce^ (O) « you » ^to^ < "生きた英語(IKITA EIGO: English { ALIVE }!)" > } > } 〛.

(aV) Don't (V) take (O) « this advice » ((too) lightly): (S) < to (wisely) (V) select 〖 ((1)((*)by (1)< school > or (2)< teacher >) or (2)((id)for yourself)) 〗 (O) « ◎English sentences { ^for^ (S) < you > ^to^ (1)(V) read (aloud) and (2)(id)(V) learn (by heart) } » > (V) is (C) 〚 the first step (in < your (w)road to < English mastery > >) 〛: (without < good selection >), (S) < you >(aV) 'll (simply) (id)(V) go (nowhere).

- ^(V) Speak^ (well), ^or^ (S) < you > (*)(aV) can^'t^ (1)(V) hear, (2)(V) read or (3)(V) write (*)(O) « English » (^(id)at all^) -

(Since (S) < English language > (*) ＼ (id)(aV) is (V) meant to ／ (1) ＼ (aV) be (V) spoken ／ , not to (2) ＼ (*)(aV) be (1)(V) seen and (2)(visually) (V) understood ／ (like (S) < Japanese >)), (S) < "sound" > (id)(V) plays (O) « a { much greater } role » (1)(in < English >) ^than^ (2)(in < Japanese >). (S) < All Japanese > (V) know (O) « that », and (S) < ‡(V) falling‡ (C) 〚 "(id)out of tune" 〛 > (V) is ◎(C) 〚 their greatest fear (in < ‡(V) speaking‡ (O) « English » >) 〛, { (S) < which > (eventually) (id)(V) leads to < (S) < their > (*)^not^ (1)‡(V) speaking‡ 〖(and (2)‡(V) mastering‡) 〗 (*)(O) « English » (^(id)at all^) > }.

(In < this author's younger days >), (S) < ^it^ > (V) was (C) 『 (quite) hard 』 ^for^ (S) < Japanese learners of < English > > ^to^ (V) confirm (O) « ^whether^ (S) < they > (*)(V) were (1)(C) 『 (id)in tune 』 ^or^ (2)(C) 『 (id)out of sync 』 (^in^ < ‡(V) speak^ing^‡ (O) « English » >) ». (There) (*)(V) was (1)(S) < no (w)Internet >, (2)(S) < no ◎multi-channel TVs { *[(S) < which > (V) were]* (C) 『 (id)full of < English ‡broadcasting‡ > 』 } >, (3)(S) < no ◎multi-media English ‡tutoring‡ programs { to (V) give (O) « you » (O) « audio guidance » } >. (Still), (S) < this author > (V) was (C) 『 (quite) (id)sure of < the correctness of < his English speech > > 』... (aV) Do (S) < you > (V) know (O) « why »? (S) < The reason > (V) is (C) 『 (*)(quite) (1)simple and (2)logical 』: (S) < he > (id)(V) made (O) « ^it^ » (C) 『 a rule 』 ^(1)to^ ^(V) cast (O) « spotlights »^ 〖 in < sound > 〗 ^on^ < semantic partitions (in < a sentence >) > and (2)never ^to^ (V) stop (absurdly) ((id)in the middle of < a stream of < meaning > >). (Since (S) < ^no^ sound (in < English >) > (^can^ ^possibly^) (id)(V) go against < meaning >), (S) < to (rhythmically) (V) connect (O) « { (meaningfully) separated } blocks of < terms > » > (aV) will (id)never (V) fail to (V) sound (C) 『 good 』 (as < English >). ((id)As for < anatomical interpretation of < English > ((w)via < (visually) conspicuous signs > ((1)< >(2)「 」(3){ }(4)( )(5)[ ])) >), (S) < this author > ↑ (aV) has (already) (V) shown ↑ (O) « you » (O) « how *[to (V) do (so)]* ». (S) < This > (V) is (C) 『 the most reliable ◎guidance { ^for^ (S) < you > ^to^ (O) « follow » (^in^ < ‡(V) speak^ing^‡ (O) « English » >) } 』. ^(V) Speak^ (O) « English » (well), ^and^ (S) < you > (aV) will (automatically) (V) understand (O) « its meaning » (well) ((id)as well).

- (*)^(V) Spend^ (1)(O) « (*){ less } (1)time and (2)energy » (^in^ < preparation >) and (2)(O) « more *[(1)time and (2)energy]* » (^in^ < recitation >); (3)least *[(1)time and (2)energy]* (^in^ < notation >) and (4)most *[(1)time and (2)energy]* (^in^ < memorization >) -

(S) < Most Japanese students > 〖 ((id)(V) try to) 〗 (V) make (O) « ◎grandiose notebooks { *[(S) < which > (V) are]* (C) 〚 (id)independent of < English textbooks > 〛 } », { (S) < the creation of < which > > ＼ (aV) is 〖 mistakenly 〗 (V) considered ／ (C) 〚 to (V) be (C) 〚 the study of < English > 〛 〛 }. (If (S) < you > (V) are (C) 〚 (id)one of < them > 〛), (S) < you > (ic)(V) are (C) 〚 bound to (id)(V) end up in < the miserable line of < English illiterates > (in < Japan >) > 〛.

NEVER (V) make (O) « notes » (outside < your English textbooks >): (S) < it > (V) is (C) 〚 an act of < linguistic suicide > 〛. (S) < Notation > (aV) must ＼ (aV) be (V) made ／ ((id)in the form of < (1)footnotes/(2)headnotes ((id)in between < the lines of < your textbooks > >) >). (Since (S) < such small space > (aV) can (V) hold (O) « { (id)only so much } information »), (S) < you > (aV) can't (id)(V) write in (O) « (id)too much info ». (S) < You > (aV) must (V) make (O) « wise selection » (here), (too): (1)◎{ what } info { to (id)(V) write down } and (2)◎{ what } others { to (id)(V) store up (in < your memory >) }, and (3)◎what { else } { to (simply) (V) ignore }.

(At < preparation stage >), (V) check (O) « unknown words », (id)(V) look (O) « them » up (in < the dictionary >), (V) confirm (O) « their meaning », and ^(V) mark^ (O) « the words » (^with^ < some tentative signs >) — (1)◎W. or w. 〖 ((id)†(V) standing† for *(= (S) < which > (V) stands for)* < "word" >) 〗, (2)!((w)exclamation), (3)?((w)question), (4)#((w)sharp), (5)*((w)asterisk), etc,etc. — but (aV) don't (id)(V) write in (O) « their meanings ». (At < ‡reviewing‡ stage >), (id)(V) check to*(= and)* (V) see (O) « if (S) < you > (aV) can (V) remember (O) « their meanings » (correctly) ». (If (S) < you > (aV) can't *[(V) remember (O) « their meanings » (correctly)]*), (V) admit (O) « your defeat » ((id)with a good grace), (V) consult (O) « the dictionary » (again) and (V) write (O) « the meanings » ((id)in between < the lines >). (Even if (S) < you > (V) can *[(V) remember (O) « their meanings » (correctly)]*), (aV) don't (id)(V) wipe out (O) « the tentative signs of < your uncertainty > »: (S) < they > (aV) will (V) serve (O) « you » (well) (in < (id)‡(V) preparing‡ for < the exam > >) (as < your { (

possibly) weak } points >).

(aV) Don't (id)(V) try to (id)(V) write down (O) « ◎grammatical info » 〖 ((S) < which > (S) < you > (id)(V) happened to (*)(V) find (1)(in < some (w)reference book >) or (2)(from < the teacher's mouth >)) 〗 ((id)in between < the lines >): (S) < you > (simply) (aV) can't *[(V) do (O) « that »]*, ((id)due to < the (*){ limited } (1)time and (2)space >). (Instead), (just) ^(V) mark^ (O) « (*)the (1)terms or (2)expressions { (S) < which > (V) demand (O) « grammatical consideration » } » ^with^ < signs 〖 (GR./gr.) 〗 *[†(V) standing†]* for < "grammar" > >. (id)What about < the grammatical information (itself) >?... (id)(V) Store (O) « it » up (in < your memory >) (◎(id)the moment { *[(that)]* (S) < you > (V) find (O) « it » })!... *[(V) Is (S) < it >]* (C) 『 Impossible 』?... (Well), (then), (just) (id)(V) write in 〖 (beside < the "gr." mark >) 〗 (O) « the ◎page of < the (w)reference book { [where] (S) < you > (aV) can (V) find (O) « detailed explanation » } > »... (id)What *[(aV) should (S) < you > (V) do]* if (S) < the info > (casually) (id)(V) comes off < the teacher's mouth >?... (Just) (V) summarize (O) « it » or (id)(V) think about < ◎(1)some snappy title or (2)keyword { to (V) remember (O) « it » (by) } >.

((id)In any case), (aV) don't (aV) let (O) « the act of < (id)‡(V) writing‡ in > » (C) 『 (id)(V) play a (O) « { major } role » (in < your studies >) 』: (id)(V) give (O) « (w)top priority » to < (*)the (1){ reading }, (2){ thinking } and (3){ memorizing } (*)process >. (^The^ more) (S) < you > (V) write, (^the^ less) (*)(S) < you > (1)(V) read and (2)(V) think: and (S) < (*){ the least } (1)reader and (2)thinker > (V) is (C) 『 most (id)likely to (V) fail in < ‡(V) mastering‡ (O) « English » > 』.

((id)As for < ◎(w)idioms { (O) « *[which]* » (S) < you > (V) found (in < sentences >) } >), ^(V) mark^ (O) « them » ^with^ < (w)IDIOM signs 〖 (ID. or id.) 〗 > and (just) (id)(V) write in (O) « ◎their meanings { (O) « *[which]* » (S) < you > (V) found (in < the dictionary >) } » (as < (1)footnotes/(2)headnotes ((id)in between < the lines of < your textbook > >) >): (S) < you > (id)don't have to (V) hide (O) « the meanings of < (w)idioms > » (for < later examination >) — (S) < (w)the test of < an (w)idiom > > (aV) does ^not^ (id)(V) lie (1)in < (correctly) ‡(V) remembering‡ (O) « the meaning » >, ^but^ (2)in < (perfectly) ‡(V) reciting‡ (O) « ◎the whole example sentence { < *[which]* > (S) < it > ＼ (aV) is (V) used ／ (in) } » >. (id)(V) Try (1)to (id)(V) store up (O) « the (w)idiom » (in < your head >) (in < the context of < the sentence > >), not (just) (2)to (V) memorize (O) « the short definition ».

(Finally), (V) give (O) « anatomical interpretation signs » ((only) to < ◎^those^ sentences { [^(O) « which »^] (S) < you > (V) find (C) 『 { ^worth^ } (O) « anatomiz^ing^ » 』 } >): (just) (V) ignore (O) « all { else } » and (V) leave (O) « them » (C) 『 untouched 』. (In < actual lessons (in < the classroom >) >), (id)(V) be (C) 『 all (1)eyes and (2)ears 』 (to (id)(V) check to*(= and)* (V) see (O) « if (S) < (O) « what » (S) < you > (V) anatomized (at < preparation stage >) > ↑ (aV) has (really) ＼ (aV) been (correctly) (V) interpreted ／ ↑ »). (id)(V) Pay (O) « attention » to < your teacher's explanation >, / for, (besides < (O) « what » (S) < you > (already) (V) marked (at < preparation stage >) >), (there) (aV) may (V) be (S) < ◎some other sentences { [(S) < which > (V) are] (C) 『 (id)worthy of < anatomical interpretation > 』 ((id)in the opinion of < the teacher >) } >: (S) < that particular opinion of < the teacher > > (aV) may (V) count (much) (in < the exam >) ((id)later on)!

(Now) (S) < you > (aV) can (V) see (O) « [that] (S) < you > (id)don't have to ^(V) spend^ (O) « (*){ too much } (1)time or (2)energy » ^in^ < (id)‡(V) preparing‡ for < an English lesson > > » — ((id)so long as (S) < you > (V) are (C) 『 (wisely) selective (*)in (1)< (O) « what » { to (id)(V) write down (on < paper >) } >, (2)< (O) « what » { to (V) inscribe (in < your memory >) } >, and (3)< what { else } { (*)to (1)(simply) (id)(V) go through and (2)(id)(aV) let (C) 『 (V) go 』 } > 』). (S) < The real battle (for < mastery >) > (V) begins (when (S) < the lesson > (V) is (C) 『 over 』): (w)(V) give ◎all { (O) « *[that]* » (S) < you > ↑ (aV) 've (V) got ↑ } to < (1)‡(V) reciting‡ and (2)‡(V) memorizing‡ (*)(O) « (O) « what » (S) < you > (aV) should (V) *[(V) recite and (V) memorize]* » >. (If (S) < you > (aV) can (V) (correctly) remember (O) « ◎all those sentences { (O) « *[that]* » (S) < you > (V) found (C) 『 (*){ ^worth^ } (O) « (1)‡(V) not^ing^‡ and (2)‡(V) remember^ing‡ » 』} »), (S) < ◎all the relevant information { [(S) < *that* > ＼ (aV) *are*]] (id)(V) related with ／ < them > } > (aV) will (V) (naturally) (id)(V) come up to < your mind > ((id)along with < the sentences >) — (1)(in < ◎sound { †(V) ringing†(= (S) < *which* > (V) *rings*) (in < your ears >) } >, not (2)(in < ◎letters { [(S) < *which* > ＼ (aV) *are*]] (V) written ／ (on < (id)sheets of < paper > >) } >))!

(S) < All knowledge of < English > — (1)words, (2)(w)idioms, (3)(w)sentence patterns, (4)(w)semantic constructions, (5)grammatical info — > (aV) ought to ＼ (aV) be ^(V) fortified^ ／ 【 in < your memory > 】 (^with^ < some particular sentences (in < the spoken form >) >), (id)so that (whenever (S) < you > (id)(V) try to (V) confirm (O) « (id)a { certain } piece of < knowledge > »), (S) < it > (aV) will (*)(id)(V) come up (1)(＼ [(aV) *being*] (id)(V) coupled with ／ < some sentence >), not (2)(as < ◎an abstract academic information { [(S) < *which* > ＼ (aV) *is*]] (V) itemized ／ (in < a (w)rule book >) } >). (S) < (1){ Preparation } and (2){ reviewing } (*)stages of < your English lessons > > (V) are (C) 『 ◎the opportunities { to ^(V) enrich^ (O) « yourself » (^with^ < such ^combination^ of < example sentences > ^with^ < (*){ related } (1)info and (2)knowledge > > }) 』. (V) Make (O) « as many couples as possible », and (V) make (O) « them » (C) 『 (perpetually) memorable 』 (by < ‡(V) reading‡ (O) « them » (aloud) ((id)over and over [again]) >).

- (S) < { English illiterate } Japanese > (invariably) (id)(V) make (O) « too much » of < (w)pronunciation > ((id)with no regard (*)to (1)< rhythm > or (2)< (w)intonation >) -

((id)Next to < the correct choice of < ◎{ what } English { (*)to (1)(V) read (aloud) and (2)(V) memorize } > >) (V) comes (S) < the question of < how to (correctly) (V) read (aloud) > >. (Here) (aV) will (S) < the Japanese > (invariably) (id) ＼ (V) get (C) 『 stuck 』 ／ ((id)due to < their queer notion of < < what > (S) < English > (aV) should (id)(V) sound like > >). (*)(S) < They > (1)(id)never (V) fail to (V) imitate (O) « "GAIJIN SOUND" » and (2)(id)(V) fail to (id)(V) sound like < English >.

(S) < Most { Japanese } notion of < anything { foreign } > > (id)(V) tends (*)to (1)(id)(V) go (C) 〚 (strangely) awry 〛 and (2)(w)(V) come back to(= and) (V) haunt (O) « them » (in < { hands-on } experience >). (To (V) take (O) « a { (rather) WESTERN } example »), (S) < { (virtually) all } Japanese citizens > (V) have (O) « no actual experience of < ‡(V) shooting‡ (O) « a handgun » > », ((id)thanks to < ◎the (id)ban on < guns > { (S) < which > (V) makes (O) « this country » (C) 〚 the safest (in < the world >) 〛 } >). ((id)Thanks to < this vacuum >), (S) < Japanese ideas (*)of (1)< wars >, (2)< combats >, (3)< weapons > 〖 (and (4)< peace >) 〗 > (V) are (all) (C) 〚 (id)out of sync with < the world (outside) > 〛. (S) < (1)Wars and (2)combats > (id)(aV) might as well not ＼ (aV) be (V) experienced ／ (personally), but (there) (V) are (S) < ◎some Japanese { (S) < who > ◎(id)(V) want to (V) experience (O) « ‡(V) shooting‡ (O) « real guns » » } >, { (S) < which > (V) leads (O) « them » (to < ◎foreign countries { where (S) < casual tourists > (id)(aV) are (V) allowed to (V) shoot (O) « this "dream weapon" { of theirs } » } >) }. (S) < Most Japanese tourists >, 〖 naturally 〗 , (V) are (C) 〚 (w)lousy shots 〛 ((id)due to < their (id)lack of < experience > >). But (S) < the worst (of < all >) > (V) are (C) 〚 ◎^those^ Japanese shooters { ^(S) < who >^ ↑ (aV) have ＼ (id)(aV) been (V) accustomed to ／ ↑ (V) imitate(= ‡(V) imitating‡) (O) « the real shooter's (id)reaction to < the violent recoil of < a handgun > > » (with < a silent (w)model gun (in < their hand >) >) } 〛. (S) < Their image of < ◎(w)Dirty Harry { [(S) < who > | (aV) is]] (V) shooting | (O) « a legendary (w)44 magnum » } > > (V) is (C) 〚 never complete (without < ◎the powerful reaction of < the bullet > { †(V) swinging†(= (S) < which > (V) swings) (O) « his right arm » (upward) (◎the moment { [that] (S) < it > (id)(V) goes off }) } >) 〛! (So), (with < a fake plastic revolver (＼ [†(V) being†] (firmly) (V) held ／ (in < their hand >)) >), (S) < Japanese (w)gun nuts > ^(V) imagine^ (O) « themselves » (1)(C) 〚 | (V) shooting | (O) « a real gun » 〛 and (2)(C) 〚 (id) | (V) dealing | with < the gigantic recoil of < ‡shooting‡ > > 〛 (^by^ < ‡(V) swinging‡ (O) « their arm » (sky-high) >)... ◎^Those^ { ^(S) < who >^ ↑ (aV) have ＼ (id)(aV) been (V) accustomed to ／ ↑ < this (id)kind of < (*){ preconceived } (1)notion and (2)reaction (*)of < "(C) 『 what 』 (S) < ‡(V) shooting‡ (O) « guns » > (aV) should (V) be" > > > } (V) are (C) 『 less (id)likely to (V) shoot (correctly) 』 than (S) < ◎^those^ Japanese shooters { (S) < ^who^ > ↑ (aV) have never (id)(V) dreamt of ↑ < ◎themselves ‡(V) shooting‡ (O) « a real gun » > } >. (S) < Japanese { would-be } shooters > (aV) will (instinctively) ^(V) add^ (O) « their imaginary (id)version of < "a real gun's recoil" > » ^to^ < the natural physical recoil of < ◎the gun { (O) « *[which]* » (S) < they > | (aV) are (actually) (V) shooting | } > >... how (*)(aV) could (S) < they > (1)(V) aim and (2)(V) shoot (correctly) (when (S) < their guns' muzzles > (aV) will (id)(V) jump up (^not only^ (1)physically ^but also^ (2)mentally))? (S) < They > (aV) will (invariably) (id)(V) end up *[in]* < ‡(V) shooting‡ ((considerably) above < the target >) >!

(S) < The same preposterous mistake > ＼ (aV) is (habitually) (V) repeated ／ (by < ◎the Japanese { (id)†(V) sticking† to *(= (S) < who > (V) stick to)* < their imaginary (id)versions of < "(C) 『 what 』 (S) < GAIJIN SOUND > (aV) should (V) be" > > } >). (S) < This author > (id)(V) has (O) « no intention of < (id)‡(V) pointing‡ (O) « them » out (here) ((id)in detail) > ». (id)(V) Suffice (O) « ^it^ » ^to^ (V) say (O) « [that] (S) < the Japanese > | (aV) are ^(V) gazing^ | 〖 ^too^ (nervously) 〗 ^at^ < trees > (^to^ (V) see (O) « the whole forest ») ».

(S) < One great source of < this Japanese farce > > (V) is (C) 『 ◎the undue ^weight^ { (O) « *[which]* » (S) < they > ^(V) put^ (^on^ < particular (w)pronunciation (in < a particular word >) >) } 』. (S) < The minor ^difference^ 〖 in < sound > 〗 ^between^ < "l" > ^and^ < "r" > > (aV) does ^not^ (V) matter so much as (S) < the innocent Japanese > (V) believe; (*[^whether^ (S) < it > (V) is]* (C) 『 "red" 』 ^or^ (C) 『 "led" 』), (S) < "(S) < His face > (V) was (C) 『 red 』 (with < shame >) (by < ＼ ‡(aV) being‡ (V) misled by ／ < preconception > >)" > (aV) will never ＼ (id)(aV) be (V) misunderstood as ／ < "His face was LED with shame by being MISS RED by preconception" >. (*)(S) < { English speaking } people > (1)(aV) will (V) understand (O) « the meaning of <

particular words > » ((id) according to < ◎the context { < [*which*] > (S) < they > ＼ (aV) are (V) used ／ (in) } >), and (2)(aV) will never ＼ (id)(aV) be (V) misled by ／ < mere sound >. (Although (S) < ^it^ > (V) is (C) 『 shameful 』 ^to^ (V) say (O) « "SHIT (here)" » (when (S) < you > (V) want (O) « someone » (C) 『 to "(V) SIT (here)" 』)), (S) < no sane person > (*)(aV) will (1)(id)(V) take (O) « your word » (1)(for < it >) 【 (or (2)for < the sound >) 】 and (2)(id)(V) sit down (before < you >) (to(= *and*) (id)(V) bring down (O) « their pants » (to(= *and*) (V) shit (there))).

(S) < Refined pronunciation > (V) is (C) 『 (certainly) (w)good news 』, but (S) < { too much } consciousness of < it > > (aV) will (id)(*)(V) do (O) « you » more (O) « (1)harm » than (O) « (2)good ». (There) (V) are (S) < ◎two ^other^ things { < [*which*] > (S) < beginners > (aV) should (id)(V) pay (O) « { much more } attention » to } ^than^ < (w)pronunciation > >. (S) < The first > ↑ (aV) has ＼ (aV) been (already) (id)(V) referred to ／ ↑ : ◎semantic blocks (in < a sentence >), { (S) < the distinction of < which > > (*)(V) is (1)(C) 『 (essentially) important 』 but (2)(C) 『 (rather) hard (for < beginners >) 』 }. (*)(S) < The second > (1)(V) is (C) 『 (also) important 』 (in < ‡(V) making‡ (O) « you » (C) 『 ＼ (V) understood *[to < others >]* ／ (in < English >) 』 >), but (2)is (C) 『 easier ((id)in a way) (for < the Japanese >) 』: (w)accentuation (in < each term (in < the sentence >) >).

- (aV) Don't (id)(V) stick to < perfect (w)pronunciation >; (S) < (*){ correct } (1)(w)accent and (2)(w)intonation > (aV) will (V) make (O) « you » (C) 『 ＼ (V) understood *[to < others >]* ／ (in < English >) 』 -

(S) < Novice learners > (aV) may not (even) (V) know (O) « the ^distinction^ ^between^ < (w)pronunciation > ^and^ < (w)accentuation > ». ^(V) Take^ (O) « the term "parallel" » (^(id)for example^). (S) < (*)The (1){ favorite } 【 (or (2){ most dreaded }) 】 (*)distinction 【 of < the Japanese people > 】 ^between^ < "l" > ^and^ < "r" > > ＼ (aV) is (V) found ／ (in < this term >): (if (S) < you > (V) say (O) « it » (like <

"paLaReRu" >)), (S) < you > (id) | (aV) are (V) making | (O) « a mistake » (in < (w)pronunciation >); (if (S) < you > (V) say (O) « it » (like < "paraLLEEEL" >)), (S) < you > | (aV) are ˆ(V) puttingˆ | (O) « a wrong ˆ(w)accentˆ » (ˆonˆ < "le" >). (S) < You > (aV) must (w)(V) accentuate (O) « "pa" » (in < "parallel" >): (S) < this knowledge > (V) is (C) 〖 much more important 〗 ˆthanˆ (S) < the (w)phonetic ˆdistinctionˆ ˆbetweenˆ < "l" > ˆandˆ < "r" > >. (S) < Most Japanese people > (aV) can (hardly) (id)(V) expect to (V) sound (C) 〖 right 〗 【 (just like < GAIJIN >) 】 (in < their pronunciation of < English words > >), / while (S) < they > (aV) can (V) make (O) « themselves » (C) 〖 (decently) ＼ (V) understood *[to < others >]* ／ 〗 (by < ‡(V) making‡ (O) « correct (w)accents » (in < each term >) >).

(V) Forget (about < (w)pronunciation >) and (just) (id)(V) remember to (w)(V) accentuate (correctly). (When *[(S) < you > | (aV) are]]* (id)(V) looking up | (O) « a word » (in < a dictionary >)), (S) < you > (aV) should (first) (id)(V) pay (O) « attention » to < (w)the primary accent of < the word > >. (V) Remember: (O) « (S) < ˆ(w)accentsˆ > (aV) can ˆonlyˆ ＼ (aV) be ˆ(V) putˆ ／ (1)ˆ(ˆonˆ < a (w)vowel >)ˆ, never (2)(ˆonˆ < a (w)consonant >) ». (If (S) < you > ↑ (id)(aV) haven't (V) got ↑ (O) « a dictionary » ((id)[near] at hand)), (V) make (O) « alphabetical anatomization of < the term > » and (id)(V) find out (O) « the position of < "(1)a, (2)i, (3)u, (4)e, (5)o" 【 (and (sometimes) "(6)y") 】 > »; (then), ˆ(V) tryˆ (O) « ˆ‡(V) puttˆing‡ˆ (O) « theatrical ˆ(w)accentˆ » (ˆonˆ < each "(1)a, (2)i, (3)u, (4)e, (5)o 【 (and (6)y) 】 " >) ((id)one by one) », and (V) see (O) « how (S) < it > (V) sounds »: (S) < { the least queer †sounding† } position > (aV) should (V) be (C) 〖 ◎the (w)vowel { to ˆ(V) putˆ (w)the primary ˆaccentˆ ˆonˆ } 〗... *[(aV) Do (S) < you > (V) feel (S) < it >]* (V) Sounds (C) 〖 (*)too (1)rough and (2)unreliable 〗 (to < your ears >)? OK, (then), (if (S) < you > (V) are (C) 〖 an authentic Japanese 〗), (here) (V) is (S) < one { (incredibly) reliable } method of < (correctly) ‡(V) detecting‡ (O) « (w)the primary accent (in < (w)any given English term > ») > > — (S) < you > ˆhave only toˆ (id)(V) go against < ◎the ˆ(w)accentˆ { (O) «

[which] » (S) < the Japanese > ^(V) put^ (^in^ < ‡(V) pronounc^ing^‡ (O) « "外来語 (GAIRAIGO: ◎Japanese terms { *[(S) < which >* ＼ *^(aV) are^]]* ^(V) derived from^ < abroad > ／ })" » >) } > (^in order to^ (w)(V) accentuate (O) « it » (right)).

(^For^ < some ^reason^ >), (S) < the Japanese people > (id)(V) have (O) « a way » of < ‡(V) changing‡ (O) « the position of < (w)the primary accent > » (in < ◎any English term { (O) « *[that]* » (S) < they > (V) introduce (to < their language >) (as < GAIRAIGO >) } >) >. (If (S) < you > (V) are (C) 〚 a Japanese 〛), ^(V) try^ (O) « (*)‡(V) say^ing^‡ (1)(O) « "display" » or (2)(O) « "endeavor" » (^both^ (1)(in < your language >) ^and^ (2)(in < English >)) » (*[in order]* to (V) see (O) « (O) « what » (S) < this author > (V) means »). (When (S) < the Japanese > (V) pronounce (O) « a foreign term » (as < GAIRAIGO >)), (S) < they > (*)(aV) will ^either^ (1)(V) kill (O) « the (w)accent » (altogether) (eg. (1)"engineer", (2)"guitarist", (3)"pioneer", (4)"pianist") ^or^ (2)(V) shift (O) « (w)the primary accent » (to < some wrong position >) (eg. (1)"accessory", (2)"curriculum", (3)"musician", (4)"success"). (S) < To (V) pronounce (O) « "display" » ([in] < the Japanese way >) ((id)as if (S) < it > (*)(V) were (1)(C) 〚 "this play" 〛 or (2)(C) 〚 "this prey" 〛) > (V) is (C) 〚 ^too^ crazy (^to^ (id)(V) make (O) « { any } sense ») 〛 (in < English consciousness >), but (S) < such > (V) is (C) 〚 the way of < the Japanese > 〛: (w)maybe*(= (S) < it > (aV) may (V) be (C) 〚that))* (S) < ^it^ > (V) is (C) 〚 in < the nature of < Japanese > >*(= natural ^for^ (S) < Japanese language >)* 〛 ^to^ (id)(V) go against < the authentic English (w)accent > 〛. ((C) 〚 Whatever 〛 (S) < the reason > *[(aV) may (V) be]*), (S) < this phenomenon > (V) is (C) 〚 ◎something { (O) « *[which]* » (S) < you > Japanese students of < English > (aV) should (id)(V) put (to < good use >) } 〛: (when *[(S) < you > (V) are]* (C) 〚 (id)in doubt about < (w)accent > (in < (w)any given term >) 〛), (id)^(V) go^ against < the Japanese way >, ^and^ (S) < you > (aV) will (probably) (w)(V) accentuate (O) « it » (right). (V) Trust (O) « me »: (S) < { anti-Japanese } accents > (rarely) (id)(V) fail to (V) sound (C) 〚 right 〛 (in < English >).

- ((id)In the end), ^(V) copy^ (O) « the whole book » (in < your brains >), ^and^ (S) < nothing > (aV) will (id)(V) stand in the way of < your (w)road to < intelligence > > -

(As (S) < you > (aV) can (V) see), (*)(S) < all the { above-mentioned } knowledge > (1)(aV) should ^not^ and (2)(aV) can^not^ ＼ (aV) be (id)(V) written down ／ (on < { "a perfect (w)guide to < English >" } notebook { (id)of { your } own ‡(V) mak^ing^‡ } >), ^but^ (simply) (3)(id)has to ＼ (aV) be (V) inscribed ／ (upon < your memory >) 【 ((id)with a little help (from < (1)footnotes/(2)headnotes { (id)in between < the lines of < your textbooks > > } >)) 】 . (S) < { ((id)Less than) intelligent } Japanese > (V) are (C) 『 (id)in the { nasty } habit of < ‡(V) being‡ (unduly) (C) 『 (id) ＼ (V) satisfied with ／ < (id)‡(V) making‡ (O) « a note » of < something > > 』 > 』: (S) < { (really) intelligent } people > (aV) will never (V) be (C) 『 ＼ (V) satisfied ／ 』 (until (S) < they > ↑ (aV) have (id)(V) succeeded (*)in ↑ < (1)‡(V) memorizing‡ and (2)‡(V) recollecting‡ (*)(O) « something (in < their own brains >) » >).

(In < this age (*)of (1)< information explosion > and (2)< mega storage ((id)in the form of < electrical devices >) > >), (S) < people > (*) | (aV) are (V) getting | (1)(C) 『 ((id)less and less) selective of < (S) < what > (V) is (really) (*){ ^worth^ } (1)(O) « ‡(V) not^ing^‡ » and (2)(O) « ‡(V) memoriz^ing^‡ » > 』, (2)(C) 『 ((id)more and more) (id)dependant on < mechanical memory > (for < later retrieval >) 』, ((thereby) †(V) making† (O) « themselves » (1)(C) 『 (progressively) unintelligent 』 or (2)(C) 『 (even) anti-intelligence 』). (To (id)(V) go against < this trend of < "mechanical deintellectualization" > >), (S) < the value (*)of < the study (*)of (1)< English 【 ((id)for that matter, (1)French, (2)Spanish, (3)Italian, (4)whatsoever) 】 > and (2)world history 【 (not just the local chronicles { of < your small country > }) 】 > > (V) are (C) 『 priceless 』. (S) < ^It^ > (*)(V) takes (1)(O) « selective intellect » and (2)(O) « (*){ constant } (1)memorization, (2)recollection, (3)reviewing and (4)rewriting » ^to^ (V) be (C) 『 (*)a (1)good linguist and (2)reasonable historian 』. (*)(S) < The task > (1)(V) is (C) 『 arduous 』, but (2)(V) is (C) 『 (well) { worth } (1)(O) « ◎the effort », 【 (id)(S) < I >

(V) mean 】, (2)(O) « { (pleasurably) enthusiastic } journey » 』. (V) Be (C)『 (1)diligent and (2)intelligent ^enough^ 』 (^to^ (id)be able to (id)(V) speak about < (S) < what > 【 (S) < you > (really) (V) believe 】 (V) is (C)『 { ^worth^ } (O) « ‡(V) mention^ing^‡ » 』 > – (with < people from < (id)all over the world > >) – (in < ◎English >, { (S) < which > (id)(V) happens to (V) be (C)『 the { (w)de facto standard } language (of < today >) 』 }, { (in < which >) (S) < you > (aV) can (id)(V) expect to (V) make (O) « yourself » (C)『 ＼ (V) understood ／ (to < the largest number of < people > ((id)all over the world) >) 』 })).

And, ((*)^in^ < (1)‡(V) study^ing^‡ and (2)‡(V) command^ing^‡ (*)(O) « English » >), (id)(V) get to (*)(V) know (better) (1)(O) « (*){ your } (1)own language, (2)own country, (3)own people » and (2)(O) « your own mind ». (S) < English > (aV) will (V) be (C)『 a good ◎mirror { to (V) reflect (O) « yourself » (in) } 』. ((*)^The^ (1)more and (2)deeper) (S) < you > (id)(V) look in, (C)『 (*)^the^ more (1)beautiful and (2)intelligent^ 』 (S) < you > (aV) can (V) be (as < a { self-respecting } citizen (of < the twenty-first century >) >).

Greeting and invitation from *author* Jaugo Noto
筆者・之人冗悟(のと・じゃうご)よりの御挨拶&御招待

Thank you very much for taking (even *READING!*) this book.

本書を手に取って(更には読んで！)いただき、感謝します。

If you found it useful, you could find it much more so by visiting **the WEB site presented by this author**:
「役に立つ本だなぁ」と感じた方は、**筆者提供の WEB サイト**に更にもっと役立つ何かを発見できますよ：

<WEB forum regarding "reversENGLISH">
本書（でんぐリングリッシュ）専用 WEB フォーラム
http://zubaraie.com/denglenglish

<WEB lesson on English constructions>
英語構文インターネット・レッスン
http://furu-house.com/sample

http://zubaraie.com ←合同会社ズバライエ(ZUBARAIE LLC.)ホームページ

— about **the author** of this book (本書の**著者**について) —

Jaugo Noto **is a professional educator in linguistics, who makes it his business to enable students to see, do, or be what he's been through and what he can see through, in ways other humans have never imagined or even thought possible. His field of business activity ranges from modern English to ancient Japanese, developing not so much on paper or in the flesh as on the WEB currently.**

之人冗悟(のと・じゃうご)は語学教育の専門家。彼本人の実践・予見の体験を、学生にも認識・実践・体得させること(それも、他者が想像もせず、不可能とさえ思っていた方法で可能ならしめること)を仕事とする彼の活動の幅は、現代英語から古典時代の日本語まで多岐に渡る。現在、紙本執筆や生身の授業よりインターネット上での事業展開が主力。

— about **ZUBARAIE** LLC. (合同会社ズバライエについて) —

Limited Liability Company

ZUBARAIE LLC. was established in Tokyo, Japan, on July 13th (Friday), 2012, as a legal vehicle for Jaugo Noto to perform such services as education, translation, publication and other activities to help enlighten people.

合同会社ズバライエ(ごうどうがいしゃZubaraie)は、2012年7月13日(金曜日(おまけに仏滅))、日本国の東京にて、之人冗悟(のと・じゃうご)が教育・翻訳・出版その他の啓蒙(けいもう)活動を遂行(すいこう)するための法的枠組として設立された。

「でんぐリングリッシュ:英文解剖編(anatomy of reversENGLISH)」
ISBN 978-4-9906908-1-6

1st edition published from ZUBARAIE LLC. 2013/01/31

= *also from the same* **author 之人冗悟(Jaugo Noto)** =

***B**eneath **U**mbrella of **Z**ubaraie LLC.*

☆！併読推奨！☆『**でんぐリングリッシュ：**英・和 対訳版』ISBN 978-4-9906908-0-9

日本の初学者&再挑戦者に贈る、英語を真にモノにするための心得(英文／和訳見開き対訳本)。

・・・本書一冊では効果半減：『英文解剖編』との併用により、真の英文解釈力の開眼を図るべし。

★本書★『**でんぐリングリッシュ：**英文 解剖編』ISBN 978-4-9906908-1-6

同書の全英文を、解剖学的解釈の詳細な構造図で「**可視化**」した古今未曾有の英文読解指南書。

英語がこの形で「見える」ようになることこそ、全学習者の理想形・・・よ一く見て、マネ(真似)ぶべし。

『**古文・和歌**マスタリング・ウェポン』ISBN 978-4-9906908-2-3

大学入試で出題される古文と和歌の知識を完全網羅。暗記必須事項は抱腹絶倒の語呂合わせで、

重要事項の全ての暗記＋確認は巻末穴埋めテストで、調べ物は詳細な索引で、完全サポート。

『**古文単語千五百**マスタリング・ウェポン』ISBN 978-4-9906908-3-0

充実の語義解説で大学入試古文にも和歌・古文書解釈にも不自由を感じぬ完璧な古語力を養成。

入試得点力に直結する受験生の福音書にして、日本語・日本文化への目からウロコの知識の宝庫。

『**ふさうがたり(Fusau Tales)扶桑語り**：古文・英文・現代和文対釈』ISBN 978-4-9906908-4-7

『古文単語千五百』の**全見出語1500**(＋**平安助動詞37**＆**平安助詞77**全用法)で書かれた22編の

擬古文歌物語で『古文・和歌マスタリングウェポン』の説く古典読解法の実践を図る英和古対釈本。

www.ingramcontent.com/pod-product-compliance
Lightning Source LLC
LaVergne TN
LVHW051626080426
835511LV00016B/2195

* 9 7 8 4 9 9 0 6 9 0 8 1 6 *